Coptic Perspectives on Late Antiquity

(Photo: by Kevin Kerdash)

Dr Leslie S.B. MacCoull

Leslie S. B. MacCoull

Coptic Perspectives on Late Antiquity

VARIORUM

Published by VARIORUM
Ashgate Publishing Limited
Gower House, Croft Road,
Aldershot, Hampshire GU11 3HR
Great Britain

Ashgate Publishing Company
Old Post Road
Brookfield, Vermont 05036
USA

ISBN 0-86078-364-2

A CIP catalogue record for this book is available from the British Library.

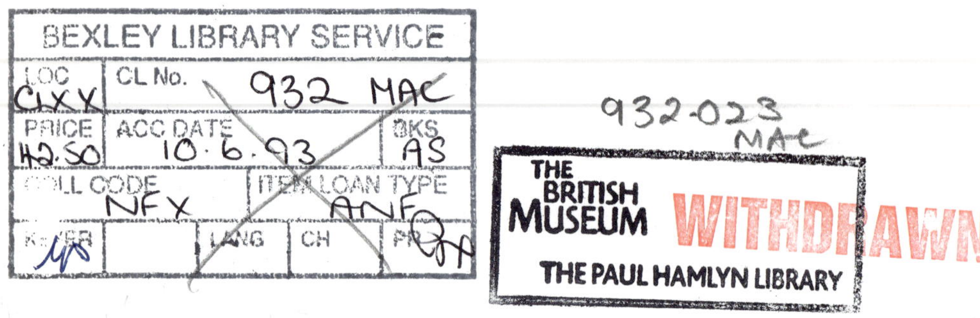

This Variorum edition is printed on acid-free paper.

Printed by Galliard (Printers) Ltd
Great Yarmouth, Norfolk
Great Britain

COLLECTED STUDIES SERIES CS398

To Mirrit

Mein Freund ist mein, und ich bin dein,
Die Liebe soll nichts scheiden.

(Bach, Cantata 140)

CONTENTS

This volume contains xii + 250 pages

PREFACE

To boldly go where no one has gone before . . . is in fact a good description of why someone goes into a specialised discipline like papyrology. It comes as a fantastic liberation to find out that classics is not just re-reading the same old works about which nothing new can possibly be said: fields exist in which one can actually discover new facts the way a scientist does, real facts about real things. From a tiny tax receipt one can come to ponder the life and death of a culture.

To collect the *disjecta membra* of one person's work is especially useful in a field like papyrology, in which short articles widely scattered in often hard-to-obtain journals usually far outnumber large-scale editions or monographs. I am grateful to Variorum and John Smedley for the opportunity to put together the present collection (and to Sebastian Brock for not minding my variation on his title). I should also like to thank the editors of the journals and volumes from which the individual papers were taken, for their permissions to reproduce them for this collection.

The volume contains twenty-nine studies, some written as early as 1978/79, and published in just over a decade from 1981 to 1992. They are framed by studies of the field of Copto-Byzantine papyri from Late Antiquity *qua* field: a survey of the history of the subject, written by one who remembers a time before Late Antiquity became respectable; and three efforts at mapping the area, pointing out desiderata, and emphasising the uniqueness of Late Antiquity as a slice of time.

The remaining twenty-five pieces fall into three categories. The first group is made up of fruits of my more than twenty years' delight in the mind of Dioscorus of Aphrodito, who sums up in his own person so much of Byzantine Egyptian culture. I remember first encountering Dioscorus' prose and poetry in the old Winchester Hall papyrology workroom at Yale, and being astonished that in the ordinary way of things one never got to read things in Greek that were so much fun. The second group illustrates the nuts and bolts that the papyrologist works with: that moment when a reading comes right is another reason why you do this, like when the lead subject in the *Kyrie I* of Bach's B Minor Mass suddenly appears in the major, pure magic. The third and largest group shows how one pushes like a topologist at those bare technical facts so as to ask questions about the society that produced the documents. The creative qualities of Coptic society in its flourishing period stand in such contrast to its loss, indeed its seeming choice of cultural suicide, that study of this area acquires a poignancy, a quality of *wabi* that haunts the researcher. Since it is the discipline of papyrology that is opening up this new terrain of human history to such a degree, a Late Antique papyrologist in the Coptic field is, or should be, an artist with a voice, one able to express the quality of the period as a gateway to intense experience. In Bird's words, "If you don't live it, it won't come out of your horn."

All of these studies were written since, and because, I became the companion of Mirrit Boutros Ghali, founder and president of the Society for Coptic Archaeology. My life in classics, early music, and *cha-no-yu* had prepared me to go to Egypt like the protagonist of the *Hymn of the Pearl* and find my *syzygos*. As Dowland sang, "That I do live it is thy power, / That I do love it is thy worth."

LESLIE S.B. MacCOULL

Washington / Cairo
May 1992

PUBLISHER'S NOTE

The articles in this volume, as in all others in the Collected Studies Series, have not been given a new, continuous pagination. In order to avoid confusion, and to facilitate their use where these same studies have been referred to elsewhere, the original pagination has been maintained wherever possible.

Each article has been given a Roman number in order of appearance, as listed in the Contents. This number is repeated on each page and quoted in the index entries.

I

TOWARDS A NEW UNDERSTANDING OF COPTIC EGYPT[1]

The year of grace 1989 marks three anniversaries that are of relevance to those who study late antiquity: the bicentenary of the publication in 1789 of the first documentary papyrus from Roman Egypt;[2] the centenary of the birth in 1889 of Helen Waddell, whose pioneering work first made a larger world aware of the seminal importance of the late antique period; and twenty years since the death in 1969 of C. Bradford Welles, who trained three generations of specialists in papyrology and the civilisation of Egypt from Alexander to the Arabs. Perhaps these three points of reference can be of use to us as we try to define the nature of our field, where it has been, and where it is going.

What we now label as "Late Antiquity" in Mediterranean history was really born just over twenty years ago. I belong to the last generation of scholars who had at first to read our material under the covers with a flashlight because it was not permitted in the regular curriculum, who were not allowed to write theses on the topics we wished because they were "too late". Now the battle has been won, the paradigm has shifted, younger scholars take up these subjects quite normally. But it was not always so, and the understanding of Coptic Egypt — and I take that to mean the civilisation of Egypt in the period of late antiquity — long suffered. There is of course no substitute for the classical education: it is the sine qua non prerequisite for anyone studying late antiquity in any form; but the older classical curriculum in Europe, Britain, and America did have very narrow spectacles through which to observe very restricted, approved, "edifying" subject-matter. Any work of writing or art later than about the reign of Hadrian (if that) was by reflex prohibited under what the Carolingian scholar Peter Godman has called "the dreary metaphor of decadence".[3] Ladies and gentlemen simply did not consider late,

---

[1]A first version of this paper was given in March 1989 as the introductory lecture at the symposium for the opening, in Providence, Rhode Island, of the exhibition "Beyond the Pharaohs: Egypt and the Copts, 2nd-7th Centuries A.D." I am grateful to Dr. Florence Friedman, Curator of Antiquities at the Rhode Island School of Design Museum of Art, organiser of the exhibit, and editor of the published catalogue of the same title, for inviting me to participate. It was published in Italian translation (by M. de Ghantuz Cubbe) as "Verso una nuova comprensione dell'Egitto copto," in Studi e ricerche sull'oriente cristiano 13 (1990) 3-17.

[2]Cf. R. Pintaudi et al., eds., Miscellanea Papyrologica in occasione del bicentenario dell'edizione della Charta Borgiana (Florence 1990) v-viii.

[3]P. Godman, Emperors and Poets (Oxford 1987) 37. What he has to say, in the first chapter of this study, about the nature and meaning of sixth-century panegyric should be taken seriously to heart by everyone working in the late antique field.

decadent material: it was Bad. (And only seminarists of whatever persuasion could work on Christian subjects, which were also regarded as slightly infra dig.) Specifically concerning Egypt, its late antique persona suffered from multiply confused identities. The Coptic language was regarded, under the influence of Victorian enthusiasm for Bible history, only as a tool for figuring out hieroglyphics. The history of the period was pigeonholed under "Early Christian" — usually seen as tales of the pseudo-Parisian wicked Alexandria in which Hypatia (pagans were always the "good guys") was lynched by a mob of fanatic, unwashed monks, and Paphnucius was wrong-headed enough to turn Thais away from her delightful life of sin. Even when documentary papyri, the very stuff of history, began to be discovered, they were largely neglected in favor of a traditional search for lost masterpieces by the accepted classical authors. And as art of the period began to be unearthed and kept — instead of simply destroyed in the search for Pharaonic levels lower down — it was regarded either as the clumsy efforts of uneducated, impoverished, nationalistic peasants, executed in crude, squalid isolation, or else, in the period of Expressionism and the rediscovery of "primitive" art by Picasso and Roger Fry, romanticised as the staring-eyed products of an ignorant, pre-Freudian "age of anxiety".[4]

So far, so bad. What we have had is a post-Gibbon school of studies on this culture that simply rang changes on Gibbon's deadly "triumph of Christianity and barbarism". The landmark studies on late antique Egypt between the 1880s and the 1950s do not look encouraging either, when they are surveyed. Bell, one of the first (along with Jean Maspero) to decipher Byzantine Egyptian papyri, called the society that produced them the "servile state";[5] while Milne, who worked on the coinage, wrote of "the ruin of Egypt by Roman mismanagement".[6] Rouillard's survey of the administration in 1928[7] imposed the vision of an all-strangling, inescapably rapacious, and paper-pushing bureaucracy; while Hardy's survey of the large estates' economy and life in 1932[8] presented the picture of the runaway "privatisation" of everything from taxes to prisons

---

[4]Perpetuated even today in R. Milburn, Early Christian Art and Architecture (Berkeley 1988) 147, 180; cf. the amateur views in BSAC 19 (1967/68) 227-290.

[5]H.I. Bell, "The Byzantine servile state in Egypt," JEA 4 (1917) 86-106.

[6]J.G. Milne, "The ruin of Egypt by Roman mismanagement," JRS 17 (1927) 1-13. Was he perhaps trying indirectly to complain of the British policies in the 1920s of neglect of education and preference for the incompetent?

[7]G. Rouillard, L'administration civile de l'Egypte byzantine, 2nd ed. (Paris 1928).

[8]E.R. Hardy, The Large Estates of Byzantine Egypt (New York 1932).

and from security guards to priests perpetrated by the obscenely rich in the face of an impotent central government. Bible texts and saints' lives were amassed only to be studied in doctrinal or philological isolation, giving the false impression that the only writing there was was religious and without social context. Even so competent a papyrologist as Zilliacus wrote of the servility[9] and cringing abjectness of a society that loved to make up ever more bombastic titles for the powerful while the poor had no choice but to escape the tax man by fleeing to enter a monastery: everything that the classical values of the classical curriculum taught upstanding people was beneath contempt. There were lights in the dark — Riegl on late Roman ornament, Marrou on education — but those scholars' work did not catch fire until, unfortunately, quite recently. The good news was the indefatigable production, by scholars such as Crum and Steinwenter, of masses of Coptic documentary and legal texts that could be used by later workers[10] with different assumptions to construct a more balanced picture of what it was like to be human in Egypt between 284 and 641 A.D.

It is obvious that it was high time to rethink our whole conceptual order and arrive at a new understanding of this place and time that had been seen through so many powerfully distorting lenses. The present generation of middle-aged scholars, such as Bagnall, Keenan, Worp and myself, has taken up the challenge of shifting the paradigm. Thanks to the persistent and increasingly influential work of Momigliano, Brown, various French _Annales_ disciples and a few North American and European papyrologists, it has become not only respectable but even compelling to investigate and characterise the world of late antiquity and of Coptic Egypt in particular. The ever-fascinating period of transition between the Roman Empire and the Middle Ages (once termed "Dark") is seen to be the most far-reaching geopolitical and psychosocial transformation of humanity before the global industrial revolution. It changed the map in ways that are still very much with us. Increasing discovery of evidence and asking of questions has led both to a later extension in time of the classical curriculum and to an awareness that this is the period when the meaning of the classical inheritance really comes into its own. Egypt in particular ought to emerge as the crucible of late antique studies, because from it we have a vast mass of documentary evidence, preserved on papyrus, equalled in no other area of the Mediterranean sphere. Historians of Greece and Italy, Europe, Syria, Armenia, Asia Minor, North Africa would give anything to have, as Coptic Egypt offers, the complete tax records of cities extending over hundreds of years, complete with birth and death certificates, production and income

---

[9]H. Zilliacus, _Selbstgefühl und Servilität_ (Copenhagen/Helsinki 1953).

[10]Cf. L.S.B. MacCoull, "Coptic documentary papyri as a historical source for Egyptian Christianity," in B.A. Pearson, J.E. Goehring, eds., _The Roots of Egyptian Christianity_ (Philadelphia 1986) 42-50.

figures, rosters of employment, legal testimony as taken down by actual court reporters, police blotters, military records, marriage and divorce contracts, medical recipes, housing deeds and leases — not to mention private letters, dinner invitations, letters home from school, curses, prayers, and even the daily horoscope.

What is the shape of this history, and how do we know it? Owing to an unknown combination of factors — destruction of manuscripts, low prestige of the written language in some periods, lack of an educated class in the Middle Ages — no original Coptic historiography has survived:[11] there are no chronicles. Our evidence comes from papyri, ostraka, inscriptions, coins, law codes, a few archaeological finds, and sometimes from the details of hagiography and homiletics. (Coptic "ethnohistory" is a field yet to be born.) This is not the place to do a precis of the history of the period from 284 to 641 (or 750): the student can be directed to A. Bowman's Egypt After the Pharaohs (Berkeley 1986) and especially to the forthcoming work of synthesis on late antique Egypt by Roger Bagnall. Suffice it to say that our time-lapse camera travels from a world of Roman strategoi and temples of Serapis to a world of great monastic landlords, pilgrimage centers, icons, and Coptic-speaking lawyers who wrote Greek poems combining Homer and the Psalms.[12]

The old spiritual writers used to say, "You are the only Christ some people may ever see". Those of us who deal in our work with the Levant are well aware of the truth of the notion "You are the only good taste some people may ever see". Upon the cultures that have been inheritors of the classical tradition there has been laid the charge "You are the only classics some people may ever see". Coptic Egypt had a special relationship to the classics. Such a charge was laid on the Copts, and they abdicated it. In the different ways of dealing with the classical paradosis, that which is handed down, can be discerned the different "socially patterned psychic structures that lie behind, give form to, and animate a more or less coherent body of cultural expressions".[13] The Orientalist C.H. Becker, one of the first scholars ever to deal with Umayyad papyri, painted a contrasting picture of the East where comparatively unbroken contact with the classics led only to

---

[11]Cf. L.S.B. MacCoull, "Coptic sources: a problem in the sociology of knowledge," BSAC 26 (1984) 1-7.

[12]See L.S.B. MacCoull, Dioscorus of Aphrodito: His Work and his World (Berkeley 1988). In 1982 a lecture on "The Coptic Period of Egyptian History" (an astonishing title considering the political climate) was commissioned by the American University in Cairo: not from a professional in the field, but from a retired former minister, an amateur. In fact a professional, I myself, had to write the lecture. Our field suffers from being regarded as a playground for the unqualified.

[13]The words are those of S. Shapin, "Understanding the Merton thesis," Isis 79 (1988) 598.

stagnation (familiarity breeding contempt?), as against the West, strengthened by a historical trajectory of loss followed by self-conscious recovery.[14] What content did the classics hold for the Copts? How did they see themselves as heirs of antiquity, and of what antiquity?

The coming of Christianity to Egypt seems to have brought with it a devaluing of the brooding presence of ubiquitous Pharaonic antiquity. The Christian writers of Egypt are singularly free from that romantic modern trait of self-taught folklorists, namely, seeing everything through the prism of the praeparatio evangelica of a land specially fitted to receive the Good News and discerning survivals of Ancient Egyptian beliefs, practices, and mind-sets in Christian guise.[15] Nothing can have been further from their minds.[16] Nor do we any longer think that Christianisation liberated a surge of "nationalism" on the part of downtrodden peasants who now had something to call their own. Far more alive to people of the fourth to seventh centuries were, first, the cultural furniture of Graeco-Roman earlier antiquity, the country's normal ambiance after five hundred years since Alexander; and, second and especially, the far-reaching timeline of Biblical antiquity.[17] Coptic Christianity is solidly Biblical, in nomenclature, discourse, piety and expression. The harmonisation of these two strands of antiquity, classical and Biblical, is what gives its distinctive flavor to the way in which Egypt dealt with the classical past.[18]

The classical curriculum remained, right up until April 641, the accepted and respected way in which an elite and self-

---

[14]See C. Essner - G. Winkelhane, "Carl Heinrich Becker (1876-1933), Orientalist und Kulturpolitiker," Welt des Islam 38 (1988) 154-177.

[15]I mean to downplay both the tired cliche of the "religiosity of Egypt" and the romantic attachment to the Ancient Egyptians characteristic both of evangelical Protestants and of Coptic nationalists.

[16]For Cyril the Great on Ancient Egypt see A. Kerrigan, St. Cyril of Alexandria Interpreter of the Old Testament (Rome 1952) 330-333, 444 with n. 3 citing E. Drioton, "Cyrille d'Alexandrie et l'ancienne religion égyptienne," Kyrilliana (Cairo 1947) 233-246. (Today it would not be permitted to commemorate a great Christian figure in Egypt.)

[17]See L.S.B. MacCoull, "Christianity at Syene/Elephantine/Philae," BASP 27 (1990); "Philoponus on Egypt," forthcoming in ByzForsch; "The growth of Holy Family pilgrimage in late antique Egypt: the case of Qosqam," forthcoming.

[18]Cf. C. Mango, "Discontinuity with the classical past in Byzantium," in M. Mullett, R. Scott, eds., Byzantium and the Classical Tradition (Birmingham 1981) 48-57.

perpetuating bureaucratic governing class, the dynatoi, was built up, and the values proper to such people carried on. Abundant studies of the classical literature known (from papyri) to the Egyptian reading public and worked on in schools are filled out by observations of the complete pervasiveness of classical diction and reminiscence in the documents of everyday life. Coupled with this is the permeation of both everyday and highbrow writing and speech by the Scriptures, known, by a process familiar to English-speakers until recently, through daily and weekly hearing in the liturgy. Late antique Egyptian writers, from philosophers to lawyers and bureaucrats, combined these two timelines of classical and Biblical antiquity in a fresh and living way. This unified curriculum gave Egyptians a practical context for understanding themselves.[19]

In the exhibit "Beyond the Pharaohs: Egypt and the Copts" we are trying to discern the nature of Coptic culture from its products. By observing the documents of a civilisation, we are trying to lay bare what has been termed "the deep structure of cultural products"[20] — in effect the whole range of what older scholars called "style" (in Schapiro's words, "... a concrete embodiment or projection of emotional dispositions and habits of thought common to the whole culture"[21]). What are the "conceptual treasures"[22] of the Coptic world? And how did they lose their content over the centuries, until recent scholarly efforts were made to reactivate this world of stopped time and uncertain meaning?[23]

We know from the survival of papyri and works of visual art that items whose intelligibility depended on a knowledge of the classics continued to be produced and consumed in Egypt even beyond the mid-seventh century. The wealth of land and cities continued to guarantee the availability of a classical education, and the inheritance of land and status was no bar to becoming learned. Patronage of ecclesiastical literature did not exclude the "nonsectarian" classics.[24] The figures in tapestry and sculpture, the personifications and cliches in poetry, even the similes in

---

[19]Cf. W. Goffart, The Narrators of Barbarian History (Princeton 1988) 15.

[20]M.A. Holly, Panofsky and the Foundations of Art History (Ithaca 1988) 181.

[21]Quoted ibid. 166.

[22]The phrase is Marvin Minsky's, The Society of Mind (New York 1986) 236.

[23]Cf. Holly, Panofsky, 192.

[24]I am indebted to M. Whitby, The emperor Maurice and his Historian (Oxford 1988, last chapter) for remarks on "the end of traditions". The useful designation "nonsectarian" is Walter Goffart's (above n. 19).

sermons and saints' lives presupposed a background unknown to many secondary-school students of today. Even in the eighth century Greek prose of the highest style continued to be written,[25] and Coptic continued to be used in letters, documents, inscriptions, colophons, and a range of writings from panegyrics to oracles: the paradoxical and so far inexplicable death of the Coptic language does not start to happen until about the eleventh century.[26] (Nonetheless, it was only Coptic culture, alone among all the cultures of the Christian Orient, that threw away its vernacular language: and in a very deep way this was the step by which continuity of the classics was broken, in a way in which it was not elsewhere.) Later a deliberate obliteration of meaning takes over what remains of the culture we see witnessed in the artifacts of the fourth to seventh centuries. In contrast to the schools and scriptoria of Mesopotamia, Armenia, and even Ethiopia, centers of learning die out in Egypt. We do not yet know how to discern the roots of this process: how to reconcile the marginal status of the late antique grammaticus[27] with the holy act that learning undoubtedly became in cultures other than Coptic, and with the liberation from the stifling Mediterranean family that was offered by institutional Christianity.[28] Coptic culture disastrously devalued learning. Yet it remains the case that the Coptic civilisation of late antique Egypt was a uniquely strong carrier, transformer, and enabler of the classical inheritance, until, somehow, it opted to bury its talent.

Every indigenous culture evolves in a place, conditioned by the nature of the local landscape and responsive to, resonant with, the special features of that landscape.[29] The Nile Valley was such a special landscape, within which unfolded a language with its

---

[25]See L.S.B. MacCoull, "Redating the inscription of el-Moallaqa," ZPE 64 (1986) 230-235; "The paschal letter of Alexander II, patriarch of Alexandria: a Greek defense of Coptic theology under Arab rule," DOP 44 (1990) 27-40.

[26]On the death of the language see L.S.B. MacCoull, "Three cultures under Arab rule: the fate of Coptic," BSAC 27 (1985) 61-70; "The strange death of Coptic culture," Coptic Church Review 10 (1989) 35-45. Cf. eadem, "The Teshlot papyri and the survival of documentary Sahidic in the eleventh century," OCP 55 (1989) 201-206.

[27]See R.A. Kaster, Guardians of Language: The Grammarian and Society in Late Antiquity (Berkeley 1988).

[28]Cf. E. Pagels, Adam, Eve, and the Serpent (New York 1988).

[29]Cf. Barry Lopez, Crossing Open Ground (New York 1988) 67, 81: important.

concomitant ways of thought, a type of human personality,[30] a response to circumstances that is worth knowing about and worth making known. Its qualities would benefit the humanities at a time when they are again in danger of losing touch with the content of the classical inheritance, with which, as Helen Waddell pointed out, "is bound up the life of human learning".

A strange paradox hangs over the field of Coptic studies. Its effects can be seen at any scholarly conference dealing with the late antique period, and in the pages of any scholarly publication covering a number of regions during this era. For example: At any of the Oxford Patristics conferences, there are at least two or three entire sessions dealing with Syriac studies, yet one is lucky if one single paper on a Coptic subject is presented during the entire meeting. In any volume of assorted studies on a particular topic in late antiquity or Byzantium, most of the articles are on Constantinople, Syria, Armenia, Gaul, North Africa, and Palestine. Egypt is left off the map, or mentioned only in passing: if there is a single essay on the Coptic dimension of the subject being treated, it is most unusual. The same is the case at the annual Byzantine studies conferences, or in conferences with titles like "East of Byzantium". The formation of a society for the study of hagiography lists an abundance of Syriacists and not a single Copticist. In a volume of essays on the effects of the Council of Chalcedon, there is only one on the Egyptian church. And these few-and-far-between papers on Coptic subjects tend to be of abysmal quality, so far below the other papers that it is painful. The top graduates in classics, the cream of the talented young people coming off a classics baccalaureate — and they are out there — , the very people whom we would wish to recruit into this potentially exciting area, do not go into Coptic. They go into Syriac and Armenian, or, if not those areas of the Christian Orient, they stay in the Greek- and Latin-speaking sphere of late antiquity and know the other sources only in translation. Brilliant young classicists do realise that where the action is in classics is in the later period, and even east of Rome. But brilliant people do not go into Coptic. Coptic attracts the autodidact, the underqualified, and what, because it deals with Egypt, can only be described as the lunatic fringe. I am embarrassed for my profession. No one wants to be associated with a field populated by the incompetent, the marginal, and the just plain weird.

Something must be done. No field can be born, let alone make progress, unless it is entered by the best minds. We must recruit the best of the best, the most talented classical graduates who fall really in love with the later period, as I did, and have a flair for asking the right questions and evaluating old evidence with new eyes. Bright people can be attracted only by prestige and by the atmosphere of institutions at the cutting edge, where it is

---

[30] Again, however, I mean to downplay the "religiosity of Egypt" syndrome so beloved of those exponents of the party line who try to insist on "Egyptian national unity". See L.S.B. MacCoull, "The myth of Egyptian national unity," The Copts (Jersey City).

obvious that exciting new work is going on.[31] Coptic studies are not yet institutionalised in our curricula: they are shunted off into departments of religion, of history, of oriental studies, treated as the vermiform appendix of Egyptology or as a dead end of Byzantine art misunderstood by clueless provincials. No. Coptic studies are a part, a vital part, of classical studies. The investigation of the civilisation of Egypt in the period between 284 and 650 A.D. falls within the purview of departments of classics and scholars of classics. This culture was the proving-ground of the classical heritage, which we can know in depth as we can no other of its contemporaries. Surely, now that the paradigm has shifted and the period of late antiquity is not only respectable but downright "hot", now that what a culture does with the classics has come to be seen as a touchstone of its achievement, the study of this Coptic culture can attract the top talented people it deserves.

A proposed title for this exhibit, one that was not used, was "Coptic Egypt: An Unknown Golden Age". The "golden" aspect, the achievement of this civilisation, I hope will be made known by what is seen and read in the exhibit and catalogue. The quality of being "unknown" is owed to many factors: the disdain of earlier classicists; the loss of continuity with the classical heritage itself; and, not least, the obliteration, the cultural genocide, that threatens the remains of Coptic culture in our own time. For "known" to replace "unknown", let these objects and words, and so many more, speak for themselves, and, above all, generate questions. From the document scholars remember that the use of original sources overturns received ideas, which is a good thing. And from the humanists remember that the human spirit survives not by the checkbook but by the scholarly book. The people who lived in the houses, gathered in the public buildings, used the utensils, wore the clothes, joined the groups, sang the melodies, prayed before the icons, paid the taxes, and looked at the environment, formed a social network that had its strengths and its weaknesses, its pressures and its high flights. They can be understood as not only passing on what we value — classics, Christianity — but also as constructing their own values. When we come to understand "the tensions and the fragilities"[32] as well as the confident solidities

[31]In Dr. Sherwin Nuland's words on the stimuli necessary to make a profession evolve, "... the improving intellectual status of entering members of the group...": S.B. Nuland, Doctors: The Biography of Medicine (New York 1988) 173. And people have to do it, have to embody the highest professional standards: cf. C. Rosenberg, "Woods or trees?," Isis 79 (1988) 568. The good intentions of amateurs are not enough. It is people to whom high standards are as natural as the air they breathe that make a difference.

[32]P.R.L. Brown, "Eastern and western Christendom in late antiquity: a parting of the ways," SCH 13 (1976) 1-24; here p. 17 n. 70.

of what the people of that place and time accomplished, perhaps we will know more of why this particular Eastern Christian culture met the fate that it did. For it was a culture that could have had a unique future as well as a unique past.[33]

As always, Chesterton said it best:

> Therefore your doom is on you,
> Is on you and your kings:
> Not for a fire in Ely fen,
> Not that your gods be nine or ten,
> But for it is only Christian men
> Guard even heathen things.

---

[33] I should also like to thank Gary Vikan, Thelma Thomas, and Lucas Siorvanes for their illuminating discussion on various topics of this paper. And, as always, Mirrit Boutros Ghali: "Ich bin ein' Flöt' an deinem Munde..."

II

The Coptic Archive of Dioscorus of Aphrodito*

In 1957 G. Malz summarised the state of our knowledge of the published Greek works of Dioscorus of Aphrodito, the sixth-century Egyptian lawyer and poet (1). Dioscorus' archive of writings, now dispersed among several papyrus collections, comes from the second find at Aphrodito (Kom Ishqaw) in the Antaeopolite nome in Upper Egypt, made by G. Lefebvre in 1905 after the collapse of a house-wall in the village (2). The first find, in 1901, had consisted of papyri dating from after the Arab conquest, including many Coptic pieces: these were published by Bell and Crum in *P. Lond.* IV (1910). Dioscorus' Greek papyri from the second find are known principally from their publications in *P. Cairo Maspero* I-II-III (1911-1913-1916) and *P. Lond.* V (1917). Only one Coptic piece from Dioscorus' hand was ever published, by Thompson, as *P. Lond.* V. 1709 : it is the record of an arbitration (ⲙⲉⲥⲓⲧⲉⲓⲁ) of an inheritance dispute by Dioscorus at Antinoë about A.D. 569. To the Greek works published since Malz's article may now be added *P. Freer* 1-4 (3), *P. Mich.* XIII. 659-674 (4), and *P. Vatic. Aphrod.* 1-26 (5). The Coptic portion of the archive remains unknown.

(*) I should like to thank Professor Gladys Frantz-Murphy, who invited me to participate in the papyrology panel of the ARCE meeting, Boston 1981 ; and, as always Ⲕ.ϣ.ⲉ., H. E. Mirrit Boutros Ghali : ϯⲛⲁϩϯ ϯⲛⲁϩϯ ϯⲛⲁϩϯ ... ϣⲁ ⲡⲓⲛⲓϥⲓ ⲛ̄ϩⲁⲉ.

(1) G. Malz, *The papyri of Dioscorus : publications and emendations*, in *Studi Calderini-Paribeni* 2 (Milan, 1957), 345-356.

(2) H. I. Bell, *An Egyptian village in the age of Justinian*, in *JHS* 64 (1944), 21-36.

(3) L. S. B. MacCoull, *Greek and Coptic papyri in the Freer Gallery of Art*, diss. Catholic University (Washington), 1973.

(4) P. J. Sijpesteijn, *The Aphrodite papyri in the University of Michigan papyrus collection* [= *Stud.Amst.* 10] (Zutphen, 1977).

(5) R. Pintaudi, *I papiri vaticani greci di Aphrodito* (Vatican City, 1980).

Dioscorus, a bilingual member of a bilingual society (1), obviously did his work and led his life in Coptic as well as Greek. The present paper is an attempt to fill the language gap.

I have outlined and underlined the importance of Dioscorus of Aphrodito as a representative figure of his time on many occasions (2). He was born about A.D. 520, and educated, as befitted the fourth generation in a Hellenised Coptic family, both in the Greek of polite culture and in the Latin needed for a legal career (the *Digest* was promulgated in his youth [A.D. 533], in the year of the condemnation of the Three Chapters and of Flavius Strategius Apion's tenure as *comes sacrarum largitionum*). After his father Apollos had attained the rank of Flavius (in connexion with a journey to Constantinople), founded a monastery at Aphrodito and died there, Dioscorus himself travelled to the capital in 551 in defence of his town's right of *autopragia* (tax collection). From 566 to 573 he lived at Antinoë, seat of the Dukes of the Thebaid, practising the notariate and writing encomiastic poetry. In his later years he served as curator of his father's monastery ; the latest dated papyrus from his archive falls in A.D. 585. His Coptic mother-tongue and his literary life were closely connected : he compiled a Greek-Coptic literary glossary, mostly of poetic (especially Epic) words (3), showing that the Coptic of his local usage sounded something like Crum's siglum « S[a] », a kind of Middle Egyptian tinged with what Professor Kasser would have us call

(1) On the bilingualism of Byzantine Egyptian society see J. W. B. Barns-E. A. E. Reymond's remarks in *Four martyrdoms from the Pierpont Morgan Coptic codices* (Oxford, 1973), 18, relying on literary material. For the texture of life in general, simply observe the range of documentary papyri and their interrelationships : e.g. A. A. Schiller, *The Budge Coptic papyrus of Columbia University and related Greek papyri of the British Museum*, in *Actes X[e] Congr. Papyrol.* (Warsaw, 1964 [1961]), 193-200. Note that *P. Lond.* V. 1709 deals with the same family as *P. Cairo Masp.* I. 67006.

(2) L. S. B. MacCoull, *Dioscorus and the dukes*, paper at the 1976 Byzantine Studies Conference, to appear in *Byzantine Studies*. See also *BSAC* 24 (to appear). Did his name, *Dios-kouros*, stem from an original translation (in his grandfather's generation) of Coptic *She-noute* « son of God »? Was there an implied reference to (Patriarch) Dioscorus I, the Monophysite culture-hero ?

(3) H. I. Bell-W. E. Crum, *A Greek-Coptic glossary*, in *Aegyptus* 6 (1925), 177-226 (= *P. Lond.* V. 1674 verso). Thompson does not note linguistic idiosyncrasies in *P. Lond.* V. 1709, e.g. ϯⲁ- for ϯⲛⲁ- 1 Future.

« Lycopolitan » (i.e. Assiut) (1). No one, not even Bell who originated the terminology (Introduction to *P. Lond.* V, p. iv n. 2), has remarked on the simple and striking fact that Dioscorus' « Hand A », the uncial hand in which he wrote his literary works, is simply his normal Coptic documentary hand. That is, he wrote Greek poems and Coptic contracts with one and the same handwriting. There is no clearer way to demonstrate the importance of Dioscorus' Coptic archive, and the unity of the archive as a whole, than to put *P. Cairo Masp.* I plates XXVIII and XXIX and a photograph of *P. Lond.* V. 1709 next to each other. Or, indeed, to turn the latter over : the recto is Dioscorus' contract, the verso is his poetry (*P. Lit. Lond.* 100 F/G = Heitsch 18). The hand is the same.

There are, I have ascertained so far, three directions in which we may turn to seek for the missing items of Dioscorus' Coptic archive. First, most logically, of course, the Cairo Museum itself (2). (Bell's preface to *P. Lond.* V does not indicate British Museum acquisition of sixth-century Aphrodito Coptic material, whereas Crum's preface to the Coptic section of *P. Lond.* IV [p. xlvii] stated that these Jkôw [Aphrodi-

(1) Most recently, R. Kasser, *Prolégomènes à un essai de classification systématique des dialectes et subdialectes coptes selon les critères de la phonétique*, in *Muséon* 93 (1980) 53-112, 237-297. Cf. Chaîne's « Assioutique ».

(2) A. A. Schiller, *A checklist of Coptic documents and letters*, in *BASP* 13 (1976), 99-123 : 103 states, s.v. « Cairo », « No recent description of the status of the Coptic collection is known ». Sadly true. For the second-find Aphrodito material, a look at Cairo Museum Journal d'entrée vol. VI nos. 35104-35105 reveals the astonishing fact that two boxes of Coptic papyri were never given accession-numbers in 1905 (the rest of the bifolium is blank), and the space allotted to them in the « Régistre provisoire » corresponds to no known place in the Museum. A check of the transactions accompanying transfers of Coptic material to the Coptic Museum in the 1930s yielded only negative results (but see below). It is hoped that a formal enquiry initiated by the International Association for Coptic Studies may put in train an official search for the whereabouts of these boxes. The whereabouts of the sixth-century Aphrodito Coptic material, as a group, is still unknown : a phenomenon all too frequent in the case of bilingual archives. (A particularly frightening case is the fate of the Coptic portion of *P. Apollônos Anô* [Greek publ. 1953]. Rémondon states that the Greek documents he found in a jar at Edfu were « ... mêlés à des documents coptes [Introduction p. v] ». Nothing more is said about the Coptic pieces that he did not touch. Could they be still at the French Institute at Cairo, after the difficult 1950s? [I am enquiring.]. For Greek strays see now J. Gascou, *Papyrus grecs inédits d'Apollônos Anô*, in *Hommages S. Sauneron* 2 [Cairo 1979], 25-34, and *Documents grecs des époques byzantine et arabe*, in *IFAO Livre du centenaire* [Cairo 1980], 323-328).

to] texts were at Cairo : repeated in his Dictionary siglum « PJkôw » [1939] (1). Cairo whereabouts are indicated in the preface to *P. Cairo Masp.* III [p. viii] : « ... plusieurs caisses provenant des fouilles anciennes de M. Lefebvre, et ne contenant ... que des papyrus coptes ».). To start with published material, as at Cairo one must, it can be noticed (and was by Malz, « Papyri of Dioscorus » 349) that the rectos of *P. Cairo Masp.* 67176, 67275, and 67351 are Coptic. Malz thought that these three (not noting 67353, which is Coptic also : see below) formed parts of a single document, which does not appear to be the case although 67351 and 67176 both have on their versos portions of the conjugation of *ποιέω*. (At any rate all three were kept together among Dioscorus' papers, as they contain paradigms from the three sorts of contract verbs in *α*, *ε* and *ο* : Dioscorus was practising his accidence). In point of fact I have found the missing lower half of 67176 r° : it is Alexandria inv. no. 689, and the whole is a cession of land (**ⲡⲁⲣⲁⲭⲱⲣⲏⲥⲓⲥ**) in Dioscorus' hand, written at Antinoë and dated Hathyr 8, third indiction in the reign of Justin II = 4 November A.D. 569. The parties to the transaction include Anoup son of Apollo and Julius son of Sarapammon : they will reappear. A complete text of both halves of the document, with commentary, is appearing in the Acta of the Second International Congress of Coptic Studies, Rome, September 1980.

I have not yet obtained permission to see the original of 67275 ; so I shall conclude my remarks on the Coptic contents of the Cairo Museum by stating that an inspection of some thirty unpublished inventory numbers (8032-6, 8044-5, 8051-70, 8074-8) has yielded nothing locatable at Aphrodito (one piece is from Akhmim, 8076) (2). It is just possible that one tiny scrap (10.6 × 5.2 cm) that did find its way to the Coptic Museum is a stray from Dioscorus' Greek literary archive, and that the « Victor the priest » who signs a Coptic harvest contract (**ⲅⲉⲛⲛⲉⲥⲙⲁ**) in the same collection is to be identified with Dioscorus' first cousin. (These texts appear in *Studia Orientalia Christiana : Collectanea*

(1) Crum adds that he knows of the Jkôw texts through copies made by Lacau : these copies are kept in Crum's archives in the Griffith Institute, Ashmolean Museum, Oxford (see below), to which (and to Miss Helen Murray, the Archivist) I express my thanks for making them available to me. One works at a set of Platonic removes from reality : copies of Crum's copies of Lacau's copies of untraceable originals.

(2) Most of these papyri have now been photographed by the 1981 Cairo Mission of the International Photographic Archive of Papyri (Dr R. A. Coles and colleagues), and so will shortly be accessible to scholars.

16 [1981] 199-206). I have also been able to see a few photographs of untraceable originals at Cairo, including a Greek tax-receipt by Dioscorus' father Apollos (a 7th indiction, probably A.D. 528 as he is not yet Flavius) mentioning two pagarchs, and a Coptic letter to an ecclesiastic containing no proper names more distinctive than John.

Second, at Oxford, the Griffith Institute's Crum archives contain, as indicated above (p. 188, n. 1), some half-dozen copies of copies of the elusive Aphrodito texts, made so that Crum could draw on them for slips for his *Dictionary*. In Group V no. 4 is to be found. with a covering letter from Ch. Kuentz dated Paris 10 October 1933, a transcription by Kuentz of *P. Cairo Masp.* 67353 recto (the verso is an *apokeryxis* of A.D. 569, the same year as Alex. inv. 689 + *P. Cairo Masp.* 67176). Sure enough, this is another document relating to the cession of land by Anoup/Apollo and Julius/Sarapammon (1) before they enter the monastic life. It appears to be framed in the first person by « *their* mother Mesiane » (Alex. inv. 689.22), who refers to the two as « my sons » (**ⲚⲀϢⲎⲢⲈ**) (1.3), by, according to their patronymics, different fathers. The place-name **ⲦⲖⲔⲈ** appears (l. 9) (cf. *Τελκε*, a *χωρίον*, *P. Lond.* IV. 1461. 33 [Hermopolite?]). The date « Mecheir 7 » occurs twice (ll. 9 and fr. b. 6), so this document appears to have been drawn up three months after its fellow (Alex. inv. 689). Apa Papnoute, known also from the corresponding contract, appears likewise (ll. 13, 14, 15, fr. b. 4). And to fit in with the archive of Dioscorus' father's monastery (cf. Alex, inv. 689.29), we next find Crum's transcription of an unnumbered Aphrodito Coptic papyrus, photographed by Brugsch in June 1907. It is a letter from Apa Phoebammon, father of the **ⲦⲞⲞⲨ** of Apa Apollo « and the whole people of God and the brothers » to a plural number of recipients whose names are unfortunately lost (the papyrus is so tattered that it looks like lace). To be found are the names Sophia, « the men of Jkôw », and Ezekiel : an Ezekiel head of the winesellers' guild turns up in *P. Cairo Masp.* 67283. III. 14 (A.D. 548). Crum's other copies (dated November 1909) reveal the existence of a letter « to Phoebammon [the same superior?] and

(1) The only Sarapammon hitherto known at Aphrodito is the *megaloprepestatos*, *endoxotatos* and *illustris* Sarapammon who was mixed up in a murder case in probably A.D. 543-4 (*P. Mich.* XIII. 660 and 661). He was accused of having both received and paid bribes in connexion with the murders of one Heraclius and a priest, Victor. There is, of course, no way to identify this shady character with Julius' father in this archive.

Dioscorus [acting as curator?] from Moses (ⲙⲱⲩⲥⲏⲥ) their son [? cf. *Μωυcῆc* son of Phoebammon, deacon, *P. Cairo Masp.* 67094. 24, A.D. 553] » and complaining of sickness : if the 550s are right, Dioscorus had just returned from the capital, where there had been plague since the 540s (1). We also have a tax document mentioning Easter signed by Apollos as protocometes; a letter stating that Dioscorus at Antinoë (hence after 566) has written to the lord Apa Victor, *ekdikos* (*defensor civitatis*) of Antaeopolis ; a letter « to my beloved fathers [*sic*] Dioscorus and ⲥⲟ̣ⲫⲓ̣ⲁ » (cf. the Sophia in the Apa Phoebammon letter described above ; and a letter from the clergy of ⲁⲅⲓⲁ ⲙⲁⲣⲓⲁ ⲛⲧⲕⲱⲟⲩ, S. Mary's at Antaeopolis (well known from *P. Cairo Masp.* 67066, a letter to Dioscorus ; cf. 67061, to Apollos as protocometes), mentioning John the ⲃⲟⲏⲑⲟⲥ (one occurs in *P. Cairo Masp.* 67090.1). Finally there is a letter from an unnamed *logistes* naming « Apollo of ⲫⲁⲣⲁⲩ », which brings us right back to Alex. inv. 689.27, the latter providing evidence for the sixth-century existence of the monastery of ⲫⲁⲣⲟⲟⲩ (hitherto known from *P. Lond.* IV) and its connexion with Dioscorus' family (2). Many new names occur, to be added to a future prosopographical study of the social structure of Aphrodito. (Its population may have been about 5000-6000).

Our third source, the richest and most promising, is the Vatican Library (3). It seems that in the process of transferring material from the Cairo Museum to the Coptic Museum, certain mostly documentary papyri never arrived at their destination, but found their way on to the

(1) Cf. T. S. Miller's analysis of plague descriptions in *GRBS* 17 (1976), 385-395 : 391-2 on Procopius on the Justinianic plague.

(2) Bell (General Introduction to *P. Lond.* IV, p. xvii n. 1) thought that this monastery was the same house as the *Φαρ̣αοῦτος* of *P. Cairo Masp.* 67003.5 (ca. A.D. 522 ?) : but the Coptic papyri show that this is not the case, as the proper name of the latter was « the Christ-bearing Apostles », rather to be associated with « the Apostles » at Aphrodito known from *P. Cairo Masp.* 67283. II. 3 (ca. A.D. 548). No one has yet tried to analyse which of the religious edifices in sixth-century Aphrodito were Chalcedonian and which non-Chalcedonian : cp. J. B. Segal, *Edessa « the blessed city »* (Oxford, 1970), 190-191 with notes.

(3) For what follows I should like to thank Professor Rosario Pintaudi and Dr Lucia Papini of Florence, for making this valuable material available to me and for sending excellent photographs (my thanks also to the Vatican Library) and transcripts. Dr Papini has graciously asked me to co-edit with her the Vatican Aphrodito Coptic material, and I am grateful to her for permission to describe and cite it here.

antiquities market, and were bought by Jean Doresse, who presented them to the Vatican Library in 1961 (1). The Greek Aphrodito pieces have been published by Rosario Pintaudi (1980) (2) ; the Coptic, so long sought for, are being studied by Lucia Papini and myself. *P. Vatic. Copti Doresse* (so Pintaudi's siglum, *PVA* p. 6) consist of 21 inventory-numbers, of which three are literary. None of the pieces appears to be in Dioscorus' own hand, but all are from either his personal archive or that of the monastery of Apa Apollos, his father's foundation.

Papyri 1 and 5, though not in the same hand, concern the same people, and both appear to be sales of land (3). They concern the family of one Tsyra daughter of Sabine, her late husband Christopher son of Pesynthius (?), and their son David, none of whom is known from the Greek documents from Aphrodito. (One is handicapped by the lack of a Coptic *Namenbuch*, but I find no identifications). The witnesses to both documents include Victor son of the late Phoebammon, Theodosius son of the late (X), Victor Apater the priest, John the hegoumenos, and one Mark. One of the notaries is called George ; no dating-clauses, unfortunately, have been preserved, though 5. II mentions « the coming D.V. 15th indiction » (A.D. 550-1 ?). No. 2 is a division of house property by one Jacob, mentioning the crops of the thirteenth indiction (549 or 564?) and including an oath « by God Almighty and the ⲟⲩϫⲁⲓ of (the emperor? cf. Seidl, *Eid* 2 [= *MB* 24, Munich 1935] p. 139) ». No. 3 appears to be a contract, referred to as a « unanimous ⲥⲩⲙⲫⲟⲛⲟⲛ », to which the witnesses include a Constantine, a George, a Paul and another Apa Victor, all very slow writers, a Phoebammon, and someone else whose name is lost who describes himself as a ⲕⲧⲏⲧⲱⲣ. And of No. 4, a long and fragmented strip from the centre of a contract, only single names or single patronymics appear in the witness list, not really enough for identifications : we have two Colluthuses, a Tribounos (cf. *P. Lond.* V. 1757. 11, dated 7th century by the editor [?]), and a ϭⲁⲙⲟⲩⲗ. All of these larger pieces are long rolls (40-95 cm) written across the fibres.

Of the smaller pieces, a good many appear to be from the correspondence archive of Dioscorus' father's monastery, Apa Apollos'. Under No. 15 we find a letter from Theodore to « the honoured father Apa

(1) Pintaudi, *P. Vatic. Aphrod.* (1980) p. 5.

(2) Cf. his paper, *I papiri vaticani di Aphrodito*, at the XVI International Congress of Papyrology, New York, July 1980.

(3) Confirmed in a letter from L. Papini, 29 December 1980.

Makare, the *oikonomos* of our lord father Apa Apollo », who is addressed as « my beloved lord father » ; a letter to « my brother Mak[» of Apa Apollo, from Apa Anoup ; and what appears to be a tax-receipt or requisition, mentioning three sailors and the monastery of Apa Apollo, dated to a sixth indiction. (Extra fragments belonging to No. 5 are to be found glassed with Nos. 13[2] and 16[1]). The first line of No. 16[2] runs tantalisingly « This is the prayer which the patriarch [N. prayed ? ?] ... » : perhaps a bit of some pro-Cyrillian writing? And under No. 20 we find the first evidence that the Apa Apollos monastery still existed after the Arab conquest : a letter from Rashîd son of Khaled (ⲣⲁⲍⲓⲇ ⲩⲓⲟ(ⲥ) ⲭⲁⲗⲉⲇ) to Peter son of Cyrus « and the brothers, the men of the monastery of Apa Apollô », with regard to the ⲕⲁⲧⲁⲥⲧⲁⲥⲓⲥ or collection of a sum upon an official's assumption of office. This Arab governor, to my knowledge, is hitherto unknown ; the name رشيد is rendered with - ⲍ - in the eighth-century Aphrodito documents in *P. Lond.* IV.

Numerous further fragments under the remaining inventory-numbers remain to be read. (E.g. No. 10 contains a letter from Sarapammon [!] to Patermoute, mentioning Apa Papnoute (1) : the same cleric as in Alex. inv. 689 and above ?). Suffice it to say that the two pieces comprising No. 9, and one from No. 19, are three leaves from an account-book bearing lists of personal names followed by placenames (« the man from ... »), headed by two lines ending « ... of the holy ... of this year, the eighth [indiction] » (A.D. 559 or 574 ?). The leaves are in an extremely tattered condition : the items listed at the right sides of the columns appear to be either types of linens (ⲡⲁⲗⲗⲓⲟⲛ, ⲕⲁⲙⲓⲥⲩⲛ) or a figure apparently preceded by an artaba-sign ; nearly all the sums are of three artabas. Could it be a record of donations to a monastery ? On the first leaf appears the name Anastasia. We know of two Anastasias from Aphrodito, both oddly enough married to men called Phoebammon : one was Dioscorus' first cousin Anastasia Tekrompia (« Dove ») (*PVA* 10), the other one of the plaintiffs in *P. Lond.* V. 1708, an arbitration by

(1) In the phrase ⲕⲓ [<ⲕⲱ ?] ... ⲡⲣⲟⲥⲟⲡⲟⲛ [*sic*] : a reference to judicial representation ? See still M. San Nicolò, *Das* ⲉⲓⲣⲉ ⲙ̄ⲡⲣⲟⲥⲱⲡⲟⲛ *als Stellvertretungsformel in den koptischen Papyri*, in *BZ* 24 (1924), 336-345 : cf. Crum's lemmata, *Dict.* 647a, for ⲕⲱ ϩⲟ / ϯ ϩⲟ / *πρόσωπον τάσσειν*. A variant legal phrase ?

Dioscorus. It is tempting to assign this account-book to the monastery of Apollos itself (1).

The Dioscorus dossier is far from closed. Prof. Pintaudi informs me (2) that he has found more Greek texts in Berlin. Further strays will doubtless be discovered (3) : and of course the bulk of the Coptic archive, the unknown remainder of what was found over the period 1905-1908, is the object of this whole exercise. I hope that the contents sketched in this progress report have been such as convincingly to depict the unity and importance of Dioscorus' œuvre. Up to the moment of writing, his works have served only to provide matter for ridicule (« ... ces bizarreries de décadent [Maspero] ... morass of absurdity [Bell] ») to the few scholars who have tried, peering through their classical spectacles, to read them. I find this attitude still. It will not do. The research of the last two decades has made us more receptive to the aesthetic and administrative achievements of Late Antiquity. The writings of Dioscorus, Coptic and Greek, are a door through which we may enter the rich and complex cultural world of that Egypt that flourished from Chalcedon to the Conquest. Its history is not yet written. With the works (in *both* the languages of his world) of a writer and civil servant who described his homeland as *τὴν ἀcτυμφέλικτον καλὴν ἐπαρχείαν*, « the beautiful eparchy wreathed in cities » (visualise the Egypt of the *Notitia Digni- tatum*, dotted with heraldic walls), with the only case remaining to us out of the whole ancient world of the actual autographs of poems from the poet's hand, with Dioscorus, is a good place to begin. *

(1) Similar in its square format is P. Yale inv. 1804, a codex of 32 leaves, which I have assigned to the Antaeopolite nome on the basis of local and monastic names : publication to appear in the series *Textes et documents* of the Society for Coptic Archaeology.

(2) Letter of 29 January 1981.

(3) Cf. Cl. Wehrli's publication of P. Gen. inv. 204 (A.D. 551), XVI International Congress of Papyrology, New York, July 1980.

* Delete "wreathed in cities" and substitute "unshakable".

III

The Imperial *chairetismos* of Dioscorus of Aphrodito

To my best student

Not appearing among the poems of Dioscorus printed in E. Heitsch, *Die griechischen Dichterfragmente der römischen Kaiserzeit* (Göttingen, 1964), 128-52, is the fragment *P.Cairo Masp.* I.67097 verso (F) part 2, lines 18-27.[1] Indeed, it is not in verse, but in a kind of heightened rhythmic prose reminiscent of imperial acclamations.[2] Its text runs:

χαῖρε, ὁλοκοττινοπερίπατε | ἀγγελοπρόσωπε,
χαῖρε, κ(ύρι)ε χρυσαργυροπιναροσμαραγ `δο´ | μαργα `ρι´ τοβελτίων,
χαῖρε, δέσπ(οτα) χρυσολιθοκαχατωνύχιε, | πρα[σ]ινοπάντιμε λαμπρόβ[ιε,

(gap of 1 or 2 lines)

χαῖρε, δέσπ(οτα) . . . θαλα]σσιοπλοιοχρυσ[ο] | γόμου,
χαῖρε, κ(ύρι)ε παναξιοκτηνοπτηναστρο | φωστηροκοσμοποιΐας,
χαίρων χορείης εἰς μυριάμφορον χρόνον.

1 — κοτ'τι —, αγ'γελο — Pap. The restorations are Maspero's.

'Hail, angelic face on the circulating *nomisma*,
hail, lord surpassing gold, silver, mother-of-pearl, emerald, and pearl,
hail, master of onyx, chrysolith, and agate, all-honoured of the Greens, bright of life,
hail, master of the golden cargo of seagoing ships,
hail, most worthy possessor of a star in the ascendant that illuminates the whole created universe,
in joy may you dance to a time of ten thousand jars of wine.'

This sort of series of formal addresses, called from its first word a *chairetismos*,[3] is well known from liturgical and hymnological contexts. The form reaches its best-known heights in the Akathistos Hymn of the East[4] and such Western parallels as the late-medieval Litany of the Virgin. In its specifically Coptic and Marian form we see it flowering in the Theotokias,[5] and also in the salutations to the Holy Cross.[6] The present piece from Dioscorus' pen is unique in the genre in that it is addressed, not to God or a saint or divine being or attribute, but to an emperor, presumably Justin II.[7] It employs expressions and esthetic effects that come straight from the heart of Byzantine Egyptian culture; and it is an important addition to our sources for knowledge of the place of the imperial image in Late Antiquity. The unusual epithets by which the emperor is hailed[8] deserve individual consideration.

The first line obviously refers to Justin II's numismatic portraiture, that ever-visible form of the imperial image.[9] To modern scholars the most outstanding issues of the reign are the double (juxtaposed) portraits of Justin and Sophia. But for something corresponding to Dioscorus' "angel-face" (with its Biblical overtones[10]) we must turn to the full-face *aurei* obverses of the mint of Constantinople (Bellinger/Grierson nos. 1-8b, Plate XLIX). Such *solidi* would have been impressive pieces in Egyptian circulation. And Dioscorus is deliberately recalling the use of "angel" as a courtesy title for an illustrious person,[11] a usage abundantly documented in Coptic.[12] Note also that the metaphor of the 'image' on a coin, the 'impression', was a favorite patristic conceit (Lampe *s.v.* νόμισμα, p. 919): Origen writes the striking sentence, 'As the *nomisma* has (ἔχει) the *eikon* of the king of the nations (τοῦ βασιλεύοντος τῶν ἐθνῶν), so he who does the works of the *kosmokrator* bears (φορεῖ) his *eikon*' (*hom. 39 in Luc.*). The emperor's face was visible everywhere as that of the First Christian of the realm.

The juxtaposition of precious elements in the second line reflects the preferences for splendid color-combinations we can see in surviving examples of Byzantine Egyptian jewellery, such as the pair of bracelets in the Metropolitan Museum, formerly in the Pierpont Morgan collection.[13] Combinations of various kinds of white—ivory, silver, pearl—with green (and blue) were regarded as especially delicious to the eye.[14] Similar appeal to the eye is evoked by the juxtaposition of precious stones in the third line.[15] Onyx and agate were both found in Egypt, as was beryl, and mother-of-pearl came from the Red Sea.[16] But there may also be an implied pun on 'onyx/fingernail' (cf. Paul the Silentiary, *Descriptio ambonis S. Sophiae*, 76ff.[17]): Epiphanius of Salamis' comparison of the onyx-stone to 'a townsman's fingernails' (*De XII Gemmis, PG* 43.301B) is known in Coptic literature (Zoega, p. 611, Sahidic: . . . ⲚⲈⲈⲒⲂ ⲚⲚⲢⲰⲘⲈ ⲚⲀⲤⲦⲒⲞⲤ). All three—chrysolith, agate, onyx—are mentioned in the Coptic Alexander Romance (a pre-conquest composition), (O. v. Lemm, *Der Alexanderroman bei den Kopten*, St. Petersburg, 1903, 43–45), in a passage recalling the stones on the breastplate of the Old Testament High Priest.

An allusion to Justin's possible allegiance to the Green faction (πρασινοπάντιμε) may have been wishful thinking on Dioscorus' part: as successor to the 'Blue' Justinian (and the 'Green' Theodora), he was determined to be neutral;[18] but perhaps Dioscorus is concealing behind this epithet a wish that the emperor will be kindly disposed toward the affairs and aspirations of the Egyptian church. Without dragging out anew the question of doctrinal labels for the factions, we may yet remember that anti-Monophysite policies were implemented starting in 571.

On foreign trade in Justin's reign (fourth line), at least so far as precious objects are concerned, we have the crosses and reliquaries[19] sent by the rulers to Rome and other great shrines of the West. (The overland trade of the 'silk road' would not have been alluded to by an epithet involving ships.)

The involved epithet of the fifth line brings us to some very characteristic Late Antique, and Dioscorian, imagery. Star imagery elevated the mind of the reader to the regions of the upper air, the sphere inhabited by saints, invisible patrons with whose glory the individual could get into immediate touch. (Think of the glory of the cross-in-stars in its three stages at Ravenna: the mausoleum of Galla Placidia, the chapel of the archbishop's palace, and San Apollinare in Classe.) One's personal star was also a sign of this heavenly companionship.[20] Dioscorus is fond of using star imagery in the context of an encomium:

Heitsch 10B.3, a poem on Victor the prefect and *domesticus*:

ὁ γὰρ σὸς ἀστὴρ νειλαγωγὸς πέφανται.

'For your star has appeared to lead the

Nile.'

Heitsch 15.5, a poem for the birthday of Constantine:

οὐκ ἀμβλυνεῖ ἄστρο[ν] τὸ σ̣[ὸν] π̣ο̣[τ'] ἐ̣κ̣ θε̣ο̣[ῦ·

'Your God-given star will not become dim.'

And again in Heitsch 17.12–13, a poem for Colluthus (on whom cf. Heitsch 13), mentioning the recipient's relatives Callinicus (Heitsch 5), count Dorotheus (Heitsch 14), and Mark the judge (Heitsch 13 again):

οὐκ ἀμβλυνεῖ ἄστρον τὸ σὸν ποτ' ἐκ θεοῦ τὸ θεῖον, . . .

'Your God-given, divine star will not grow dim.'

Obviously here the star of the emperor, the *kosmokrator*, takes first place in the universe.[21]

For the last line, Dioscorus often uses dance imagery (think of all the poems that begin θήβη πᾶσα χόρευσον: Heitsch 9.1, 10.1, 11.1; also 3.9, 5.53; and cf. 21.1 and 22.1 in the epithalamia; and, in the same papyrus just before the present piece, 28.1). But it seems that μυριάμφορον is a *hapax* (Maspero restores it in *P.Cairo Masp.* III.67317.19 from the present line: repeated in the text and apparatus of Heitsch 3.22, adducing Aristophanic parallels). When used as an epithet for χρόνον, it conjures up a pleasing picture of scenes of imperial feasting like those of the Sassanian court, with which Justin II inherited Justinian's rivalry.[22] Feasts in which the emperor impressed his magnates and subjects with his grandeur were a fit subject for Dioscorus' fanciful praise.

". . . The more we put a poem into the past, establish it in its historical context, and interpret it by its own age's aesthetic canons, the more its uniqueness and individuality appear. When we are unfamiliar with the art of an epoch all its products tend to seem alike. The better we come to know a period, the less its products appear 'period pieces'."[23] As we become more familiar with the aesthetic as well as the administrative achievements of the Late Antique Egypt, we shall become more able to appreciate the originality, the *Lebensgefühl*, the world picture, of a local writer like Dioscorus of Aphrodito. His imperial praises carry 'the full overtones of late-Roman relationships of generosity, dependence, and solidarity'[24] to the heart of an Egyptian village with all 'the deep joy of proximity'.[25]

POSTSCRIPT

'The article by Barry Baldwin, 'Dioscorus of Aphrodito and the circus factions,' *ZPE* 42 (1981) 285–286 became available to me only after the previous study was completed. Baldwin has not taken into account the dated acknowledgements of payment on the same side of the papyrus: the seventh and eighth indictions must be 573–574, under Justin II. Perhaps the time will come when this sort of late antique literary production will not be referred to as "doggerel".'

Research for this paper was begun during my tenure of an ARCE fellowship; hence I am particularly grateful to the American Research Center in Egypt; the Franciscan Center for Christian Oriental Studies, Cairo; and, as always, Mirrit Boutros Ghali (Mt. 13:46).

[1] Cairo Museum Journal d'entrée No. 40833.

[2] The juxtaposition of divine and imperial salutation was a perfectly natural one, as is to be the point of this paper. See E. Wellesz, *A History of Byzantine Music and Hymnography*[2] (Oxford, 1961/1980) 1, 193, 333, 369 (especially on 'Salutations'). (Henceforth *HBMH*[2])

[3] A. Baumstark, *s.v.* 'Chairetismos' in *RAC* 2.993–1006 (Stuttgart, 1954).

[4] E. Wellesz, "The 'Akathistos': a Study in Byzantine Hymnography," *DOP* 9/10 (1956) 141–74; *idem*, *The Akathistos Hymn* (Copenhagen, 1957). Exhaustive bibliography in J. Szövérffy, *A Guide to Byzantine*

Hymnography, I (Brookline/Leiden, 1978), 116–35. Wellesz, *HBMH*[2], 193, n.1, cites Cyril of Alexandria's encomiastic praises of the Virgin (= *PG* 77.1032D–1033C) as an early, and quite developed, Marian example (cf. Wellesz' Excursus to p. 191, on p. 369).

[5] For example, see DeL. O'Leary, *The Coptic Theotokia* (London, 1923), pp. 4, 74–75 (Sunday office); 29, 31 (Tuesday); 35 (a fragment from the monastery of S. Macarius); 36, 41 (Wednesday); 60–61 (Saturday).

[6] Cf. Baumstark, *op. cit.*, 993–94, 996–97 for ancient Egyptian roots; 999, 1001, 1003–05 for Ethiopic parallels.

[7] *P.Cairo Masp.* I.67097 recto contains a land-lease from Hermauos to Isaac, son of George; and section (A) of the verso records Dioscorus' payment of grain to shepherds for a 7th/8th indiction, most likely to be placed in A.D. 573/4 (R.S. Bagnall and K. A. Worp, *Chronological Systems of Byzantine Egypt, Stud. Amst.*8 [Zutphen, 1978], 90): hence Justin II. The whole papyrus appears to have been a sort of work-sheet, repeatedly re-used: other poems on the verso are Heitsch, nos. 4 (B–C), 9 (E), and 28 (F), while section (D) is the famous draft of an *apokeryxis*. Athanasius (Heitsch 4) was Duke of the Thebaid ca. A.D. 567–570, so the papyrus comes from the end of Dioscorus' "Antinoë period" of encomium-writing and practising his profession of νομικός; or perhaps he used it in Antinoë and brought it back with him to Aphrodito in 573, where, by November of that year (cf. *ZPE* 26 [1977], 279), he was acting as agent for his father's monastery, Apa Apollos', when a monk of that house, Psates, donated a building site and two *solidi* to found a *xenodocheion* (*P.Cairo Masp.* I.67096).

[8] Maspero's note *ad. loc.* (p. 154), '. . . ces composés ridicules . . .', can be set aside. Compare the polysyllables in school exercises, e.g. as in H.-I. Marrou, *A History of Education in Antiquity*, 3rd ed., English trans. by G. Lamb (London & New York, 1956), 342.

[9] For what follows, see A. R. Bellinger and P. Grierson, *Catalogue of the Byzantine Coins in the Dumbarton Oaks Collection* I: *Anastasius I to Maurice (491–602)* (Washington, 1966), 195–263 and pls. XLIX–LIX. (My thanks to Mr. Francis D. Campbell Jr., Librarian of the American Numismatic Society, New York, for photocopies of Justin II material.)

[10] Stephen in Acts 6:15.

[11] P. R. L. Brown, *The Making of Late Antiquity* (Cambridge, 1978), 72, with n. 64, p. 121; idem, *The Cult of the Saints* (Chicago, 1981), 51.

[12] Among many examples, Ep 113.3–6:. . . ⲉⲓ̈ⲁⲥⲡⲁⲍⲉ . . . ⲙⲛ̄ⲡⲉⲧⲛ̄ⲁⲅⲅⲉⲗⲟⲥ.

[13] K. Weitzmann, ed., *The Age of Spirituality* (New York, 1979), pp. 323–24: No. 300, in which alternating emerald paste and sapphires are aligned between rows of pearls. (Color plate in the 1977 catalogue, No. 52).

[14] G. Mathew O.P., *Byzantine Aesthetics* (New York, 1971), 88–89.

[15] Maspero's interpretation ('. . . aux ongles de topaze et d'agathe') is overly literal (although we do know of ancient Egyptian, though not imperial Byzantine, use of fingernail-lacquer: R. J. Forbes, *Studies in Ancient Technology*[2] III (Leiden, 1965), 2, 20–21, 41–42).

[16] A. Lucas, *Ancient Egyptian Materials and Industries*, ed. J. R. Harris (London, 1962), 386–87, 389–90; cf. 38, n. 5, for a Coptic mother-of-pearl necklace supposed to have been in the Cairo Museum. (I have not been able to check its present whereabouts.) Compare the juxtaposition of pearl, emerald and agate in Ryl. 72 36, f.2r, v.4: A. van Lantschoot, "A propos du Physiologus," *Studies . . . W. E. Crum* (Boston, 1950), 353–54, seemingly a peculiarly Egyptian addition to the popular *Physiologus* we know. (In the homiletic context, it is in a set of metaphors for the Virgin Mary.)

[17] C. Mango, *The Art of the Byzantine Empire* (Englewood Cliffs, 1972), 92.

[18] Alan Cameron, *Circus Factions* (Oxford, 1976), 127–28; cf. Averil Cameron, *Corippus: In Laudem Iustini Augusti minoris* (London, 1977), 173–75.

[19] Averil Cameron, "The Artistic Patronage of Justin II," *Byzantion* 50 (1980), 62–84.

[20] Cf. e.g. Symmachus *Relatio* X.3: . . . *benign(a salu)tis meae sidera*; P. R. L. Brown, *The Cult of the Saints*, 73.

[21] Note that the epithet φωστήρ was used by Eusebius of Constantine (Lampe *s.v.*); otherwise, among human beings, only for ecclesiastics and theologians. Could there also have been a hidden play on the (Egyptian-)Gnostic notion of *illuminator*?: P. Bellet O.S.B., 'The colophon of the *Gospel of the Egyptians*,' in R. McL. Wilson, ed., *Nag Hammadi and Gnosis* (= *NHS* 14) (Leiden, 1978), 48: '. . . a technical word in gnostic theology for the divine element of the ogdoad.'

[22] On Justin II's coronation banquet, Averil Cameron, *Corippus: In Laudem Iustini*, 183–84. Sassanian banquets were 'part of the ceremony of rule . . . splendor (was) a sign of legitimacy': P. R. L. Brown, 'The Sassanian Empire in the Near East' (typescript), 8–10. Besides the descriptions of coronation ceremonial in Corippus and the lavish imperial gifts, we know of Justin's taste for adornment and display, so necessary in the highly visible world of the sixth century; he placed the famous icon of Christ above the Chalke Gate (G. Stričević, review of K. Weitzmann, *The Monastery of S. Catherine at Mount Sinai: the Icons*, I [Princeton, 1976], in *AJA* 82 [1978], 268); and he adorned the Liturgy with the introduction of the *Cherubikon* (Wellesz *HBMH*[2], 166) in A.D. 574.

[23] Dame Helen Gardner, *The Business of Criticism* (Oxford, 1959), 20.

[24] P. R. L. Brown, *The Cult of the Saints*, 90.

[25] *Ibid.*

IV

A Trinitarian formula in Dioscorus of Aphrodito*

Scholars are becoming increasingly aware both of the aesthetic achievements of the poetry produced in Byzantine Egypt[1] and of the importance of documentary phraseology as a witness to the religious and institutional life of the period[2]. The present study calls attention to an instance of poetic usage that foreshadows the shape taken by official language half a century to a century later, to endure long after the Arab conquest and be reflected in the formulary of three tongues.

Poem 6 of Dioscorus of Aphrodito[3], an encomium addressed to an unknown recipient[4], is a fully-developed specimen of its type, praising the ancestry:

κυδαλίμων πατέρων ἀπὸ ῥίζης ὀλβιστήρων (line 2),

the virtues: τοσσατίην ἀρετήν, ἅπερ ἀστέρες ἄκριτοι ἦσαν (line 14),

and the wisdom: τῆς πολυκαλλιστῆς σοφίης (line 10)

of the addressee. The mythological parallels (Achilles, Ajax, Diomedes) are interwoven with pure Homeric tags (ἁλὸς ἀτρυγέτοιο, line 15) to create an atmosphere of classical song and story like that of a Coptic textile. But in the most prominent place at the head of the poem, Dioscorus praises above all other qualities that of orthodox faith, in the arresting line (sc. σὺ)

πίστιν ἀερτάζων Τριάδος μονοειδέος ὀρθήν

'exalting the right faith of the Trinity, single in essence.'

One is immediately struck by the epithet μονοειδής. Dioscorus uses it in one other place, in 3.41 Heitsch, a panegyric on John, Duke of the Thebaid *ca* A.D. 574-576[5]:

ἀχράντου Τριάδος μονοειδέος ἔλλαχε δῶρον.

'you have obtained as your portion the gift of the undefiled Trinity, single in essence.'

The choice of word is not determined simply by the requirements of metre. Schubart and Wilamowitz comment (*BKT* V 119) 'ΟΜΟΟΥCΙΟC', quoting Justinian *Codex* 1.5, which is precisely what does *not* occur here. (By way of comparison, the Creed in the liturgy of the Coptic church simply borrows ΟΜΟΟΥϹΙΟϹ: it neither adopts another Greek word -- after all the doctrinal battles fought over that one -- nor translates into a purely Coptic periphrasis or equivalent.) Ὁμοούσιος —◡◡ Τριάς would end a hexameter line perfectly well[6]. In this epithet (and the words it carries along with it), with its Platonic overtones, Dioscorus is making a theological statement: both a Trinitarian one and a Christological one. In Dioscorus's poetic world Christology and the classical tradition meet, and we are the richer for it.

As a philosophical word μονοειδής can be traced back to Plato's *Timaeus* and other dialogues (*LSJ s.v.*). It and its derivatives appear down the centuries in writers as different as Theophrastus, Ptolemy, Sextus Empiricus, Polybius, and Iamblichus. Eusebius and Gregory of Nyssa use it of the Deity (Lampe *s.v.*). In a specifically Trinitarian context its principal appearance is in Maximus the Confessor, in the seventh century *(PG* 91: 1196B):

> [If anyone comes]... πρὸς μίαν καὶ μόνην ... κίνησιν [in God ...]... μακάριος ὄντως ἐστὶ τῆς ἀληθοῦς τε καὶ μακαρίας τυχὼν οὐ μόνον ἑνώσεως τῆς πρὸς τὴν ἁγίαν Τριάδα, ἀλλὰ καὶ ἑνότητος τῆς ἐν τῇ ἁγίᾳ Τριάδι νοουμένης, ὡς ἁπλοῦς καὶ ἀδιαίρετος καὶ μονοειδὴς κατὰ τὴν δύναμιν πρὸς τὴν ἁπλῆν καὶ ἀδιαίρετον κατὰ τὴν οὐσίαν γεγενημένος ...
> [The section title runs ... καὶ τίς ἡ ἐν τῇ Τριάδι νοουμένη ἑνότης. Latin: 'uniformis'.]

Dioscorus is here anticipating Maximus by three generations and more.

The unity of the Trinity, and the unity of the Son: absorbing subjects in the sixth-century East[7]. (It must be remembered, of course, that Arianism was no longer a burning issue, and ὁμοούσιος no longer needed to be invoked as a victory-cry. Other matters were at stake.) The Trinity is mentioned, with varying epithets and attributes, in papyrus invocations and oaths[8] in both Greek and Coptic[9]. In the documents (in particular those of the seventh and eighth centuries) we find ἐν μόναδι (cf. *P.Stras.* 397, reclassified as 8th-c. Coptic: Bagnall/Worp *BASP* 15 (1978) 244) in Trinitarian formulae[10]. As an epithet in Trinitarian contexts μονάς occurs from the Cappadocians to Sophronius of Jerusalem (Lampe *s.v.*). The point is that no special non-Chalcedonian emphasis can be placed on this particular word[11]. Dioscorus is praising orthodoxy (πίστιν ὀρθήν) *per se,* not a special or particularistic interpretation of it. (It must be noted that ὀρθὴν πίστιν is a favorite phrase in Nonnus's ***Paraphrasis of the Gospel of John,*** always with Christological overtones[12].) (This is in contrast to the typical non-Chalcedonian employment of the epithet 'the orthodox' to mean 'Us' as opposed to 'Them'!) It tells us something about the priorities of sixth-century society in Egypt that a local ruler is expected to possess this virtue above all[13].

We may note in passing the epithet ἄχραντος as applied to the Trinity, which turns up infrequently in documents (*P.Apoll*. 61.9)[14], very often in liturgical contexts (Ryl 35; Ep 592 A 5, 597 r° 1): Dioscorus is again our earliest instance after Theodoret (Lampe *s.v.*), in either prose or poetry. And the other two adjectives by which Dioscorus describes πίστις are θεοδέγμονα κυδιανείρην (1 v° 6 Heitsch): 'divine and glorifying mankind': a beautiful phrase for the orthodox concept of θείωσις[15]. Christological sources for the sixth-century East are abundant[16], but direct evidence from Egypt itself is hard to find (the 'standard' theological writers are thirteenth- and fourteenth-century encyclopaedists writing in Arabic[17]). The point is to ask whether Dioscorus in the 550's A.D., very close to the time of the Council of Constantinople II, is making some sort of a statement about the person of Christ. Let me state that this is not the place to become involved with the fate of the word εἶδος, its translations and interpretations, at the hands of the Arabic Platonic commentators: a subject in itself. This is also not the place to get entangled with questions of (i) words for 'essence' and 'attribute' (by the time of the Egyptian encyclopaedists everyone in the East had had his ears filled with the *kalam* for six and a half centuries); or (ii) the supposedly 'Monophysite' 'farced Trisagion' as a doctrinal rallying-cry in the East[18]. We may interpret μονοειδής Christologically, as a poetic compendium of the Cyrillian 'four touchstones of orthodoxy' on the hypostatic union:

> 'without confusion: ἀσυγχύτως,
> without change: ἀτρέπτως,
> without division: ἀδιαιρέτως,
> without separation: ἀχωρίστως.'

In Coptic cf. Zoega 225, a dialogue between an emperor and a cleric: ⲁϫⲛ ϣⲓⲃⲉ, ⲁϫⲛ ⲡⲱϣ, ⲁϫⲛ ⲧⲱϩ, ⲁϫⲛ ⲡⲱϣⲛⲉ[20]. Dioscorus is stating that a right faith (in the Person of Christ) is framed in terms of this sort of unity of εἶδος. His formulation has a respectable Cyrillian background[21], and a Platonic atmosphere appropriate in the works of one of his education and career as poet and scholar.

All this helps, I hope, to show that Dioscorus's implied Christology is an extrapolation from his Trinitarian conception as expressed in a single poetic epithet[22]. The Trinity in Egypt is 'life-giving' and 'undefiled': it is also 'single in *essence*[23]', a proleptic echo of that ⲉⲓⲥ ⲑⲉⲟⲥ that is to persist for centuries in Coptic inscriptions[24].

Dioscorus's poems yield much when placed in and understood within their historical context.

> 'An informed, avid awareness of the history of the relevant language, of the transforming energies of feeling which make of syntax a record of social being, is indispensable. One must master the temporal and local setting of one's text, the moorings which attach even the most idiosyncratic of poetic expressions to the surrounding idiom.'
>
> -- George Steiner, *After Babel* (Oxford 1975) 25.

The sixth century in Egypt was a time of no small cultural ferment and no mean accomplishment[25]. The achievements of this culture shape the papyri produced by it: their physical make-up, their handwritings, their phraseology where institutional life and the life of the creative mind interpenetrate. A single word chosen by Dioscorus of Aphrodito can be reverberant with the history and the sensibility of his times.

A Trinitarian Formula in Dioscorus

NOTES

* I am grateful to the American Association of University Women for fellowship support in the initial stages of my work for this paper; to the libraries of the German Archaeological Institute and the Franciscan Institute for Christian Oriental Studies, Cairo; and to Mirrit Boutros Ghali: ϩⲉⲛϩⲓⲟⲟⲩⲉ ⲉⲛⲁⲛⲟⲩⲟⲩ ⲛⲉ ⲛⲉϥϩⲓⲟⲟⲩⲉ· ⲁⲩⲱ ⲛⲉϥⲙⲁ ⲙ̄ⲙⲟⲟϣⲉ ⲧⲏⲣⲟⲩ ϩⲛ̄ⲟⲩⲉⲓⲣⲏⲛⲏ.

1. A. Cameron, 'Wandering poets: a literary movement in Byzantine Egypt,' *Historia* 14 (1965) 470-509; *idem*, '*Pap.Ant*. III.115 and the iambic prologue in late Greek poetry,' *CQ* 64 (1970) 119-129; R.C. McCail, 'P.Gr.Vindob. 29788C: hexameter encomium on an unnamed emperor,' *JHS* 98 (1978) 38-63.

2. Z. Borkowski, 'Formules de datation dans les papyrus de la fin du VIe et du début du VIIe siècle,' given in English as '*Invocatio* in papyri under Maurice, Phocas and Heraclius,' paper at the XV International Congress of Papyrology, Brussels 1977; and now R.S. Bagnall/K.A. Worp, 'Christian invocations in the papyri,' to appear in *Cd'E*.*By the same latter two authors, 'Chronological notes on Byzantine documents I,' ('CNBD') *BASP* 15 (1978) 233-246, esp. 240-244; and their *Regnal formulas in Byzantine Egypt (RFBE)* (*BASP* Suppl. 2) (Missoula 1979) and *The chronological systems of Byzantine Egypt (CSBE)* (*Stud.Amst*. 8) (Zutphen 1978). Such things were noticed as far back as H.I. Bell, 'A dating clause under Heraclius,' *BZ* 22 (1913) 395-405; for the religious implications of documentary phraseology see L.S.B. MacCoull, 'Child donations and child saints in Coptic Egypt,' *EEQ* 13 (1979) 409-415.

3. Cited from the edition of E. Heitsch, *Die griechischen Dichterfragmente der römischen Kaiserzeit* (=*Abh.d.Akad.d.Wiss. Göttingen, phil.-hist. Kl.*, F. 3 nr. 49) (Göttingen 1963/4). Poem 6 is dated to around A.D. 554, the year after Dioscorus's journey to the Pentapolis; the year of Justinian's Edict XIII reorganising Egypt. I am preparing a monograph on Dioscorus's life and work: the outdated treatments by Maspero (*REG* 24 (1911) 426-481) and Bell (*JHS* 64 (1944) 21-36) do nothing but view him through much too 'classical spectacles' and use over-emotive words: '... ses bizarreries de décadent' (Maspero *loc.cit*. p. 472).

4. The prose and verse encomium/panegyric of the later empire has recently come in for its share of scholarly attention: T. Viljamaa, *Studies in Greek encomiastic poetry of the early Byzantine period* (=*Soc.Scient.Fenn. Comm.Hum.Litt*. 42.4) (Helsinki 1968); S.G. MacCormack, 'Latin prose panegyrics,' in T.A. Dorey, ed., *Silver Latin II: Empire and aftermath* (London 1975) 143-205; for Syriac, K.A. McVey, *Memre of George, bishop of the Arabs* (diss. Harvard 1978). One must bear in mind that the Byzantine/Coptic writer of encomia may have been influenced, in addition to his classical models, by the hagiography he had heard and read.

5. L.S.B. MacCoull, 'Dioscorus and the dukes,' *Second Byzantine Studies Conference* (Madison, Wis., 1976) *Abstracts* pp. 3-4 (to appear in *Byzantine Studies*). The *ed. princ*. of this poem is *BKT* V (1907) 117-122.

*NOTE: *Cd'E* 56 (1981) 112-133.

6. See now A. Saija, 'La metrica di Dioscoro di Afroditopoli,' *Studi ... A. Ardizzoni* 2 (Rome 1978) 823-849.

7. P.T.R. Gray, *The defense of Chalcedon in the East (451-553) (=Stud.Hist.Chr. Thought* 20) (Leiden 1979): a useful and timely study. See his treatment of the so-called 'double consubstantiality', pp. 100 ff.

8. E. Seidl, *Der Eid im römisch-ägyptischen Provinzialrecht* 2 *(=MB* 24) (Munich 1935) 137-160, esp. 140-144; cf. E. Springer in *ZÄS* 23 (1885) 132-144. Seidl renders ⲞⲘⲞⲞⲨⲤⲒⲞⲤ as 'vom einheitlichen Wesen', Springer as 'von gleichem Wesen'. The former is really closer to being a translation of μονοειδής.

9. E.g. *P.Lond.* V.1675.2 (a petition to the duke of the Thebaid, written by Dioscorus at Antinoë, A.D. 566-573), in an oath formula. It is interesting to observe the interaction and interpenetration of Dioscorus's documentary phraseology and his poetic imagery. In this petition the parties ask to receive the Duke's mercy 'as those in Hades received the *parousia* of Christ'. For the Trinity in the eighth century (ⲈⲚ ⲘⲞⲚⲀⲀⲒ) cf. *P.Lond.* IV.1494 (A.D. 709), 1496 (A.D. 708), 1508.1 (Kurrah ibn Sharik). In Coptic cf. *ROC* 19.72: He became man ϩⲚⲞⲨⲘⲚⲦⲀⲦⲠⲰⲰⲚⲈ ⲘⲚ-ⲞⲨⲘⲚⲦⲀⲦϢⲒⲂⲈ: interesting for what follows. The Dioscorus petition would be dated to just before his Poem 3. Bagnall/Worp in *BASP* 15 (1978) 241: 'Trinitarian formulas first appear under Phocas' (i.e. A.D. 602/3 sqq.): not quite without exception. Cf. also Borkowski, 'Formules,' p. 6 with n. 16.

10. See the references to *P.Lond.* IV in the preceding note.

11. Seidl *Eid* (above note 8) p. 144 with n. 8 comes down heavily on the supposedly 'Monophysite' wording of KRU 3.15-17: ...ⲘⲠⲞⲨⲬⲀⲒ ⲚⲦⲈⲦⲢⲒⲀⲤ ⲈⲦⲞⲨⲀⲀⲂ ⲚϩⲞⲘⲀⲞⲨⲤⲒⲞⲚ [*sic*] ⲠⲈ ⲒⲰⲦ ⲘⲚⲠϢⲎⲢⲈ ⲘⲚⲠⲈⲠⲚⲀ ⲈⲦⲞⲨⲀⲀⲂ ⲦⲘⲚⲦⲞⲨⲀ ⲈⲦϩⲚⲞⲨⲦⲢⲒⲀⲤ. (See below for ⲘⲚⲦⲞⲨⲀ as a Christological word.) Affirmation of the Unity does not presuppose one position or the other.

12. Nonnus *Paraphrasis* ed. A. Scheindler (Leipzig: Teubner, 1881) 1.18-19 (=John 1:76); 3.(90-)92 (=John 3:18); 6.122-3 (=John 6:29); 11.146 (=John 11:40, to Martha at Bethany); 17.65 (=John 17:20). We look forward to the forthcoming edition of this work by Professor E. Livrea.

13. The whole doctrinal and social imbroglio is sorted out and summed up with admirable clarity by W.H.C. Frend, 'Old and New Rome in the age of Justinian,' in D. Baker, ed., *Relations between East and West in the Middle Ages* (Edinburgh 1973) 11-28. Compare the switching of sides by the *patricius* Apion 2, who went over to the Chalcedonians (*PLRE* II.111-112).

14. Cf. *P.Lond.* V.1675, written by Dioscorus (above note 9); *SB* I.4669; and Bagnall/Worp, *BASP* 15 (1978). On ἄχραντος , Borkowski, 'Formules,' p. 11 with n. 28.

15. There appears to be no specifically Egyptian iconography for the Trinity (*Lexikon d.christl. Ikonographie* I (Freiburg i/Br 1968) 525-537). Nonnus's other epithets for πίστις are ἑκούσιον, *Paraphrasis* 3.84, ἀκαμπέα, 3.167, ἀστεμφέα , 6.145 and 14.50, θεουδέα , 12.155, and ἀτίνακτον , 12. 183. (Cf. 7.145.)

16. D. Evans, *Leontius of Byzantium, an Origenist Christology* (Washington 1970); R.C. Chesnut, *Three Monophysite Christologies* (Oxford 1976); the *Cathedral Homilies* of Severus of Antioch, in 17 volumes of *PO* and still appearing; etc.

17. John ibn Siba' (late 13th c.) and Abu 'l Barakat (early 14th c.): respectively in *PO* 16 (1924) ed. J. Perier, re-ed. V. Mistrih O.F.M., *Juhanna ibn Abi Zakaria ibn Siba': Pretiosa margarita de scientiis ecclesiasticis* (Cairo 1966); and *PO* 20 (1926) edd. L. Villecourt et al.
Abu 'l Barakat in his commentary on ὁμοούσιος in the Creed (*PO* 20.700-701) was translating from a lost Coptic original: he repeatedly states that 'the word *"jawhar"* ['substance'] is not in the Coptic'. Ibn Siba' on the divine unity uses the term *"dhat"* for 'essence': *PO* 16.597, Mistrih p. 5. Two points are to be made: one, that *tawhid* (= 'act of making one') in describing the unity of the Godhead is very different from *ittihad* (= 'result of unification') in describing the hypostatic union within Christ, the Second Person. Two, that both these words come in the Arabic sources trailing their full associative weight and aura from centuries of classical Eastern philosophy's almost 'high-Scholastic' age. They do not reflect the Trinitarian and/or Christological thought of the sixth century. (See the summary in *LexTheolK* III (1959) 549-560.) (For help with the Arabic I again thank M. Boutros Ghali.) Be it remembered that *jawhar* 'essence, substance' is a Persian loan-word.
For Syriac see A. de Halleux, 'La philoxénienne du Symbole,' *SympSyr 1976* (=*OCA* 205) (Rome 1978) 295-315, esp. 301-302 on Syriac renderings of the elements in ὁμο- + -ούσιος. On 'etymological translation', i.e. precisely what the Coptic creed did *not* do with ὁμοούσιος , see S. Brock, 'Aspects of translation technique in antiquity,' *GRBS* 20 (1979) 69-87.

18. Our best summary is in H. Quecke, *Untersuchungen zum koptischen Stundengebet (= Publ.Inst.Or. Louvain* 3) (Louvain 1970) pp. 302-304 with notes 11-23.

19. Denzinger *Enchiridion Symbolorum* (Barcelona 1950) 71 gives the Definition-of-Chalcedon version.

20. Three of the four, with a difference, are echoed in the 'Confession' after the Consecration in the Coptic Eucharist: ⲙⲉⲧⲁⲧⲙⲟⲩϫⲧ; ⲙⲉⲧⲁⲧⲑⲱϧ; ⲙⲉⲧⲁⲧϣⲓⲃϯ [Boh.] (ⲡⲓϫⲱⲙ ⲛⲧⲉⲡⲓⲉⲩⲭⲟⲗⲟⲅⲓⲟⲛ..., Cairo n.d., p. 321). We are reminded that this passage in the Mass, these three particular technical words *in Coptic*, were an addition of the twelfth century (!): O.H.E. Burmester, 'The canons of Gabriel ibn Turaik,

LXX Patriarch of Alexandria,' *OCP* 1 (1935) 5-45; cf. *idem* in *Muséon* 46 (1953) 44 with n. 10. See now I.-H. Dalmais, 'Symbole et confession de la foi dans les églises orientales,' *La Maison-Dieu* 134 (1978) 31-36. A monastic-party synod prevailed upon the patriarch to introduce the new phrase, *in Coptic* (Burmester 1935: 8-9). What influences can have been at work in twelfth-century Egypt to bring this about?
The Coptic emphasis and choice of terms are subtly different from the straight Chalcedonian formulation (Dalmais 1978 p. 36 oversimplifies). The Greek has two adverbs to express similar ideas of 'division/separation': this is what they did not want people to think they were doing to Christ. The Coptic has two negative abstract nouns to express similar ideas of 'mixing/mingling': corresponding in effect to **ⲥⲩⲙⲙⲓⲅⲛⲩⲛⲁⲓ/ⲥⲩⲅⲭⲉⲉⲓⲛ** (the latter going with ἀσυγχύτως). This is what the *Copts* did not want people to think they were doing to Christ. Two different sets of preoccupations here. Cf. Cyril Ep. 45 (*PG* 77.232A): [neither] σύγκρασις [nor] σύγχυσις .

21. See N. Charlier, 'Le "Thesaurus de Trinitate" de S. Cyrille d'Alexandrie,' *RHE* 45 (1950) 25-81. Coptic versions of the work existed (p. 35); the Bohairic Catena quotes it. Cyril's Trinitarian thought was alive and well in post-Conquest Egypt too. And it was fidelity to Cyril's thought that mattered above all: Gray, *Defense of Chalcedon* (above note 7) pp. 5-6, 104, 119.

22. Cf. J. Pelikan, *The Christian Tradition II: The spirit of Eastern Christendom (600-1700)* (Chicago/London 1974) 55 (on 'economy' and 'theology'), cf. 199: '... the debates between Chalcedonian orthodoxy and the Jacobite and Nestorian christologies had to relate the issue of the unity of Christ to the issue of the unity of God.'

23. On *eidos* see also Gray, *Defense*, p. 148 with n. 172.

24. A. Mallon, 'Copte (Epigraphie)' in *DACL* III.2 (1948); cf. M. Cramer, *Archäologische und epigraphische Klassifikation koptischer Denkmäler* (Wiesbaden 1957) nr. 55, p. 33.

25. DeL. O'Leary, *The Coptic Theotokia* (London 1923) p. xi points out the probable early sixth-century origin (in Syriac) of liturgical poetry of no mean complexity: this sort of thing doubtless found its way into Coptic without delay, and original Coptic compositions must have belonged in such a milieu. It is only the bad fortune of our transmission that everything we have is so late.
Borkowski, 'Formules,' p. 5 with n. 11, prefers not to attribute variations in religious documentary phraseology to variations in religious orientation. I think that for the sixth century, before the official introduction of the *invocatio* as a required element in documents, we must try to draw what parallels we can. *Who* was trying to convince *whom* of a theological *what*, in such choices of words and epithets as we see in work like that of Dioscorus?

V

μονοειδής IN DIOSCORUS OF APHRODITO: AN ADDENDUM*

In the previous number of this *Bulletin*[1] I commented upon the epithet μονοειδής applied to the Trinity by Dioscorus of Aphrodito in his poems 6.8 Heitsch, *ca.* A.D. 553/4 (or a little earlier), and 3.41 Heitsch, *ca.* A.D. 574-576. Some further remarks may be of help in identifying the source or sources from which Dioscorus drew this unusual and telling word.

First, the Egyptian Christian culture hero, Cyril of Alexandria.[2] Cyril's rhetoric -- tropes, figures, stylistic orientation -- is, as I hope to show in a chapter on prose style in my forthcoming monograph *Dioscorus of Aphrodito,* a basic key to understanding Dioscorus' *Geschäftsprosa*. Traces of Cyril are to be found in the poetry as well. In Cyril's dialogue *Quod unus sit Christus*[3] the neuter τὸ μονοειδές is applied to the unity of a human being:

> A. Ἆρ' οὐχ ἕνα φαμὲν τὸν καθ' ἡμᾶς νοούμενον ἄνθρωπον, καὶ μίαν αὐτοῦ φύσιν, καίτοι τὸ μονοειδὲς οὐκ ἔχοντος, συντεθειμένου δὲ μᾶλλον ἐκ δυοῖν, ψυχῆς δὴ λέγω καὶ σώματος;
> B. Φαμέν.

Here is a passage, seminal for any post-Chalcedon Egyptian thinker, in which the word is used in a train of thought leading, albeit obliquely or by a kind of reversal (τὸ μονοειδές is what a human being does not have), into the familiar notion of 'for as the reasonable soul and flesh is one man: so God and man is one Christ'. By a well-known progression, the unity of the Second Person leads to the unity of the Trinity (and *vice versa*).[4] Dioscorus could have hardly have failed to be aware of this first Cyrillian formulation.

Second, the Alexandrian philosopher, John Philoponus, the probable addressee of Dioscorus' verse epistle in *P.Berol.* 13894.[5] The word μονοειδής in various forms is frequently found in Philoponus' Aristotelian commentaries,[6] as well as in his theological work. Citation of these passages will, I believe, demonstrate whence and how the epithet found its way into Dioscorus' poetic mind.

i) *in Categ.* 3.11–14 (ed. Busse, *CAG* 13.1 [1898]): on Aristotle's different writings:
τῶν καθόλου πάλιν τὰ μὲν ὑπομνηματικὰ τὰ δὲ συνταγματικά, καὶ τῶν ὑπομνηματικῶν τὰ μὲν μονοειδῆ τὰ δὲ ποικίλα· καὶ μονοειδῆ μὲν ὅσα περὶ ἑνὸς αὐτῷ θεωρήματος ἐγράφη, ποικίλα δὲ ὅσα περὶ πλειόνων ἐσημειώσατο.

ii) *in Categ.* 4.6–8 (*ibid.*):
τῶν δὲ ὑπομνηματικῶν τὰ μὲν μονοειδῆ ἔλεγον, ἐν οἷς περὶ ἑνὸς μόνου πράγματος ἀπεσημειοῦντο, οἷον περὶ ψυχῆς ἢ οὐρανοῦ ἤ τινος ἄλλου, τὰ δὲ ποικίλα, ἐν οἷς περὶ πλειόνων ἀπεσημειοῦντο πραγμάτων.

iii) *in Analyt. prior.* 18.11–14 (ed. Wallies, *CAG* 13.2 [1905]): on analysis of a logical proposition:
ἤρκει γὰρ καὶ οὕτως ὁρίσασθαι, ὅτι πρότασίς ἐστι λόγος τινὸς κατά τινος· ἀλλ' ἐπεὶ μὴ μονοειδεῖς εἰσιν αἱ προτάσεις (διαιροῦνται γὰρ εἴς τε τὰς καταφατικὰς καὶ ἀποφατικάς), εἰς διάκρισιν τῶν διαφόρων εἰδῶν προσέθηκε τὸ καταφατικὸς ἢ ἀποφατικός,...

iv) *in De anima* 33.6–10 (ed. Hayduck, *CAG* 15 [1897]): on analysis of the soul:
ἀμφίβολον οὖν τέως τὸ γένος· ἀλλ' ἐπειδὰν εὕρωμεν ὅτι οὐσία ἐστί, πάλιν ζητοῦμεν πότερον σῶμα ἢ ἀσώματον, καὶ εἰ σῶμα, ἁπλοῦν ἢ σύνθετον, καὶ εἰ ἀσώματον, χωριστὸν ἢ ἀχώριστον· καὶ πότερον μία ἐν ἑκάστῳ ψυχὴ ἢ πολλαί, καὶ εἰ μία, μονοειδὴς ἢ πολυδύναμος, καὶ τίς ἡ τῶν δυνάμεων διαφορά...

v) *in De anima* 528.5–9 (*ibid.* [attributable to Stephanus of Alexandria?]):
πρῶτον μὲν γάρ, ὡς εἴπομεν, ἔσται διπλοῦς ὁ μονοειδὴς καὶ ὁ αὐτὸς νοῶν καὶ νοούμενος, καὶ μὴ πάντα ἑαυτὸν γινώσκων· καθὸ γὰρ νοεῖται, νοεῖ ἑαυτόν, καὶ οὐ καθὸ νοεῖ.[7]

Finally, the word μονοειδής appears twice in Philoponus' *De opificio mundi*,[8] usually dated to A.D. 546–549 from the dedication to Sergius, patriarch of Antioch, but pushed to as late as A.D. 557–560 by *PLRE* II *s.v.* Ioannes 76 (a more likely hypothesis). The work is a defence of Cappadocian theology (especially Basil's *Hexaemeron*) against the Nestorian tendencies of the Antiochenes (especially Theodore of Mopsuestia),[9] wrought in terms of Aristotelian/Neoplatonic physics. The relevant passages:

i) 81.20 ... εἰς μίαν καὶ μονοειδῆ τοῦ σφαίρου φύσιν ..., in a context of comment upon Empedocles' 'love and strife'.

ii) 191.26–192.1 ... ἐκείνη (*sc.* σελήνη) μὲν γὰρ μονοειδὴς οὖσα σκιὰν ποιεῖ ..., describing the moon.

The Philoponian corpus, that rich storehouse of sixth-century Alexandrian thought and learning, seems the obvious source from which Dioscorus, *poeta non indoctus*, took an epithet that was to resonate in his poetry and reflect his world.

NOTES

*I am grateful to the libraries of Duke Divinity School and the University of North Carolina at Chapel Hill; and, as always, to Mirrit Boutros Ghali (ϫⲓⲧ ⲉϩⲟⲩⲛ ⲉⲡⲏⲓ̈ ⲙ̄ⲡⲏⲣⲡ· ⲥⲙⲓⲛⲉ ⲛⲁⲓ̈ ⲛ̄ⲟⲩⲁⲅⲁⲡⲏ [Cant. 2:4]).

1. 'A Trinitarian formula in Dioscorus of Aphrodito,' *BSAC* 24 (1982) 103-110.

2. Cf. *BSAC* 24 (1982) 106 with n. 21. Underlying both Cyril and Dioscorus is the phenomenon that both were writing while listening, as it were, with one ear to Coptic syntax: a point I hope to develop elsewhere.

3. Ed./tr. G.M. de Durand, *Cyrille d'Alexandrie: deux dialogues christologiques* [=*SC* 97] (Paris 1964) at 736b of *Le Christ est un* = pp. 374-375. For Ethiopic see B.M. Weischer, ed./tr., *Cyrill von Alexandrien: der Dialog "Dass Christus einer ist" (äthiop.)* (Bonn 1966) 67-68 (tr.).**

4. *BSAC* 24 (1982) 106 with n. 22.

5. *Ed.princ.* by R. Keydell in *ByzNgrJbb* 10 (1934) 341-345. I hope to have shown in my forthcoming study 'Dioscorus of Aphrodito and John Philoponus' that the lawyer/poet of Aphrodito had studied philosophy with the eminent Alexandrian ecclesiastic. [Now published in *Studia Patristica* 18 (1987); in this volume Study IX.]

6. Various editors, in *Commentaria in Aristotelem Graeca* (Berlin) (hereafter *CAG*).

7. Cf. also (α) Michael of Ephesus (formerly attributed to Philoponus), *in De Gen.anim.* 236.19-21, on the food of bees; and (β) Elias *in Categ.* 113.26-29 and 114.8-9 (ed. Busse [*CAG* 18]), on Aristotle's writings. The word had a respectable philosophical *Nachleben*.

8. Ed. W. Reichardt, Leipzig (Teubner) 1897.

9. Cf. W. Wolska-Conus, *La topographie chrétienne de Cosmas Indicopleustès* (Paris 1962) 161-192 on the world of the controversies before the Constantinopolitan council of A.D. 553; also now A. Cameron in *JRS* 71 (1981) 184-185. Philoponus himself of course became a Monophysite culture hero -- and

a controversial figure. Remember that Dioscorus' father Apollos, already a monk, had visited the capital in 541: J.G. Keenan, 'Aurelius Apollos and the Aphrodito village elite,' paper at the XVII International Congress of Papyrology, Naples, 25 May 1983; while Dioscorus had gone there in 551 (*P.Cair.Masp*. 67032). [See J.G. Keenan in *Atti XVII Congr. Papirol*. (Naples 1984) 957-963.]

** See also R.A. Norris, 'Christological models in Cyril of Alexandria,' *Studia Patristica* 13 [*TuU* 116] (Berlin 1975) 255-268.

VI

THE PANEGYRIC ON JUSTIN II BY DIOSCORUS OF APHRODITO

'Of the bureaucrats who composed correct Greek epigrams in the middle of the sixth century, and were thus certainly classically educated and surely an élite, some at least were ready to admit Christian material in their poems, and it is to one of them that we owe one of our earliest testimonies to the growing cult of icons' ([1]). Indeed yes : this sentence was written referring to Agathias ; while it is the purpose of this paper to show that exactly the same words apply to Dioscorus of Aphrodito and his poem preserved in *P. Cair. Masp*. II 67183, entitled by Heitsch 'Encomium Justini II' ([2]). The existence of these verses has been noticed once or twice, in the context of the *adventus* of an imperial image ([3]) (since the *ed. princ.* by Maspero it has been assumed that an image was in question here, since Justin II never visited Egypt in person). Dioscorus' work has

For their assistance in preparing this paper I should like to thank Prof. Francis T. Gignac S.J., Catholic University, Washington ; Mr Francis D. Campbell Jr., Librarian, The American Numismatic Society, New York ; the library of the German Archaeological Institute, Cairo ; and, as always, Mirrit Boutros Ghali, εἰκὼν ἄγραφος ἀγράφου μορφώματος (*Christus Patiens* 923).

(1) Averil Cameron, *Images of authority : élites and icons in late sixth-century Byzantium*, in M. Mullett/R. Scott, edd., *Byzantium and the classical tradition* (Birmingham 1981) 227 (with n. 123) (originally published in *Past and Present* 84 [1979] 3-25).

(2) E. Heitsch, *Die griechischen Dichterfragmente d. röm. Kaiserzeit I* (= *Abh. d. Akad. d. Wiss. Göttingen*, philol.-hist. Kl., Folge 3, Nr. 49) (Göttingen 1964) XLII, 128-129. The Cairo papyrus we possess was Dioscorus' working copy, as can be seen from the marginalia in r 11 and v 2, and the alternative lines in v 2/3.

(3) H. Kruse, *Studien zur offiziellen Geltung des Kaiserbildes im röm. Reiche* (= *Stud. z. Gesch. u. Kultur d. Altertums* 19.3) (Paderborn 1934, repr. 1968), 41-42 ; and now R. Browning, *The Byzantine empire* (London 1980) 33. Av. Cameron in *BMGS* 3 (1977) 5 places the arrival of the image wrongly at Alexandria, not Antinoë, and does not credit the poem to Dioscorus.

found mention in at least one literary survey of the period (4) – when it has not simply been matter for ridicule (5). With the recent entry into prominence of the figures and achievements of Justin II and his successors (6), and now that the scholarly world is beginning to explore the sensibility of this period on its own terms, it is of value to examine this text, with particular openness to what it provides us of Christian imagery and of the atmosphere surrounding the veneration of images, specifically the imperial image.

I reproduce here the text and apparatus of Heitsch, with corrections based on work with the original papyrus (7) :

(4) T. Viljamaa, *Studies in Greek encomiastic poetry of the early Byzantine period* (= *Soc. Scient. Fenn. Comm. Hum. Litt.* 42.4) (Helsinki 1968) 33ff., 87ff., 122ff. Dioscorus is at least mentioned after a fashion (cf. note 5 below) in Al. Cameron, *Wandering poets : a literary movement in Byzantine Egypt*, *Historia* 14 (1965) 478-480, 483, 490, 493, 509. See also A. Saija, *La metrica di Dioscoro di Afroditopoli*, [disregarding the incorrect form of the place-name] in E. Livrea/G. A. Privitera, edd., *Studi ... A. Ardizzoni* 2 (Messina/Rome 1978) 823-849.

(5) '... morass of absurdity ...', Bell in *Aegyptus* 6 (1925) 177 ; 'ce jargon grotesque ... bizarreries de décadent', Maspero in *REG* 24 (1911) 472 ; '... cattivo gusto ...', Calderini in *Aegyptus* 2 (1921) 151. This will no longer do. The articles of J. Maspero, *Un dernier poète grec de l'Égypte, Dioscore, fils d'Apollos*, *REG* 24 (1911) 426-481, and of H. I. Bell, *An Egyptian village in the age of Justinian*, *JHS* 64 (1944), 21-36 are hopelessly out of date. They will be superseded by my
* monograph, *Dioscorus of Aphrodito : his life, his work, his world,* currently in progress, and by the *Guide to the sixth-century Aphrodito archives* being planned by Prof. K. A. Worp of Amsterdam and a team of associates. For a general evaluation of Dioscorus in his cultural context see L. S. B. MacCoull, *Dioscorus and the dukes : an aspect of Coptic Hellenism in the sixth century*, to appear in *Byzantine Studies/Études byzantines* ; cf. *eadem*, *The Coptic archive of Dioscorus of Aphrodito*, *CD'E* 56 (1981), 185-193. At least the paper-title of B. Baldwin (XVII Congress of Papyrology, Naples 1983), *Dioscorus of Aphrodito, the worst poet of antiquity ?*, ended with a question-mark.

(6) Opened up above all by Averil Cameron, ed., *Corippus : In laudem Iustini Augusti minoris* (London, 1977) ; and now we have S. Antès, ed., *Corippe : Eloge de l'empereur Justin II* (Paris, 1981). Earlier on a section of a scholarly collection entitled 'The Turning-Point of the Late Sixth Century' (Mullett/Scott, above n. 1) would have been difficult to conceive.

(7) I thank the author, Prof. Dr. Heitsch, and the Göttingen Academy of Sciences for their permission to reproduce this material ; and the Cairo Museum authorities for finally allowing me access to the papyrus.

* Monograph published by Berkeley 1988.

recto ↑

Ἰούστι]νος ἄμμνι ἵκανε φερέσβιος ἐσθλοσυνάω[ν,
Ἰούστινος] ἄμμιν ἵκανεν, ἐλευθερίης καὶ ἀρωγ[ῆς
δεινῶν σφ]αλμάτων λαθικηδέος ἤγαγε τέρψιν
ἀνδράσι τε κρατ]εροῖς πολυτ[ερπ]έσιν ἠδὲ γυναῖξι[ν.
[λώιόν ἐστιν ἑὸν παναοίδιμον οὔνομα μέλψαι],
[ὅττι χάρις καὶ] χάρμα καὶ ε[ὐε]πίης [φίλον] ἄνθο[ς,
ὑμνε]ῦσαι νέον υἷα πολυσκήπτρου παλλατίου,
τὸν πολυ]κυδήεντα φιλόχριστον βασιλῆα,
οἷον δῶρο]ν ἐπήρατον ὃν θεὸς ὤπασε κόσμῳ.
ἤλυθεν] οὐ κατὰ [κ]όσμον ἀληθέα πάντα ν[ο]μεύει[ν].
κλεινότ]ατον δ' ἀτίταλλε θ[εοφρ]αδέεσσιν βουλαῖς
σώφρον]ος εὐσεβίης Θεοδοσίου πάνσοφον ἄσθμα,
ἐκ γέν]νης μεθέποντα θεοῦ δέος ἠδὲ καὶ θεσμούς,
θείω]ν χριστοφόρων ὃς ἁλουργίδα οἶδε φορῆναι.
σπεύδεο] νῦν, στρατίαρχε, σέθεν καλέειν ναετῆρας.
. . . . .]ος ἔπλ[ε]ο μοῦνος, ἀ[γ]ακλυτὰ δῶρα κομ[ί]ζῃς.
πάντ]ῃ κοιρανίης σκοπιάζετε πυθμένα [ῥ]ίζης
σώφ]ρονα, κυδαλίμης σοφίης ἐγκύμονα θεσμῶν,
τοῖς προτέρο]ι[ς] βασιλεῦσιν ἀοίδιμον ἐς θρόνον υἷα.

Iustinus II (aa. 565-578) Aegyptum numquam adiit ; quare carmen ad adventum effigiei imperatoriae pertinet. – omnia sup. Ma. – **5**s e 20,5s sup. Ma, cf. 3, 13 **7** cf. E. Kornemann, Weltgesch. d. Mittelmeerraumes II 445 **10** cf. 2, 23 ; 3, 50 ; (14, 2) ; 21, 26 ; B 214 **11** *θεορρητοι[ς σεο* in margine dextro sup. Cr **12** Theodosius I. (379-395) **16** *αφθιτος* sup. Ma | cf. Nonn. D. 37, 103 **18** cf. 6, 10

verso →

χαίρε]τε μο[ι], βασιλῆες, ἐπὶ χρόνον ἄσπετον εὕδῃς.
κοιρα]νίης [ἀ]πάνευθε τεῆς φθόνος αἰὲν ἀλάσθω.
ἐκ σέο] κο[ιρα]νίης φθόνος ἕρπελος α[ἰ]ὲν ἀλάσθω
. . . .]λιν ὑμετέρῃσιν ὑ[πέ]σσε[τ]αι χέσμια χερσίν
. . . . . . π]εφρικότα τραγικώτερα δάκρυα λείβειν.
πίστ]ιν ἀερτάζεις θεοδέγμονα κυδιανείρην.

1 de confusione plural. et sing. cf. e.g. 5, 33 ; 6, 9s ; 17, 14s ; 23, 14 ; 24, 18. 21 | *ευδεις* II **2**s alter versus delendus, cf. 8. 10 ; 2, 2. 7s-11s ; 4, 3 ; 10, 33 ; 12 B 5s ; 13, 9s ; 17, 15s. 23s ; 19, 8. 11 ; 24, 12s | cf. 23, 21 et 12, 3 **5** cf. Nonn. D. 47, 228 **6** cf. 6, 8

μὴ τ]ρομέοις, σκηπτοῦχε, τὸ σὸν κλέος οὔποτ' ὀλεῖται·
ὡς] στέφος [ὑ]ψι[κ]άρηνον πάμφυλον ἔσσι κίβωτιν,
ἀκτ]ῖνες ἀστράπτουσ[ι τε]ῆς περικαλλέος μορφῆς
ὡς στ]έφος ὑψικά[ρηνο]ν .λαυ. . τα . . .κατ . . αφ. . .[

. . . .]. .ς ἱμ[εί]ρων φιλο[π]άρθενος ε. . . . . . .τιν
οὐδαμὸς] δὲ ἄγαξ πανομο[ῖι]ος ἔπλετο σεῖο.
οὐραν]οθεν θε(ὸ]ς ὔμμι πόρεν διαδήματα φωτός
. . . . . .]. . . . .λεν . . . . .αφθιθαι. . ατα . ε[
. . . .] . . . [. . . .]λη[. . χθον]ὸς ἠδὲ θαλάσσης
. . . .]τατου τ[. . . . . . ὑπει]ρόχη [

7 *τρομεεις* II, cf. Nonn. D. 29, 56 | cf. 4, 7 ; 7, 10 ; 20, 1 **8** *κιβωτιν* = arca Noae (Ke) ; cf. 12 B 5.9 **9** *ομφης* II, cor. Ke cl. 20, 3

Further notes :
r 1 : read *ἄμμιν*
11 : in apparatus add *[σιν* Ma.
13 : *εκ γεν]* *`γε´* Pap.
v 2 : *ερπελος εια.* in right margin

> 'Justin is come to us, the life-giver, bringer of good, Justin is come to us : he has brought to brave men and their happy wives the joy of freedom to banish care and of help for our painful failures. It is a fine thing to celebrate his name, worthy of poetic praise, as Grace does and Joy and the lovely flower of Eloquence, to sing the young son of the many-sceptred palace, the much-praised Emperor who loves Christ, which delightful gift God has granted to the world. He has come to shepherd all truth, not according to worldly standards. He has cherished with his divinely-spoken counsels the most renowned wise breath of prudent and pious Theodosius, following from his birth the fear and the ordinances of God, and he knows how to wear the purple robe of the holy bearers of Christ. Come now, Duke of the Thebaid, call your subjects. You alone are ..., and you bring gifts of renown. Behold everywhere the wise root of the stock of sovereignty, big with the statutes of glorious wisdom, a splendid successor to the throne of former Emperors. Rejoice with me, O sovereigns ; may you reach a boundless length of life. May the evil eye ever be banished far from your reign (may creeping Envy ever be banished from your reign). It is in your hands to loose our bonds ... (as) in our fear we shed tears of sorrow. You exalt the divine faith which glorifies mankind. You who bear the sceptre, do not fear, your glory shall never fade : like a crowning garland, you are the universal Ark of the Covenant, and the rays of your beautiful voice flash out, like a crowning garland ... lover of Our Lady ... Never has there been a ruler like you. God has sent you from heaven a crown of light ...'

We may take it as read that Dioscorus was an eyewitness to the festivities that called forth this poem. He moved from Aphrodito to

Antinoë between May and 28 September A.D. 566 (*P. Cair. Masp.* 67161) (Bell on *P. Lond.* V 1674, p. 56); thus almost surely overlapping with Photeinos' mission to Egypt (with a view to ecclesiastical union) which lasted until 31 August 566 (8). It would have been quite fitting for the ruling power that was trying to bring about such a *rapprochement* to send its own image (9) to the seat of the Duke of the Thebaid, a notable locus of power (10); and for that image to be received with appropriate ceremonial.

Individual points in the poem require further attention.

R 1 *φερέσβιος*, cf. NONNUS, *Paraphr.* 5.105, 7.99, 117, 18.132 (10a).

3 *σφ]αλμάτων* cf. *P. Cair. Masp.* 67115.5; *P. Flor.* 284.9. An accustomed word for 'troubles' (usually economic) at Aphrodito.

6 *ἄνθο[ς* : used in the Planudean Anthology in the sense of 'choice bits of rhetorical embellishment' or the like (*LSJ s.v.*): we shall see that Dioscorus shares much of his vocabulary, as might be expected, with the sixth-century epigrammatists (who have been the subject of so much recent exact scholarship). For comparisons to the work of Paul the Silentiary, Agathias, and Corippus, see my forthcoming

(8) THEOPHANES 242.4-7; JOHN OF NIKIOU 94 (p. 401 Zotenberg); F. DÖLGER, *Regesten d. Kaiserurkunden d. oström. Reiches* 1 (Munich, 1924), Justin II, no. 2. (Justin II's reign is reckoned from 15 November 565 : R. S. BAGNALL/K. A. WORP, *The chronological systems of Byzantine Egypt* [= *Stud. Amst.* 8] [Zutphen, 1978] 89). On Photeinos and his mission cf. P. GOUBERT, *Les successeurs de Justinien et le Monophysisme*, in GRILLMEIER/BACHT, *Das Konzil von Chalkedon* II (Würzburg, 1953), 182 with n. 4a. J. MASPERO, *Histoire des patriarches d'Alexandrie (518-616)*, (Paris, 1923) points out that the death of the exiled patriarch Theodosius on 22 June 566 called for direct measures : cf. pp. 212-228 on the chaotic succession problem. It was hoped that the new reign might bring about some measure of Chalcedonian/non-Chalcedonian reconciliation : hence Dioscorus honoured the new accession with a poem in high style.

(9) Cf. D. BULLOUGH, '*"Imagines regum" and their significance in the early medieval West*', in G. ROBERTSON/G. HENDERSON, edd., *Studies in memory of David Talbot Rice* (Edinburgh, 1975), 223-276, esp. 224, 227-228. We cannot infer from Dioscorus' text what the image might actually have looked like, except that it probably showed the emperor with purple robe and sceptre (r 14, V 7).

(10) R. S. BAGNALL/K. A. WORP, *Papyrus documentation in Egypt from Justinian to Heraclius*, *BES*, 1 (1979), 5-10, esp. 6-7.

(10a) Cf. R. C. MCCAIL, *P. Gr. Vindob. 29788C : hexameter encomium on an un-named emperor*, *JHS*, 98 (1978), 38-63, esp. 46-47 on *φερέσβιος* and the use of the emperor's name at the beginnings of lines.

monograph *Dioscorus of Aphrodito : his life, his work, his world* (above n. 5). (Cf. 5 *παναοίδιμον*, 8 *πολυ]κυδήεντα*, 10 *νομεύειν*, 11 *θεοφραδής*. For this last cf. NONNUS, *Paraphr*. 3.9, 38, 8.154, 12.177, 20.113. The new edition of this poem, to replace the Teubner edition of 1881 by A. Scheindler, being made by E. Livrea, is eagerly awaited).

7 *πολύσκηπτρον* is used by AGATHIAS, *Anth. Pal*. 4.3^{b}.17, and PAUL. SIL., *Ekphr*. 281. Cf. *Anth. Pal*. 1.10.11.

παλ(λ)άτιον had been a respectable loan-word since Eusebius (and is used in the *Apophthegmata Patrum*). In Dioscorus' world cf. *P. Lond*. V 1679.4 (from Aphrodito, perhaps from the papers of Dioscorus' father Apollos) ; *P. Cair. Masp*. III 67320.1, (a 5th indiction : A.D. 541 ?), an order from Thomas, *praeses* of the lower Thebaid, to do with the *annona* of the Antaeopolis garrison. And Dioscorus the lawyer was making an effort to make administrative Latinisms acceptable in poetry, using such terms as *δομεστικός*, *ἐξκουβίτωρ*, *καγκελλάριος*, *δίπλωμα*, *ὀφφίκιον* (see Maspero's indices). The capital was a living presence to Aphroditans and especially to Antinoites in their civic tradition : the imperial presence was represented in microcosm by the ducal palace, and no citizen could have failed to be aware of the *palatium* when the annual grain shipment was loaded at the quay of Antinoë. Moreover, Dioscorus had seen Constantinople with his own eyes.

8 *φιλόχριστον βασιλῆα* : here it is in all its glory, the formulation that is to flower under Heraclius (cf. I. SHAHID, 'The Iranian factor in Byzantium during the reign of Heraclius', *DOP* 26 [1972] 293-320, esp. 302-303 ; *idem*, 'Heraclius *πιστὸς ἐν Χριστῷ βασιλεύς*', *ibid*. 34-35 [1980-81] 225-237) (11). But the epithet has quite a history. In imperial titulature the first to use it was, it seems, Justinian (*Chron. Pasch*. I 636.1-4 Dindorf, in which the word has been added in the margin by what may be the same hand (12) ; followed by the Prologue to the *Edictum de recta fide* of 551 = *PG* 86A. 993) (13).

(11) Cf. also E. K. CHRYSOS, *The title ΒΑΣΙΛΕΥΣ in early Byzantine international relations*, *DOP* 32 (1978), 29-75.

(12) For the history of this term great help is offered by the work of G. RÖSCH, *Onoma Basileias* (= *Byz. Vindob*. 10) (Vienna, 1978) : see pp. 62 and 168 (Anhang Nr. 48) for the *Chron. Pasch*. textual problem.

(13) RÖSCH p. 65 (and p. 103, n. 58), for the *Edictum* and references to recent scholarship on its transmission. (Elsewhere I have tried to suggest a possible

The earliest epistolary use of the word is by Cyril of Alexandria to Theodosius II, in the acts of the Council of Ephesus (RÖSCH pp. 145-146) ; while similarly in the acts of Chalcedon itself the word was used in addressing Theodosius and Valentinian by Eutyches, and to Valentinian III and Marcian by the bishops of Egypt (and others) (RÖSCH, pp. 147-148). It is also addressed to Justinian by the bishops of Syria Secunda in an undated petition (RÖSCH, p. 152). It seems that this word may have carried some weight of significance in the great Christological controversies. Dioscorus is using great delicacy in inserting it into a salute to the new emperor.

10 *οὐ κατὰ [κ]όσμον* : Maspero distorted the sense by trying to read *οὖ*. The apparatus quite rightly recalls Dioscorus' other uses of this phrase (like a Baroque composer, he often borrowed from himself). It certainly fits in with the desired image of the emperor as being the bearer of Christian values (*χριστοφόρων*, 14), not just an arch-bureaucrat (lines 8, 9, 11, 13, 14, and especially v 6).

12 *Θεοδοσίου πάνσοφον ἄσθμα* : a hopeful, proleptic reference to what Justin's legislative programme would be (note also that, as we are aware, any epithet involving forms or compounds of *σοφία* is a complimentary pun on the name of the empress : cf. *σοφίης*, line 18 below) (14). *πάνσοφος* is Cyril of Alexandria's favourite epithet for biblical personages, especially in the later period of his style : see G. M. DE DURAND, ed./tr., *Cyrille d'Alexandrie : deux dialogues christologiques* [=*SC* 97] (Paris 1964) 58 n. 1. *ἄσθμα* is used by Agathias, Colluthus, Nonnus : quite expected and natural models for Dioscorus' phraseology. A study of the attitude towards law and the sources of law implicit in Justin II's legislative activity (*Novellae* etc.) would be desirable.

v 6 Again the imperial role : to lift up the faith. Elsewhere in Dioscorus' poetry he specifies *πίστις* as *μονοειδέος Τριάδος* (see L. S.

connexion with Dioscorus and his teacher, John Philoponus : L. S. B. MACCOULL, *Dioscorus of Aphrodito and John Philoponus*, Ninth International Conference on Patristic Studies, 1983). We are also reminded (p. 103, n. 58) of the Alexandrian connexions of this epithet : citing J. IRMSCHER, *Alexandria, die christusliebende Stadt*, *BSAC* 19 (1967/68), 115-122. *

(14) Averil CAMERON, *Corippus : In laudem Iustini* (above n. 6), pp. 204-205. The allusion must be to Theodosius' outlawing of paganism (*C. Th.* XVI, 10.11, of 16.vi.391).

* Published *Studia Patristica* 18 (Kalamazoo 1987) 163–168. In this volume study IX.

B. MacCoull, 'A Trinitarian formula in Dioscorus of Aphrodito', *Bulletin de la Société d'Archéologie copte* 24 [1982] 103-110 and 25 [1983] 61-64). Here faith is valued for what it can do for humankind.

7 *σκηπτοῦχος* Nonnus, *Paraphr*. 3.80, 18.162, 19.113.

8 *ὑψικάρηνον* : a Homeric/Callimachean word often used by Nonnus, see especially *Paraphr*. 6.7.

πάμφυλον ... κίβωτιν (for *-ιν/-ιον* see F. T. Gignac, *Grammar* II [Milan 1981] 27-29) : the central motif that in effect gives tone to the entire poem. Surely not, *pace* Keydell (attempting to correct Maspero's bizarre notion of Pandora's box [!]), Noah's ark (though the LXX word is the same) (15) : but patently the Ark of the Covenant. Here a figure, not, as it would become later, of the Blessed Virgin (16), but of the emperor. The closest parallel to this usage occurs later, in George of Pisidia's *In restitutionem S. Crucis* (ed. A. Pertusi [Ettal 1959] p. 228) 73-74 (A.D. 630) :

ὁ σταυρὸς ἐν σοὶ τοῖς ἐναντίοις νέα
κιβωτὸς ὤφθη, τῆς δὲ κιβωτοῦ πλέον · ...

True Cross imagery was of course deeply involved with Heraclius and the glorification of his exploits (17) : but even in the later poet it is not the emperor himself who is compared to the Ark. (Note *πάμφυλον* : the palladium of all the tribes of Israel : hence the emperor as world-Ark). Dioscorus has achieved a poetic 'first' ; and,

(15) A glance at the lemma *s.v.* in Hatch/Redpath will show that the vast majority of uses are of 'the Ark of the Lord', i.e. of the Covenant. Would Dioscorus have been familiar with the interpretation by Clement of Alexandria (*Strom*. V.35.5, 36.3 ; ed. A. Le Boulluec [=*SC* 278-279, Paris, 1981]) of the Ark as the *νοητὸς κόσμος*, and the Ogdoad with its (Coptic-)Gnostic overtones ? (*SC* 279.148-150). Cyril (*De adoratione* 5.9) uses the Ark of the Covenant as a type of Christ's humanity.

(16) For Egypt see G. Giamberardini, *Il culto mariano in Egitto II* : *s. VII-X* (Jerusalem 1974) 346, cf. 325ff. The epithet is used in the Coptic liturgy in the Theotokia for Sundays and the psalmody for Choiak (December), the month of the Virgin ("ed." Cl. Labib, Cairo 1911-1921). Cf. De L. O'Leary, *The Coptic Theotokia* (London, 1923), p. 39(a) line 1 : †ⲕⲩⲃⲱⲧⲟⲥ ⲛ̀ⲗⲟⲅⲓⲕⲏ ; also pp. 4, 29, 31, 35-36, 41, 60-61, 74-75.

(17) For the Ark of the Covenant, the True Cross, and Heraclius, see S. S. Alexander, *Heraclius, Byzantine imperial ideology, and the David plates*, *Speculum* 52 (1977), 217-237, esp. 227 with n. 52, cf. 224.

after all, Old Testament imagery is a typically Coptic way of embodying one's picture of the world.

For *ΚΙΒωΤΟϹΙΟΝ* in Coptic documents, see *Berliner Koptische Urkunden* III 383.16, 390.9 ; Bal 52.72 ; Ep 111.2, 5 (a letter from Pesynthius to Epiphanius, quoting Old Testament incidents) ; BM 511 (a prayer : '... behold the holy Ark that gives salvation ...' : Middle Egyptian) (18).

9 *ἀκτ]ῖνες* suppl. Maspero, here surely rightly. See the outstanding paper of J. Christensen at the 1977 Dumbarton Oaks Symposium, 'The optical theory of John Philoponus', on the Alexandrian philosopher's innovations in the theory of visual rays (he denied their existence) vs. light rays. In Philoponus light functions across space *ἀχρόνως* : here the picture is that of the universe immediately filled with the directives of the emperor's voice (see next note). I have tried to show elsewhere (19) that Dioscorus had studied philosophy with Philoponus at Alexandria. There may be a deliberate reference here to Philoponian ideas.

μορφῆς / *ομφης* Pap. The papyrus reading is clear, and the emendation (Keydell's parallels notwithstanding) is unnecessary. This strong synesthesis is perhaps Dioscorus' boldest poetic stroke. Compared to his uses of similar purely visual figures (Heitsch 2.18, 5.22, 21.19) the mixture of 'sound and light' is peculiarly telling (20). The event was, after all, an imperial *adventus* (21). The imperial

(18) The Coptic fathers do not seem to have commented on Ex 25 : 10ff. : cf. R. Devreesse, *Anciens commentateurs grecs de l'Octateuque*, *SeT* 141 (1948), 25-27, for Theodore of Mopsuestia, who would have been understandably unpopular with Egyptian Monophysites ; there are no surviving papyri of him (J. van Haelst, *Catalogue des papyrus littéraires juifs et chrétiens* [Paris, 1976]). See J. Quasten, *Patrology* III (Utrecht/Antwerp 1975), 403-404.

(19) L. S. B. MacCoull, *Dioscorus of Aphrodito and John Philoponus*, Ninth International Conference on Patristic Studies, Oxford 1983. *

(20) G. Mathew O.P., *Byzantine aesthetics* (New York, 1971), p. 30, for notions current in Late Antiquity of how 'rays' from the object seen interact with 'rays' coming from the eye (and cf. pp. 36, 88-90 on colour perception) ; and see the paper of J. Christensen mentioned above, on how the characteristics of physical and of metaphysical light were thought to influence on another.

(21) S. G. MacCormack, *Change and continuity in Late Antiquity : the ceremony of adventus*, *Historia* 21 (1972), 721-752 (cf. Mathew [above n. 20] p. 81 for images of Justin II). Antinoë was a city where this sort of thing mattered very much : think of the great ceremonial spaces described in E. Kühn,

* Published *Studia Patristica* 18 (Kalamazoo 1987) 163–168. In this volume study IX.

portrait was probably set in a gold mounting, accompanied in its procession by the music of gilded brass instruments giving an effect of double brilliance in the Egyptian sunshine and clear air. Dioscorus with his paradox is aptly describing the 'divine voice' as it rang ('flashed') upon the ears of the crowd at Antinoë. Nonnus uses *ὀμφή* of the voice of Christ : *Paraphr.* 3.49, 53, 5.106, 6.196, 8.104 and many other places ; and of Scripture prophecy, *Paraphr.* 1.93, 7.162, 10.127, 12.152, 166, 15.103. Note *Paraphr.* 5.127 : *θεοδέγμονος ἔγκυον ὀμφῆς* !

11 *φιλο[π]άρθενος* : an epithet supremely applicable to Justin II and his reign. The word was used to mean 'loving virginity' in Palladius *HL* (ed. Butler [Cambridge 1898] p. 84) and in Nonnus' *Dionysiaka* (cf. Heitsch 5.26) ; but also by Nonnus in his *Paraphrasis*, 19.139 and 141, in a beautiful play-on-words between this meaning and that intended here by Dioscorus, 'loving the Blessed Virgin' : the Nonnus *Paraphrasis* passage in question is that rendering the interchange ' "Woman, behold thy son" – "Behold thy mother" ' (*John* 19 : 26-27). We are now aware of the great flowering of the cult of the Virgin in the later sixth and seventh centuries, thanks to the brilliant work of Averil Cameron (22). Marian invocations appear at the head of documentary papyri in Greek and Coptic, especially in the Arsinoite nome of Egypt (23). At the beginning of the new reign Dioscorus is stressing a key element in Justin's piety.

Antinoopolis (Göttingen, 1913) 60ff., the quay where one disembarked facing the 'Triumphal' Gate flanked by colonnades. See Missione archeologica in Egitto dell'Università di Roma, *Antinoe (1965-1968)* (Rome, 1974), and the paper by M. Manfredi to appear in the proceedings of the XVII International Congress of Papyrology, Naples 1983. Antinoë was the seat of both a non-Chalcedonian and a Chalcedonian bishop (Maspero, *Histoire des patriarches* [above n. 8] 177) ; one wonders how, if at all, this state of affairs affected the imperial ceremonial. (Cf. Av. Cameron, *Corippus : In laudem*, p. 199).

(22) Averil Cameron, *Images of authority* (above n. 1), 207-208, 218-224 ; and Eadem, *The cult of the Theotokos in sixth-century Constantinople*, *JTS* n.s. 29 (1978), 79-108.

(23) R. S. Bagnall/K. A. Worp, *Christian invocations in the papyri*, *Cd'E* 56 (1981), 112-133, 362-365 ; L. S. B. MacCoull, *P. Alex. inv. 647 : a contract with Trinitarian/Marian invocation*, to appear in *Studi in onore di Ugo Monneret de Villard* (Rome). [Now published in *Rivista degli studi orientali* 58 (1987) 49–54.]

PLATE I

P. Cair. Masp. III 67183r.

PLATE II

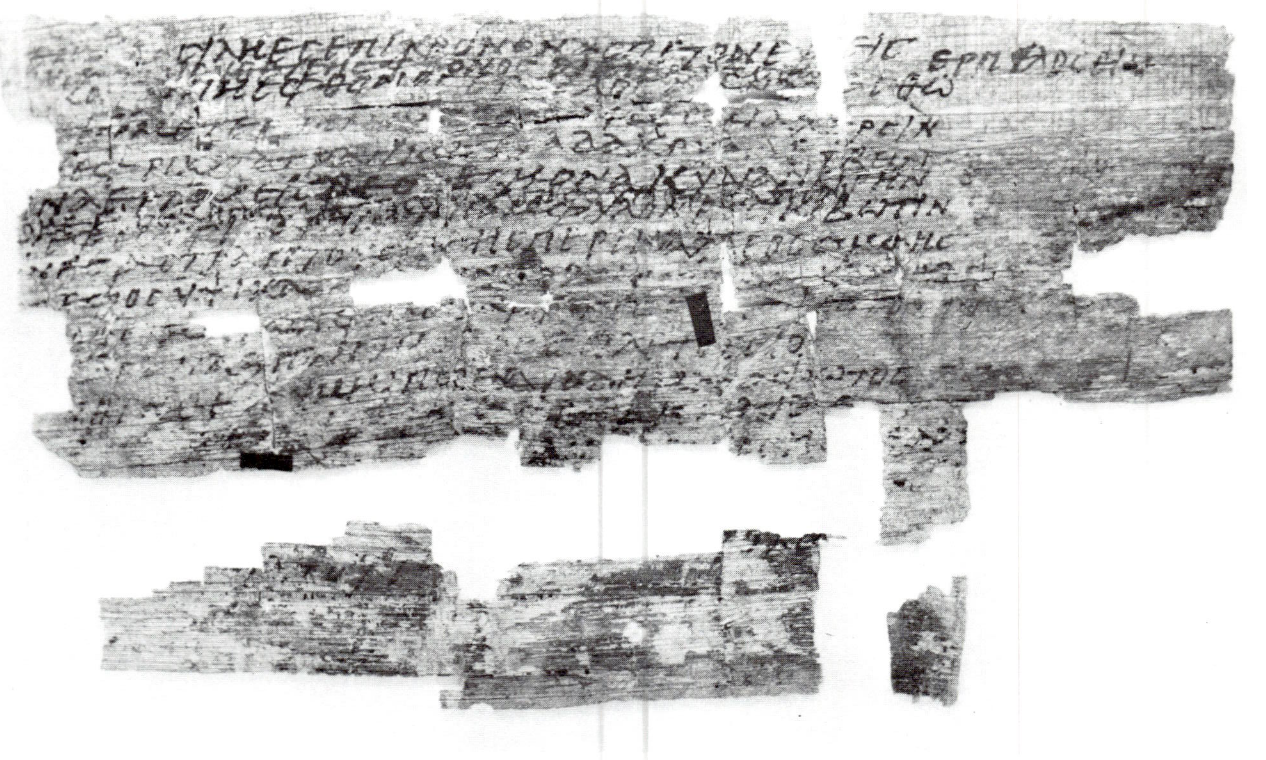

P. Cair. Masp. III 67183v.

The classical and Christian imagery of this poem, fragmentary as it is, affords new light on the imperial image, both the mental image of imperial authority and the visible image of the emperor's person as it was welcomed at the provincial capital with civic praise. Byzantine Egypt felt itself to stand in need of benefits that the new reign could bring, both in the economic and in the ecclesiological sphere. Hence *χάρις* and *εὐσεπία* mix with emphatically Christian epithets to express hope for the future, hope that is fixed upon the depiction of the purple-clad (r 14) and sceptred (v 7) emperor. In Dioscorus' lines that most ephemeral of events, a pageant, is frozen, brought back to life, and displayed with all the Christian pre-occupations that mattered to the original audience. The all-embracing *praesentia* of the Christian emperor is seen to move among his Coptic people. It is the merit of this forgotten local poet to have celebrated this *praesentia* in the ceremonial terms of his own place and time.

VII

A COPTIC CESSION OF LAND BY DIOSCORUS OF APHRODITO: ALEXANDRIA MEETS CAIRO

The papyrus collection of the Graeco-Roman Museum at Alexandria contains 48 inventory numbers of Coptic documents (one is literary, No. 698, a leaf from a codex) of which four are on parchment, the remaining 44 on papyrus [1]. I am editing these 44 items, with text and commentary, for publication. In the present paper I am happy to take the opportunity to reunite two long-separated halves of a hitherto unknown contract in the hand of Dioscorus of Aphrodito. The lower half of this document graces the Alexandria collection under the inventory number 689; the upper half is Cairo Journal d'entrée 40906, the recto (⟶) of *P.Cairo Masp.* II 67176 [2].

I: CAIRO 40 x 30 cm.

(Beginning lost)

Ⲙ̣[
.ⲘⲚ ⲞⲨⲠⲀⲢⲀⲬⲰⲢⲎ̣Ⲥ̣Ⲓ̣Ⲥ̣ ⲈⲤⲞⲠ
Ⲛ̄ⲀⲠⲀ ⲠⲀⲠⲚⲞⲨⲦⲈ { [Text } ⲈⲦⲈⲦⲚⲢ
ⲈⲦⲢⲈⲂⲢ̄ ⲠⲈⲤϪ { lost by } ϨⲈ̣ ⲚⲞⲘⲞⲤ ϢⲀ ⲈⲚⲈ[Ϩ
ⲈⲤϨⲞⲘⲞⲖⲞⲄⲈⲒ { abrasion] } ⲈⲤⲐⲀ
ϪⲞ̣ⲞⲤ ϪⲈ ϢⲀⲚ ⲚⲀϢⲎⲢⲈ ⲀⲨⲰ Ϣ̣
ⲈⲢ̄ ⲘⲞⲚⲀⲬⲞⲤ ⲈⲨ̣ⲀⲔⲖⲎⲢⲞ̣ⲚⲞⲘⲈⲒ .Ⲡ̄ⲢⲒ
Ⲙ̄ⲚⲦⲀⲨ ϨⲰⲂ ⲚⲈⲘ̇ⲀⲤ ⲀⲤϪ̇ⲞⲞⲤ ⲞⲨ̄Ⲛ̄ ϨⲚ̄ ⲦⲠⲀⲢⲀⲬⲰⲢⲎⲤⲒⲤ
ϪⲈ ⲈⲨϢⲀⲚⲢ̄ ⲘⲞⲚⲀⲬⲞⲤ ⲈⲨⲀⲔⲞⲒⲚⲰⲚⲈⲒ Ⲛ
ⲈⲒϨⲈ̣ ⲘⲎ ⲄⲈ ⲘⲚ̄Ⲛ̣ⲈⲖⲀⲀⲨ Ⲛ̄ⲔⲖⲎⲢⲞⲚⲞⲘⲞⲤ ϨⲰⲂ
ⲈⲠⲰⲒ̈ⲎⲈ ⲞⲨⲦⲈ ϢⲘ̄ⲘⲞ ⲈϢⲰⲠⲈ ⲆⲈ ⲈⲢϢⲀ̣Ⲛ̣
ⲈⲒ̈Ⲉ ⲦⲘⲚ̄Ⲧ
... [4 lines washed out; part of paradigm
... of ποιέω written at 90-degree angle]
...
...
..ⲀⲚ ⲈⲒⲤⲐⲀⲒ ⲚⲀⲨ̣
Ⲛ̄ⲚⲈⲚⲦⲀⲨⲦⲀ..
Ⲛ̄ϨⲎⲦⲞⲨ Ⲛ̄ⲦϬⲒ
Ⲛ̄ⲦⲀⲤϢⲰⲠⲈ ⲈⲦⲎⲘⲈ Ⲕ̣Ⲉ ϨⲈⲂⲆⲞⲘⲎ Ⲛ̄ⲦⲠⲈⲚⲦⲈ
ⲆⲈⲔⲀⲦⲎ ⲦⲢⲞⲘⲠⲈ Ⲛ̄ⲠⲀϨⲞ̄Ⲩ ⲚⲀⲒ̈ ⲆⲈ Ⲛ̄ⲦⲈⲢⲈⲨⲤⲰⲦⲘ̄

ϵΡΟΟΥ Ν̄ϭΙ ..ⲁΝΟΥΠ ΠϢΗΡϵ Ν̄ⲁΠΟΛΛⲰ ΜΝ̄ ΪΟΥΛΙΟC
ΠϢΗΡϵ Ν̄CⲁΡⲁΠⲁΜΜⲰΝ ⲁΥⲁΝΤΙΔΙΚΟΛΟΓϵΙ ϨⲰ..
ϢⲁΡΟΟΥ ϪϵΤΜⲁΛ....ϪΟϵΙC ΜΝ̄ ⲁΛΛⲁ Ν̄ϢΗΡϵ Νϵ
ⲁΥΜ̄ ΘΟΜΟΛΟΓΙⲁ [Broken by
fold-line] ΠⲁΡⲁΧⲰΡ[ΗCIC ?
ΤⲁC CΜΝΤ̄C Ν̄ⲁΠⲁ ΠⲁΠΝΟΥΤϵ ⲁΙϨϵ ..[
CΗΜⲁΝϵ ϵΤΡϵ ⲁΠⲁ ΠⲁΠΝΟΥΤϵ ϨΟΜΟΛΟΓϵΙ ΝΝϵ
Μϵ.....ϵΗ ΜΝ̄ ΝϵΚΛ[ΗΡΟΝΟ]ΜΟC ... ΝϵϢΗΡϵ Νϵ
ΜΝ̄ ΠϵΥΡΟC Δϵ .... ΟC ⲁΝΟΚ ΠⲁΠΝΟΥΤϵ
ΝⲁΥ ΝΙΜ ϵΤϵΤΝⲁ [Text
ΜΗΤΝ ϵΤΡΙ ⲁΥⲰ abraded ϵΛⲁⲁΥ
ϨΝ ΤϵΦΙΛΟΚⲁΛΙⲁ away] ...ΤΟC
ϭϵΡⲰΜϵ

II: P. ALEX. INV. 689 30.6 x 39.5 cm.

ΤϵⲰ [..] ⲁΤΝϵΠΟ [.] ΤΟΟΥ .. [..] Abraded
Ō Πⲁ [..] ⲁΡ ϵΤΒϵ [.] ΜΝ̄ΤϨΗΜ [..] ⲁΥΤΙ ϵΒΟΛ ⲁCΚΟΠⲰ[C
ⲁΝ ⲁΥⲰ [..] ϵΝ ⲁCΚΟΠⲰC [......] ΗΤϵ ΗΝ ΦΟCCΗⲁ[
ΒϵΒⲁΙ[Ⲱ]C Ν̄ΜⲁΥϵ ϵΤΒϵ Π[.....] CΚΟΠΟΥΝ ϵΤΒ[ϵ
Τⲁ ΠϪΟϵΙC ΝⲁϪϤ̄ ϵΠⲁϨΗΤ ϵΤΡϵ ΝΚΛΗΡΟΝΟΜ.[
Ν̄ⲁΠⲁ ΠⲁΠΝΟΥΤϵ ΜΝ̄ ⲁΝΟΥΠ ΠϢΗΡϵ Ν̄ [
ⲁΠΟΛΛⲰ ΜΝ̄ ΪΟΥΛΙΟC ΠϢΗΡϵ Ν̄CⲁΡⲁΠⲁΜΜⲰΝ [
ΚΛΗΡΟΝΟΜϵΙ Ν̄Πϵ ϨΙΟΥCΟΠ Ν̄ΠⲁϢϵ ΚⲁΙ ΠⲁϢ[ϵ
ΚⲁΤⲁ ΠΔΙΚⲁΙΟΝ Ν̄Τϵ ΝⲁΗΙ Μϵ...ΒΙ ΤΠⲁϢϵ Ϩϵ[
ⲁΠⲁ ΠⲁΠΝΟΥΤϵ ΝΤϵΝⲁϵΙ ϵΒΟΛ Ϣϵ Ϩⲁ ΤϵΥΠΡⲁCΙC[
ΤΜΤΟΥ [....] ΥΠΟΘϵΤΟΥ ΝΝϵΥϵΡΗΥ ϵΤΒϵ ΠϵϨΟΥ.[
Ϫϵ ⲁΝⲁ Η...Β - Η ϵΤΒϵ ΠϵΒΚϵ Ϫϵ ΝⲁΪ ΤⲁⲁϤ
ΜΟΝΟΝ ϵϢⲰΠϵ ⲁ ΛⲁⲁΥ Ν̄ΦΙΛΟΚⲁΛΙⲁ ϢⲰΠϵ
ϨΝ̄ΤΡΙΤΜ̄Τϵ Νⲁ ΠⲁΠΝΟΥΤϵ .... ϵϢϢΙΝϵ
Ν̄Cϵ .. Ν̄ΤΟΟΤΟΥ ΤⲁΡϵΤΡΙ Ν̄ΠϵΥΡΟΤ Ν̄ΟΥΟϵΙϢ
'ΝΙΜ' Ρ̄ⲁΛⲰΤΝ̄ ϨⲁΜΟΟΥ ϵΠΟΡΔΙΝΟΝ ϵΥ... Μ̄ΜΟC
ΜΝ̄ΝϵΥϵΡΗΥ ⲁϪΝ ΜΙϢϵ [...]. Ν̄ΗΙϵΥ ΜΦⲰΝϵ
ΓⲁΡ ΚⲁΤⲁ ΤϵΝΔΟΚΙΜⲁCΙⲁ .Ϩ [...] Ϫϵ ϵΙC [.] ϨΝ ΚⲁⲁΥ
]ΟCϵΝΤ[ ]ϵΪϵ ΠϵΝ
ϢΟϪΝϵ Ν̄ΤϵΝΝΟΠ̄C [.]ⲁΡ Ϫϵ ⲁΝΟΥΠ ΜΝ̄ ΪΟΥΛΙΟC
Ν̄ϵ Ν̄ϢΗΡϵ Η̄ Πϵ..ΟΡ Ν̄ΤⲁΥϵΪ ϵΤΜΝ̄ΤΜΟΝⲁΧΟC
ΚⲁΤⲁ ΝΙϢΟϪΝϵ Ν̄ΝϵΜϵCΙⲁΝΗ ΤϵΥΜⲁⲁΥ ΜΝ̄
ΠϵΥ Ρ.[......]. ϵΙⲰΤ ϵϢⲁΥΜϵΤϵΧϵ ΜΝ̄Νⲁ [.]
ⲁ ΠⲁΠΝΟΥΤϵ ΟΡΘⲰC ΚⲁΙ ΔΙΚⲁΙⲰC ϵΤΡϵΥΠⲁϢϵ
ΚⲁΙ ΠⲁϢϵ ϨΙΟΥCΟΠ ΛΟΙΠΟΝ ΟΥΝ ΚⲁΤⲁ ΠϵΙΤΥΠΟC
ⲁΘΚΡΙΝϵ ⲁϪΝ̄ ϨΥΠΟΚΡΙCΙC † ΤⲁⲁC Ν̄ΝΜⲁΪΝΟΥΤϵ
Ν̄ΝΟϭ Ν̄ΡⲰΜϵ Ν̄ΠΤΟΟΥ Ν̄ΦⲁΡΟΟΥ ΜΝ̄ ΝⲁΠϯΜ[ϵ
ΤΗΡϤ̄ ϨΙΤΝ ΔΙΟCΚΟΡΟC ΠΙϵΛⲁΧ/ ΠϢΗΡϵ Ν̄ⲁΠⲁ
ⲁΠΟΛΛⲰ Ν̄ΦⲁΡΟΟΥ † Η ⲁΓΙⲁ ΤΡΙⲁC Κ(ⲁΙ) ΔΙ ϵΥΧⲁΙ ΥΜⲰ[Ν
ϵΜϵ ΔΙⲁΦΥΛⲁΤΤⲰΙ ⲁΝⲰΘϵΝ ΠⲁΝ[
ΚⲁΤΟΥ ϵΡϵ...Θϵ ϨϵΝ ...[

+ Ἀθὺρ νεομηνίᾳ τρίτης ἰνδ ἔτ[ο]υς [τεταρ]του τῆς
βασιλίας κα[ὶ] / ὑπατείας τοῦ θειοτ ἡμῶν δεσπ/ Φλ/
Ἰουστίνου τοῦ αἰωνίου αὐ[γ(ούστου)] / αὐτοκρά(τορος)

[On reading of dating clause, last line:] = 4.xi. A.D.569 (thanks to Prof. K. A. Worp).

I.2,8; cf. 26 ⲠⲀⲢⲀⲬⲰⲢⲎⲤⲒⲤ: 'cession', usually of land. For explications of παραχωρητικὴ ὁμολογία and the like see D.S. Crawford's comments on *P. Michael.* 41, a cession of two parcels of church land in the Antaeopolite nome by a bishop named John to Apollos son oh Joseph: esp. lines 19, 50, 63; cf. 30. P. 80: '... there seems to have been no real distinction between πρᾶσις and ἐγχώρησις or παραχώρησις.' Not quite: ⲠⲢⲀⲤⲒⲤ especially as a loan-word in Coptic documents becomes more or less a general word for 'contract' of any kind, and we find this loose popular usage perpetrated even by the scribes themselves, e.g. *KRU* 106.37 (cf. below, II.10). As a Coptic loan-word it occurs 21 times in the Jeme documents. It is found in parallel phraseology with φιλοκαλία (below, 33, II.13) in Till *CPR* IV 26 and 27.: cf. Schiller *CLT* 7.30, 31. Used in the Greek documents from Aphrodito, e.g. *P.Cairo Masp.* I 67111.15, lease of land, A.D. 585; 67118.34, A.D. 547, by Dioscorus. In *Ness.* 24.10 of A.D. 569, the same date as the present document (see below), it is used in an official notice to the land-office.

3 ⲀⲠⲀ ⲠⲀⲠⲚⲞⲨⲦⲈ: One of the principals of the contract; an ecclesiastic by this name is known at Aphrodito only in the Coptic text of *P.Cair.Masp.* III 67353r, which also mentions Anoup and Julius (as below). Cf. L. S. B. MacCoull in *Chronique d'Égypte* 56 (1981) 185-193 and in BSAC 25 (1983) 91-94.

11 ϢⲘ̄ⲘⲞ: used in the customary phraseology ensuring that 'no one can sue you, neither relation nor stranger...': cf. *CLT* 1.70, 7.46. Not here, apparently, in a prohibition involving an oath, like *CLT* 5.128, 6.42, 9.13; cf. Seidl *Eid* II.146-147.

33ⲪⲒⲖⲞⲔⲀⲖⲒⲀ: used most often in connection with improvements in leased property. Well known in Aphrodito usage: *P.Cairo Masp.* II 67151.185, the testament of the physician Fl. Phoebammon, A.D. 570; I 67006 II 104 and 67020 II 8; and, from Syene, *P.Lond.* V,1727.36 (A.D. 583/4): requests and dispositions of property. Used in the Apion archive: *P.Oxy.* XIX.2239.11 (A.D. 598), '... every care and efficiency in the cultivation of your estate...' (p. 112); XXVII.2478.17-18, deed of surety, A.D. 595-6 (same phrase).
Well known in Coptic documents since L. Stern, 'Zwei koptische Urkunden aus Theben auf einem Papyrus des ägyptischen Museums zu Berlin', *ZÄS* 22 (1884) 157 n.3. pointed out its use as 'verbessern'. The noun is rarer in Coptic than the verb: see *ST* 181.6 in a letter,

CO 87 with Crum's note *ad loc.* p. 11, and *Ryl* 159, a land-lease. This usage persists in the sixth and seventh centuries: e.g. *P.Michael.* 46.21 (Aphrodito, A.D. 559; participial); *P.Ant.* II.105.7; and for the early reign of Heraclius, *P.Lond.* II.483.41, 75: emphyteutic lease, A.D. 616, from Apollonos Anô (the monastery of Abba Patois) (H. Comfort, 'Emphyteusis among the papyri', *Aegyptus* 17 [1937] 3 - 24, does not specifically explicate φιλοκαλία).
In the eighth century it comes to mean rigging and accoutrements for ships, often occurring in the lengthy requisitions for naval equipment in the Arab period: *P.Lond.* IV. 1346.6, 1371.1, 1386.1, 1391.4, 1410.2, 1433 (register of *dianomai* or requisitions), 31 times (A.D. 706/7); and fifteen more occurrences of the same type. Compare *P.Apoll.* 32.7: ... καὶ ἄλλους δύο μῆν[α]ς θέλουσιν εἰς τὴν φιλο[καλε]ίαν, 'Et ils veulent deux autres mois par la réparation': in a letter to the pagarch of Apollonos Anô about ship repair, A.D. 713.
Du Cange *s.v.* reminds us that it is the word used by Theophanes (8th c.) to describe what Justinian did to the dome of St. Sophia: 'he made it over better'.
From its use in sixth-century Palestinian monastic writers (Lampe *s.v.*) one can see how φιλοκαλία subsequently came to mean 'piety, excellence in the monastic life': tending one's garden, in fact.

II.9 ΝΑΗΙ: 'My houses', i.e., those monastic establishments for which Dioscorus was acting as administrator and arbitrator, Apa Apollos and Pharoou (see below for the latter).

16 ϵπ ΟΡΔΙΝΟΝ: a strange Latino-Graeco-Coptic loan-phrase. See N. Van der Wal, "Die Schreibweise der dem lateinischen entlehnten Fachworte in der frübyzantischen Juristensprache," *Scriptorium* 37 (1983) 29-53. A survey of Coptic Latinisms would be useful.

22 ΜЄCΙΑΝΗ: the name ΜЄCΙΑΝΗ (f.) is listed by Heuser (*Die Personennamen der Kopten* [Leipzig 1929]) p. 109 n. 1, without giving a reference: I cannot find it in published sources. Cf. MacCoull in *BSAC* 25 (1983) 91-94.

27 ΦΑΡΟΟΥ: this monastery is hitherto unattested. Etymologically from ϨΡΟΟΥ 'voice'?

28 ЄΛΑΧ(ΙCΤΟC): in no other document does Dioscorus refer to himself by the monastic/ecclesiastical title of humility.

32 ff. The third indiction in the regin of Justin II, Hathyr 8, comes out to A.D. 569 (R.S. Bagnall/K.A. Worp, *The Chronological Systems of Byzantine Egypt* [Zutphen 1978] 89, with postconsulates possibly to be read in line 33). In this year Dioscorus was living at Antinoë, practising the notariate and writing poetry. He drew up several other contracts in this year: *P.Cairo Masp.* 67169 (+ *bis*), a sale of land by Fl. Victor son of Phoebammon the *scholasticus* to Aur. Melios; 67164, a loan of money between two tradesmen at Antinoë; and 67309, a loan of money by Aur. Maria to Fl. John, son of Acacius, *logisterios* of Lycopolis (Assiut). *P.Cairo Masp.* 67353 verso, a contract, is also in Dioscorus's hand. It should be noted thet *P.Vatic.Aphrod.* 14 has been redated to the reign of Justin I, not Justin II: so it does not belong with Dioscorus's papers for this year.
As far as the juristic aspect of this document is concerned, it would seem that Dioscorus is arbitrating, on behalf of the monastery of Pharoou, an action in which Anoup son of Apollo and Julius son of Sarapammon (I.22-23, II.6-7, 20) on the one hand, and Apa Papnoute on the other hand, are dividing (*pashe kai pashe*) some land before the former two enter the monastic life (see now M. Krause, * 'Zur Möglichkeit von Besitz im apotaktischen Mönchtum Ägyptens', paper at the II Congress of Coptic Studies, Rome, September 1980; cf. A. Steinwenter, 'Byzantinische Mönchstestamente', *Aegyptus* 12 [1932] 55-64). Neither Anoup nor Julius is previously attested at Aphrodito (the Anoup and Sarapammon in *P.Michael.* 34 are unrelated to the present document, the latter being in a place-name) they appear also in *P.Cair.Masp.* III 67353r. There also appears to have been a woman party to the matter, but a feminine proper name as subject of ⲉⲥϩⲟⲙⲟⲗⲟⲅⲉⲓ (I.5) cannot be read. As for Mesiane ⲧⲉⲩⲙⲁⲁⲩ, *'their* mother', is it the case that Anoup and Julius are both her sons, half-brothers, by two different fathers, Apollo and Sarapammon? Is she the female party? The state of the fibres in the upper half of the document does not permit a restoration.
For Dioscorus as an arbiter in Coptic see *P.Lond.* V.1709. together with Steinwenter's remarks on arbitration (cf. II.26, ⲁⲛⲕⲣⲓⲛⲉ ⲁϫⲛ ϩⲩⲡⲟⲕⲣⲓⲥⲓⲥ) in *Das Recht der koptischen Urkunden* (Munich 1955) 53-55; and M. Krause, 'Ein Fall friedensrichterlicher Tätigkeit im ersten Jahrzehnt des 7.Jhdts. in Oberägypten', *Rev. d'Eg.* 24 (1972) 101-107 for a slightly later instance.

* Krause's paper in *Acts 2nd Congress* is pp. 121–134.

NOTES

I am grateful to Dr Dia Abou-Ghazi of the Cairo Museum and Dr Joseph Ghariani of the Alexandria Museum, for permission to study and publish these documents; and to Mr Sami Mitri of the Egyptian Antiquities Organisation for photographs.
As always, my thanks to Mirrit Boutros Ghali, President of the Society for Coptic Archaeology (cf. Jer 42:14 and Is 54:1).

1. An attempt at publishing five of the Alexandria documents was made by de Ricci and Winstedt in *Sphinx* 10 (1906) 1-4, with many errors.
2. An unknown hand has written in French on the label of the Alexandria document that possibly it belongs with 'Catalogue Maspero No. 67176'. I have not been able to ascertain who the writer was: the ink appears quite old.

APPENDIX – *English translation of Coptic text*

. . . in a cession . . . Apa Papnoute . . . you will renew its . . . in law for ever . . . she agrees saying . . . my sons, if they become monks, are to inherit the cell and are not to go to law with her. She said accordingly in the cession that if they become monks they are to share in the fields, with no heir nor stranger going to law with them. And if they enter into the monastic life . . . But there intervened another week of the past fifteenth indiction. But when they heard these things, viz. Anoup son of Apollo and Julius son of Sarapammon, they filed a countersuit against them, the mother not being the owner. But being sons they made an agreement . . . a cession . . . which was concluded with Apa Papnoute; I have found (cause) to show that Apa Papnoute should agree with the heirs . . . they being sons . . . with satisfaction.

I, Papnoute, have seen everything which you (have done?) . . . in improvement of the property . . . They did not sell it without cause . . . (but) firmly to consider what the Lord has put into my mind, that they should inherit . . . Apa Papnoute with Anoup son of Apollo and Julius son of Sarapammon are to inherit it all together, half and half, according to the *dikaion* of our house . . . Should Apa Papnoute exceed the terms of their document (lit. "sale"), let them not make a deposit with one another on account of profit (?) . . . (or) wages. It is to be sold only if no property improvement has been made . . . Let Papnoute seek to . . . them, to satisfy their every wish to set everything in order among them without quarrelling. For they are in agreement according to our opinion and our advice. . . . That Anoup and Julius, being sons, entered into the monastic life according to the advice of Mesiane their mother, with their fathers (being deceased?), they are accustomed to have a share with Apa Papnoute rightly and justly, to go half and half at once. For the rest, according to this *typos*[1] we have made judgement without dissembling. ⳩ Give it to the God-loving superior of the monastery of Pharoou and its whole community (lit. "village") from Dioscorous, the most humble son of Apollo of Pharoou. ⳩ The Holy Trinity. And may I be guarded from above by your prayers. Hathyr, at the new moon, third indiction, fourth year of the reign and consulship of our most divine master Fl. Justin semper Augustus and imperator.

1. Cf. L.S.B. MacCoull, "*Typos* in Coptic legal papyri," *ZSS* Kan. Abt. 75 (1989) 408–411.

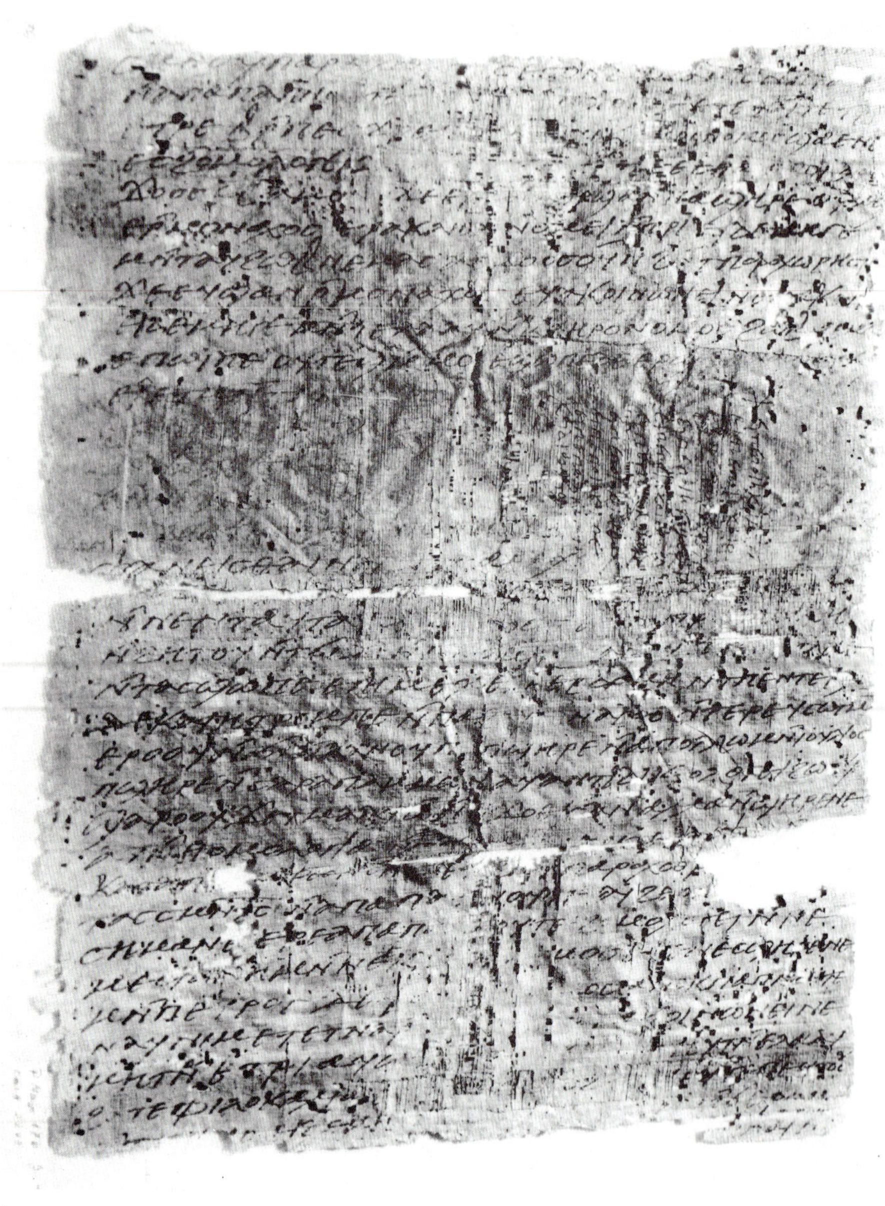

1

2

VIII

Further notes on the Greek-Coptic Glossary of Dioscorus of Aphrodito*)

The recent article of Barry Baldwin[1]) is a reminder that the bilingual glossary of Dioscorus of Aphrodito, preserved on the verso of *P. Lond.* V 1821, is indeed an editorial aid to his poems.[2]) It is also an index of Dioscorus' wider culture. The paramount fact to be borne in mind is that Dioscorus was Coptic-speaking, and that it is the Greek words that he was glossing into Coptic, explaining them, as in any student's vocabulary list, by their Coptic equivalents. As Baldwin is not a Copticist, it may be useful to raise some further points from the angle of Coptic philology and cultural history, based on autoptic work with the original papyrus.

I cite according to the line numbers of the original edition.[3])

27. The notion of 'daughter' [*κόρη*] 'of the eye', unexceptionable in Coptic usage, should be compared to the gloss in 25, *κόρη ὀφθαλμοῦ* = **ϫⲛ̄ⲣⲱⲙⲉ ⲛ̄ⲛⲃⲁⲗ**, where **ϫⲛ-** = **ϣⲛ-**, construct form of **ϣⲏⲣⲉ/ϣⲉⲉⲣⲉ** (Crum *Dict.* 585 b). **ⲕⲉⲕⲉ/ⲕⲁⲕⲉ**, 'child', can be of either gender (Crum *Dict.* 101 b with lemmata): here it is feminine and appears in the short form **ⲕⲁⲕ**. (The Sahidic of Psalm 16: 8, 'Keep me as the pupil of the eye', varies between **ⲕⲉⲕⲉ** and **ⲕⲁⲕⲉ**; the London MS. [6th–7th c.] has corrected **ⲕⲁⲕⲉ** to **ⲕⲉⲕⲉ**. We have no Lycopolitan (Subakhmimic) witness for this Psalm text.) For 'man of the eye' compare the Bohairic **ⲫⲣⲱⲙⲉ ⲙⲡⲓⲃⲁⲗ**, 'pupil', in Kircher's scala (*Lingua Aegyptiaca Restituta,* 1636) 75, rendered *ansan al-'ayn*. The notion of 'maiden of the eye' persists as late as the early fourteenth-century *Triadon*,[4]) 288.2, a passage which punningly rhymes **ⲕⲁⲕⲉ**

---

* I am grateful to Mr. Thomas Pattie of the British Library for the opportunity to work with the original of *P. Lond.* V 1821v descr. The inventory number is 1727 (1–3). I should also like to thank Ms. Monica Blanchard of Catholic University and Dr. Stephen Morse of The Rockefeller University for help with references; and, as ever, Mirrit Boutros Ghali (Ps 80: 8).

[1]) B. Baldwin, 'Notes on the Greek-Coptic glossary of Dioscorus of Aphrodito,' *Glotta* 60 (1982) 79–81.

[2]) As Baldwin pointed out in *Atti del XVII Congresso Internazionale di Papirologia* (Naples 1984) 327–331. Compare his *Anthology of Byzantine poetry* (Amsterdam 1985) 100–105, which does not cite this writer's commentary in *Byzantion* 54 (1984) 575–585.

[3]) By Bell and Crum in *Aegyptus* 6 (1925) 184–198 (text).

[4]) Newly ed. by P. Nagel (Halle 1983).

'darkness' with кеке 'pupil'. It seems that the pun is not so much in the Greek (*κόρη*) as in the Coptic: since there exists the masculine noun каке/кеке, 'darkness', this has influenced the secondary meaning of 'dark part of the eye'. To Crum's lemma in *Dict.* 101 b I would add that as a proper name какваλ would be more likely to mean 'apple of (the parent's) eye' than the descriptive 'bare-eyed' (101 a).[5])

161 ff. Coptic words for the sexual organs are abundantly attested. So far as terms for 'penis' are concerned, ваϩ is of uncertain etymology; ϯмє is 'the giver of urine'; снт is 'tail' (Crum *Dict.* 47 b, 158 b, 359 a). The Coptic ϫаϫ renders not only 'sparrow' but also 'ostrich', which would give rise to a clever slang usage for 'the one that hides its head'. Baldwin passes over the most interesting word in this semantic field, 163 *σαρακοιτιν* = саракωтє, 'wanderer'.[6]) The usage 'wandering monk' was intelligible as late as, again, the *Triadon*, 471.1–2, in the amusing rhyme оүрм̄ракотє/н̄ϩєнсаракотє: 'Are you an Alexandrian?' – 'Do I look like a wandering bum?' This too would be an excellent slang word for 'penis'. The Coptic rendering of 164–166, тωнє, means 'the stone', which would more logically mean 'testicle' rather than 'penis': it translates 'bull-roarer', *rhombos*. The more usual Coptic term for 'testicle' is ϫоєιт, literally 'olive' (there are also a few Bohairic late hapaxes). Then, in the glossary, *ψωλή* resumes the order of words for 'penis'.

190, *ὑδρόκομος*. Technical terms for parts of well equipment and irrigation machinery are well-known in both Greek and Coptic from Dioscorus' documentary papyri. *Hydrokomos* is glossed by the Coptic оүєιрє н̄ϣнї, an *eire* of a well. From Crum *Dict.* 84a, an єιрє appears to be a plaited leather strap which functions rather like a fan-belt in a typical water-wheel, including at the present day in Egypt. The Greek term being explained by Dioscorus is not so much a 'well-bucket' (Crum), i.e. a *shaduf*-bucket, as rather the drive-cable of a *sakiyeh.* It is apparent from the present grouping of terms that it is the *sakiyeh* or water-wheel that is being discussed. Other sections of the glossary text that deal with tools and matters to do with agriculture and irrigation are lines 111–123, 350–374, and 386–400, all of which lie near one another across the columns (see below on

---

[5]) See also P. de Lagarde, *Aegyptiaca* (Göttingen 1883) 242.27 (Canones ecclesiastici § 12), a proverbial usage. Heuser's 'wimpernlos' is erroneous.

[6]) See L. S. B. MacCoull in *Actes du XVe congrès international de papyrologie* 2 (Brussels 1979) 116–123.

how the text is organized and laid out on the papyrus). Comparable terms are found in Coptic in P. Vat. Copti Doresse 1 and 5.[7])

343 (misprinted in Baldwin's article as 340), *ἀννουάλια*. Baldwin is apparently not acquainted with the numerous legal Latinisms in Dioscorus' documentary papyri. In fact three Latinisms are glossed all together here as a group: *ἀννουάλια, λήγατον,* and *πεκούλιον (λήγατον).* The parallels from Dioscorus' other writings are: *ἀννουάλια*: *P. Lond.* V 1706.11 n.; *λήγατον*: *P. Lond.* V 1706 11 n., *P. Cair. Masp.* II 67151.295, 299, III 67312.110, 67314.33, II.5, III. 18.26; *πεκούλιον*: *P. Cair. Masp.* III 67312.101, 102, 67313.68, 67314.20, 29, 33, III. 18. The juxtapositions are apparent. I have commented on these legal Latinisms in *Dioscorus of Aphrodito: his work and his world* (Berkeley, to appear), chapter III. By the reign of Justin II they have become completely at home in the scholarly jargon of Egyptian Greek.[8])

The editors of the glossary, Crum and Bell, point out (p. 180, cf. 184) that Dioscorus organized his glossary by subjects, working horizontally across three main columns as they stand on the papyrus. (Organizing a wordlist by subjects is a familiar practice, going back even to Ancient Egyptian parallels.[9]) This means that when writing he had the entire piece of papyrus unrolled vertically in front of him - or else, more logically, he worked by unrolling it as he went along. Now P. Lond. inv. 1727 (1-3) is, so to speak, doubly a rotulus, or a *transversa charta* roll twice over. That is to say: The first thing Dioscorus wrote on it, on the so-called recto, i. e., *transversa charta* across the fibres (which on that side run the long way, parallel to the long edges of the roll), is *P. Lond.* V 1674, a draft of a petition to Athanasius Duke of the Thebaid, which is written in short lines parallel to the short edge of the papyrus roll. Then, to write the glossary, he turned the roll over, and began writing again across it, i. e., this time *with* the fibres, parallel to the short edge, making three short double columns of Greek and Coptic word lists that cohere horizontally by

---

[7]) See L. Papini, 'Notes on the formulary of some Coptic documentary papyri from Middle Egypt,' *BSAC* 25 (1983) 83-89; eadem, 'Annotazioni sul formulario giuridico di documenti copti del VI secolo,' *Atti del XVII Congresso Internazionale di Papirologia* (Naples 1984) 767-776. Compare line 392, **ⲧⲃⲓⲛⲉ**, found in Hall p. 108.

[8]) See s. vv. in S. Daris, *Il lessico latino nel greco d'Egitto* (Barcelona 1971).

[9]) Compare *P. Rainer Cent.* Kopt. 12 (pp. 206-213 and Tafel 17), and the editorial remarks on this 7th-c. Greek-Coptic word list from the Fayum, with the literature there cited. Cf. also H. Satzinger in *Cd'E* 47 (1972) 343-345.

subjects. The Greek words and their Coptic equivalents are separated either by a colon (:) or by just a space. Thus the lines numbered, in Crum and Bell's publication, 4–58, 131–180, 272–312, all dealing with parts of the body, go together to form a section that coheres horizontally across the papyrus. So too do the sections on farming and irrigation equipment referred to above. Lines 1–3, the beginning of the leftmost column, are glosses on 'man', 'animal' and 'death'. In the space to the right of them, above columns 2 and 3, Dioscorus has written what Crum and Bell identified as question-and-answer aphorisms deriving from the 'Secundus' corpus.[10]) Baldwin has offered no remarks on this anomaly in the glossary, which deserves attention.

Instead of 'man', 'animal', and 'death', the three Secundine excerpts appear to respond to queries about the definition of 'man', 'the sea', and 'death', in that order. It is possible that the points in which Dioscorus' text differs from the known Greek texts of Secundus (but are closer to the Arabic) derive from a possible Coptic version of this popular work.[11]) In particular we should notice 130, *ἀπέρατον διάστημα*, 'boundless separation' as an epithet of Death. This equals the **ϫⲓⲛⲡⲱⲣϫ** of Coptic epitaphs,[12]) the yawning gap that knows no closing. Dioscorus may well have known in a Coptic version the school text that was to be put, in the West, even into the mouths of Pippin and Alcuin.

As described above, Dioscorus' glossary was written on the other side of a draft petition to the Duke of the Thebaid, dated by Bell to between A.D. 567 and 573. It would seem logical to infer that the glossary was written later than the petition, when Dioscorus was back home at Aphrodito and doing some serious work on his Greek poetic vocabulary, relating it at every turn to the world around him and the landscape of his ancestral village. Dioscorus' glossary is a kind of genre sketch, with its topographical terms, names for local animals and Nile fish, the typical occupations of the late antique Upper Egyptian countryside, and, in happy celebration, words for Dionysiac festival figures and the poetry of drinking songs. He may have compiled it with a view to writing dedicatory epigrams for vari-

---

[10]) See B.E. Perry, *Secundus the silent philosopher* (Ithaca 1964).

[11]) In spite of the many faults of the study of E. Revillout in *CRAIBL* ser. 3 no. 1 (1872) 256–355, his postulation of a sixth-century Sahidic Coptic version of Secundus makes sense.

[12]) M. Cramer, *Die Totenklage bei den Kopten* (Vienna/Leipzig 1941).

ous occupations. As a document, Dioscorus' glossary summons up a picture of the life and seasonal round of the estate of a Coptic landowner, at a point where prosperity and opulence were informed with a deep-rooted sense of the vitality of classical culture in both the languages of Christian Egypt.

IX

DIOSCORUS OF APHRODITO AND JOHN PHILOPONUS*

The Christological, Trinitarian, and philosophical ideas expressed in the poetry of Dioscorus of Aphrodito, the sixth-century Egyptian lawyer, reveal much about his educational and cultural background, especially when regarded in the light of recent research.[1] I have called attention elsewhere[2] to the implications of Dioscorus' Trinitarian epithet μονοειδής. Further examination of texts of the period[3] may establish a hitherto unsuspected connexion between the two figures of the Alexandrian Christian philosopher, John Philoponus, and the provincial Coptic man of letters, Dioscorus.

Dioscorus used the phrase μονοειδὴς Τριάς in two poems, the chronology of which should be kept in mind. First, Heitsch 6 (line 8 is in question) was written to a recipient whose name is only partly preserved on the papyrus, some time between A.D. 551 and 553, upon Dioscorus' return from Constantinople. The phrase recurs considerably later, in an encomium (Heitsch 3, line 41) addressd to John, duke of the Thebaid A.D. 573-576. Now in the sixth century the unusual adjective μονοειδής appears in the *De opificio mundi* (81.20 and 192.1)[4] of John Philoponus, the anti-Chalcedonian commentator on Aristotle, the implications of some of whose writings were being attacked in the 570s within Monophysite circles themselves.[5]

This work of Philoponus, also referred to as the *Hexaemeron* from its subject-matter, was formerly dated to ca. 546-549, on the grounds of its dedication (in the proemium, ed. Reichardt 1-2) to patriarch Sergius of Antioch: but Sergius' patriarchate, and hence this work, are now placed in 557-560 (*PLRE* II: Iohannes 76). Its approach to the Mosaic account of creation as handled by an experienced Aristotelian (with a Neoplatonic background as well; see below) fits in well with what we know of the intellectual atmosphere of Alexandria in the years around and after the Constantinopolitan council of 553.[6] Philoponus applies μονοειδής to the nature of the planetary globe (II.13, in a context where he is discussing the Empedoclean φιλία and νεῖκος) and, somewhat oddly to our view, to the moon (IV.16, in an explanation of Gen 1:14-17, the moon as the lesser of the two great lights). It is an epithet he had to have found in Plotinus *Enn.* VI.9.3.43 H.-S., quoting Plato *Symposium* 211B: Οὔτε οὐν τι οὔτε ποισὸν οὔτε νοῦν οὔτε ψυχήν· οὐδὲ κινούμενον οὐδ' αὐ ἑστώς, οὐκ ἐν τόπῳ, οὐκ ἐν χρόνῳ, ἀλλ' αὐτὸ καθ' αὐτό μονοειδές, μᾶλλον δὲ ἀνείδεον πρὸ εἴδους ὂν παντός, πρὸ κινήσεως, πρὸ στάσεως· ταῦτα γὰρ περὶ τὸ ὄν, ἃ πολλὰ αὐτὸ ποιεῖ. We do well to remember that at least this portion of the *Symposium*, not a popular school-text of Late Antiquity, had been known in Roman Egypt (*P. Oxy.* V 843 [= Pack² 1399], *ca.* A.D. 200). Philoponus does not cite Plotinus by name in his work: but it is only Philoponus who uses this word in the first three-quarters of the sixth century.[7]

We are coming to know more about John Philoponus and his place in sixth-century thought.[8] As a pupil of Ammonius, he was in the direct line of Neoplatonic teaching and tradition, a heritage he made use of both in his Aristotelian commentaries and in his directly theological works. Thanks to papyrological sources we even have a better understanding of the meaning of his *Beiname*.[9] A **ϕιλοπονος** in the Coptic papyri was a church volunteer worker,[10] usually a member of an organised charity guild attached to a church or monastery.[11] It is doubtless his Trinitarian thought, nurtured in such a background, that underlay such verbal usages as that of μονοειδής; and his Christian Platonism (and proto-scholastic Aristotelianism) that must have impressed his students at Alexandria with such memorable formulations as φιλοσοφία ἐστὶν ὁμοίωσις θεῷ (*De opif. mundi* 242.11-12 Reichardt = VI.7).

This Trinitarian thought is preserved and transmitted principally in Syriac,[12] in particular in the Διαιτητής or *Arbiter* of perhaps before 553 (and in the epitome of it made just after the Council of 553),[13] and the *Letter to Justinian* of *ca.* 560-65[14] (a reply to the *De recta fide* of 551). We may assume that Philoponus wrote these works originally in Greek. Whether they were ever translated into Coptic, and whether Philoponus himself was bilingual, are questions we cannot answer for lack of evidence. (It is extraordinary how many works by Egyptian thinkers are transmitted in Syriac and not in Coptic.) It is illuminating to combine the terms (often Greek loanwords)[15] used in these works with Philoponus' uses of terms like ὁμοειδής (four times in the *De opificio mundi*, nine times in the *De aeternitate mundi contra Proclum* [ed. Rabe, Teubner 1899]) to arrive at a notion of the nuances of his Trinitarian vocabulary. A singularity of εἶδος[16] was a natural thing for an Alexandrian Monophysite to insist on.

And the connexion with Dioscorus of Aphrodito, the only other sixth-century author to employ this Philoponian word? It can be seen in a papyrus at Berlin, P. Berol. 13894, an epistle in iambic verse addressed to someone Dioscorus obviously thought of with affection as the ideal teacher of 'divine philosophy'.[17] It runs:

Δέχου, φέριστ̣ε̣, τοῦ φίλου τὰ γράμματα
ἐμοῦ φιλοῦντος, ὥς ἄνυδρος την θεά[ν
προϊκάνων ἔνερα θεωρῆσ[α]ι ῥάθους.
τῆς σῆς, ἐράσμιε, γλυκ[υτ]άτης τριβῆς
Θεοῦ τὸ δῶρον, οὐκ ἀν[θρώ]π[ο]υ . . ποτε
ὅθεν διδάχθεις τὴν . . . .
ṫύχαις πεσόντων [. .] ατων πανουργίαις
καὶ ὡς δικαίως α . . . . . . ν . . . . ης αἰσχρῶς
. . . . τησας τύχην
. . . . ηω . . . .
. . . . ἀκούσαις προσκυνῶν . . . .
κ̇ινδ[υ]ναίμην τοῖς λόγ[οις] σοφίσματα

. . . ε. . . . . . . ἀκριβῆ. . . . .
κάλαμος ἐμὸς τὴν σὴν ἄνϊσον περιβαλεῖν
τιμαῖς παναυτάδελφον ἱλαροφυῖαν.
ἐστὶν δὲ μίκρον ὄρνεον τῷ σώμ[α]τι
τέτ'τιξ, ἀνύμνει τὸν Θεὸν τὸν φέρ[τ]ερον.
τὰ νῦν σύ γ' αὐτὸς ταῖς ἀμοιβαῖς ἔντυχε,
ὅτως μαθῶ φιλαιτάτην σωτηρίαν.

'Receive, O best of men, a letter from me, your friend, who loves you, the way a thirsty, dead (land) (loves) to see the free gifts of God (i.e. rain) upon her body. (For,) dear friend, the gift of your dearest care is of God, not of man, whence you taught . . . attacked by bad luck and trickery, justly . . . shamefully . . . making obeisance . . . I would dare to reply to (their) sophisms with (my) arguments . . . (for) my pen worthily to clothe in words your matchless, brotherly joyfulness. Though the cicada is but a small winged creature in body, it hymns great God (Himself). So you now in recompense pray for me, that I may learn most beloved salvation.'

This is a letter to a religious philosopher who has been involved in a controversy. Several points in the text are noteworthy, and were not noticed by Keydell (or other commentators on Dioscorus):

1 φέριστε, cf. φέρτερον in line 18.

2–3 sc. γῆ: the reference is above all scriptural, Ps 142:6b LXX: ἡ ψυχή μου ὡς γῆ ἄνυδρός σοι; and cf. Ps 62:2b LXX: ἐδίψησέν σοι ἡ ψυχή μου . . . ἐν γῇ ἐρήμῳ καὶ ἀβάτῳ καὶ ἀνύδρῳ. (Sahidic of Ps 142:6b: ⲁ ⲧⲁⲯⲩⲭⲏ ⲣ̄ ⲑⲉ ⲛ̄ⲛⲓⲕⲁϩ ⲉⲧⲟⲃⲉ ⲛ̄ⲛⲁϩⲣⲁⲕ.[18]) A beautiful figure of longing to use in an affectionate letter. And further: ἄνυδρος land had an Egyptian documentary signification as well. In fact this poetic usage is a telling juxtaposition of the desert imagery of the Psalmist with the Nile-valley imagery that was bred in Dioscorus' bone. Ἄνυδρος land is 'land from which the inundation had receded' (*P.Lond.* V 1693.5, from Aphrodito, signed by Fl. Theoteknos who is known also from *P.Flor.*, *P.Cair.Masp.*, and *P.Freer* 1.5.15, 6.6, 21, 7.26, 2.2.10; the 'coming third indiction' is probably either A.D. 524 or 539 [*CSBE* 86–87]; and note *ad loc.*; cf. *P.Lond.* V 1686.12, 1689.12).[19] In writing to his respected recipient Dioscorus is looking out over his own land and seeing both its present reality (cf. Menander Rhetor § 346.2–4) and its aspect under the Biblical cast of his mind (cf. Ps.-Apoll. *Metaphr.Pss.* 142.66 [ed. Ludwich, Leipzig 1912]).

4–6 A description of the addressee's inspired teaching; followed in 7f. by what appears to be a reference to opponents' tactics in a controversy, and, in 13–14, a defence against the opponents' σοφίσματα.

16 ἱλαροφυῖα, a coinage of Dioscorus': cf. μεγαλοφυΐα in Theodoret, ὁμοφυΐα in Cyril; and above all the term of address often found in the papyri, (ἡ σὴ) ὑπερφυΐα: cf. Buck *RI* pp. 165, 754 for such compounds (Zilliacus, *Abstrakte Anredeformen* . . . [Helsinki 1949] p. 91). The joy is παναυτάδελφον, that of a fellow Monophysite no doubt.

17ff. A favourite image in Dioscorus' poetry, that of the hymn-singing cicada: see Heitsch 5.15–16 (A.D. 570–573) and 7.5–6 (between A.D. 565 and 573).[19a] Compare Synesius' Hymn I (=IX) 45-46 (ed. Lacombrade, 1978); Theophylact Simocatta *Ep.* 1 (ed. Boissonade, 1835). Dioscorus has turned a Hellenistic conceit from the Ptolemaic court into a delightful Christian image—rather like one of the lovable insects in the *haiku* of Issa.[19b]

19-20 ἔντυχε here surely in the sense of 'intercede for': a graceful close to a letter from disciple to former master. The phrase μαθῶ . . . σωτηρίαν well expresses the intellectual concern with Christian truth that animated the best minds of Late Antique Egypt.

Clearly the internal evidence of this verse letter by Dioscorus points to his having written it to a revered master (of Alexandria, one would think), a teacher of philosophy in the Christian vein who was also involved in a controversy. This identity would fit that of John Philoponus, whose lifetime chronology would easily permit him to have been Dioscorus' teacher of philosophy.[20] The polemics levelled against Philoponus by Cosmas Indicopleustes,[21] Patriarch Damian,[22] and numerous others could certainly be described as πανουργίαι.[23] I propose that in this verse letter, which I would date in the mid-570s after Dioscorus' return from Antinoe to Aphrodito, the provincial Egyptian lawyer and man of letters was paying a graceful compliment to his old teacher, saying that he still thought well of him in spite of the attacks of others. It is a pleasing document of ties of loyalty in the intellectual life of Byzantine Egypt. 'But in Alexandria unity of love was of necessity linked with passion *and* theology . . .'.[24]

Notes

*I am deeply indebted to the libraries of the American School of Classical Studies and the British School of Archaeology at Athens, of the École française d'Athènes, and of the Pontificio Istituto Orientale at Rome, without whose unparalleled resources my work would have been impossible. For their valuable help and advice I also thank Dr Sebastian Brock, Fr Robert Murray S.J., and, as always, Mirrit Boutros Ghali (Cant 6:3).

1. E.g. L. Abramowski, 'συνάφεια und ἀσύγχυτος ἕνωσις als Bezeichnungen für trinitarische und christologische Einheit,' in *Drei christologische Untersuchungen* (Berlin/New York 1981) 63-109, esp. 66ff., 105ff; R.Y. Ebeid/A. van Roey/L.R. Wickham, *Peter of Callinicum: anti-tritheist dossier* (Leuven 1981) esp. ch. 3.

2. L.S.B. MacCoull, 'A Trinitarian formula in Dioscorus of Aphrodito,' *Bulletin de la Société d'Archéologie Copte* 24 (1982) 103-110 and 25 (1983) 61-64.

3. Including resonances and efforts in the West: H. Chadwick, *Boethius: The Consolations of Music, Logic, Theology, and Philosophy* (Oxford 1981) 211-222.

4. Ed. W. Reichardt, Leipzig (Teubner) 1897 from the unique Vienna MS.

5. Ebeid/van Roey/Wickham, *Peter of Callinicum* (above n. 1) 23, 25-33. The texts are set out in A. van Roey, 'Les fragments trithéites de Jean Philopon,' *Orientalia Lovaniensia Periodica* 11 (1980) 135-163; cf. *idem*, 'Fragments antiariens de Jean Philopon,' *ibid.* 10 (1979) 237-250. See P. Allen, *Evagrius Scholasticus the church historian* (Louvain, 1981) 36-40.

6. Cf. W. Wolska-Conus, *La topographie chrétienne de Cosmas Indicopleustès* (Paris, 1962) 161-

192. Philoponus was much concerned to refute the notions of the Antiochene theologians, especially Theodore of Mopsuestia, as popularised by Cosmas. His Trinitarian thought was built on foundations and examples from the scientific understanding of his time and tradition: cf. W. Boehm, *Johannes Philoponos: christliche Naturwissenschaft im Ausklang der Antike* (Paderborn, 1967) 29, 411-37, 450 n. 119. As an anti-Chalcedonian he was equipped to fight with his opponents' weapons: the Roman-law and especially Neoplatonic antecedents of terms in the definition of Chalcedon could not have been lost on such a mind. Abramowski (above n. 1) calls attention to the work of E.L. Fortin, 'The *definitio fidei* of Chalcedon and its philosophical sources,' *Studia Patristica* 5 = *TU* 80 (Berlin, 1962) 489-98. I am grateful to the Franciscan Center for Christian Oriental Studies at Cairo for the opportunity initially to follow up this reference. - On the atmosphere of 553 see Av. Cameron, 'Cassiodorus deflated,' *JRS* 71 (1981) 183-86 esp. 184-85.

7. For usage of this word in Philoponus' Aristotle commentaries see L.S.B. MacCoull in *BSAC* 25 (1983) 61-64.

8. See now *PLRE* II (Cambridge, 1980) 615-6, Ioannes 76. The older accounts are given by Th. Hermann in *ZNTW* 29 (1930) 209-264 (see esp. 211 n. 10, 219ff. on Trinitariology); E. Evrard in *Bull. Cl. Lettres Ac. Belg.* 5.39 (1953) 299-357; H.D. Saffrey in *REG* 67 (1954) 396-410. His life, formerly variously dated, is now seen to have continued into the reign of Justin II (as A. Sanda, *Johannis Philoponi opuscula monophysitica* [Beirut, 1930] p. 7 already discerned). See now G.A. Lucchetta in *Studia Patavina* 25 (1978) 573-593. Surely he was a cradle Christian (a cradle Monophysite), not a convert as older scholars liked to believe. He was born in a city called Caesarea: perhaps the Egyptian ⲡⲟⲗⲓⲥ ⲡⲟⲩⲣⲟ: Amelineau, *Géographie de l'Egypte à l'époque copte* (Paris, 1893) 366.

9. As Usener (*RE* 18 [1916] 1793n.) had already seen in 1892 in a review of the *CAG* (*Kl.Schr.* III 210 n. 36); so Boehm (above n. 6) p. 26; Maspero *Histoire des patriarches d'Alexandrie* (Paris 1923) 198. See E. Wipszycka, 'Les confréries dans la vie religieuse de l'Égypte chrétienne,' *Proc. XII Intl. Congr. Papyrol.* [= *ASP* 7] (Toronto 1970) 511-525; *eadem, Les ressources et les activités économiques des églises en Egypte* (*ive-viiie siècle*) [= *PapBrux* 10] (Brussels, 1977) 150.

10. *CPR* IV 195.4, 196.6; Bal 32.35, p. 423 n. 6; Ep 649n; BM 514 r° 13, 1013.10, 1023.3. Cf. *Vit.Joh. Eleem.* 1.5, 2.16, 4.18, 37.6.

11. Called a ⲫⲓⲗⲟⲡⲟⲛⲉⲓⲟⲛ in *CPR* IV 195.2, 5, cf. BM 423a, 435, 1013. The ⲫⲓⲗⲟⲡⲟⲛⲉⲓⲟⲛ of the monastery of S. Theodore of Panore makes out the 12th-indiction receipt for wheat in Push 1.1, 6. Cf. Krall 103, 204. (References to Coptic papyri are according to A.A. Schiller, 'A checklist of Coptic documents and letters,' *Bulletin of the American Society of Papyrologists* 13 [1976] 99-123.) *Philoponoi* tend to be found in a Monophysite milieu: see T.S. Miller, *The birth of the hospital in the Byzantine Empire* (to appear) ch. 7, 26f.

12. In addition to the works of van Roey (above n. 5) and Sanda (above n. 8: a rare and indispensable book), the articles of Furlani (below nn. 13-14) and Hermann (above n. 8) give an overview of these writings. An edition of British Library MS. Add. 12171 (containing the *Arbiter*), with a philosophical and historical commentary, would be a desirable project. Cf. H.-G. Beck, *Kirche u. theol. Literatur im byz. Reich* (Munich, 1959) 391-92; P. Allen, *Evagrius Scholasticus* (above n. 5) 13 with citations.

13. In Greek partly *apud* John Damascene (*PG* 94:743-54); see G. Furlani, 'Il contenuto dell'Arbitrio di Giovanni il Filopono,' *Riv.trimestr. di studi filos. e relig.* 4 (Perugia, 1922) 385-405.

14. From Ms. Vat.syr. 144 (8th c.): see especially Sanda *Opuscula monophysitica* pp. 125-26 (Syriac), 175-76 (Latin tr.) for key Trinitarian word-usages esp. of οὐσία. See also G. Furlani, 'Una lettera di Giovanni Filopono all'imperatore Giustiniano,' *Atti R.Ist.Veneto* 79 (1920) 1247-1265; 1427-1465. Also *idem*, 'Sei scritti antitriteistici in lingua siriaca,' *PO* XIV (1920) 673-766, esp. 706-7.

15. Especially μονοούσιον, as kindly explicated for me (in the passage in *PO* XIV 706-7) by Fr Robert Murray SJ in a letter of 18 May 1982: '. . . μονο- . . . excludes the possibility of multiplicity.' This is exactly the force behind μονοειδής in Dioscorus: there is only one εἶδος possible in the Godhead, namely the Idea of God.

16. The word is variously rendered in Coptic (see Crum *Dict.*, Greek Index), usually by ⲥⲙⲟⲧ 'form, likeness'. A person like Dioscorus who thought, and worked, in both languages was concerned to find the right equivalent: see his glossary in *Aegyptus* 6 (1925). Boethius' use of *forma* in his *De Trinitate* (II, cf.

VI) shows how the leading Western thinker of the period tried to make this sort of usage assimilable by his readers.

17. Originally published by R. Keydell in *ByzNgrJbb* 10 (1934) 341–45. I give a text (in modern form) of the portions that can still be connectedly read, differing in some places from Keydell. I am grateful to Dr G. Poethke of the Berlin Museum (DDR) for providing a photograph. Dioscorus' characteristic hand is unmistakable: the upright working hand, not the more slanted 'fair-copy' hand.

18. From E.A. Wallis Budge, *The earliest known Coptic Psalter* (London, 1898) 147. The Sahidic uses a form of EIBE 'to be thirsty', while the Bohairic renders ἄνυδρος literally by ⲁⲑⲙⲱⲟⲩ, 'without water' (Crum, *Dict.* 76a).

19. See D. Bonneau, *Le fisc et le Nil* (Paris, 1971) 80–81, cf. 84 n. 418 with references.

19a. Dioscorus may have got the image from Menander Rhetor (edd. Russell/Wilson [Oxford, 1981] 118–19, 299.

19b. Could Dioscorus have known Alcaeus' tettix (347a) from Proclus' commentary on Hesiod *WD*? For a charming first-hand view of the Mediterranean cicada see Norman Douglas, *Birds and beasts of the Greek Anthology* (London, 1928) 190–96. See R. B. Egan, 'Jerome's cicada metaphor (*Ep* 22.18).' *CW* 77.3 (1984) 174–6, with the literature cited, p. 175, n. 2: P. Antin, 'Le cigale dans la spiritualité, *Rev. asc. myst.* 37 (1961) 486–92; *idem*. 'Cigales littéraires', *Bull. Budé*, ser. 4.1 (1982) 338–46, and in *Recueil S. Jérôme* (Brussels, 1968) 283–90. Diocorus' image emphasizes the insect's musicality, of course, but also is unique to him in its original picture of the tiny creature whose voice reaches God.

20. There is no direct evidence in the papyri from his archive as to where Dioscorus studied either rhetoric (he wrote no encomia 'on the professors of Alexandria' or the like) or law; but I think Alexandria as the place of his pre-law formation is an inescapable conclusion (see A. Cameron, *Agathias* [Oxford 1970] 140–41, opposing Maspero's notion that he might have studied law as well at Alexandria in spite of Justinian's ruling in *C. Omnem*). See also S.L. Karren, 'A late ancient Neoplatonic biography and its reflections of Coptic culture,' *Sixth BSC* (Oberlin 1980) 43 (on encomia of professors). I would like to suggest the possibility that *PSI* XIV 1400 might be a missing portion of Philoponus' lost *Contra Aristotelem*. See E. Garin in *PSI* XIV (Florence, 1957) pp. 89–100, quoting the remarks of A. Barigazzi in *Aegyptus* 29 (1949) 59–75 (cf. A. Körte in *Archiv* 13 [1938] 110); and J. L. Kraemer, 'A lost passage from Philoponus' *Contra Aristotelem* in Arabic translation,' *JAOS* 85 (1965) 318–327. See E. Evrard, *Philopon, Contre Aristote, livre premier* (thesis, Liège, 1943). The piece is from a deluxe codex. Is there also a chance that Dioscorus on his return from Constantinople in 551 brought with him a copy, destined for his old teacher, of Justinian's *De recta fide*, the work to which Philoponus replied in his *Letter to Justinian*?

21. W. Wolska-Conus, *La topographie chrétienne* (above n. 6) 273–80; he called him 'the pretended Christian'.

22. Ebeid/van Roey/Wickham (above n. 1), *Peter of Callinicum* 78 (Syriac), 51 (Eng. tr.)

23. On the Tritheist controversy see P. Allen, *Evagrius Scholasticus* (above n. 5) 36–40 (once more), with the sources and literature there cited.

24. J.L. Pinchin, *Alexandria still: Forster, Durrell, and Cavafy* (Princeton 1977) 142. Cf. also A.H. Armstrong, 'Later Platonism and its influence,' in R.R. Bolgar, ed., *Classical influences on European culture A.D. 500–1500* (Cambridge, 1971) 200.

ADDITIONAL NOTE

On Philoponus see now R. Sorabji, ed., *Philoponus and the Rejection of Aristotelian Science* (London – Ithaca 1987), esp. H. Chadwick, pp. 41–56, and K. Verrycken, "The development of Philoponus' thought and its chronology," in R. Sorabji, ed., *Aristotle Transformed* (London 1990) 233–274.

p. 167, note 11: Miller's monograph published Baltimore 1985.

p. 167, note 12: See, with reservations, the 1987 dissertation of J.E. McKenna, *The Life-Setting of the Arbiter* by *John Philoponus* (Fuller Theological Seminary).

p. 168, note 20: See L. MacCoull and L. Siorvanes, "*PSI* XIV 1400: A papyrus fragment of John Philoponus," forthcoming in *Ancient Philosophy* 12 (1992).

X

*DIOSCORUS AND THE DUKES: AN ASPECT OF COPTIC HELLENISM IN THE SIXTH CENTURY**

To quote Sir Harold Bell: "If the still scanty band of papyrologists [that was in 1925—there are a few more of us now, though we are not exactly thick on the ground] . . . should ever compile a calendar of their own, it would be necessary to assign a red letter day to the memory of Dioscorus, the poetical advocate of Aphrodito . . . his services to papyrology are immense."[1] Dioscorus has for the most part been held up to ridicule by the two or three people who have troubled to write about him (the British Museum exhibit of 1974 titled "The Written Word on Papyrus" referred to him as "the McGonagall of the ancient world"), mostly because, like most people, he had occasional trouble when doing Verse Composition. But the fact remains that we owe to his archive, the second of the two sizeable groups of papyri discovered at Aphrodito (Kom Ishgaw, Coptic χκωογ) in the Antaeopolite nome in Upper Egypt, most of our information about how Byzantine Egypt worked: how the administration and day-to-day activities worked, and how people's minds worked. I am concerned in this essay with how Dioscorus interacted with the holders of the important office of duke of the Thebaid in the 560s and 570s. The papyri we have from Antinoe, the ducal seat, especially those written by Dioscorus' own hand, give us, together with the recent Italian excavations at the site of Antinoe itself,[2] our best picture of

* This essay grew out of presentations to the Byzantine Studies Conference in 1976 and to the American Research Center in Egypt in 1979. I should like to thank Prof. Water Hanak, Roberta Chesnut, Elizabeth McVey, Marie Taylor Davis, Mary Whiting, and, as always, Mirrit Boutros Ghali (Cant. 7:10).

1. H. I. Bell and W. E. Crum, "A Greek-Coptic Glossary," *Aegyptus*, 6 (1925), 177.

2. Missione archeologica in Egitto dell'Università di Roma, *Antinoe (1965-1968)* (Roma: Istituto di Studi del Vicino Oriente, 1974). See also now M. Manfredi, "Notizie sugli scavi recenti di Antinoe," *Atti XVII Congr. intl. di papirologia* (Naples, 1984), pp. 85-96; cf. *IACS Newsletter*, 12 (iii. 1983), 9-10.

how life in the administrative centre of Upper Egypt operated between Justinian's thirteenth edict and the Arab conquest.

We can date Dioscorus' lifetime, from his datable papyri, from about 525 to a little after 585.[3] He was fourth generation in a hellenised Coptic family: his great-grandfather was called Psimanobet (etymology still uncertain, but we know it was a name associated with the Aphrodito area, for example from an inscription in the monastery at Bawit).[4] His father Apollos and his uncle Besarion had both been *protokometai*, village headmen, of Aphrodito in the second decade of the sixth century;[5] Apollos, after functioning as *riparius* off and on in the 520s and 530s and then serving as *dioicetes* of Count Ammonios, the great landowner of the neighbourhood, attained to the rank of Flavius,[6] made a journey to Constantinople in 541, and then retired to a monastery he had founded, of which he appointed his son Dioscorus lay ad-

3. A good deal of information on Dioscorus's life and times is contained in H. I. Bell, "An Egyptian Village in the Age of Justinian," *JHS*, 64 (1944), 21-36. Both this study and that of Maspero (1911; *infra* n. 15) are, of course, hopelessly out of date. Thanks to recent research, a whole new scholarly sensibility is in the air, one receptive to the aesthetic and administrative achievements of the fourth to the seventh centuries. The work of Dioscorus, in his creative art and in his recording of the transactions of everyday life, can serve as our introduction to society and letters in the many-textured, colorful, and exuberant world of late antique Egypt. See now L. S. B. MacCoull, "The Coptic Archive of Dioscorus of Aphrodito," *Chron. d'Eg.*, 56 (1981), 185-93; *eadem*, "A Trinitarian Formula in Dioscorus of Aphrodito," *BSAC*, 24 (1982), 103-10, with addendum in *BSAC*, 25 (1983), 61-64; J. G. Keenan, "Aurelius Phoibammon, Son of Triadelphus: A Byzantine Egyptian Land Entrepreneur," *BASP*, 17 (1980), 145-54, and details in "On Village and Polis in Byzantine Egypt," *Proc. XVI Intl. Congr. Papyrol.* (Chico, 1981), pp. 479-85; L. Papini, "Notes on the Formulary of Some Coptic Documentary Papyri from Middle Egypt," *BSAC*, 25 (1983), 83-89. J. G. Keenan has recently referred to "an Aphrodito renaissance in the making," (*infra* n. 7). A guide to the Aphrodito archives is now in progress.

4. J. Maspero and E. Drioton, *Fouilles exécutées à Baouît* [= *Mémoires IFAO*, 59] (Cairo: IFAO, 1931-43), n. 128. Perhaps = "the man from the place of geese," from WBT "goose," Crum, *Dict.* 519a.

5. Later: e.g., *P. Cair. Masp. II* 67125.2-3 (14 July A.D. 525); *I* 67114.A.2-4. Cf. Freer Gallery of Art papyrus 08.45a II.3.

6. *P. Cair. Masp. II 67126.3-4*. See J. G. Keenan, "The *Nomina* Flavius and Aurelius: A Question of Status in Byzantine Egypt," unpublished Ph.D. dissertation, Yale Univ., 1968, pp. 175-77; with the updating in *idem*, "The Names Flavius and Aurelius as Status Designations in Later Roman Egypt," *ZPE*, 11 (1973), 33-63; 13 (1974), 283-304.

ministrator.[7] Dioscorus was trilingual: he had had to learn Latin for his training as a lawyer, which we assume took place at Alexandria (he had little reason to travel as far afield as Beirut). In 551, ten years after his father, he himself travelled to Constantinople to present a petition in defence of the autopract tax rights of Aphrodito village, which had been threatened by the rapacious tactics of Julian and Menas, pagarchs of Antaeopolis.[8] He returned with two ἐκβιβασταί (*exsecutores negotii*) in tow to do the job for his home town. Then in 566, a year after the accession of Justin II, Dioscorus moved to Antinoe, seat of the dukes of the Thebaid, to set up in practice as a notary (as Bell pointed out in the preface to *P. Lond. 1674*, he probably was not licensed as a νομικός until 567, allowing time for the wheels of bureaucracy to revolve) and to put his penchant for writing poetry at the service of the dukes and their subordinates.

Why Antinoe? It was, of course, a Hadrianic foundation, a city most Hellenic in temper, whose inhabitants had enjoyed special tax exemptions particularly in the third century. It had been the seat of the duke of the Thebaid, combining military and civil authority, at least since the administrative reorganisation of Egypt by Justinian's Edict 13 in 554.[9] Twelve years later Antinoe, with its great centrally-crossing Roman streets, its memorial to Antinous, its church (which was probably an episcopal see), and its surrounding monastic complex,[10] was an up-and-coming capital. It is probably just at this time that an imposing new official office-complex (of which traces have survived) would have been built for the duke and his staff. Dioscorus was just over forty, and he needed a better job and more money. In 549/550 the duke of the Thebaid (old-style, before the reorganisation) had been one Apion II, kinsman of the Fl. Strategius who had been *comes*

7. *P. Cair. Masp. I* 67096; cf. Bell, "Egyptian Village," (*supra* n. 3), p. 26. J. G. Keenan, "Aurelius Apollos and the Aphrodito Village Elite," *XVII International Congress of Papyrology* (Naples, 1984), pp. 957-63.

8. *P. Cair. Masp. III* 67283; *I* 67024. Cf. V. Martin, "A Letter from Constantinople," *JEA*, 15 (1929), 96-102; R. G. Salomon, "A Papyrus from Constantinople," *ibid.*, 34 (1948), 98-108.

9. See G. Malz, "The Date of Justinian's Edict XIII," *Byzantion*, 16 (1942-43), 135-41; R. Rémondon, "L'édit XIII de Justinien a-t-il été promulgué en 539?," *Chron. d'Eg.*, 30 (1955), 112-212.

10. M. Martin, *La laure de Dêr el Dîk à Antinoé* [= *Bibl. d'études coptes*, 8] (Cairo: IFAO, 1971).

sacrarum largitionum in the 530s:[11] both of them were members of the "divine house" of the Apions from Oxyrhynchus, the most powerful land-owning family we know from Byzantine Egypt.[12] We may speculate as to the possible relations between the local country-gentry family of the Psimanobets of Jkow and their rich northern neighbours the Apions. At any rate, Dioscorus must have known where to go and to whom to apply for his own advantage.

The succession and the chronology of the dukes of the Thebaid have remained puzzling. Jean Maspero tried to construct a list in 1910,[13] and corrected himself in 1912[14] (in the course of publishing his comprehensive article on Dioscorus, one of the few studies dedicated to him individually);[15] while Bell, Gelzer, and Remondon made a few further updatings and suggestions.[16] The puzzle largely remains. The dating-clauses in papyri are not always as explicit as one might wish (and often contradictory), while those in Egyptian inscriptions are usually incomplete (giving, e.g., only an indiction-number). And we need to know still more about the titles and functions of the duke during these hundred or so years. His title was usually, earlier on, *spectabilis* [περίβλεπτος], and later *clarissimus* [ἐνδοξότατος]. The duke was at the top of the military, judicial, and financial pyramid of Upper Egypt. He administered eleven cities directly, and ten more indirectly through the *praeses* or ἡγεμών. He controlled eight wings of cavalry, Byzantine and native, eight legions, sixteen *alae*, and ten cohorts in the smaller towns toward the southern frontier. He had under him a *schola* of *agentes in rebus*; *numerarii*; a private secretary or *commentariensis*; and a staff

11. *P. Oxy.* XVI 1928; cf. E. R. Hardy, *The Large Estates of Byzantine Egypt* (New York: Columbia Univ. Press, 1932), pp. 30-31.

12. See J. Gascou, "Les grands domaines, la cité et l'Etat en Egypte byzantine (5e, 6e et 7e s.)," *Travaux et mémoires*, 9 (Paris, 1985), 1-90. Further material may remain among the posthumous papers of E. R. Hardy.

13. J. Maspero, "Etudes sur les papyrus d'Aphrodité, 2. Flavios Marianos, duc de Thébaïde," *BIFAO*, 7 (1910), 97-119.

14. *Idem*, "Les papyrus Beaugé," *ibid.*, 10 (1912), 131-57, esp. 143.

15. *Idem*, "Un dernier poète grec de l'Egypte, Dioscore, fils d'Apollos," *REG*, 24 (1922), 426-81. This has been superseded by my monograph, *Dioscorus of Aphrodito: His Work and His World* (Berkeley, 1988).

16. H. I. Bell, "The Aphrodito Papyri," *JHS*, 28 (1908), 97-120; M. Gelzer, "Altes und Neues aus den byzantinischen-ägyptischen Verwaltungsmisere," *ArchPf*, 5 (1913), 346-77; R. Rémondon, *Papyrus grecs d'Apollônos Anô* (Cairo: IFAO, 1953), p. 5 (introduction to nº 1). See also *infra* n. 33.

of scribes (*exceptores*).[17] He even had a state boat for making splendid official visitations up and down his stretch of the Nile.[18] Most importantly, he managed from the top level the collection of taxes in kind and in money, and ensured their safe conveyance to the capital. He also, as we know from the lives and discourses of Coptic saints, heard cases at law.[19]

In the sixth century, at any rate, the duke was a man decidedly of the upper class. Serving in the office in about 553/4 and again for a second term from about 568 to 570 (hence one of Dioscorus' bosses) was on Fl. Triadios Marianos Michael Gabriel Constantine Theodore Martyrios Julian Athanasius.[20] This sort of string of baptismal names (often with pairs of patron saints, like Michael Gabriel or Sergius Bacchus [see below]) was not uncommon among the very noble, including some members of the house of Apion. One had, in such a station in life, many heavenly patrons and many godparents. (It is all rather like the second act of *Der Rosenkavalier*, where Sophie says "I know all your names: you are called Octavian Maria Ehrenreich Bonaventura Ferdinand Hyazinth.") As we shall see, this was in the mid-seventh century to some degree to change.

My list of the dukes under whom Dioscorus worked runs (provisionally) as follows:

Cyrus	?-567
Athanasius (2nd time)	567-70
Callinicus [fl. 570-73; Marianos Michael Gabriel Sergius Bacchus Narses Conon Anastasius Domninus Theodore Callinicus][21]	

17. For the pre-reform duchy, see O. Seeck, ed., *Notitia dignitatum* (Berlin, 1876; rpt. Frankfurt a/M, 1962), pp. 63-66. In general, G. Rouillard, *L'administration civile de l'Egypte byzantine*, 2nd ed. (Paris: Geuthner, 1928), pp. 33-34, 37-38, and elsewhere (see index).

18. *P. Cair. Masp. II* 67136; cf. M. Merzagora, "La navigazione in Egitto nell'età greco-romana," *Aegyptus*, 10 (1929), 117.

19. See, for example, Shenoute's discourses on the "idols" of Pneueit, in J. Leipoldt, ed., *Sinuthii Archimandritae vita et opera omnia*, III [= *CSCO*, 42; Scr. copt. 2] (Louvain: CSCO, 1908), 84-90; cf. J. W. B. Barns, "Shenute as a Historical Source," *Actes Xe Congr. intl. de papyrologues* (Varsovie, 1964), pp. 151-59.

20. *P. Cair. Masp. I* 67002.1.

21. *Ibid., I* 67005 *verso*.

Romanos[22] 574?
John II 574-76?
(there had been a John I in the 530s)
Theodore the δεκουρίων[23] 577/8 +
(the meaning of this title in the sixth century, as applied to a duke of the Thebaid, is unclear)

About the frequency of turnover of the office I cannot comment: for example, the degree to which it was dependent upon imperial favor or the like. A prosopography of Byzantine Egypt has not yet been made.

The papyri from Dioscorus' hand written at Antinoe fall into two groups, literary and documentary. Of the documents we know, for example, that Dioscorus was retained by one Aurelia Athanasia in an inheritance case on 28 September 566; in 567 (31 March) he drew up the will of Fl. Theodore, *exceptor* on the ducal staff (who incidentally left a large part of his lands to Shenoute's monastery at Sohag). In 568 he was busy with partnership contracts for a firm of carpenters; in 569 with loans, sales of land, a disinheritance, and contracts in Coptic; and in 570 with the business accounts of one Aurelia Tekrompia and her daughter (24 September), divorces, and, probably, the will of Fl. Phoebammon, the public doctor of Antinoe.[24]

As a poet Dioscorus began his "Antinoe period" in 566 with an encomium on the arrival at the ducal seat of the image (the statue or, very likely, the panel-painted ikon) of Justin II, and the accompanying festivities.[25] He also wrote a poem to Victor, *praeses* in 566. For Duke Athanasius he wrote an encomium praising his

22. XLII: Dioscorus, no. 12, in E. Heitsch, ed., *Die griechischen Dichterfragmente der römischen Kaiserzeit*. Abh. d. Akad. d. Wiss. Göttingen, 3 Folge, Nr. 49 (Göttingen: Vandenhoeck & Ruprecht, 1961), I.141-42 [= *P. Lond. Lit.* 98 and *P. Rein.* 2070].

23. G. Lefebvre, *Recueil des inscriptions grecques-chrétiennes d'Egypte* (Cairo: IFAO, 1907), p. 584 (A.D. 578). To be identified with the Fl. Marianos Michael Gabriel John Theodore George Marcellus Julian of *P. Monac.* 2.4-5 (A.D. 578)? Probably the dedicatee of Agathias' preface to his *Cycle*, in 567/8: A. and Averil Cameron, "The *Cycle* of Agathias," *JHS*, 86 (1966), 23.

24. *P. Cair. Masp. II* 67161; *III* 67312; *II* 67158, 67159; *III* 67353ᵛ; *II* 67156; *III* 67151. *P. Cair. Masp.* `*III* 67353ʳ is a Coptic arbitration hearing (parallel to *P. Lond. V* 1709) in Dioscorus's hand: text and commentary published by the present writer, *Dioscorus*. (above n. 15)

25. *P. Cair. Masp. II* 67183 = Heitsch (*supra* n. 22), Dioscorus, no. 1. For a full commentary on this poem, see MacCoull in *Byzantion*, 54 (1984), 575-85.

God-given legal judgment, his military leadership, and, in particular, his defensive ability against the Blemmyes and Saracens.[26] Duke Callinicus he honored with an encomium praising his noble ancestry (with all sorts of appropriate—or odd—comparisons with mythological heroes), and with an epithalimium on the occasion of the duke's wedding with one Theophile χρυσοστεφάνη, praised for her beauty and σωφροσύνη (and repeating many of the same mythological figures).[27] Romanos is addressed and described as ὄλβιε πανόλβιε τῷ γένει κ[α]ὶ τοῖς λόγοις . . . σοφὸς σοφωτάτων.[28] Next, Dioscorus wishes he could have an adequate portrait of Duke John (for whom he borrows not a few of the same mythological comparisons as he used for Callinicus; Dioscorus was like Handel: he stole from himself very often). John is described as a "new Solomon" in an Egyptian landscape.[29] Theodore we know only from a fragment. Further, on the sub-ducal level, Dioscorus wrote, for example, poems to one Hypatius of the ducal τάξις,[30] and to one Paul of the ὀφφίκιον (the latter word much less common, at least in documents).[31]

It is possible to see that even these verse-composition cliches have something to tell us about the difficulties and the perquisites of the office of duke of the Thebaid. Someone at least cared enough to refer to Aphrodito elegantly as the "Paphian land".[32] An ability to turn out verse using approved classical forms helped Dioscorus in his job (he mentions his need of money fairly often)

---

26. *P. Cair. Masp.* I 67097 *verso B-C* = Heitsch, Dioscorus, no. 4.

27. *P. Cair. Masp. III* 67315 verso = Heitsch, Dioscorus, no. 5; *P. Cair. Masp. II* 67179 A-Heitsch, Dioscorus, no. 21.

28. Heitsch, Dioscorus, no. 12 (*supra* n. 22).

29. *P. Cair. Masp. I* 67055 *verso* = Heitsch, Dioscorus, no. 2; *BKT* V. 1 (Berlin, 1907), 117-26 = Heitsch, Dioscorus, no. 3. I am grateful to Dr. G. Poethke for a photograph of the Berlin papyrus.

30. *P. Cair. Masp. II* 67185 verso A = Heitsch, Dioscorus, no. 19 (Hypatius is an *excubitor*).

31. *P. Cair. Masp. II* 67185 verso B = Heitsch, Dioscorus, no. 20 (Paul is a *cancellarius*).

32. *P. Cair. Masp. I* 67120 *verso B.15, C.34*: "Constantine the *dioicetes*" and "To Count Dorotheos" respectively. In fact the title of the first poem is an error: it is actually addressed to Colluthus, pagarch of Antaeopolis (remember that Saint Colluthus was the patron of Antinoe and the whole area: L. Papini, commentary on nos. 20-21 of M. Manfredi, ed., *Trenta testi greci da papiri* . . . [Florence: Istituto Papirologico "G. Vitelli," 1983], pp. 68-70.)

as it might have helped an official of the T'ang dynasty or perhaps a minor administrator of the British Raj.

Dioscorus returned to Aphrodito in 573/4, to resume serving as *curator* of the monastery founded by his father, and to live on into the reign of Maurice. Just as a postscript, it might be well to give an introduction to the man holding the office of duke of the Thebaid in 642/43, at the time of the Arab conquest. He bore the emotionally associative, quintessentially Coptic name of Shenoute. We know him from Patriarch Benjamin I's *Homily on the Wedding at Cana*:[33] "I wrote a letter to the God-loving Shenoute at Antinoe." This fact may well show that, as the social structure of Byzantine Egypt evolved, the office of duke could become open to men of truly Coptic culture and sympathy, as well as to hellenised aristocrats with long strings of names. After the conquest the office of duke, like so much else of the Byzantine administrative structures, continued, as we know, for example, from the eighth-century papyri from Apollonopolis Ano (in 704-06 the duke was an Arab called Wā'iz, Ουοειϑ),[34] and from the correspondence of Basilius, pagarch of Antaeopolis, with the Arab governor Qurrah ibn Sharik.[35]

I have chosen Dioscorus of Aphrodito as a kind of type in little, a microcosm if you will, of the life of Byzantine Egypt, cultural and public, and have tried to present him in his interactions with his world from village to capital as a Late Antique man inside whose head we can get to a surprising depth. His archive still has much more information to yield if only one asks the right question. I have also tried to present vignettes of a few of the holders of the office of duke of the Thebaid, showing them to be more than just faceless bureaucrats trapped in a sterile jungle of red tape and meaninglessly elegant nonsense. They were men

33. C. D. G. Müller, *Die Homilie über die Hochzeit zu Kana u. weitere Schriften des Patriarchen Benjamin I. von Alexandrien* (Abh. Heidelberger Akad. d. Wiss., phil.-hist. Kl., 1968), pp. 174-76. See now J. Gascou and K. A. Worp, "Problèmes de documentation apollinopolite," *ZPE*, 49 (1982), 83-95, for an up-to-date listing of post-conquest officials.

34. *P. Apoll.* (*supra*, no. 16), *1.2*, *3*, *6*, *8*; see p. 5, and now Gascou and Worp in *ZPE* 49 (previous note). In A.D. 699 Flavius Titus (how Roman!), Bell in *P. Lond. IV*, p. xix, citing Wessely; in A.D. 709, one Zora ibn al-Wasal (*P. Lond. IV 1440.6*)

35. See especially *P. Ross.-Georg. IV* (Tiflis, 1927; rpt. Amsterdam: Hakkert, 1966). Papyri from the Qurrah archive in both Greek and Arabic are numerous and scattered among several collections. See H. Cadell, "Nouveaux fragments de la correspondance de Kurrah ben Sharik," *RechPap*, 4 (1967), 107-60; Y. Ragib in *JNES*, 40 (1981), 173-87.

who did a difficult job in a uniquely bicultural world, and they changed as their governmental and cultural worlds changed. A man like Dioscorus worked for men like them. At the end of a day of writing out long, complicated legal phrases in his office, he sat down and wrote (and perhaps read aloud to his friends) things like

> Ἀεὶ χαίρω χορεύειν,
> ἀεὶ θέλω λυρίζειν. . . .
> στρατηγὸν νέον ἔραμαι,
> ποθοβλήτην Ἡρακλέα,
> δαμάζοντα τοὺς λέοντας·
> ἀεὶ τὰς πόλεις σαῶσαι.[36]

One wonders what he might have looked like—even in Dioscorus' imagination: probably a cataphract-mailed figure with great dark eyes.

It is well for us to look carefully at what Dioscorus' Anacreontic poetry is really all about.[37] The drinking-song is, of course, a universal form for all centuries. Though it is later in time, Dioscorus' skolion reaches us across somehow greater spaces than those that separate us from the model, Anacreon himself, with his Hellenic colonising activity and his involvement with the Athenian state. Songs like Dioscorus' have a different background: they were sung above mosaic pavements like the great circle-arcs at Khirbet Majfar, under carved ceilings where faces looked down from amongst whorls of trailing foliage, in the summer palaces of Hellenised Coptic nobles whose echoes we find in the Umayyad villas like Mshatta and Qusayr Amrah. The remains of such buildings have not yet been unearthed in Egypt, but it is only a question of time, now that archaeologists are beginning to treat the Coptic period as something more than an annoying layer to be removed. A family like the Apions did not hold their yearly patronage-feasts without a suitable architectural surrounding, accompanied by the Greek and Coptic equivalent of the lost art of the Sassanian court dinner minstrels. One had to be

---

36. *P. Cair. Masp. I 67097 verso F* = Heitsch, Dioscorus, no. 28.1-2, 13-16.

37. Th. Nissen, *Die byzantinische Anakreonteen*, SB. Bayer. Akad. d. Wiss. (München, 1940), does not mention Dioscorus at all; B. Baldwin in *Mus Phil Lond* 8 (1987), 13-14 simply notices the borrowing from Anacreon.

seen to celebrate, to give and receive, with clothing of appropriate colors and music of appropriate modes, as in Heian Japan: and Dioscorus' poems of wine and of praise fit into this world of high visibility.[38]

Among his papers, Dioscorus put together a Greek-Coptic glossary heavily poetic in content.[39] Perhaps, as papyrological discovery proceeds (the new pieces from Antinoe are still being worked on by their discoverers), and as more attention is paid to Coptic material alongside the Graeco-Roman, we shall find that one day Dioscorus expressed his duty towards and his feelings about one of his ducal patrons in Coptic, in spite of the fact that we know almost nothing, the Manichaean psalms notwithstanding,[40] about Coptic verse style or metre, apart from popular hagiographical ballads of the tenth century. At any rate, anyone who in the sixth century managed to coin one of the three longest words in Greek[41] certainly merits our continued attention.

Dioscorus' work and career illustrate the latest pre-Arab-conquest phase of the process of unification of the two cultures, Greek and Egyptian, a unification which bore a different stamp and proceeded along different lines in different eras, from the earliest Ptolemies, to the Hadrianic Baroque praised by Gibbon, to the two hundred years from Shenoute of the White Monastery to the fall of Alexandria. Different elements from the two cultures were stressed and combined in differing ways: a classical and a Christian education in a thoroughly bilingual society formed the minds of successive generations of Egyptians. No one now considers Nonnus of Panopolis, author of the *Paraphrase* of St John's Gospel that underlies so much of Dioscorus's own poetry, "the last pagan." In Dioscorus' work, after the trilingual conversation-manuals for upward social mobility and the pervasiveness of the

---

38. W. Crönert in *Gnomon*, 2 (1926), 663-66, noted poignantly that this poem was to be Egypt's last drinking-song before the Moslem conquest wiped out such pleasures. There are many Dionysiac and wine words in Dioscorus's Coptic glossary.

39. *Supra*, n. 1: 177-226.

40. C. R. C. Allberry, *A Manichaean Psalm-book* (Stuttgart: Kohlhammer, 1938); T. Säve-Söderbergh, *Studies in the Coptic Manichaean Psalm-book* (Uppsala: Almqvist & Wiksell, 1949). For the late period see H. Junker, *Koptische Poesie des 10. Jhdts.* (Berlin: Curtius, 1908); cf. S. Gaselee, "Hymnus de Sinuthio," *Parerga Coptica* (Cambridge: Cambridge Univ. Press, 1912), pp. 17-24.

41. χρυσαργυροπιναροσμαραγδομαργαριτοβελτίων: *P. Cair. Masp. I.* 67097 verso F 19-20. See the commentary on this piece by the present author, "The Imperial *chairetismos* of Dioscorus of Aphrodito," *JARCE*, 18 (1981, appeared 1984) 43-46.

grammarian's art, the fusion of "the Mediterranean *koine*" is complete and has flowered.[42]

When Dioscorus asked his servant (in Subakhmimic Coptic) to bring him his Nonnus or his Menander, and then sat down to glorify the Duke of the Thebaid for whom he worked, he was going through the process known to us all in classical verse composition, the transmutation of his own inheritance. They are not the grave elder gods and heroes, these Diomedes and Bellerophons in his poetry, the "young Heracles" whom he loves, but figures who might have sat for their portraits in encaustic or danced through the interwoven colors of a Coptic tapestry wall-hanging. And the praise of family, of lineage, in the hands of Dioscorus great-grandson of Psimanobet had become a means of stating his deepest beliefs about the society to which he belonged.

---

42. Everything in late antique Egypt has been viewed as pairs of opposites: Alexandria vs. The Valley, city vs. countryside, Christian vs. pagan, illustionistic Hellenism vs. abstract Copticism, classical rhetoric vs. native vehemence, rich vs. poor. There is supposed to be nothing classical about Shenoute, and none of the taint of "Coptic" about Nilotic tapestries. But even Bell was closer to the nature of things in his intuition of "its queer jumble" (*JHS* [1944], 30-31, cf. 36). It was simply a question of the total vocabulary with which one worked.

XI

The Coptic Papyri from Apollonos Anô

The compiler of the most recent reference work on Christian Egypt,[1] Dr Stefan Timm of the *Tübinger Atlas des Vorderen Orients*, has reminded us that the history of Christian Edfu (Apollonos megale/Apollonopolis Magna) remains to be written on the basis of both the archaeological evidence and all of the documentation found in all languages. To pretend that Coptic papyri do not exist is both unscholarly and irresponsible. The documentary papyrus material for the history of this Late Antique Egyptian city has undergone the fate that commonly has befallen bilingual, or multilingual, archives: the Greek pieces are published and well-known;[2] a few Arabic pieces, the province of Semitists or Islamic specialists, have appeared singly in periodicals or as part of large collections like *APEL*;[3] the Coptic pieces were put away in a drawer and forgotten. (I began looking for them in 1980 [see *Chr.Ég.* 56 (1981), p. 187 n. 2], and Jean Gasou called attention to their existence and to their unedited state in *ZPE* 49 (1982), p. 95.) Attempts at transcriptions of some of the Coptic pieces had been made by Remondon and Fr Pierre du Bourguet, but those scholars were not documentary Coptic specialists, and no results were obtained. I am grateful to P. Posener-Krieger and Dr Guy Wagner of the French Institute at Cairo for granting me permission to transcribe, edit, and publish the Coptic portion of the Apollonos Ano papyri, thus helping to make more complete the dossier of life in late antique Edfu, whose name, ⲧⲃⲟ/ⲧⲃⲱ, means "tree" or "wood."

Sixty-seven paper folders in Drawer 22 of the papyrus store-room at the French Institute, bearing the pencilled designation "Edfu Copte," contain over eighty-five unmounted, partially numbered papyri, mostly in a fragmentary state. One folder contains a document supposed to have been found at Edfu but identified by Gascou as coming from Aphrodito on the basis of toponymy and prosopography. The actual Edfu Coptic papyri formed the topmost layer of the papyrus material contained all together in a large jar (still preserved in Cairo) that was found by the first French excavations at the site during the season of 1921/22. The jar contained the archive of the well-known

1. S. Timm, *Das christlich-koptische Ägypten in arabischer Zeit* (I-III so far) (Wiesbaden 1984--): here III.1154. (Edfu = 1148-1157.)

2. *PApoll.*: R. Remondon, ed., *Papyrus grecs d'Apollonos Anô*, Cairo 1953.

3. Bibliographies and lists in J. Gascou-K. A. Worp, "Problèmes de documentation apollinopolite," *ZPE* 49 (1982), p. 95, and in Timm, *Ägypten*, III.1156 n. 7.

Apollinopolite pagarch Papas, who flourished, as Gascou and Worp have shown,[4] in the last third of the seventh century. The papers of Papas appeared to have been sorted according to language,[5] in a way that corresponded to subject-matter, Greek public documents as against Coptic private letters. In fact we shall see that such a hard-and-fast demarcation of content by language does not obtain.

None of the Coptic documents bears a complete absolute date. But we can plunge directly into Papas' administrative activity as pagarch with a document partially reconstructable from fragments numbered as being from papyri ## 29, 33, 35, 78, and 82 (Plate I). Since it uses the phraseology ϯⲣⲏⲛⲏ ⲛⲁⲕ it can be inferred as coming from the amir's office (cf. *PApoll.* 5.3, 7.4, 8.5; and see below.) (This also shows that the amir's office was employing official Coptic scribes.) It is an official letter concerning the *διανομαὶ τιμήcεωc*, articles requisitioned which are included in the official assessment or quota for the Upper Thebaid (as in *PLond.* IV 141; Bell, *ibid.*, p. 124). No mention is made of an *ἀπαργυριcμόc* or money commutation. The articles requisitioned and to be sent include ⲁⲕⲩⲣ = *ἀγκύρια*, anchor-cables (as in *PLond.* IV 1414.45 *et alibi*) and ⲁⲕⲑ = *ἄκανθα*, acacia wood used for shipbuilding, a desirable Thebaid commodity (as in *PLond.* IV 1433.24 *et alibi*, and especially *PApoll.* 11.6 with note and references): items know to be in demand by the Arab government for constructing its fleet. Part of an incompletely preserved word can be restored ⲡ– + as ⲉⲡⲁⲛⲁ[ⲗⲏⲯⲓⲥ or –[ⲗⲩⲙⲯⲓⲥ the *epanalepsis* or taking over of a required payment (cf. *PCair.Masp.* II 67151.136): the amir's office is enjoining upon Edfu that the quota be met. (One incomplete line reads "...I shall see to it that the amir has it in writing," ⲧⲁⲣⲓⲥϩⲁⲓ ⲛⲁϥ ⲛ̄ⲡⲁⲙⲓⲣⲁ.) Part of a date appears to be preserved, which may be either Phamenoth 15 or Pharmuthi 15. Only a fragment of the opening formula remains.

PApoll.Copt. 5 (so numbered) (Plate II) is also a letter to Papas from a member of the amir's staff, the subject-matter of which is similar to that of *PApoll.* 29, namely the requisition of ⲛ̄ⲉⲣⲅⲁⲧⲏⲥ /*ἐργάται* or unskilled workmen, the *ἀλλαγή* or changeover of work personnel, and the complications entailed by having to reconcile the demands of the requisition system on the one hand with the necessities of carrying on basic local agriculture and transport of produce on the other. In question are keels and masts for boats, sailors, foodstuffs (bread and wine), and the logistics of having workmen in the right place at the right time. "The *paneuphemos* amir is seeking for them according to

4. Gascou-Worp, "Documentation apollinopolite," pp. 83-89.

5. Remondon in *PApoll.* p. vi.

the reward for fugitives," writes Papas' (unnamed) correspondent, indicating the presence of a perennial problem of control (cf. *PApoll.* 9 and 13); it can be gathered that we are in the 660s to the 670s A.D. The ship-masters ⲚⲚⲒⲤⲦⲒⲔⲞⲤ of Edfu witness to the requirement of a total of eight καράβια (ⲔⲀⲢⲀⲂⲈ, cf. again *PApoll.* 9.7 and 29.9), presumably furnished by them to the government. "You carried out your personnel shift (*allage*) without listening to me," writes the official; "let my lord not find fault with me": "my lord" being presumably the duke (here ⲦⲞⲨⲜ) of the Thebaid, Jordanes (fl. 669 to 675/6, as again in *PApoll.* 9: GASCOU/WORP, "Documentation apollinopolite," p. 90). The writer refers to "being a slave (ϬⲀⲨⲞⲚ) in this city": we shall shortly see further evidence of the condition of slavery in post-conquest Apollonos Ano. The writer closes with a polite salutation to "the footstool of your [Papas'] feet" and the formula Ⲟ[Ⲩ]ϪⲀⲒ ϨⲚⲦϬⲞⲘ ⲚⲦⲈⲦⲢⲒⲀⲤ ⲈⲦⲞⲨⲀⲀⲂ, "Farewell in the power of the Holy Trinity" (a formula known from the Fayum, Ashmunein, Thebes, and elsewhere: BM 468.6-7, 1104.19; Ep 238^{r} 10-11; Herm 43.10; Pleyte-Boeser 10a^{r} 2-3).[6] Papas, and/or his house (the more usual phraseology, as here in Apoll. Copt. 103), is addressed with the honorific epithet ⲈⲨⲖⲞⲔⲈⲘⲈⲚⲞⲤ (εὐλογημένος), "blessed:" cf. Bal 205.2, 265.1, 395.8; Ryl 199.8, 300.3; BM 666, 1103.2, 30, 1119.3, 1240^{v}; Herm 37.2, 39.8; *MPER* V 25, 26, 55.

Slavery recurs in Apoll. Copt. 25, a letter (in two fragments, Plate III) with parallels to *PApoll.* 51 and 9 (hence probably also datable to the 660s-670s), which contains the phrase ... ϨⲚ̄ⲂⲀⲂⲨⲖⲰⲚ ⲈⲦⲢⲈ Ⲣ̄ϬⲀⲨⲞⲚ, "...in Babylon (Fustat) in order to serve as a slave." In post-conquest Coptic texts the terms ϨⲘ̄ϨⲀⲖ, "servant," and ϬⲀⲨⲞⲚ, understood by some jurists as "chattel slave," are not always clearly distinguished.[7] The χριστιανὰ ἀνδράποδα of *PApoll.* 51.5 (cf. 37.5 and 66.7) are also being sent to Fustat. When the Greek term *andrapodon* is used in the Aphrodito texts of the Arab period (*PLond.* IV 1433.17, 1435.39, 1438.9, 1441.65, 1447.172) it refers to slaves of the *symboulos* or Arab governor of Egypt, of his *familia*, of the Commander of the Faithful, or of the *Moagaritai/muhajirun* ("emigrants"). The slaves in *PApoll.* 51 are the former property of deceased Chri-

6. See A. BIEDENKOPF, *Koptische Brieftormular*, Würzburg 1983, pp. 106-107, Type I(f).

7. A. STEINWENTER, *Das Recht der koptischen Urkunden*, Munich 1955, pp. 16-17. KRU 95.6 juxtaposes both terms: "serving it (the monastery) in all slavery," Ⲣ̄ ϨⲘϨⲀⲖ ⲈⲢⲞϤ ϨⲘⲘⲚ̄ⲦϬⲀⲨⲞⲚ ⲚⲒⲘ. KRU 104.33 indicates that ϬⲀⲨⲞⲚ are obliged to do work enjoined upon them by the master who has legal power over the disposal of their persons.

stians, who are now being confiscated by the Arab government. The Coptic document refers to the sums of a trimesion and half a holocot, and to the period of seven months. Its fragmentary state does not yield a connected enough text for it to be clear what these amounts refer to. Slaves also appear in Apoll. Copt. 3, 23, and 74.

Over a dozen fragments from folders nos. 10 and 27 belong to a document (Plate IV) referring to the *demosion* and mentioning the well-known ⲕⲩⲣⲓⲟⲥ ⲭⲣⲓⲥⲧⲟⲫⲟⲣⲟⲥ, identifiable with the Christophoros of *PApoll.* 86.2 (7th indiction probably = A.D. 678/9), 37.8, 39.9, 10, 41.4, 48.4. Remondon classified this personage as a *topoteretes*, occupying an official position intermediary between the duke of the Thebaid and the pagarch. (This title appears in Apoll. Copt. 99, the ⲉⲩⲕⲗⲉⲉⲥⲧⲁⲧⲟⲥ ⲧ.) The writer of the present Coptic document addresses Papas – assuming him to be the recipient – as both ⲧⲉⲧⲙ̄ⲙⲛ̄ⲧ̄ϣⲏⲣⲉ "your sonship," and ⲧⲉⲧⲙ̄ⲙⲉⲅ(ⲁ)ⲗ(ⲟⲡⲣⲉⲡⲉⲓⲁ), "your magnificence." The document contains the interesting phrase ⲉⲓⲧⲉ ⲉⲓⲥ ⲩⲡⲟⲗⲩⲙⲯⲓⲛ ⲉⲓⲧⲉ ⲉⲓⲥ ⲩⲡⲟⲥⲧⲁⲥⲓⲛ (in context) "...having written (them) down/inscribed (them) [the responsible taxpayers of Edfu] either for good repute or for property" (cf. *Nov. Just.* 3 on qualifications for *ἀξιόπιστοι* witnesses), Under discussion is Papas' present (ⲉⲧⲃⲉ...ⲡⲕⲁⲓⲣⲟⲥ) ⲇⲓⲟⲓⲕⲏⲥⲓⲥ a term which Remondon regarded as synonymous with "pagarchy" (*PApoll.* 9.10, note *ad loc.*).

In accordance with the pattern found in the Greek documents in *PApoll.*, Papas is addressed by his correspondents who write on behalf of the amir/duke of the Thebaid by the title *peribleptos* = *spectabilis* (twenty occurrences in *PApoll.*; e.g. Coptic papyri nos. 11 and 28 [Plates V and VI]). The notarial style of post-conquest Edfu appears to have gone one step further in coining, as an inner-Coptic development, the abstract term of address (ⲧⲉⲕ)ⲙⲛ̄ⲧⲡⲉⲣⲓⲃⲗⲉⲡⲧⲟⲥ corresponding to the Augustinian and juristic *spectabilitas vestra*: the unique *περιβλεπτ[τότης* in *BGU* II 547.3 is a restoration by Krebs.[8] The Coptic abstract noun first appears (correct reading by Crum of a scribal error) in BM Or. 8903.20 (Crum in *ZÄS* 60, 1925, p. 106 with n. 8), a document of professional guilds and the pepper monopoly written in Edfu on 24.×.649 (Gascou/Worp, "Documentantion apollinopolite," p. 94). In Apoll. Copt. 11 there appears three times the deacon Severus, who may possibly be identified with Papas' agent Severus in *PApoll.* 63.3, 65.7, 8, 101.2. The writer of the Coptic document says that he has sent two accounts to Papas, one of money

8. Not recorded by L. Dinneen, *Titles of Address in Christian Greek Epistolography*, Washington 1929.

(in gold and copper currency, ⲛⲟⲩⲃ and ϩⲟⲙⲛⲧ) and one of seed-grain; and that the deacon Severus is to perform various services in connexion with them. We also encounter a Stephanos, and two brothers called Stephanos and Severus appear in *PApoll.* 79.4 as dependents of Papas.

In Apoll. Copt. 2 (Plate VII) and 52 we find the title ⲡ̄ⲉⲡⲁⲣⲭⲟⲥ, "the eparch." Apropos of *PApoll.* 66.1, *τοῦ ἐπάρχου*, Remondon remarked "...nous voyons mal ce que peut être un *ἔπαρχος* à cette époque" (p. 145). The title is attested in Coptic documents mostly in a Nubian context, in *CPR* IV 28.6 and BM 449, 450, and 452. It survives in a stereotyped notarial formula at Jeme in the eighth century in KRU 66.53, the testament of Susanna, in which the testator declares that "no one shall be able to destroy this will, neither archon nor hegemon, neither eparch nor *lashane*, neither bishop nor cleric, neither relative nor non-relative..." No. 52 preserves, in its fragmentary docket, part of a name plus title,]ⲟⲭⲓⲟⲥ ⲡⲉⲡⲁⲣⲭⲟⲥ: I am not able to suggest a restoration for the proper name. It is not clear from the context whether an "eparch" was equivalent to a pagarch or to a duke of the Thebaid: from the literary use of *ἐπαρχία* (as in George of Çyprus), possibly the latter.

Papas the pagarch of Apollonos received a variety of requests and complaints in his official capacity. The Coptic documents preserve a selection of them, involving camels and other livestock, money, "balancing the books" (ⲥⲩⲛⲁⲣⲥⲓⲥ, no. 29), and members of the local monastic communities ("the brothers," no. 31). Personal names not hitherto attested at Edfu include Komes and Demetrius. All these texts are fragmentary.

Many of the letters addressed to Papas are concerned with trade and local commodities, as they formed the backbone of Edfu's economic life as a town and a tributary part of the Umayyad state. Acacia wood remains attested as a sought-after building material (nos. 37, from an ecclesiastic, and 30). Monasteries raised livestock and carried out improvements to their property (no. 34); while ropes were a valuable article of requisition (account, no. 10). Further personal names appearing in the correspondence are Markos (cf. *PApoll.* 87.11), Iannakis (cf. BM Or. 8903), Philotheos (cf. *PApoll.* 27.5, 63.23), Andreas (cf. *PApoll.* 61.7), Athanasius (cf. *PApoll.* 74 B 6), Zacharias (cf. *PApoll.* 63.18), and Colluthus (cf. *PApoll.* 49.11, 50.5: a notary).

There are many more fragmentary Coptic pieces belonging to this archive. Most are small fragments of letters, the subject-matter of which covers the usual range of everyday life: greetings, money payments, dealings with officials (e.g. a ⲭⲁⲣⲧⲟⲩⲗⲁⲣⲓⲟⲥ in no. 99, cf.

PApoll. 25.2, 54.4, 91.11, 97 A 11) and functions (e.g. a γραματαφορος, *sic*, in no. 8: cf. *PApoll.* 3.1, 23.1, 24.1, 54.1, 55.1, 61.2), household objects such as jars and other containers, ropes, livestock, and foodstuffs. No. 1 even complains of "disturbance and confusion in this life," ϣτορτρ̄ ϩι ταραχη ⲛ̄τⲉ ⲡⲉⲓⲃⲓⲟⲥ : could this be from after AD 685, when the reforms of 'Abd-al-Malik were troubling the monastic communities of Upper Egypt? Interesting Greek loanwords occur, e.g. ⲇⲓⲁⲥⲧⲣⲟⲫⲏ in no. 12 (cf. KRU 92.46, ST 202.9, Ep 142.8), ⲑⲉⲟⲧⲏⲣⲏⲧⲟⲥ in no. 14 (cf. BM 1240), ϋⲡⲉⲣⲏⲫⲁⲛⲉⲓⲁ in no. 18 (used in *PApoll.* 69.17), ⲥⲧⲉⲛⲱⲥⲓⲥ in no. 19A (cf. *PApoll.* 26.4), ⲕⲉⲫⲁⲗⲁⲓⲟⲛ in no. 19B (cf. *PApoll.* 29.3). No. 30 coins the Copto-Greek form *ⲥⲩⲛⲕⲣⲟⲧⲓⲁ (for an equivalent to *συγκρότημα* or *-τησις*) to mean "community." We gain a few more examples of the Coptic dialectal peculiarities of Edfu:[9] ⲃⲓ for ϥⲓ (e.g. in no. 5), ϣⲁϣϥ for ⲥⲁϣϥ = 7 in n. 25, ϣⲟⲙⲉⲧ = 3 in no. 2. The common documentary Sahidic of the time was functioning well as a medium of communication.

Edfu came through the Arab conquest as a viable city (think of the activities of the physician Dios, from VC 5 [626/7] to BM Or. 8903 [649], and of Philemon, Thekla, and John in *PBu*, from about 620 to 645). Both Remondon and Gascou and Worp noticed the absence of Arabicisation in our extant sources from early Umayyad times.[10] (The present collection, of course, being the Papas papers, has no items of later date.§ By the Abbasid period our picture is a much more complex one. In *PLouvre* s.n. (Y. Ragib in *AnnIsl* 14 (1978), pp. 6-9, Pl. III) (A.D. 834) Afiya son of Boutros, a Copt, has called in five Moslem witnesses to sign his *iqrar* (deed of confirmation or acknowledgement), and part of two lines written in Coptic remain at the head of the document. (I have tried to get a date out of what is visible on the plate, but without success.) In *APEL* I 56.27-29 (A.D. 854), a Copt, Moses son of Aaron, signs in Coptic as a witness to an Arabic sale contract executed among Moslems; the property boundaries include (l. 5) the house of Pilatos the physician. In *APE* V 299.7-8 (10th c.) appear two Coptic estate agents (*wakils*), Hippolytos and Stephen, and Abu Pgol, a Coptic carpenter (l. 4). We know from manuscript colophons that by the late tenth to early eleventh century the Edfu monastery of St. Mercurius (a popular post-conquest saint) had become an active Coptic scriptorium, producing hagiographical and

9. See Crum, *ZÄS* 60 (1925), pp., 103-111; Schiller, *JARCE* 7 (1968), pp. 112-113 with nn. 10-12.

10. Gascou-Worp, "Documentation apollinopolite," 85 with nn. 14 and 16, citing Remondon.

homiletic texts.[11] The rest of the history of Christianity in Edfu remains to be written; at the present day there is one Coptic Orthodox church, of the Virgin Mary.[12] A survey of a collection, such as the present paper, is bound to give the impression of a rag-bag of miscellaneous information. But it is hoped that these Coptic papyri, when full texts and commentaries are published, will contribute to our knowledge of the life and administration of Apollonos/Edfu during a period that saw the beginnings of profound cultural transition in Egypt.[13]

11. van LANTSCHOOT, colophons nos. 110, 111, 112, 120.
12. S. TIMM, *Christliche Stätten in Ägypten*, Wiesbaden 1979.
13. I should like to thank, as always, Mirrit Boutros Ghali (Jer 42:16).

Plate I

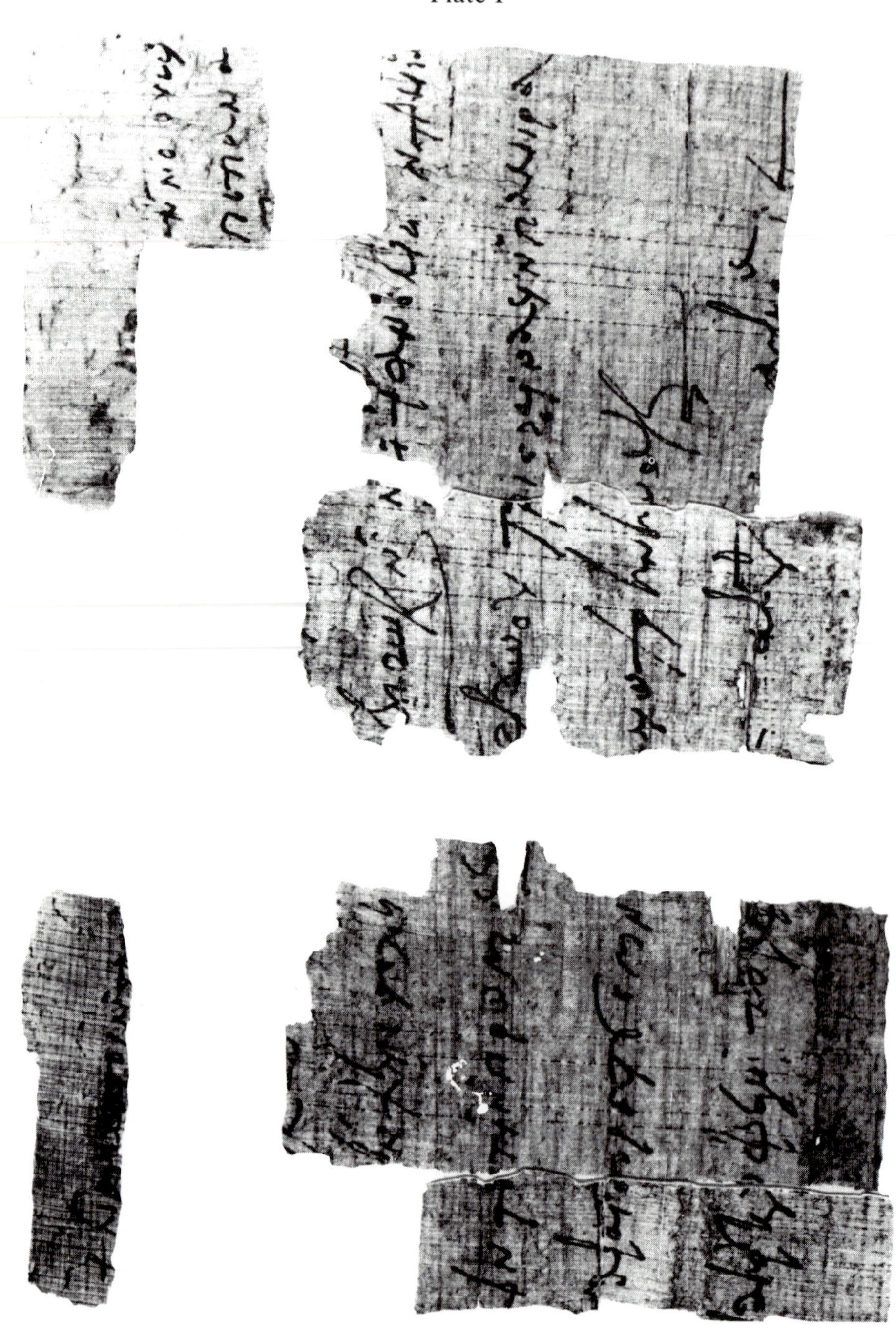

Plate IIa

Plate IIb

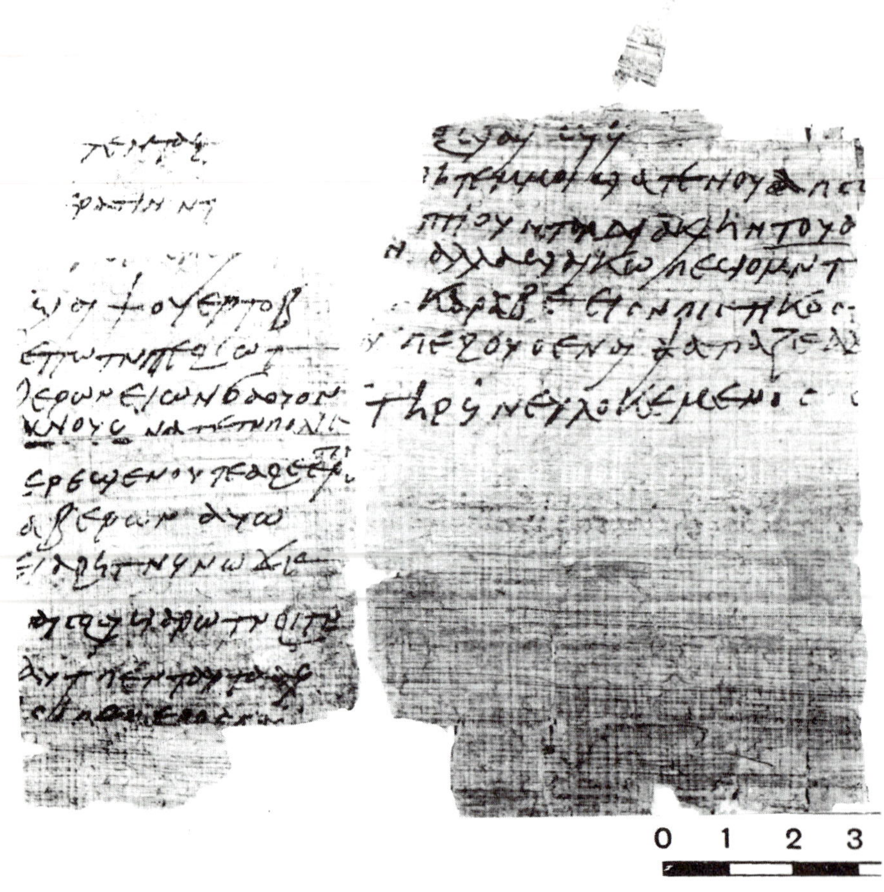

Plate IIc

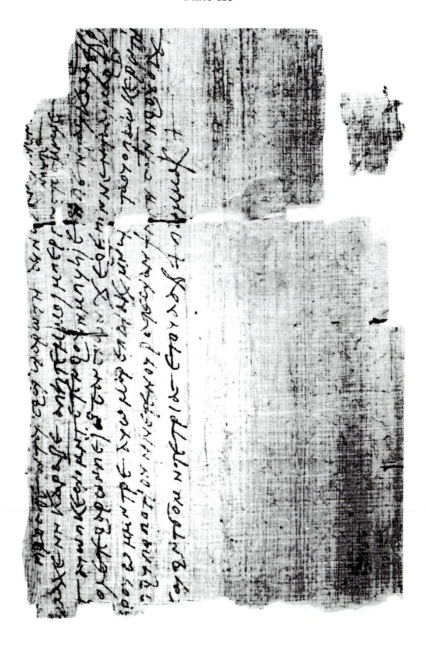

Plate III

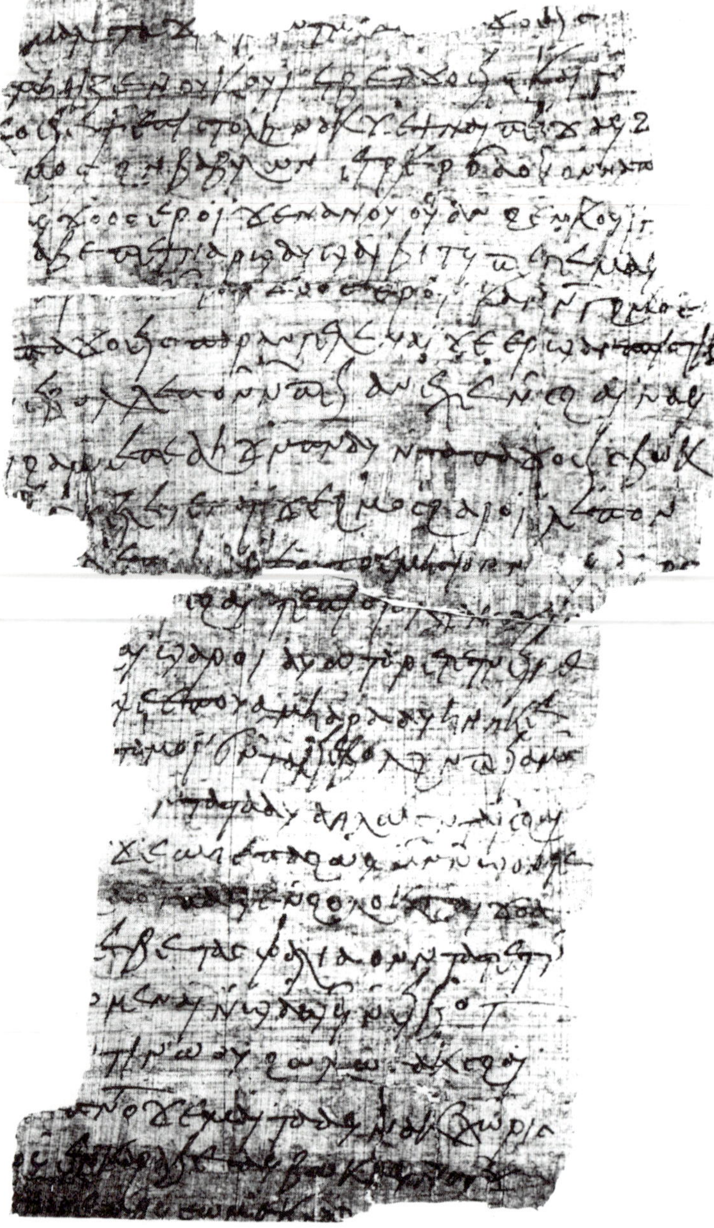

Plate IVa

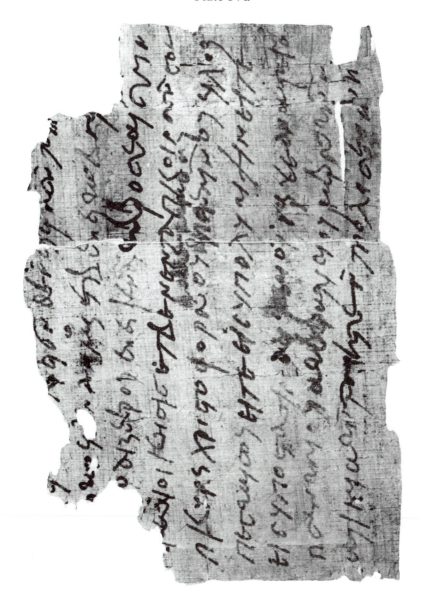

Plate IVb

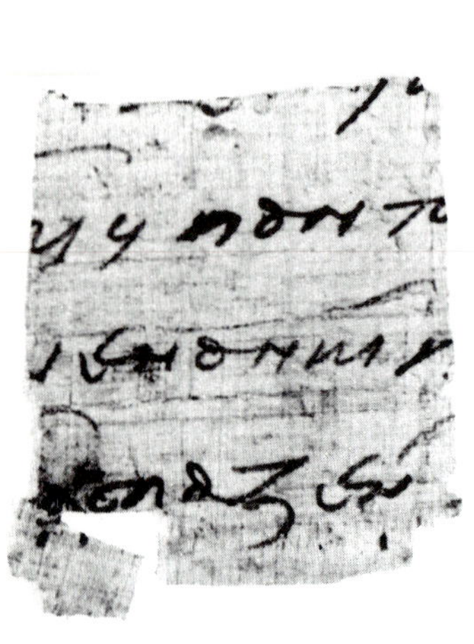

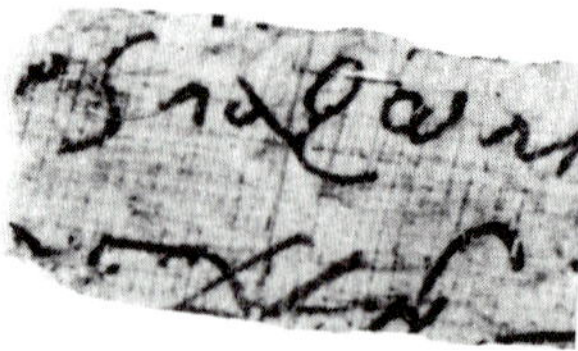

Plate IVc

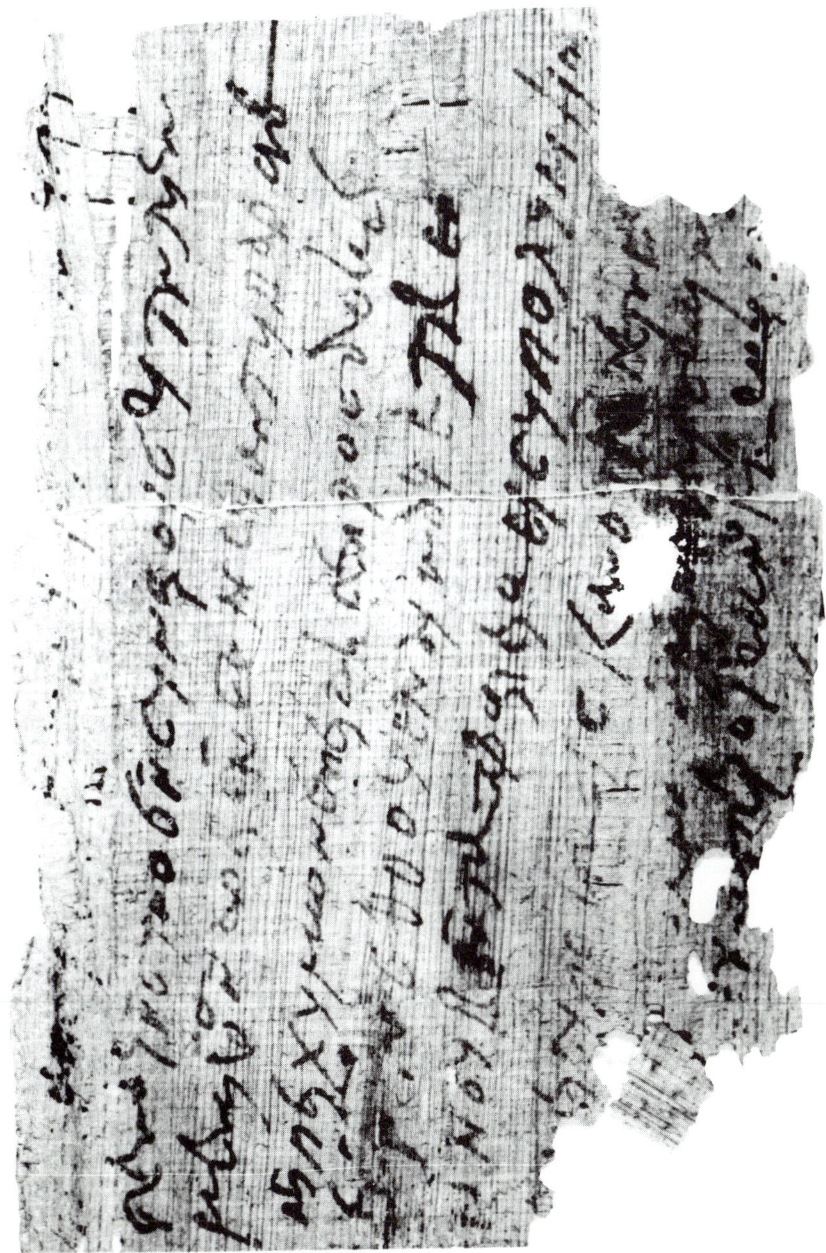

Plate IVd

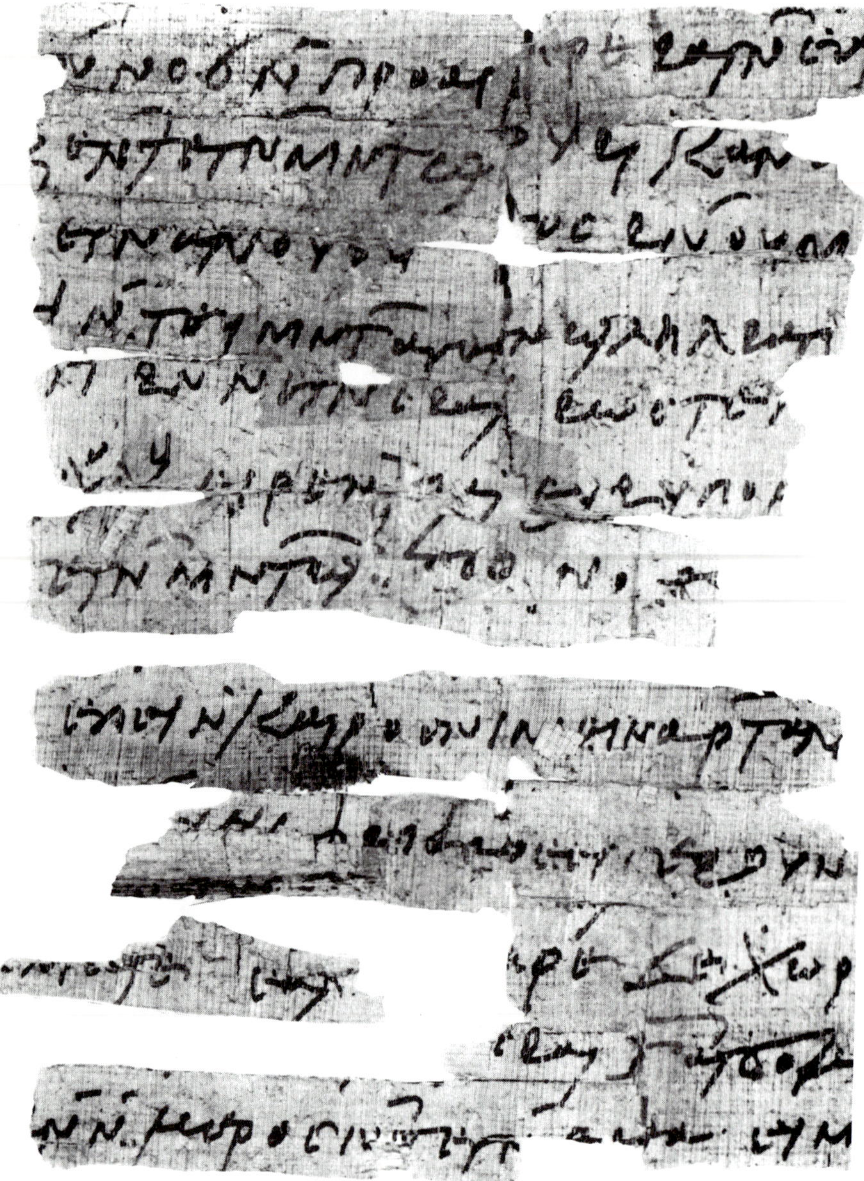

Plate Va

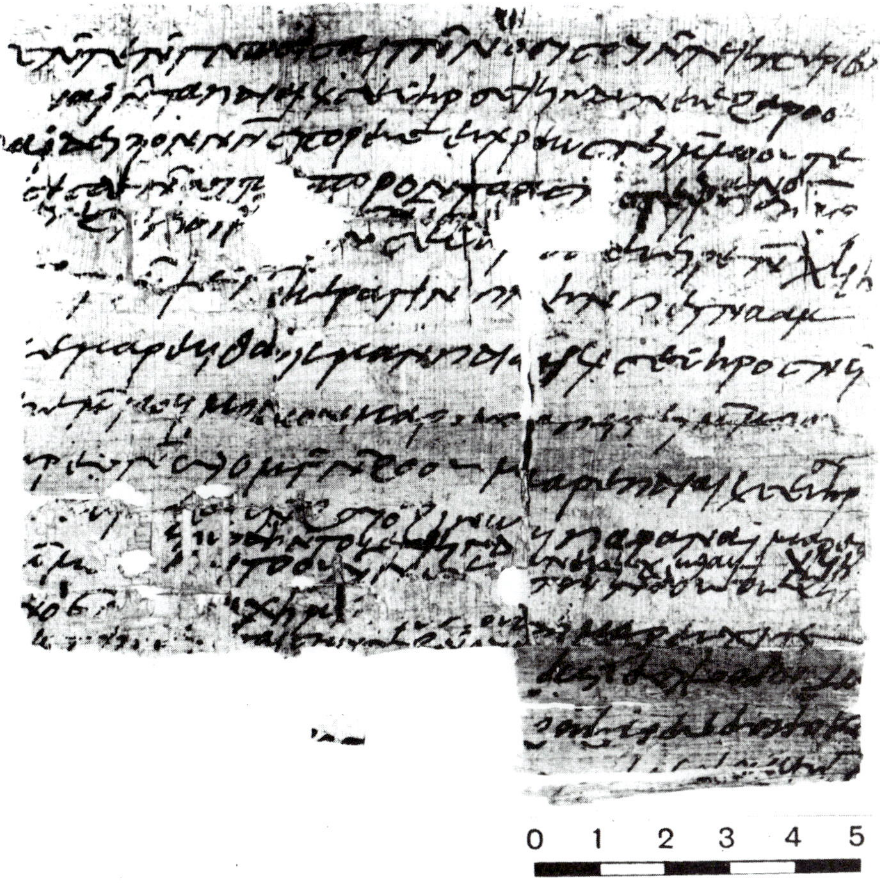

Plate Vb

Plate VI

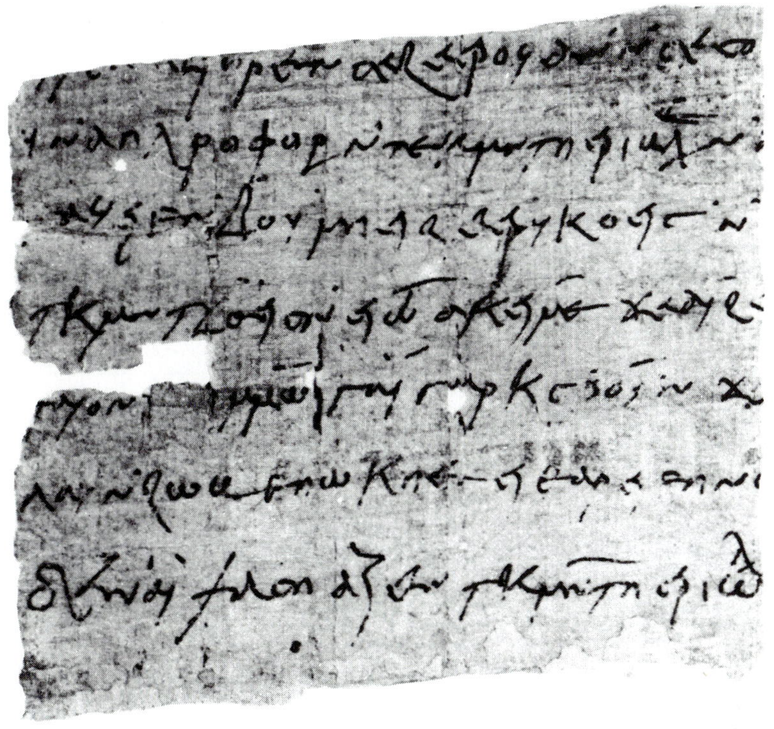

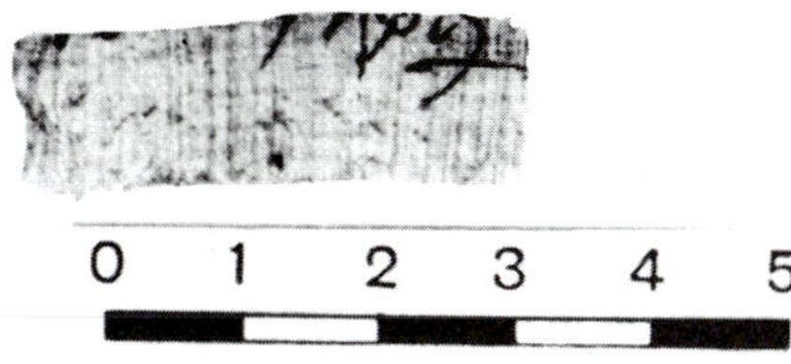

Plate VII

0 1 2 3 4 5

XII

COPTIC EGYPT DURING THE PERSIAN OCCUPATION

THE PAPYROLOGICAL EVIDENCE

In recent scholarship, the disruption casued by the Sasanian Persian invasion and occupation of parts of the Near East has increasingly been seen as *the* first great discontinuity of the seventh century. This event has been studied principally in Syria / Palestine and Asia Minor, from a combination of archaeological evidence and narrative sources. So far as Egypt is concerned, the period A. D. 619-629 has not been the object of extensive research, except in passing, as a prelude to considering the Arab conquest of the 640s; and historians have continued to rely on narrative sources[1] combined with hagiography[2]. From this period, however, comes hard evidence in the form of numerous documentary papyri in Greek, Coptic, and Persian[3], originating in several regions of Egypt. Examining their content should yield much-desired information about the actualities of daily life and administration in Egypt during its ten years of Sasanian rule[4].

Dating information[5] is sometimes *ex silentio*, arising from the

1. A. J. Butler, *The Arab conquest of Egypt*² (rev. P.M. Fraser; Oxford 1978) LVIII-LIX, 69-92; C. D. G. Müller, 'Benjamin I, 38. Patriarch von Alexandrien', *Muséon* 69 (1956) 313-340, esp. 314-317.

2. G. Gabra Abdel-Sayed, *Untersuchungen zu den Texten über Pesyntheus, Bischof von Koptos (569-632)* (Bonn 1984) 314-317, with the references cited in p. 314 n. 261; N. H. Baynes / E. Dawes, *Three Byzantine saints* (Oxford 1948) 254-256; H. Gelzer, *Leontios' von Neapolis Leben des hl. Johannes des Barmherzigen* (Freiburg / Leipzig 1893).

3. Preliminary lists in Butler / Fraser (above n. 1), XLVII (Greek), XLIX (Coptic), LIII-LIV (Persian): corrected in the present paper.

4. Older accounts conjured up an unwarranted and false picture of Persians favoring Monophysites at the expense of Chalcedonians, and of Copts welcoming Persians as 'liberators': e. g. Ch. Diehl, 'L'Egypte chrétienne et byzantine', in G. Hanotaux, ed., *Histoire de la nation égyptienne* 3 (Paris 1931) 538-540: a chapter which must be replaced by a competent synthesis based on recent research.

5. R. S. Bagnall / K. A. Worp, *Chronological systems of Byzantine Egypt* (Zutphen 1978) 128 gives '619-631 no papyri'; so too their lists of addenda and corrigenda through 1983: for the Greek material only.

absence of a regnal formula in the opening phraseology of a given papyrus[6]. Not dating by the regnal year of the Byzantine emperor might well imply that another authority has taken over. What follows is as complete as possible a list of papyri datable to indictions 8 through 2, of the just over ten-year span of the Persian presence. The list is both fuller and less full than has been thought.

We see the *argumentum ex silentio* method at work in material from Apollonopolis Megale (Edfu). In *P. Edfou* I 3 and *SB* I 5112, both datable to 618, which are respectively an acknowledgement of a debt of one solidus and a sale of a house, the regnal year is given, 9 Heraclius (6th indiction): the emperor is acknowledged as reigning; nothing out of the ordinary[6a]. But in *P. Edfou* I 2, an acknowledgement of a debt with a Trinitarian invocation, there is no regnal formula: only the seventh indiction is specified, equated with 619. Editors have taken this as the first indication of Persian occupation forces causing the notariate to leave off dating by the regnal year of the Byzantine emperor. And Edfu is far south, just north of Aswan. Then in *SB* I 4483, from Arsinoe, E. K. Chrysos has interpreted the added title «King of Kings» applied to Christ in the opening Christological invocation[7] as an echo of the Persian ruler's title, and combined it with the absence of a regnal formula (and presence of the ninth indiction) to date the document, a land-lease, to 620/21. So far, one document each for the first two years of Persian rule. *

Next comes *P. Oxy.* XVI 1921, which was formerly dated on the basis of its ninth indiction also to 620/21. This misdating caused E. R. Hardy[8] to construct a fanciful picture of the «last of the Apions» happily collaborating and doing business with the Persian occupiers out of «Egyptian nationalistic» motives. However, this papyrus, an account listing a couple of entriers for textiles as λόγῳ τῶν Περσῶν, has been convincingly redated

6. R. S. Bagnall / K. A. Worp, *Regnal formulas in Byzantine Egypt* (Missoula 1979). Cf. Z. Borkowski in *Alexandrie II* (Warsaw 1981) 132-133.

6a. So too *P. Iand.* III 49 is dated by its regnal formula to Heraclius 9, Epeiph 11, ind. 7 = 5. VII. 619 (from Oxyrhynchus).

7. E. K. Chrysos, 'The date of papyrus SB 4483 and the Persian occupation of Egypt', *Dodona* 4 (1975) 343-348.

8. E. R. Hardy, 'New light on the Persian occupation of Egypt', *JSOR* 13 (1929) 185-189.

* Add now *P. Oxy.* LVIII 3959, dated 12.i.620: no regnal dating clause, only invocation.

by J.-M. Carrié[9] to either 560 or possibly 575 (ninth indictions). So it can be struck off our list.

So too can another piece of the Apion archive, *SPP* XX 209 = *SB* I 5270, whose thirteenth indiction led Bell[10] to date it to 27. II. 625, since this document (payments to a brickmaker, from the estate of Strategius, the *paneuphemos* patrician) has an invocation but no regnal formula. However, Jean Gascou[11] (relying on Bagnall / Worp and Borkowski[12]) has redated this Arsinoite document to 610, thus placing it earlier than the Persian period[12a].

Mentioning «Persians» and dated by its editor to shortly after 621 is a problem-filled Coptic document, BKU III 338 (ed. H. Satzinger, Berlin 1968). On the basis of numerous editorial restorations its text has been understood as mentioning a violent uprising (ἀνταρσία, a word known from John Lydus' *On Portents*) and a hostage situation in Middle Egypt «since the Persians came». This interpretation is open to serious doubt, and a thorough revision of the text on the basis of, at least, a complete photograph is desirable. The text seems to fit more comfortably in the post-Arab conquest period (e.g. the presence of **ⲁⲡⲉ** in the plural), and examination of both the protocol and the Greek text on the verso will be necessary. Who these «Persians» are is in this case not at all clear[12b].

9. On the basis of its reckoning by *folleis*: J. -M. Carrie, 'Monnaie d'or et monnaie de bronze dans l'Egypte protobyzantine', in *Les dévaluations à Rome* 2 (Rome 1980) 260 n. 4. In the papyrus 'To the account of the Persians' most probably refers to the type of (Sasanian) textile.

10. In *Aegyptus* 3 (1922) 102.

11. J. Gascou, 'Les grands domaines, la cité et l'Etat dans l'Egypte byzantine', *Trav. et Mém.* 9 (Paris 1985) 61-75, esp. 70-71 with n. 392, and p. 75 addendum; stemma of the Apion family on p. 69. (Earlier stemmata of the Apions in *PLRE* II p. 1325, and note on *P. Oxy.* XVI 1829. 24 by Grenfell and Hunt).

12. R. S. Bagnall / K. A. Worp, 'Christian invocations in the papyri', *Cd'E* 56 (1981) 119; Z. Borkowski in *Alexandrie II* (Warsaw 1981) 133-134.

12a. Possible additions to the list on the *ex silentio* basis of their omission of regnal formula are *P. Würzb.* 19 (Hermopolite; Phamenoth 7, ind. 10, = 3. III. 622: Borkowski, *Alexandrie II*, p. 132 n. 22), and *SB* I 5681 (Arsinoite; Payni 14, ind. 11, = 8. VI. 623: *ibid.* p. 133 n. 24; cf. Bell in *JEA* 6 [1920] pp. 131-132 n. 13).

12b. The **ⲥⲉⲗⲗⲁⲣⲏⲥ** (σελλάριος? σελλαριώτης?) of line 1 is probably an official of the *cursus velox*, the public post, later to be in the hands of Arabs: cf. J. Gascou in *Travaux et Mémoires* 9 (Paris 1985) 53-59.

Real and interesting evidence does come from a Coptic document in the Pushkin Museum in Leningrad, Push 37/38[13], from the Fayum, datable to 25. X. 626. The recto side (with the fibres) and part of the verso bears an account (unfortunately missing the left margin) of «wheat of the fifteenth year», i. e., a slightly anomalous way of saying the 15th indiction. The account mentions, seven times, various days of «the month Dawsati» (ⲇⲁⲟⲩⲥⲁϯ), and what appears to be the Persian proper name Siavush (ⲥⲓⲁⲟⲩϣ). Amounts of wine are repeatedly listed along with the wheat. This sort of thing accords very well with the contents of most of the Persian papyri (see below). The rest of the verso side contains part of a letter written by the *anagnostes* Menas, with the phrase «I asked the Persians to ...»; it appears to deal with the reception of the monastic habit or *schema* (in Coptic ϩⲱⲕ) by two men called Peter and Anoup, and is dated 28 Phaophi (25. X). Jernstedt equated «Dawsati», via the form *nausard*, with the Zoroastrian nomth Fravarti (= 22. III – 21. IV), the first month of the Persian year, roughly equivalent in time to the Egyptian Pharmuthi[14]. Clearly a fifteenth indiction in conjunction with all the explicit Persian material dates this document securely to 626.

13. First published by P. Jernstedt in *VizVrem* n.s. 12 (1957) 221-231. I am grateful to Dr Stephen Morse of The Rockefeller University and Ms. Lee Perkins of Washington for help with the Russian. Jernstedt seems to have misunderstood the references to the monastic *schema*.

14. Cf. W. Hartner, 'Old Iranian calendars', in I. Gershevitch, ed., *CHI* 2 (Cambridge 1985) 760; M. Boyce, 'Iranian festivals', in E. Yar-Shater, ed., *CHI* 3 (Cambridge 1983) 814. I thank Dr Stephen Reinert of Rutgers University for his help with Persian. On Dawsati, J. Drescher, «A new Coptic month», *JEA* 46 (1960) 111-112, equated it, via a form ⲧⲁⲯⲁⲧⲉ, with Epeiph, on the basis of monastic accounts and *kalandologion* texts in Cairo. (This interpretation is very shaky; the Coptic Museum text, paper n. 3808, needs to be reedited, if it still exists and can be found.) It is frightening that the Greek and Coptic (especially Coptic) material once in the Michaelides collection will now never be known to the scholarly world owing to the conditions of persecution in Egypt. Two years of enquiring in the Greek community of Alexandria brought the present writer no results in trying to trace their whereabouts. If those monastic accounts were really eleventh-century, and in Coptic at that, that evidence is effectively lost to posterity. On Till's *Bauernpraktik* and its Cairo and Michigan *kalandologion* parallels see now the definitive work of G. M. Browne, *Michigan Coptic texts* (Barcelona 1979), n. 13 and Appendix, pp. 45-63.

Also from 626, 12 Hathyr = 8. XI, comes the Coptic document *CPR* II 5, from the Hermopolite. In it fourteen illiterate villagers from Pousire in that nome declare, via their scribe (ⲡⲥⲁϩ ⲛ̄ⲧⲓⲙⲉ, *komogrammateus*) Apollo, that they have received 36 gold solidi from the lord ⲡⲉⲣⲏⲥ ⲕⲱⲥⲣⲱⲓ, Firuz Khusro, as the price of 1980 loads (*phorai*) of linen cloth (i. e. 55 *phorai* cost 1 solidus, and each *phora* is stades to contain 25 *litrai*). They promise to deliver the goods in two weeks' time, by 26 Hathyr, swearing to do this «by God and the health (ⲟⲩϫⲁⲓ, *salus*) of the King of Kings (ⲡⲉⲣⲱ ⲛⲉⲣⲱⲟⲩ). Here are ordinary Coptic villagers selling their product to a Persian magnate instead of a Byzantine Egyptian one. Business as usual. Two of the names, John son of Taurine and Enoch son of Victor, are paralleled in *CPR* IX 50 R 8, 14, a tax register of the first half of the seventh century, also Hermopolite[15].

Back in Edfu we again find another document that omits the regnal year formula. *P. Edfou* I 4, with a Trinitarian invocation and giving the ἀρχή of the first indiction, is an acknowledgement of a loan of two solidi drawn up by five brothers and sisters. This first indiction has been equated by the editors with 628. And, from the Persian material, Hansen 53[16] mentions a «Year 2». If this is not a Persian king's regnal year or a year of the occupation, but rather a second indiction by the local reckoning, it would be equivalent to 628/29.

Two Greek papyri do not bear absolute dates, but explicitly mention the Persian occupation. *P. Iand.* I 22 is a letter from one Serenus, apparently an estate agent, to his *despotes*, in which the writer explains that he cannot carry out his assigned task because he has fallen «into the hands of the Persians». And *P. Ross.-Georg.* IV Anhang, pp. 97-105, from Latopolis (Esneh), is a letter in which the writer describes how the Persian beat him up, threw him into a ditch, and took away his children. (Both these Greek letters contain many Coptic calques and Coptic-influenced phraseology and grammatical features, indicating

15. There are, however, no parallels in the roughly contemporary tax list BM 1077. Some may lurk in the unpublished P. Sorb. inv. 2227 + P. Strasb. inv. 1445-1485, being edited by J. Gascou. See Till in *CPR* IV no. 48 (pp. 49-51, pl. II / 2), giving 8. XI. 625.

16. O. Hansen, *Die mittelpersischen Papyri der Papyrussammlung d. Staatlichen Museen zu Berlin* (= Abh. Preuss. Akad. d. Wiss., Phil. -hist. Kl. 1937, Nr. 9) (Berlin 1938).

that their writers' first language was Coptic). The occupying soldiers' behavior was running true to expected form.

Also not exactly datable, but providing evidence of the Persian period, are some Coptic documents from the monastery of Epiphanius[17] and the Budge legal papyrus from Thebes[18]. Ep 433 is a papyrus letter from a woman to the abbot, asking him to tell her «what to do about the Persians, for they are coming south». Ep 324 says that the writer had asked someone to write to the Persian official of the garrison at Thebes for travel permisson. The coming of the Persians was, expectedly, the sort of traumatic event that people dated happenings in their own lives by: the writer of Ep 300 says, «Before the Persians came south, my late husband gave the priest grain, and I still haven't been paid»[19]. The parties to the seventh-century lawsuit in P. Bu complain also of the difficult conditions of travel during the Persian occupation: the late Thekla, previous owner of the property that is under dispute, had had to travel by land «in the time of the Persians», since ship transport was unobtainable (perhaps commandeered by the occupying forces) (P. Bu 64-65, cf. 6-7).

Those occupying forces themselves left behind a bulk of paperwork, the Persian papyri, collected (alas, without textus) by the late Fr J. de Menasce[20]. Most are requisitions and lists of goods ordered: grain, wine, sheep, donkeys, chickens, eggs, doves, larks (300 larks!), pigs, millet, basil and other herbs. A papyrus in Basel[21] appears to list manpower levies from various towns in Egypt: Aswan, Heracleia, Oxyrhynchus, Theodo-

17. W. E. Crum et al., *The monastery of Epiphanius* (New York 1926) I 99-103 gives an account of the Persian-period material.

18. A. A. Schiller, 'The Budge papyrus of Columbia University', *JARCE* 7 (1968) 79-118, esp. p. 117.

19. Ep 200 exclaims, 'God preserve us from these men that have come into the district!', assuming them to be the Persians. Cf. Ep 198.

20. J. de Menasce O. P., *CII* 3. 4/5, *Ostraca and Papyri* (London 1957). Photographs only; the editor left no disciple to prepare texts. For an up-to-date summary of the field see D. Weber, 'Pahlavi Papyri und Ostraca: Stand der Forschung', in W. Skalmowski / A. V. Tongerloo, edd., *Middle Iranian Studies* (= *OLA* 16; Louvain 1984) 25-43; Idem, 'Die Pehlevifragmente der Papyrussammlung der Österreichischen Nationalbibliothek', *P. Rainer Cent.* (Vienna 1983) 215-228.

21. J. de Menasce, 'Recherches de papyrologie pehlevie', *JA* 241 (1953) 185-196: P. Bas. Pers. inv. M. I. 18 (p. 190).

siopolis, Hermopolis, Antinoe, Cusae, Lycopolis (Assiut), Diospolis, and Maximianopolis. Hansen 12 and 31 list Oxyrhynchus, Touphis, Lycopolis, Apollonopolis Kato, and Hypselis. Three Persian documents are bilingual with Greek, mentioning the κόδειξ (account– or tax-book) of Basileios, the *epoikion* of Kepha..., and George the *collectarius*. These documents, mostly found in the 1870s in the Fayum, do not bear absolute dates, though they occasionally mention a Zoroastrian day-name (with one exception, «Year 2», cited above). But clearly their evidential value cannot be overestimated.

This brief sketch of the extant papyrological evidence is intended simply as a papyrologist's contribution to a better understanding of this comparatively blank period in the history of late Byzantine Egypt. It is to be hoped that archaeological investigation will one day fill out the picture. What was life like in Oxyrhynchus, Hermopolis, Aphrodito, while they were in Sasanian hands? Perhaps city life in Egypt at the end of antiquity followed a path different from that perceived in Syria and Asia Minor. Identifying the physical results of Persian occupation at such sites could help give us an answer[22].

22. In this paper Greek papyri are cited by J. F. OATES et al., *Checklist of editions of Greek papyri and ostraca*[3] (Atlanta 1985); Coptic by A. A. SCHILLER, 'A checklist of Coptic documents and letters', *BASP* 13 (1976) 99-123. I should also like to thank Dr. Levon Avdoyan of the Library of Congress; Robert Bagnall Esq. of Washington; and, as always, Mirrit Boutros Ghali (Lam 3: 11).

XIII

STUD. PAL. XV 250ab: A MONOPHYSITE TRISHAGION FOR THE NILE FLOOD

THIS parchment leaf probably from the White Monastery of Shenoute at Atripe (Sohag), Vienna Coptic MS. K9740, published by Carl Wessely in 1914 in *Studien zur Paläographie und Papyruskunde XV: Griechische und koptische Texte theologischen Inhalts IV* (Leipzig), was noticed by D. Bonneau in her treatment of the Christianization of the observance of the Nile flood,[1] and called by her a prayer to St Shenoute. In fact it is a 'farced' or troped Trishagion, with the added Monophysite phrase 'who was crucified for us', embedded in a responsory with refrain, and both incorporating petitions for a good flood and a successful harvest.

[1] D. Bonneau, *La crue du Nil* (Paris, 1964), 421–39, 'Christianisation du culte de la crue du Nil': esp. 435–7, 'Prière à saint Sénouthios'.

First, let us consider a regularized text with translation.

(*a*) ποιηκόν[2]
ἀρχὴ καὶ τῶν μοναχῶν, ἅγιε Σενο[ύθιε,
μὴ εἰς τέλος ἐπιλάθου τῆς διαθή[κης
σου˙ ἀλλὰ μνήσθητι τῆς συναγ[ω-
γῆς σου˙ ἧς ἐκτήσω ⟨ἀ⟩π' ἀρχῆς, καὶ
πρεσβεῦε πρὸς τὸν Σωτῆρα κ(ύρι)ον τ[οῦ
σωθῆναι τὰς ψυχὰς ἡμῶν. (Ποιηκόν)
ἀναστάντες εἰς ὀρθρὸν δοξολογοῦμεν
σοι τῆν ἀνάστασιν, κ(ύρι)ε˙ καὶ τὴν
φωνὴν τῶν ἀγγέλων ἀναπέμπω-
μεν, λέγοντες˙ δόξα ἐν ὑψίστοις Θεῷ
καὶ ἐπὶ γῆς εἰρήνη{ς} ἐν ἀνθρώποις
εὐδοκία σου. (Ποιηκόν)
ⲁⲅⲓⲟⲥ ⲟ ⲑⲉⲟⲥ · ἀρχαγγελικαὶ δυνάμεις καὶ
χόρος ἁγίων ἱκετεύουσίν σε, φιλάν-
θρωπε.
ⲁⲅⲓⲟⲥ ⲉⲓⲥⲭⲩⲣⲟⲥ · γένος †ανθρωπος†
μὴ {α}θανατώσῃς, μήτε πόλις
ἐρημός, δίκ(αι)ος, ἄγαθε.
ⲁⲅⲓⲟⲥ ⲁⲑⲁⲛⲁⲧⲟⲥ · ἀνάγαγε, δεόμεθα, τὰ ποτάμια ὕδα-
τα˙ εὐλόγησον, δεόμεθα, τοὺς καρ-
ποὺς τοῦ ἐνιαυτοῦ˙ ὅτι πάντ[α
πρὸς τὴν τροφὴν προσδό[κω-
μεν.
ⲟ ⲥⲧⲁⲩⲣⲱⲑⲉⲓⲥ ⲇⲓ'ⲏⲙⲁⲥ · ἐ[λεῆσον
ἡμᾶς. (Ποιηκόν)
ⲁⲅⲓⲟⲥ ⲟ ⲑⲉⲟⲥ · ὃν ὑμνοῦν τὰ Χερουβ[ὶν καὶ
προσκυνοῦν τὰ Σεραφίν.
[ⲁⲅⲓⲟⲥ ⲉⲓⲥ]ⲭⲩⲣⲟⲥ · τῶν ἀσωμάτων [
ⲁⲅⲓⲟⲥ ⲁⲑⲁⲛⲁⲧⲟⲥ · ὁ ἐπιβλέπων [
τὴν γῆν, καὶ [

(*b*) ταῖς ἱ]κεσίαις τῶν ἀρχαγγέλων, τρισ-
άγιο]ς.
ⲟ ⲥⲧⲁⲩⲣⲱⲑⲉⲓⲥ ⲩⲡⲉⲣ ⲏⲙⲱⲛ · ἐλεῆ-
σον] ἡμᾶς. (Ποιηκόν)
καὶ] τοὺς πτώχους, κ(ύρι)ε, τοῦ λαοῦ σου, διὰ
τὴ]ν χῆραν καὶ τῶν ὀρφάνων, ἀνά-
γ]αγε, δεόμεθα, τὰ ποτάμια ὕδατα˙ (Ποιηκόν)
τ]ῶν στεναγμῶν τῶν πενητῶν
μὴ παριδείς, κ(ύρι)ε˙ ἀλλὰ ἐλεῆσον ἡμᾶς,
τοὺς καρποὺς τῆς γῆς αὔξησον. (Ποιηκόν)

[2] On this liturgical technical term for a refrain in Coptic see H. Quecke, 'Zukunftschancen bei der Erforschung der koptischen Liturgie,' in R. McL. Wilson (ed.), *The future of Coptic studies* (Leiden, 1978), 190.

Κ(ύρι)ε, κύριε, μὴ ἀποστρέψεις ἡμᾶς ἀπὸ τοῦ
προσώπου σου· ἀλλὰ ἐπληθῦνον τὰ γε⟨ν⟩-
νήματα τῆς γῆς, ὡς ἄγαθος καὶ φι-
λάνθρωπος. (Ποιηκόν)
Ἐγ]ένετο [sic], κ(ύρι)ε, τὸ ἐλεός σου ἐφ᾽ ἡμᾶς· ἀνάγαγε, δεόμεθα, τὰ ποτάμια ὕδατα ἐπὶ
τῶν μέτρων αὐτῶν· ἐλεῆσον
ἡμᾶς. (Ποιηκόν)
τὸν ἱερέα τοῦ Σωτῆρος ἐν τοῖς ὀρθροῖς
δοξάσομεν, ὅτι καὶ ἀθλόφορος· καὶ
]ώσε⟨ὶ⟩ ποιμὴν ἐγένετο ὀρθῶς γὰρ
] τησεν τὸν σταυρωθέντα Θ(εὸ)ν
π]λανῆς τὴν ἀσεβείαν καταλη
] νῦν πρεσβεῦ⟨ε⟩ σωθῆναι τὰς
ψυχὰς ἡ]μῶν· (Ποιηκόν)
]τριάδος κῆρ⟨υ⟩ξ ὀρθοδόξου
] τμα συνλιτουργοῦ⟨ν⟩του
]·†διεμαραριε† Χ(ριστὸ)ν τῷ [sic] ποίμνῃ
σταυ]ροῦ τιμίου

Founding chief of monks also, holy Shenoute, do not finally forget your covenant; but remember your congregation which has been yours since the beginning, and pray to the Saviour, the Lord, for the salvation of our souls.

Standing and facing the east, we glorify thy resurrection, O Lord; and we offer up the angels' song, saying: Glory to God in the highest, and on earth peace, among men with whom he is well pleased.

HOLY GOD: the archangelic powers and the chorus of the saints make supplication to thee, O lover of man.

HOLY AND MIGHTY: thou wilt not put the human race to death, nor make the city a desert, O just and good one.

HOLY AND IMMORTAL: make, we beseech thee, the waters of the river to rise; bless, we beseech thee, the fruits of the year; for we expect them all for our nourishment.

WHO WAST CRUCIFIED FOR US: have mercy upon us.

HOLY GOD: whom the Cherubim hymn and before whom the Seraphim bow down;

HOLY AND MIGHTY: the (chorus?) of the incorporeal ones (praises thee?);

HOLY AND IMMORTAL: who beholdest the (whole?) earth (or: who lookest down from heaven) and (hearest), thrice-holy one, the supplications of the archangels;

WHO WAST CRUCIFIED FOR US: have mercy upon us.
And (upon) the poor of thy people, O Lord, and on behalf of the widow and the orphans, make, we beseech thee, the water of the river to rise.

Do not disregard the groans of the poor, O Lord: but have mercy upon us, increase the fruits of the earth.

O Lord, O Lord, do not turn us away from thy face: but multiply the harvests of the earth, since thou art good and the lover of man.

Let thy mercy, O Lord, be upon us: make, we beseech thee, the waters of the river to rise up to their full measure: have mercy upon us.

Let us glorify the priest of the Saviour at dawn, for he is the prize-bearer as well: and . . . as a shepherd, for he rightly became . . . the crucified God . . . the impiety of error . . . now pray for the salvation of our souls.

. . . Herald of the orthodox Trinity . . . joining together in worship . . . Christ to the flock . . . the venerable Cross . . .

(p = parchment)

(*a*) 2 ⲙⲟⲛⲁⲭⲟⲛ P; 4 ⲁⲗⲗⲏ P; 5 P om. ⲁ; 8 ⲁⲛⲁⲥⲧⲁⲛⲧⲁⲥ P; 9 ⲥⲉ P; 11 ⲇⲟⲍⲁⲛ P; ⲩⲯⲓⲥⲧⲏⲥ P; ⲑ̄ⲩ̄ P; 12 ⲉⲓⲣⲏⲛⲏⲥ P; 14 ⲁⲣⲭⲁⲅⲅⲉⲗⲓⲕⲏ P; 15 ⲁⲅⲓⲟⲛ P; ⲓⲕⲉⲧⲉⲟⲩⲥⲓⲛ P; 16–17 *l.* ⲁⲛⲑⲣⲱⲡⲓⲛⲟⲛ or ⲁⲛⲑⲣⲱⲡⲱⲛ; 17 ⲁⲑⲁⲛⲁⲧⲱⲥⲏⲥ P; 18 ⲇⲓⲕϗⲓⲥ P; 20 ⲉⲩⲗⲏⲅⲉⲥⲟⲛ P; 22 ⲡⲣⲟⲥⲇⲱ[ⲕⲱⲙⲉⲛ P; 25 ⲩⲙⲛⲓⲛ P; 26 ⲡⲣⲟⲥⲕⲩⲛⲉⲓⲛ P; restore [ⲁⲅⲓⲟⲥ ⲉⲓⲥ-]; 27 [ⲡ̄ⲛ̄ⲁⲧⲱⲛ] Wessely; 28 [ⲟⲗⲏⲛ] Wessely, [ⲉⲍ ⲟⲩⲛⲱⲛ] MacCoull, cf. Dmitrievskii *Opisanie* 2, p. 989 l. 24

(*b*) 1 ⲓⲕⲉⲥⲉⲓⲁⲓⲥ P; 2 *l.* -ⲉ ; 6 ⲡⲟⲇⲁⲙⲓⲁ ; 7 ⲡⲟⲓⲛⲏⲧⲟⲛ P; 11 ⲉⲡⲗⲩⲑⲓⲛⲟⲛ P; ⲅⲉⲛⲏⲙⲁⲧⲁ P; 14 ⲉⲅⲉ]ⲛⲉⲧⲟ Wessely, *l.* ⲅⲉ]ⲛⲉⲧⲟ (for ⲅⲉⲛⲟⲓⲧⲟ); 19 ⲁⲑⲣⲟⲫⲟⲣⲟⲥ P (Fayumic influence); 25 ⲕⲩⲣⲍ P; 26 ⲥⲩⲛⲗⲓⲧⲟⲩⲣⲅⲟⲩⲧⲟⲩ P; 27 ⲡⲟⲓⲙⲏⲛ P

These spellings and vowel interchanges are not unexpected according to the patterns assumed by Greek words in Coptic, owing to interference from spoken Coptic: see F. T. Gignac, *A Grammar of the Greek Papyri of the Roman and Byzantine Periods*, I (Milan 1976). Interchanges seen here are ⲟ-ⲱ, ⲏ-ⲁ, ⲁ-ⲉ, ⲉ-ⲟⲓ, ⲏ-ⲟⲓ, ⲩ-ⲱ, ⲏ-ⲁⲓ, ⲉ-ⲉⲩ, ⲉⲓ-ⲓ, ⲇ-ⲧ, ⲟⲓ-ⲏ, ⲏ-ⲩ, ⲓ-ⲩ, ⲣ-ⲗ. If this indicates the state of the knowledge of Greek in the White Monastery in the ninth century, it was not too incompetent (e.g. very little itacism in dative plural endings). The accents on the parchment—grave, acute, circumflex, tremata—may serve more to indicate method of recitation in the liturgy. In all cases but one (b 10) *nomina sacra* are written compendiously: ⲕ̄ⲛ̄, ⲕ̄ⲉ̄, ⲑ̄ⲱ̄, ⲑ̄ⲥ̄, ⲭ̄ⲛ̄. The word καί is written out, but in a 18 the syllable *kai* in the middle of the word *dikaios* is written ϗ.

(*a*) 3 Cf. Deut 4: 23, μὴ ἐπιλάθησθε τὴν διαθήκην κυρίου τοῦ θεοῦ ἡμῶν; Deut 4: 31, (God) οὐκ ἐπιλήσεται τὴν διαθήκην τῶν πατέρων σου. In the LXX Psalms the verb ἐπιλανθάνω is often used with εἰς τέλος. Here the reference is to a very special διαθήκη, the promise made by monks in Shenoute's monastery. The text, preserved in a Paris Ms., is found in J. Leipoldt, *Schenute von Atripe* (Leipzig 1903), pp. 195–6. In the Shenoutean *diatheke* a monk promises not to defile his body, steal, and so forth, thereby not disrupting the community. The abbot Shenoute is invoked in the Vienna text as intercessor, in the hope that the devotion towards his monastery evinced by the people of the area will combine with his prayers to ensure a good Nile flood and harvest.

4–5 The Scriptural phrase is Ps. 73: 2 (LXX), Μνήσθητι τῆς συναγωγῆς σου ἧς ἐκτήσω ἀπ᾽ ἀρχῆς.

11–13 The *Gloria in excelsis* is also used in the Nile liturgy contained in MS. no. 92 in A. A. Dmitrievskii, *Opisanie liturgitseskich rukopisei*, 2 (Kiev 1901, repr, Hildesheim 1965), a sixteenth-century Chalcedonian euchologion from Sinai: p. 689, ll. 7–8 (Ordo for the blessing of the Nile waters).

14–24 The Trishagion[3] is here repeated twice. In the same Sinai euchologion cited above, *Opisanie*, 2 p. 686, ll. 17–26, only the phrase **ⲁⲅⲓⲟⲥ ⲟ ⲑⲉⲟⲥ** is repeated several times with added invocations.

Zoega's Sahidic MS. no. CII, Borgia copto 109, cas. 24, fasc. 102, is cited by one liturgical scholar[4] as the only (other) example of a Trishagion possibly for the Nile flood: it is called **ⲧⲣⲓⲥⲁⲅⲓⲟⲥ ⲉϫⲙ ⲡⲙⲟⲟⲩ**,'Trishagion upon the water', and listed as bilingual, Greek/Coptic.[5] Until photographs of the Naples MS. can be obtained for comparison, this clearly non-Chalcedonian transmission appears the only place in which the formula is used in a Nile liturgy.

23–4 The Monophysite addition appears here for the first time ending in δι᾽ ἡμᾶς, and for the second time ending in ὑπὲρ ἡμῶν (b. 2).

26–7 Wessely restored [**ⲕⲁⲓ ⲟ**], thinking **ⲭ︦ⲩ︦ⲣⲟⲥ** (l. 27) was a spelling of **ⲭⲟⲣⲟⲥ**, not recognizing that the text was a Trishagion requiring [**ⲁⲅⲓⲟⲥ ⲉⲓⲥ**]**ⲭ︦ⲩ︦ⲣⲟⲥ**.

27 Restore something like [τὸ τάγμα ἐπαινεῖ σε, space permitting.

28 My restoration comes from an eighteenth-century Cairo Greek Orthodox Patriarchate MS. given by Dmitrievskii, his no. 160, *akolouthia* for the rising of the Nile: *Opisanie*, 2, p. 989, l. 24.

29 Restore [ἀκούων] or the like.

(*b*) 7 For the Scriptural reference cf. Ps. 11: 6. . . . ἀπὸ τοῦ στεναγμοῦ τῶν πενητῶν.

10–11 Cf. Ps. 26: 9 and Ps. 142: 7, Μὴ ἀποστρέψεις τὸ πρόσωπόν σου ἀπ᾽ ἐμοῦ, here reversed; the verb in Ps. 50: 13 is different, Μὴ ἀποῤῥίψῃς με ἀπὸ τοῦ προσώπου σου.

3 See H. Quecke, *Untersuchungen zum koptischen Stundengebet* (Louvain, 1970), 302–4.

4 H. Engberding, 'Der Nil in der liturgischen Frömmigkeit des Christlichen Ostens', *Oriens Christianus* xxxvii (1953), 75, 'Ein Trisagion "über das Wasser"'.

5 G. Zoega, *Catalogus codicum copticorum MSS.*, p. 221.

11–12 Cf. Ps. 64: 10, ἐπλήθυνας τοῦ πλουτίσαι αὐτήν (sc. τὴν γῆν). The same phrase as in the Vienna text is found in Dmitrievskii's MS. 92, *Opisanie*, 2 p. 684, fourth line from bottom: πλήθυνον τὰ γεννήματα αὐτῆς (sc. τῆς γῆς).

14 The phrase is that of Ps. 32: 22, Γένοιτο τὸ ἔλεός σου, κύριε, ἐφ' ἡμᾶς.

18 ff. The text returns to praising and invoking Shenoute, to whom is applied the favourite epithet of Coptic martyrs, ἀθλόφορος. Although the leaf is damaged in this passage and the continuity is hard to reconstruct, Shenoute is apparently being held up as a defender of Monophysite orthodoxy (as against 'the impiety of error') as well as an intercessor.

25 In Dmitrievskii's MS. 92, *Opisanie*, 2 p. 691, ll. 1–5, θεοκῆρυξ is applied to St Mark, 'imitator of thine only-begotten Son, Our Lord and God and Saviour Jesus Christ; thou didst bring upon him the power of thy Spirit the Paraclete, and gavest him the grace to be a divine herald (θ.) and evangelist for the *oikoumene* . . . do thou guard the orthodox faith heralded by him'. Here Shenoute is the *theokeryx*.

26 λειτουργεῖν can be found three times in the works of Shenoute (see T. Orlandi, *Shenute Contra Origenistas* (Rome, 1985)). In Coptic the Cyrillian compound word συλλειτουργεῖν would be calqued with ϣⲃⲏⲣ. ϣⲃⲣ̄ⲗⲓⲧⲟⲩⲣⲅⲟⲥ, 'fellow-liturgizer', as an epithet of an ecclesiastic (referred to as a contemporary of Patriarch Cyril II, 1076–90), is found in the colophon to MS. Paris copte 132[1], fo. 66[r]: A. van Lantschoot, *Colophons des MSS. chrétiens d'Egypte* (Louvain, 1929), no. 72(2) (D).

27 On 'flock' cf. Dmitrievskii's MS. 92, *Opisanie*, 2. p. 690 l. 26: ἔπιδε ἐπὶ τὴν ποίμνην σου.

28 Apparently this recalls the description in Dmitrievskii's MS. 92 of how the Patriarch blesses the Nile waters holding a hand-cross: *Opisanie*, 2, p. 691.

Scholars have commented[6] on the fact that the liturgy for the Nile flood seems to have been transmitted only in Chalcedonian traditions, Syro-Palestinian and Egyptian. Here in the Vienna MS. can be seen part of such a liturgy in Monophysite transmission. In Engberding's words, 'Also hat auch der koptische Ritus bzw. seine griechischägyptische Urgestalt einmal eine eigene Weihe des Nilwassers gekannt.'[7] It would seem that the

[6] Engberding 'Der Nil' (above n. 4), 69–79; cf. A. Hermann, 'Der Nil und die Christen', *Jahrbuch für Antike und Christentum*, ii (1959), 30–69.

[7] Engberding, 'Der Nil', 72.

White Monastery of Shenoute played a part in that original form of the observance.[8]

[8] The Naples text appears to come from the same batch as the leaves that comprise Dom E. Lanne's Great Euchologion of the White Monastery.

I should like to thank, as always, Mirrit Boutros Ghali ('dass ich seine Wohnung werde, / O wie selig werd' ich sein!').

Redating the Inscription of El-Moallaqa*

The carved wooden lintel from the Coptic church of el-Moallaqa in Old Cairo, at present kept in the Coptic Museum,[1] which combines a lengthy Greek inscription with two pictorial scenes from the life of Christ, has been discussed by various art historians.[2] It is, however, necessary both to read the dating-clause that is preserved on the object correctly, making clear the chronological and prosopographical information it contains, and to evaluate the phraseology of the inscription as a whole, in order properly to place this monument in its historical context.

I first give the text in a diplomatic transcription, following the long lines in which it appears on the original wood (the lintel itself measures 2.65 metres long). Then I reproduce the text with division into cola, accents and breathings.[3] Note that throughout the inscription (except for 4.4 where once it is written out in full) καὶ is rendered by the symbol ∫. *Nomina sacra* are not marked by any specific abbreviation-sign. Abbreviated

---

*I am grateful to the Dumbarton Oaks Research Library, to the Society for Coptic Archaeology, to Roger Bagnall for reading a draft of this paper, and especially to Professor Ludwig Koenen for his valuable suggestions. I should also like to thank Ms. Helene Roberts and her staff at the Fogg Museum of Art (below n.3) for the photograph of the right-hand end of the inscription, and Dr. Stephen Morse of The Rockefeller University for help with references. Taf.XIII.

[1]Inv.no. 753. I thank G. Daoud of the Coptic Museum staff for the opportunity to study the piece at first hand.

[2]The following references will be used:

Strzygowski 1898: J.Strzygowski, "Die christlichen Denkmäler Ägyptens," *RömQ* 12 (1898) 1-41, esp. 14-22 (transcription by K. Krumbacher)

Lefebvre 1907: G. Lefebvre, *Recueil des inscriptions grecques chrétiennes de l'Egypte* (Cairo 1907), no.69

Dewald 1915: E.T. Dewald, "The iconography of the Ascension," *AJA* 19 (1915) 277-319, esp. 290-291

Simaika 1937: M. Simaika, *Guide sommaire du Musée copte* (Cairo 1937) (transcription by P. Jouguet)

Simaika 1938: M. Simaika, *Guide to the Coptic Museum* (Eng. tr. G.H. Costigan; Cairo 1938)

Kitzinger 1938: E. Kitzinger, "Notes on early Coptic sculpture," *Archaeologia* 87 (1938) 181-215

Sacopoulo 1957: M. Sacopoulo, "Le linteau copte dit d'al-Moâllaka," *CahArch* 9 (1957) 99-115.

Beckwith 1963: J. Beckwith, *Coptic sculpture* (London 1963)

Coquin 1974: Ch. Coquin, *Les édifices chrétiens du Vieux-Caire* I (Cairo 1974)

CSBE: R.S. Bagnall/K.A. Worp, *The chronological systems of Byzantine Egypt* (Zutphen 1978)

[3]The rythmical structure created, in principle, by sequences of cola with the same number of stressed syllables (frequently with a longer final clause) can be explained by both the Egyptian and the Hebrew tradition; cf. L. Koenen, *Antidoron Martino David*o, P.Lugd.Bat.17 (Leiden 1968), 31-52; idem, *APF* 17 (1960) 91-99 and *ZPE* 31 (1978) 71-76; I.Seiler, *Didymos der Blinde, De trinitate II*, Beitr. z. klass. Phil. 52 (Meisenheim 1975), pp. VIII-XIII; for the Egyptian tradition see e.g.G. Fecht, *Literarische Zeugnisse zur "persönlichen Frömmigkeit" in Ägypten*, Abh. Heidelb. Akad., phil.-hist. Kl. 1965. 1 (Heidelberg 1965). The rhythmical analysis of the present prose hymn is hampered by its fragmentary status (part of the first and second lines is missing) and by a scribal error in 3.5 (haplography; see the following edition of the text). In the latter passage, it makes little sense to connect "being invisible to the manifold powers." Except for the unusual connection of ϲυναναϲτραφῆναι with ἐν ἡμῖν, one also could reconstruct lines 3.4-4.1 as follows:

3.4 ὅτι ἐν οὐ(ρα)νοῖϲ ἀώρατοϲ (2)
⟨ϲυν⟩ὼν ποικί⟨λ⟨α⟩ιϲ δυνάμεϲιν (3)
ἐν ἡμῖν εὐδόκηϲαϲ (2)
4.1 τοῖϲ βρωτοῖϲ ϲυν|αναϲτραφῆναι (3)

In this footnote and generally in the matters of the rhythm of our piece, I follow suggestions by L. Koenen.

case endings in the dating-clause are indicated by a raised letter or letters at the end of a word.

1.[☧ ... (±22) Ο Ο]Υ̣(ΡΑ)Ν̣ΟC ΑΓΛΑΩC ΛΑΜΠΡΕΙΝΕΤΑΙ ΑΧΛΥC ΠΑΝΤΕΛΩC ΜΗ ΚΕΚΤΗΜΕΝΟC ΕΝΘΑ ΚΑΤΩΚΕΙ ΠΑΝ ΤΟ ΠΛΗΡΩΜΑ ΤΗC ΘΕΟΤΗΤΟC ΩC ΕΠΟΥΡΑΝΙΟΝ CΙΝΑΙ ΑΝΩ[

2. [(±20) ΟΙ ΑΓ]ΓΕΛΟΙ (ΚΑΙ) ΑΠΑΥCΤΩC ΑΥΤΟΝ ΓΕΡΕΡΟΥCΙΝ ΕΝ ΤΡΙCΑΓΙΑ ΦΩΝΗ ΑΔΟΝΤΕC (ΚΑΙ) ΛΕΓΟΝΤΕC· ΑΓΙΟC ΑΓΙΟC ΑΓΙΟC ΕΙ Κ(ΥΡΙ)Ε· ΠΛΗΡΗC Ο ΟΥ(ΡΑ)ΝΟC (ΚΑΙ) Η ΓΗ ΤΗ[C ΑΓΙ-

3. ΑC CΟΥ [ΔΟ]ΞΗC· (ΚΑΙ) ΓΑΡ ΠΕΠΛΗΡΩΝΤΑΙ ΤΗC ΜΕΓΑΛΙΟΤΗΤΟC CΟΥ ΠΟΛΥΕΥCΠ(Λ)Α(Γ)ΧΝΕ Κ(Υ ΡΙ)Ε ΟΤΙ ΕΝ ΟΥ(ΡΑ)ΝΟΙC ΑΩΡΑΤΟC ΩΝ ΠΟΙΚΙΛΟΙC ΔΥΝΑ̣ΜΕCΙΝ ΕΝ ΗΜΙΝ ΕΥΔΟΚΗCΑC ΤΟΙC ΒΡΩΤΟΙC CΥΝ-

4. ΑΝΑCΤΡΑΦΗΝΑΙ CΑΡΚΩΘΕΙC ΕΚ ΤΗC ΑΠΙΡΑΝΔΡΟΥ ΘΕΟΜΗΤΟΡΟC ΜΑΡΙΑC ΕΠΙΚΟΥ ΡΟC ΓΕΝΟΥ ΑΒΒΑ ΘΕΟΔΩΡΟΥ ΠΡΟΕΔΡΟ(Υ) (ΚΑΙ) ΓΕΩΡΓΙΩ ΔΙΑΚ(ΟΝΩ) ΚΑΙ ΟΙΚΟΝΟ(Μ Ω). **Μ̣(ΗΝ)Ο̣C Μ̇-Π̣ΑΧ̣(ΩΝ) Ι̅Β̅ ΙΝ̣(ΔΙΚΤΙΩΝΟC) Γ̅ ΔΙΟΚ̣(ΛΗΤΙΑΝΟΥ) Υ̣̅Ν̅Α̅**

1. 1 ☧ (± 22)
ὁ ο]ὐ̣(ρα)ν̣ὸc ἀγλαῶc λαμπρείνεται (3 [?] stresses)
ἀχλῦc παντελῶc μὴ κεκτημένοc, (3 or 4)
ἔνθα κατῳκεῖ (2)
4 πᾶν τὸ πλήρωμα τῆc θεότητοc (3)
ὡc ἐπουρανίου Cιναὶ ἄνω.| (3)
2.1 (± 20) οἱ ἄγ]γελοι
(καὶ) ἀπαύcτωc αὐτὸν γερέρουcιν (3)
ἐν τρισαγίᾳ φωνῇ (2)
ᾄδοντεc καὶ λέγοντεc: (2)

4 ἅγιοc, ἅγιοc, ἅγιοc (3)
εἶ κ(ύρι)ε, (2)
πλήρηc ὁ οὐ(ρα)νὸc (καὶ) ἡ γῆ (3)
3.1 τῆ[c ἁγί]|ac σου [δό]ξηc· (2)

(καὶ) γὰρ πεπλήρωνται τῆc μεγαλιότητόc cου, (2)
πολυεύcπ‹λ›α‹γ›χνε κ(ύρι)ε, (2)
4 ὅτι ἐν οὐ(ρα)νοῖc ἀώρατοc ὢν (3)
ποικίλοιc δυνάμεcιν ἔν‹ει› (3)
ἡμῖν εὐδοκῆcαc (2)
4.1 τοῖc βρωτοῖc cυν|αναcτραφῆναι (3)
cαρκωθεὶc ἐκ τῆc ἀπιράνδρου θεομήτοροc Μαρίαc. (4)

ἐπίκουροc γένου Ἀββᾶ Θεοδώρου προέδρο(υ)
4 (καὶ) Γεωργίῳ διακ(όνῳ) καὶ οἰκονό(μῳ).
Μ̣(ΗΝ)Ο̣(C) Μ̇Π̣ΑΧ̣(ΩΝ) Ι̅Β̅ ΙΝ̣(ΔΙΚΤΙΩΝΟC) Γ̅ ΔΙΟΚ̣(ΛΗΤΙΑΝΟΥ) Υ̣̅Ν̅Α̅

1.1 suppl. tentatively by Koenen | *read* λαμπρύνεται **1.5** ω λειτουργουcιν αι ανω cπα *Krumbacher, Lefebvre* **2.2** γεραίρουcιν **3.2** *read* μεγαλειότητόc | *read* ἀόρατοc **3.4-6** ‹cυν›ὼν --- ἐν ἡμῖν εὐδόκηcαc --- *or* ὢν --- ἔν‹ει› ἡμῖν εὐδοκῆcαc *Koenen (cf. n. 3)* **3.5** *read* ποικίλαιc **4.2** *read* ἀπειράνδρου

...The heaven shines splendidly
having no darkness at all.

There dwells
all the fulness of the Godhead,
on the peak of truly heavenly Sinai.
...the angels
and they ceaselessly honor him
with thrice-holy voice (i.e. in the Trishagion)
singing and saying:

"Holy, holy, holy
are you, O Lord:
heaven and earth are full
of your holy glory."

For they are filled with your greatness,
O Lord of great mercy,
as you are invisible in the heavens
amidst manifold powers,
and you were content
to dwell together with us mortals,[4]
having become incarnate from the Mother of God, Mary, who has never known man.
Be a helper to Abba Theodore the patriarch
and George the deacon and oeconomus.
Pachon 12, indiction 3, year of Diocletian 451.

Of primary importance is the last part of the fourth long line of the inscription. The wood at the end of the inscription is almost completely gone (since Jouguet read NA in 1937, which led to confusion, see below). What is left of a vertical element or hasta in the first part of the three numerals might be interpreted as being consistent with the remains of either P or Y; but there are traces of a V-shaped element higher up which make the eye incline toward an upsilon. The upper left part of the Y is more visible in a raking light when one is actually looking at the inscription itself (I examined it autoptically in May 1983). Even Sacopoulo's figure 6 (1957: p.105) shows the remains of the Y. In fact the Y is quite visible in a photograph (see plate) taken in Cairo by A. Kingsley Porter,[5] of which a print exists at Dumbarton Oaks. The space fits that required by three numerals, and I read **ỴNⲁ** Diocletian year 451. It is noteworthy that in the dating formula the carver switched from a rather elegant Greek to a purely Coptic set of letter-forms (**Ṁ** with its late diacritical mark as a connective element before the month-name).

The complete dating-clause thus gives Pachon 12, indiction 3, year of Diocletian 451. There are in any case only two third indictions corresponding to a Diocletian year that ends

[4]Or: "for although in heaven you were invisible
among manifold powers,
you were content among us,
among mortals to dwell."

[5]The negative is kept at the Fogg Museum of Art, Cambridge (Mass.), number M 7140/670/C 04/1(c)3 (Coptic woodwork). The original photograph was taken *in situ* by A. Kingsley Porter ca. 1900-1910. I thank Charlotte Burk and Claudia Vess of the Dumbarton Oaks Photo Collection for helping me find and obtain this plate, which was kindly supplied by Ms. Helene Roberts and her staff.

with the digits -51:[6] year 151 (A.D. 434/5, *CSBE* p.81) and year 451 (A.D. 734/5, W.C. Till, *Datierung u. Prosopographie der koptischen Urkunden aus Theben* [Vienna 1962] p.238). We have already seen that the visual evidence does not point to the vertical hasta as belonging to a rho = 100. The second alternative is to be read as the correct date, equal to 7.V.735. Also, the gamma for the indiction number is quite clear. The indiction was previously either misread (Krumbacher *apud* Strzygowski 1898:15-16 as F = ς̄ or unnoticed (Jouguet *apud* Simaika 1937-38; Sacopoulo 1957:112;[7] Beckwith 1963:13-15). By now the correct date should be clear: and this fact should help to place the object as a whole.[8] The prosopography works out clearly as well: the Monophysite patriarch of Alexandria in A.D. 735 was Theodore (reigned 731-743), the only one of that name.[9]

A couple of observations on particularities of the Greek text are also in order. τὸ πλήρωμα τῆϲ θεότητοϲ is a christological concept as lines 1.3-5 are a quotation of Colossians 2:9, ὅτι ἐν αὐτῷ [sc. Χριϲτῷ] κατοικεῖ πᾶν τὸ πλήρωμα τῆϲ θεότητοϲ, omitting the final scriptural word ϲωματικῶϲ. This passage was of importance in Monophysite Christology: it was used by Cyril of Alexandria in his third letter to Nestorius (of A.D. 430), 4.14-19 (ed. L.R. Wickham, Oxford 1983). It was equally important in eighth-century thought, for Christians living under Umayyad rule, to insist on what kind of κατοίκηϲιϲ took place in the incarnate Christ. Compare the verb ϲυναναϲτροφῆναι in line 4.1, the typical verb used of Christ's dwelling among human beings in his full humanity (e.g. by Sophronius of Jerusalem at *PG* 87.3177D, c. ἀνθρωπίνωϲ ἡμῖν.)

The poetic and exact expression describing the Incarnation in line 4.2 has eighth-century parallels in P.Berol. 10677, the Greek Paschal letter of the Monophysite Coptic patriarch Alexander II (reigned A.D. 704-729), edited by Schmidt and Schubart in *BKT* VI, *Altchristliche Texte* (Berlin 1910) 55ff. (As the letter mentions Easter as falling on 16.iv, it must date from either A.D. 713, 719, or 724; the beginning of the text, which might have carried an indiction number, is lost.) Line 173 reads ϲαρκωθεὶϲ ἐκ παρθένου: in this passage the patriarch is quoting the letter of Pope Felix to Maximus of Alexandria that was cited by both Cyril and the Council of Ephesus, and that became important in Monophysite tradition. And line 189 reads ϲαρκωθεὶϲ ἐκ παρθένου Μαρίαϲ: in this passage the patriarch is quoting the inauthentic letter supposedly from Pope Julius to Prosdocius, that was also picked up by Cyril, the Council of Ephesus, and the later Egyptian Monophysite tradition (see Schmidt/Schubart, pp.75-77). The text of our inscription is less a 'farced' Trishagion[10] than it is an explicit continuation of the Egyptian Monophysite tradition of Christological formula-making.

Aided by knowledge of its date, we can look at the carved lintel as a whole. Below the inscription lie the juxtaposed depictions of the Entry into Jerusalem and the Ascension, which have been discussed by art historians in purely stylistic terms without attention

[6]Sacopoulo 1957:100 read "51(?)", which is of course impossible. See *CSBE* pp.43-49, and note 7 below. This text is not listed in *CSBE* p.49 n.24 as being one of the instances of a Diocletian year with a numeral lacking. In any case the era of Diocletian is not found in inscriptions as early as year 51.

[7]P.112: "L'année 335 confirme avec une précision mathématique la date avancée par Pierre Jouguet..." But A.D. 335 was a ninth indiction (*CSBE* p.73): the mathematics works out quite differently.

[8]In fact we have another dated document (Coptic) from indiction 3 = Diocletian year 451. It is *SB* I 5607 = KRU 106; *CSBE* p.49; cf. R.S. Bagnall/K.A. Worp, 'Christian invocations in the papyri,' *Cd'E* 56 (1981) 22 with note *ad loc.* dating it to A.D. 734.

[9]B. Evetts, *History of the Patriarchs of the Coptic Church of Alexandria* III = PO 5.1 (Paris 1947) 86-88.

[10]For ϲαρκωθεὶϲ δι' ἡμᾶϲ or ὑπὲρ ἡμῶν in trishagia hymns see L. Koenen, *locc. citt.* (n.3).

being paid to the dating formula.[11] A post-conquest date will serve more clearly to explain this monument. The Coptic liturgy delights in juxtaposing Christ who sits above the Cherubim with Christ seated on a donkey.[12] The Palm Sunday scene placed next to the Ascension creates a triumphal portal (cf. Sacopoulo 1957:115): a door for the triumphal entry of Patriarch Theodore, and an expression of hope for the future triumph of a church that was beginning to live under persecution. The language of the el-Moallaqa inscription had special resonances in Umayyad times, stressing as it does the completely real divinity of the incarnate Christ.[13] Redating this monument to the eighth century will both revise our received ideas about style in Coptic visual art and provide valuable evidence for the persistence of epigraphic Greek of high quality in post-conquest Egypt.

[11]E.g.Kitzinger 1938:213 n.2; Coquin 1974:83. Dewald 1915:291 asserted that Strzygowski dated it to the eighth century, which in fact he did not (1898:21, sixth century). H. Kessler in *Age of Spirituality* (New York/ Princeton 1979) 502 opts for "... as late as the 6th century."

[12]Cf. A.A. el-Muharraqi, ed., *Dalil osbu' al-ālām (Ordo for Holy Week)* (Cairo 1971) 73, 80, 81-82, 87-88, 101; also 21, 24, 52, 58.

[13]Sacopoulo 1957:114 commented: "Son épigraphie retient un émouvant credo où vibre l'ardeur des luttes théologiques..." Indeed yes: the credo, the ardor, of Christians living under Muslim pressure, in an atmosphere of defensive argument.

TAFEL XIII

Inschrift aus der koptischen Kirche von El-Moallaqa, Alt-Kairo, Koptisches Museum Inv. no. 753; zu L. S. B. MacCoull S. 230ff.

XV

Coptic Alchemy and Craft Technology in Islamic Egypt: The Papyrological Evidence

The documents I shall be describing in this paper embody a three-way cultural interaction: the carrying over into medieval times of an ancient Greek tradition of speculative thought and Egyptian practical craft, from Greek into Coptic, and the taking over of words and terms from the language of the Arab conquerors of Egypt into Coptic, as the latter gradually ceased to be the everyday language spoken by Egypt's Christians. These interactions took place in the practical context of the textile industry and in the area of that experimental search for first principles and how they work that became known as alchemy, "the Egyptian art." As will be seen, much of what was disguised with occult-sounding language as "alchemy" was in fact simple craft technology—trade secrets.

The odd amalgam of hermetic-religious doctrine, magic, natural-philosophy speculation, and craft technology that has long gone under the name of alchemy is deeply rooted in the Egyptian cultural background. The recent work of R. Halleux[1] and M. Mertens[2] on the Greek alchemical papyri and manuscripts has done much to sort out the mass of material that has survived to the present day and to begin to understand it in its social and historical setting. Most of the written material of ancient and early medieval alchemy is, however, in Greek; very little has come down to us in Coptic, the other principal language of late antique Egypt. Other than some leaves of a thirteenth-century parchment codex published in 1885,[3] few alchemical texts in the Coptic language are known.

All the more valuable, then, are the two long papyrus rolls numbered A(2)P and A(3)P in the collection of the Bodleian Library at Oxford (Department of Oriental Books and Manuscripts).[4] They contain recipes for various metallurgical and dyeing operations, mostly preparations of metals for making mordants for use in the dye trade.[5] The Coptic texts are written *transversa charta,* across the long direction of the fibers and parallel to the short edge of the roll.[6] The Bodleian Library card index assigns no specific provenance to the papyri; but apparently W. E. Crum, the polymathic Coptic scholar, who cited some words from the texts in his *Coptic Dictionary* (Oxford, 1939), was of the opinion that they, like the medical papyrus mentioned above, now at the French Institute in Cairo, were found at el-Meshaikh (Lepidotonpolis) near Girga,[7] across the Nile just south of Akhmim. A Panopolite/Akhmimic origin for these texts would make sense, considering the importance of Akhmim for both the textile industry and Hermetic arcane philosophy in Byzantine and Islamic times.[8]

From burials at Akhmim, the ancient Panopolis, have come a great many of what art historians generically term Coptic textiles.[9] Both Greek and Arabic papyri attest to the presence of weaving and dyeing facilities in the city and its surrounding area.[10] And Panopolis, the "city of Pan," whose old Egyptian tutelary deity had been that Min (Bes) whose images were smashed by the abbot Shenoute in the fifth century, was the city of Zosimus the alchemist.[11] Panopolis had gained the reputation of a continuing center of "arcane philosophy," i.e., craft technology, which combined with surviving Christianity and a memory of Hellenistic philosophy. Panopolis also had been the city of the poet Nonnus and the home of pagan poets and diplomats.[12] Moreover, the cultural force of the famous monastery of Shenoute at Atripe (Sohag), just across the river from Akhmim,[13] as a Christian pilgrimage center in Islamic times was considerable. It was a thriving monastic site complete with library, scriptorium, and tradespeople, as evidenced by the many manuscripts produced in it, the extent of its fortifications, and the pilgrims' graffiti on its walls.[14] Early Islamic Akhmim was a region of Christian survival and of the textile industry and a heritage of alchemical thought.

The Bodleian texts are in the Sahidic dialect of Coptic, but forms like ⲙⲁⲭⲁⲛⲉ recall the ⲁ-vocalization so characteristic of the Akhmimic dialect in earlier centuries. I should like to postulate that these papyri were written in the area of Akhmim; and, by comparison of the hands with those of the Apa Apollos papyri in the British Library (Bodleian Library Manuscript Or. 6204 and related texts), possibly in the ninth century A.D.[15]

The first text of the two contains over nine separate recipes, in seventy-two lines (much of the beginning is damaged by abrasion). Three of them end with the approving remark ⲟⲩⲇⲱⲕⲓⲙⲟⲛ ⲡⲉ ("It is a tested recipe," i.e., "tried and works"). Some ingredients used are: bronze, copper, the potassium hydroxide found in ashes of saltwort, uterine and bladder tissue, *mahaleb* plant, lettuce, metallic sulfur, salt, alum, white vinegar, arsenic?, borax, milk, mercury, and pigeon dung (a widely used fertilizer for which pigeons have long been raised in Egypt, presumably for the nitrates). Among the *Decknamen* or code names for substances we find (line 28) ⲙⲟⲟⲩ ⲛⲕⲏⲙⲙⲉ ,which can be either "black water" or "water of Egypt." The writer does not specify most of the purposes or products for which the recipes are designed, but in one case we seem to find ourselves in the realm of what sounds like traditional alchemy. Lines 32ff. state, "If you wish gold, take two portions of *al-boraq* (ⲁⲗⲡⲱⲩⲣⲁⲕ) with water, one portion of soda-ash . . . put in a good vessel of bronze or silver. It is a rigid body." But in the context of most of the other recipes, which seem to have to do with metallic preparations to be used on fabrics (such as lines 63ff., flax and mercury to be put into an *ampulla* with pigeon dung), we might rather think that what the crafter wants to produce is an inexpensive golden-colored pigment to be used on fabric for decoration.[16]

Indeed, one of the principal searches in ancient and medieval dyeing technology was for cheaper substitutes for the prized murex purple, in Byzantine times a closely guarded imperial monopoly. Less expensive substitutes for actual gold for textile additives such as gold-leaf-wrapped thread for embroideries, or gold foil for stamped ornaments, also were sought for by craftsmen working for the less wealthy market.[17] Also cheaper yellow dyes were desirable, in place of the expensive saffron gathered in Islamic times from crocus.

The second Bodleian text uses a characteristic phrase to introduce its fifteen or so recipes: "The master (ⲡⲥⲁϩ) says" or "The master told me" (sc. "as follows"). Sometimes it is "the wise master" (ⲡⲥⲁϩ ⲛⲥⲟⲫⲟⲥ): lines 27ff. give "The wise master says, Rinse out your cup seven times and another three times, until it is properly clean and well prepared (for use) in dyeing a white garment. And find a good measure of the substance [literally "drug"] to be used on the garment." This text is clearly a collection of master-craftsman's technological how-tos for use by Coptic-speaking craft workers being trained in the textile and dyeing industry. Sample processes include: (lines 33ff.) "Take the white garment which you wish to dye. Spread it out in a thin sheet. Put a human bone on it [!] [perhaps this is where the less practical aspect comes in] and add salt. . . . Then take a measure of silver filings, a measure of vinegar, mercury, verdigris and water. . . ." One process uses a substance referred to unfortunately only as "the wise man's dye" or "the philosopher's dye" (ⲡⲥⲱⲛ ⲛⲥⲟⲫⲟⲥ). One is to dissolve a half-portion of this wonderful substance in water for seven days, then gradually add more water and put on an old garment one wishes to recondition. "For white garments, they become a fine golden color" (line 61). The papyrus ends with allusions to ⲧⲙⲁⲭⲁⲛⲏ ⲛⲥⲟⲫⲟⲥ,"the wise man's (or "philosopher's") apparatus," which appears to be not so much a search for the universal solvent ("to undo— ⲃⲱⲗ ⲉⲃⲟⲗ—any body or ⲥⲱⲙⲁ," line 73) as a way of getting usable salts of iron for use as mordants (cf. line 67).

As can be seen, these texts are filled with names of substances that are Arabic loanwords, simply Arabic words transcribed into Coptic letters. Most have been taken over complete with the Arabic definite article *al-*, to which the Coptic article is then prefixed. Of the over twenty of these terms so far seen in the texts, not all have been securely identified. ⲁⲗⲙⲁⲣⲕⲁϣⲓⲑⲉ, according to Ullmann,[18] is metallic sulfur; ⲁⲧⲓⲛⲁⲭⲁⲣ is borax; ⲁⲗⲙⲟⲩⲡⲟⲩⲗⲉ is a chamber pot or urinal (a glass chamber pot is specified for one reaction); ⲁⲗⲙⲉⲑⲉⲛⲉ is a bladder (a goat's bladder is used for another reaction of which the context is far from clear). Other as yet unsolved Arabic puzzles are probably *Decknamen*, such as ⲁⲗⲕⲁⲗⲁⲕⲁⲛ, "the restless one," i.e., quicksilver? The papyri—both of which are in the same hand—use the well-known visual symbols for gold and silver, [symbol] and [symbol] . There are four instances of cryptographic writing in number A(3)P.[19]

I am far from having established a complete, definitive, annotated text of these two papyri, but I think enough has come out of them to start considering their historical and social background. They are on papyrus, not parchment; and most important, they are in the Coptic language, at a time when presumably the pressure of the use of Arabic as the *lingua franca* of the public and governmental sphere was beginning to weigh on the use of Coptic as the language of daily life and private correspondence among the Christians (who were by any reckoning still a majority in the country). The story of the replacement of Coptic by Arabic in the record-keeping and speech of Egypt's Christians is an extremely complicated one, which has not yet been written;[20] it certainly did not happen by decree or all at once. But numbers of Panopolite (Akhmimic, not in the narrow dialect sense) Coptic papyri do survive from that region,[21] attesting to the strength and self-consciousness of the local Christians. Even if later, by the tenth to eleventh century, Copts had to speak Arabic in the workplace, they still kept some records in Coptic.[22] The Coptic master craftsperson who put together these texts, obviously thoroughly familiar with the Arabic names for technical matters in the trade, used good Sahidic to record what amounts to trade secrets, the empirical arcana of his craft technology. We can assume that the craftsperson intended them to be intelligible to other Coptic-speakers, initiates versed in the craft.

We have already considered the locality of Akhmim for its importance in the textile industry in late Byzantine and Islamic Egypt, especially for decorative textiles that made use of many dyes and technological processes: many remains of these products are extant, though unfortunately none come from a controlled archaeological context. From recent research in Arabic papyrology we are coming to know more about the role of the indigenous Christians in the textile trade in early Islamic Egypt,[23] especially in centers such as Akhmim (the old Panopolite nome) where Coptic Christianity and the Coptic language persisted in predominance and strength (judging from the remains of documentary papyri) longer than in some other areas of Egypt. Documentary compendia like the Bodleian papyri were well characterized by Pfister as collections of research hints,[24] of pointers towards further work on technological processes and "tricks of the trade" to be worked on by trained craftspeople. We may surmise that the papyri I have described in this paper were written in ninth-century Akhmim, the textile center that also preserved its earlier reputation for arcane philosophy, as collections of research hints by and for Coptic Christian professionals in the fabric trade. These were people who, while they had learned the language of their political masters, carefully preserved their own ancient language, the language of liturgy and the Fathers, as a vehicle of identity and of professional pride.

Notes

*I should like to thank the authorities of the Bodleian Library, Oxford; Dr. Marlia Mundell Mango for checking information in Oxford; Dr. J. Malek of the Griffith Institute, Oxford; Professor Sidney Griffith for help with Arabic; and, as always, looking forward to a new life, Mirrit Boutros Ghali (Ezekiel 32:15).

1 R. Halleux, *Les alchimistes grecs* (Paris, 1981); idem., *Indices chemicorum graecorum* 1 (Rome, 1983).

2 M. Mertens, *Traité gréco-égyptien d'alchimie: la lettre d'Isis à Horus* (Diss. Liège, 1986). I am grateful to Dr. Mertens for illuminating discussions on alchemy.

3 Published by L. Stern in *Zeitschrift für Ägyptische Sprache und Altertumskunde* 23 (1885): 102-19. The content, dealing largely with dyes, is not dissimilar to that of the Bodleian papyri.

4 Dimensions of Manuscript A(2)P: 64.1 x 24.8 cm. Dimensions of Manuscript A(3)P are being checked in Oxford. I thank the Griffith Institute and Dr. Marlia Mundell Mango for access to Crum's transcriptions of these papyri. The Arabic texts on the versos are being gone over by Professor Sidney Griffith of Catholic University (to whom my thanks) in search of further information on provenance and date. According to Professor Griffith, the Arabic texts appear to have been written first: the Coptic writer turned the rolls over to inscribe his Coptic alchemical texts on the other sides.

5 Cf. R. Pfister, "Teinture et alchimie dans l'Orient hellénistique," *Seminarium Kondakovianum* 7 (Prague, 1935): 1-59. The Leiden and Stockholm Greek papyri also contain dyers' recipes.

6 It is interesting that these texts, like the Coptic medical papyrus published by E. Chassinat in Cairo in 1921, are in roll, not codex, form. Perhaps this form of information storage was thought more secure by Coptic craftsmen and professionals practicing their trade under Islamic rule.

7 See E. Chassinat, *Le MS. magique copte 42573* (Cairo, 1955).

8 See G. Frantz-Murphy, "A new interpretation of the economic history of medieval Egypt: the role of the textile industry, 254-567/868-1171," *J. Econ. Soc. Hist. Orient* 24 (1981): 274-97; C. H. Becker, "Akhmim," *Encyclopaedia of Islam* 1, 1 (1913): 234; G. Weit, "Akhmim," *Encyclopaedia of Islam* 2 (1960): 330.

9 See the publications of R. Forrer, e.g., *Die Gräber und Textilfunde von Achmim-Panopolis* (Berlin, 1891). It is hoped that Professor Sheila McNally's excavations at Akhmim will establish good stratigraphy

and proper archaeological contexts for the Akhmim textiles.

10 For documentation see A. Calderini and S. Daris, *Dizionario dei nomi geografici e topografici dell' Egitto greco-romano* 4.1 (Milan, 1983), p. 43, s.v. *Panos polis*, citing *P. Beatty Panop.*, pp. 1-2 (T. C. Skeat, *Papyri from Panopolis in the Chester Beatty Library* [Dublin, 1964]) and P. Berol. 16365+P. Gen.inv. 108 (Z. Borkowski, *Une description topographique des immeubles à Panopolis* [Warsaw, 1975]). For Arabic see C. H. Becker, *P. Schott-Reinhardt I* (=P. *Heidelberg* 3; Heidelberg, 1906): A. Grohmann, *Arabische Papyruskunde* (Leiden, 1966), p. 58 and *Einführung und Chrestomathie zur arabischen Papyruskunde* (Prague, 1955), p. 24. Further Heidelberg Arabic papyri are being published by R.-G. Khoury, and items from Akhmim may be among them.

11 See H. M. Jackson, *Zosimos of Panopolis: On the letter omega* (Missoula, 1978). See also the remarks of M. Plessner on Akhmim the city of adepts of arcana in his *Vorsokratische Philosophie und griechische Alchemie in arabisch-lateinischer Überlieferung: Studien zu Text und Inhalt der Turba Philosophorum* (Wiesbaden, 1975), pp. 130-31 with p. 131, note 322.

12 Triphiodorus; the bishop Cyrus; Harpocration, on whom see G. M. Browne, "Harpocratian panegyrista," *Ill. Class. Stud.* 2 (1977): 184-96.

13 For the medieval period see B. T. A. Evetts, *The Churches and Monasteries of Egypt . . . attributed to Abu Salih the Armenian* (Oxford, 1895), pp. 235-40; A. Mallon, "Copte: épigraphie," *Dictionnaire d'archéologie chrétienne et de liturgie* 3.2 2870-72 for inscriptions (including those from Akhmim itself).

14 For Nachleben see S. Timm, *Das christlich-koptische Ägypten in arabischer Zeit* (Weisbaden, 1984), s.v. "ad-Der al-Abyad," 2:601-34, esp. 610-15 on the monastery's superiors and scriptorium, 616-24 on its survival in the Arab period. On the patronal feast, a great occasion, see H. Quecke, *Untersuchungen zum koptischen Stundengebet* (Louvain, 1970), pp. 488-505, the Paris Manuscript B.N. Copte 68.

15 Cf. also *BKU* 3.436 (P.Berol. 22178).

16 Compare the inexpensive pigments in P.Berol. 8316: A. Erman, *Aus den Papyri der königlichen Museen* (Berlin, 1899), pp. 255-56. This sort of thing is found in the second papyrus also.

17 As in notes 3, 5, and 16 above. Even a late Arabic "alchemical" test like the *Turba Philosophorum* (above, note 11), probably from the tenth-century Akhmim, deals with inexpensive purple and gold dyes. See the English translation (from the Latin) by A. E. Waite, *The Turba Philosophorum* (London, 1876): reprint ed., New York, 1976).

18 M. Ullmann, *Katalog der arabischen alchimistischen HSS. der Chester Beatty Library II: Wörterverzeichnis* (Wiesbaden, 1976).

19 See F. Wisse in *Enchoria* 9 (1979): 101-20 for Coptic cryptograms. Unfortunately, working from the known systems of substitution in these examples, I have not been able to solve the cryptograms in the Bodleian papyri. Four lines from the bottom of papyrus A(2)P appears an Arabic term written in Arabic letters, of uncertain transcriptions (*ā-q-h-ā-n-k-eh*). It seems to be the name of an apparatus or device (*wusūl*). The lexicon of A. Siggel, *Arabisch-deutsches Wörterbuch der Stoffe . . . in arabischen alchemistischen HSS. vorkommen* (Berlin, 1950) is useful in these puzzles. Perhaps in some cases Arabic itself was used as a kind of code (when not transcribed).

20 See L. S. B. MacCoull, "Three cultures under Arab rule: the fate of Coptic," *Bulletin de la Société d'Archéologie Copte* 27 (1985): 61-70; idem., "The strange death of Coptic culture," *Proceedings of the London Colloquium on Late Antiquity and Early Islam* (June 1986; to appear). [Now published in *Coptic Church Review* 10 (1989) 35–45. In this volume study XXVI.]

21 For documentation see S. Timm, *Christlich-koptische Ägypten* (above note 14) 1 (Wiesbaden, 1984), 1:80-96, esp. 84-90.

22 The Teshlot papyri from the Hermopolite are an example; see L. S. B. MacCoull, "The Teshlot papyri and the survival of documentary Sahidic in the eleventh century," to appear in *Orientalia Christiana Periodica*. [Now published in *Orientalia Christiana Periodica* 55 (1989) 201–206.]

23 See Y. Ragib, *Marchands d'étoffes du Fayyoum au IIIe/IXe siècle*, 1-2 (Cairo, 1982-85); review (of 1) by G. Frantz-Murphy in *J. Econ. Soc. Hist. Orient* 27 (1984): 219-23.

24 Pfister, "Teinture et alchimie" (above note 5), p. 59.

XVI

COPTIC DOCUMENTARY PAPYRI IN THE COLLECTION OF THE SOCIETY FOR COPTIC ARCHAEOLOGY, CAIRO

In the summer of 1982 we succeeded in opening the safe in which it was hoped would be found the originals of the papyri unearthed in the Phoebammon excavations in 1948, on which I reported at the 1980 Congress in New York.[1] Unfortunately the safe proved not to contain the Phoebammon papyri, whose whereabouts remain unknown. But in point of fact it did contain several other papyri whose existence had not been suspected and which are not without interest.

The first group, immediately identifiable, are five leaves of a Sahidic text of Job, including the title of the book ιωβ πδικδιος. They are written in a fine book-hand and appear to belong together as leaves from the same codex; one leaf bears the pagenumber δ (4). They appear to have been purchased from the Cairo dealer Phocion J. Tano in about 1938. This text is being studied and published by G.M. Browne.

Inv. 4

Most of the rest of the papyri, already mounted under glass as are the Job leaves, are documentary. Bearing the number 4 in an unknown Arabic hand is a Sahidic letter dealing with Wenofer the *riparius* (the title is translated into Coptic as λπε cποτογ),[2] a holocot, the

* Society for Coptic Archaeology; Photos courtesy K.S. Diradour and M.B. Ghali

[1] L.S.B. Mac Coull - L. Koenen, *Papyrus fragments from the monastery of Phoebammon*, in *Proc. XVI Int. Congr. Papyrol.* (Chico, 1981), pp. 491-498.

[2] On *riparii* cf. *PCairo Masp.* I 67091-67093.

sale of wine, the receipt of a pledge, and the remission of a debt. As follows: inv. 4 32 × 9.2 cm

† ⳩ ϩⲁⲉⲑⲏ ⲙⲉⲛ ϩⲱϥ ⲛⲓⲙ ⲧⲛϣⲓⲛⲉ ⲁⲩⲱ ⲧⲉⲛⲁⲥⲡⲁⲍⲉ ⲛⲧⲉⲕⲙⲛⲧⲓⲱⲧ ⲉⲧⲧⲁⲓⲏⲟⲩ
ϩⲛⲡⲉⲭ̅ⲥ̅ ⲓ̅ⲥ̅ ⲡⲉⲛϫⲟⲉⲓⲥ ⲭⲁⲓ̈ⲣⲉ ϫⲉ ⲉⲓⲥ ⲟⲩ[ⲉ]ⲛⲟⲃⲣ ⲡⲁⲡⲉ ⲥⲡⲟⲧⲟⲩ ⲁⲃⲉⲓ̣ⲛ̣ ⲉ̣ⲧ̣ⲃⲉ
ⲟⲩϩⲟⲗⲟⲕⲟⲧⲧⲉ ⲛⲉϫⲛ ⲕⲟⲩⲫⲟⲩ ⲉⲓⲥ ϩⲏⲏⲧⲉ ⲙⲡⲛϯⲏⲣⲡ ⲉⲃⲟⲗ ϣⲁ ⲧⲉⲛⲟⲩ ⲟⲩⲇⲉ
ⲙⲡⲛϫⲓ̈ ⲁⲣⲏϥ ϯ ⲫⲟⲗⲟⲕⲟⲧⲧⲉ ⲙⲡⲉϥⲣⲱⲙⲉ ϩⲁⲙⲟⲓ ⲡ̄ⲁⲣⲱⲙ ⲙⲁⲣⲏ ⲉⲙⲙⲟⲛ ⲉⲃⲟⲩⲱϣ
ⲧⲁⲁϥ ϩⲁϩⲟⲓⲧⲉ ϩⲛⲡⲁⲟⲩⲏⲧ ⲟⲩϫⲁⲓ ϩⲛ̅ⲡ̅ϫⲟⲉⲓⲥ

→ ⲡⲁ̣ⲡⲛⲟⲩⲧⲉ ⳩

Before all else we greet and salute your honoured fatherhood in Christ Jesus our Lord: greetings. Look, Wenofer the *riparius* has gone about a holocot... Look, we did not sell wine until now, nor did we receive a pledge. Give the holocot to his man. Would that... lest he wish to give it for (a) garment for my remission (of debt). Farewell in the Lord. Papnoute.

Number 5 is a Fayumic letter of post-conquest date (a *dirhem* is mentioned as being returned) that closes with the formula 'peace be with you'.
inv. 5 14 × 18 cm

ⲑ(ⲉⲱ)
† ⲥⲏⲛ ⲧⲓϣⲓⲛⲉ ⲗⲁⲕ ⲕⲁⲗⲟⲥ ⲙⲉⲛⲥⲁ ⲛⲏ-
ⲓ ⲛⲁⲕ ϯⲛⲁⲥϩⲉⲓ ϩⲏⲓ. ⲁⲣ^ⲑ ⲁⲛ ϩⲟⲗⲟⲕⲟⲧ-
ⲥⲓ ⲁⲓⲧⲁⲟⲩⲁⲥ ⲛⲏⲕ ⲙⲉⲙ^ⲗ
ⲁⲡⲓⲁⲕⲟⲩ ⲛⲕⲧⲉⲓ ⲧⲟⲩⲛⲉϩ ⲛⲏⲩ ⲉϩⲟⲩ-
ⲛ ⲡⲉⲛⲏⲓ ⲛⲉ ϩⲉⲃ ⲙⲁⲛⲕⲃⲁⲗ ⲧⲓⲥⲁⲟⲩⲛ
ⲛϫⲉ ⲧⲁⲕ ⲡⲉⲛⲗⲟⲙⲓ ⲛϩⲁⲙⲉⲗⲉ ⲗⲟ-
ⲙⲓ ⲥⲗⲧⲉ ⲛⲁⲡⲟⲕⲣⲉⲥ ⲉϣⲟⲡ ⲛⲉⲛⲗⲟⲙⲓ
ⲉⲛⲛⲉ ⲁϩⲁ ⲙⲁ ⲧⲓⲥⲁⲟⲩⲛⲉ ⲛϫⲉ ϣⲁⲕⲉⲗⲧⲁ
ⲁⲡⲟⲕⲣⲉⲥ ⲧⲟⲩϣⲏ ⲡⲛⲟⲩⲧⲓ ⲛⲉⲓ ⲥϩⲉⲓ ⲛ-
ⲏⲕ ϩⲟⲗⲟⲥ ⲁϩⲁ ⲡⲓⲥϩⲉⲓ ⲛⲏⲕ ϩⲉⲟⲩⲛⲁ
ⲧⲛⲁⲡⲟⲕⲣⲉⲥ ⲁϩⲁ ⲁⲓⲧⲁⲟⲩⲁ ⲛⲡⲓⲧⲉⲣϩⲁⲙ
ⲛⲏⲕ ⲕⲧⲁⲟⲩⲁϥ ⲛⲏⲓ ⲉϩⲏⲧ ⲙⲉ ⲡⲓⲁⲕⲟⲩ
ⲃⲁⲗ ⲙⲉⲛⲉϩ ⲉϩⲟⲩⲛ ⲡⲏⲓ ⲧⲉⲩⲧⲓ ⲉⲡⲓⲉϩⲧⲓ
ⲗⲓⲡⲟⲛ ⲉⲗⲡⲛⲁ ⲧⲡⲉⲧⲛⲁⲛⲟⲩⲃ ⲧⲁⲟⲩⲁϥ
ⲛⲏⲓ ⲃⲁⲗ ⲉⲓϩⲏϣⲙⲁϥ ϣⲁⲛⲧⲉⲕⲧⲓ ⲧϩⲟⲗ-
ⲟⲕⲟⲧⲥⲓ ⲛⲏⲓ ϩⲓⲧⲉⲛ ⲛⲉⲓⲥϩⲉⲓ ⲧⲓⲣⲏⲛⲏ ⲛⲏⲕ ⳩

With God. I greet you fairly. After these things I shall write to you ... I sent it to you ... into our house ... I know ... our man is negligent ... I know ... until you send my reply ... and I have sent the *dirhem* to you (which) you sent to me ... For the rest, be so kind as to return the favour ... until you give the holocot to me from this writing. Peace be with you.

Number 6 is a letter to one Apa Anoup asking for various favours;

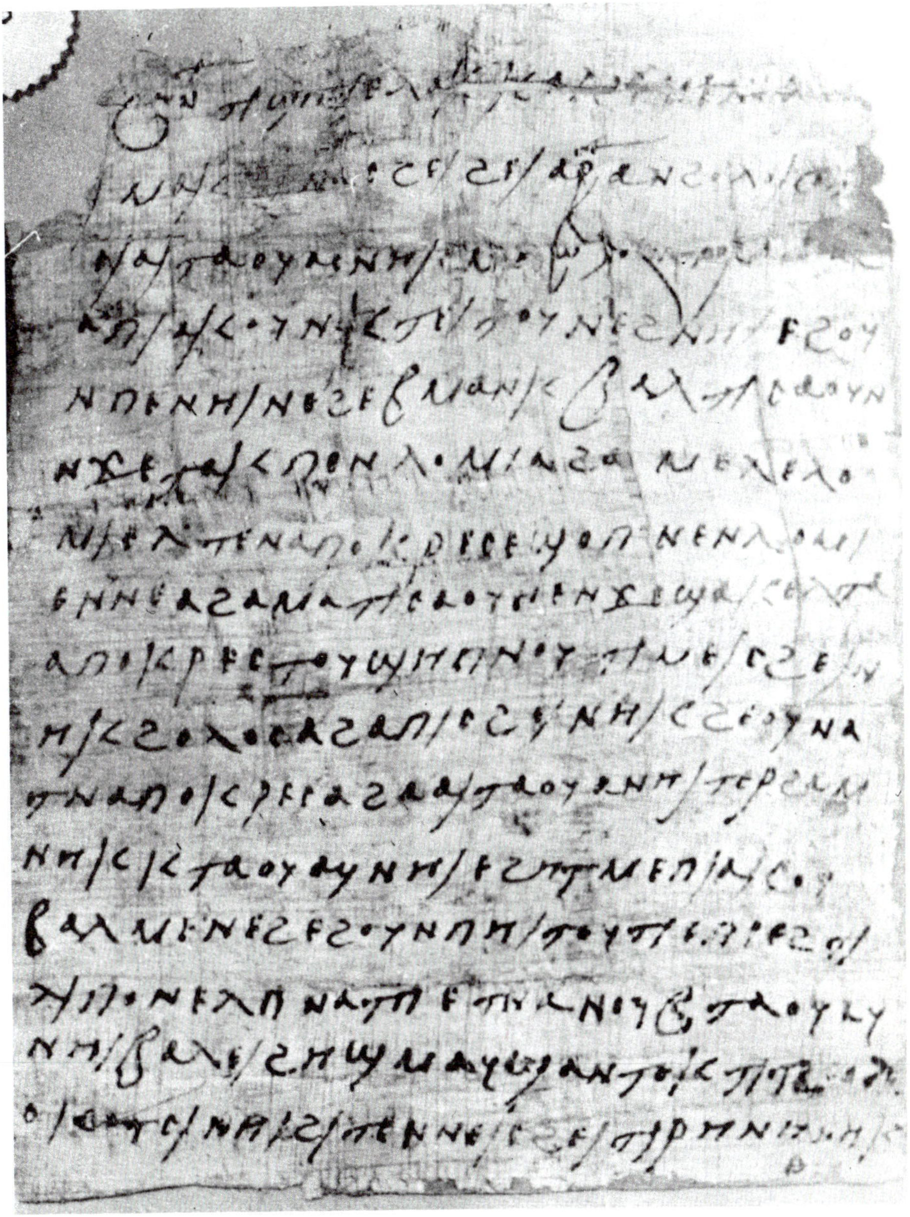

Inv. 5

780

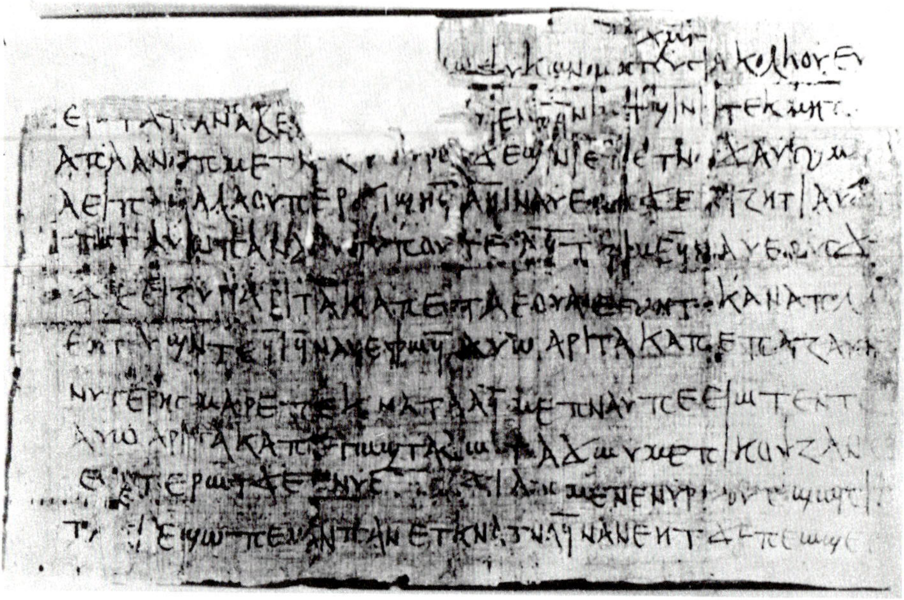

Inv. 6

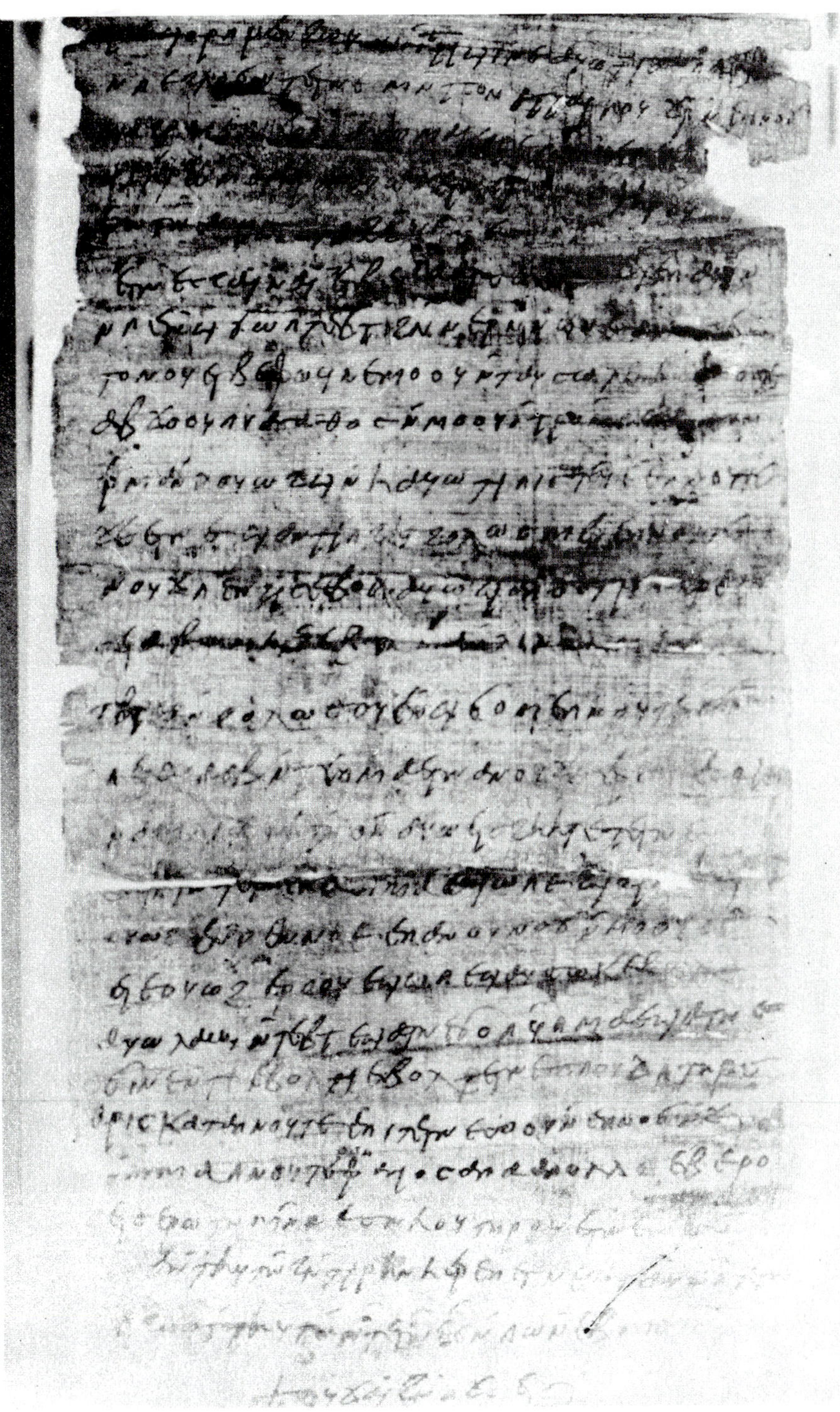

Inv. 7

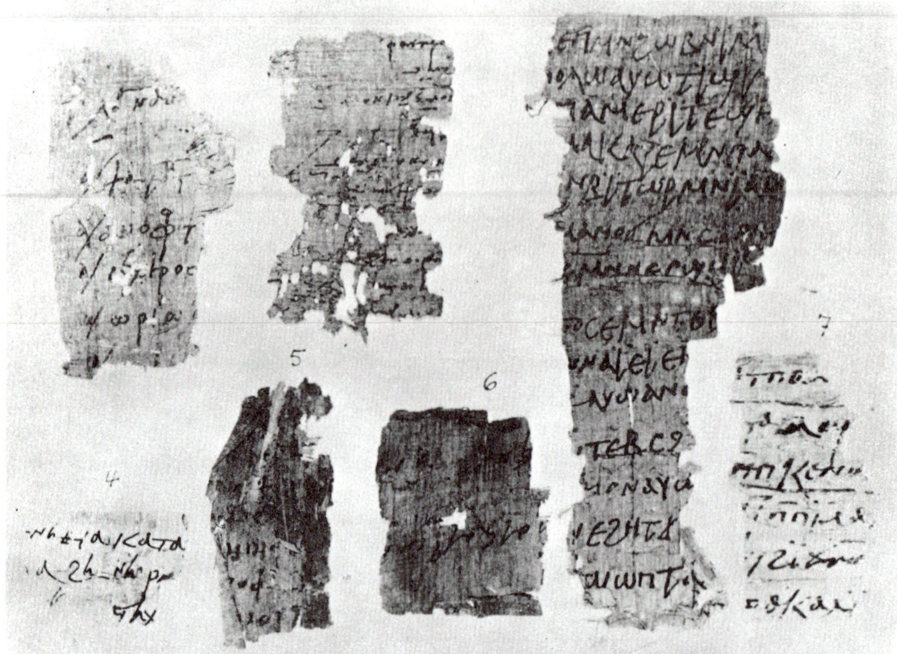

Misc. (a)

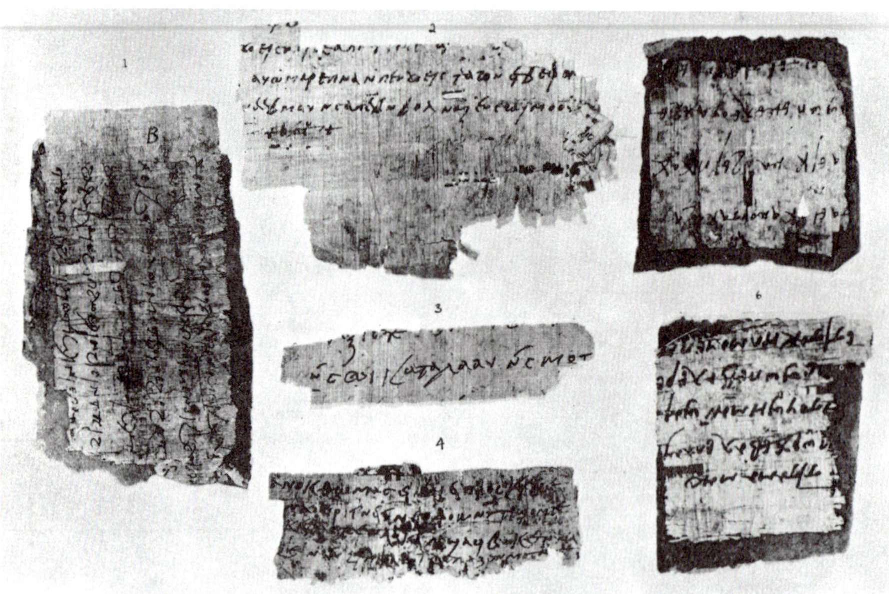

Misc. (b)

Psalter

it is in a curious upright, square, thin hand, somewhat resembling some of the Rylands hands.

inv. 6 23.5 × 14.9 cm

†

ⲭⲙⲅ
]ⲓⲱ ⲫⲩⲕⲱⲛⲟⲙⲟⲥ ⲧⲉⲩⲥⲓⲁ ⲕⲗⲟⲏⲟⲩ ⲉⲩ
ⲉⲓ..ⲁⲡⲁⲛⲁⲃⲉ [ ]..ⲉⲣ.ⲁⲛ .. ϯϣⲓⲛⲓ ⲧⲉⲕⲙⲏⲧ
ⲁⲡⲁ ⲁⲛⲟⲩⲡ ⲙⲉⲧⲛ ...... ⲉ ϣⲓⲛⲓ ⲉⲡⲉⲧⲛⲟϫ ⲁⲩ ⲙ
ⲁⲉⲓ ⲡ..ⲁⲗⲗⲁⲥ ⲩⲡⲉⲣ ϭⲓϣⲏϥ ⲁϥⲓ ⲛⲁϯ ⲉⲃⲟⲗ ϫⲉ ..ϩⲏⲧⲓ ⲁⲩⲱ
ⲡⲱϯ ⲁⲩⲱ ⲡⲁⲛⲁ ⲛⲉⲧⲉⲡⲁⲩⲧⲉ ⲁϥⲧ ⲓⲙⲉϥ ⲁⲩⲉⲣ ⲉ
ϫⲉ ⲉⲓ ϩⲩⲛ ⲁⲣⲓⲧⲁⲕⲁⲡⲉ ⲧⲁⲉⲟⲩⲁ ⲉ..ⲏⲧⲟⲕ ⲁⲛ ⲁⲡⲟⲗⲗⲱ
ⲉⲕ..ϣⲛⲧⲉϥ̄ⲓϥ̄ ⲛⲁⲩ ⲉϥⲱϥ̄ ⲁⲩⲱ ⲁⲣⲓⲧⲁⲕⲁⲡⲉ ⲡⲁⲧϩⲁⲩ ⲛ
ⲛⲩⲥ ⲉⲣⲏⲥ ⲙⲁⲣⲉ ⲡⲉⲕⲛⲁⲧⲁⲁϥ̄ ⲙⲉ ⲡⲛⲁⲩ ⲡⲉ ⲉⲓⲱⲧ ⲉⲛⲧ
ⲁⲩⲱ ⲁⲣⲓⲧⲁⲕⲁⲡⲉ ⲅⲓⲱϣ ⲧⲁϫⲱ ⲧⲁϫⲱⲩⲙⲉ ⲡⲓⲕⲟⲩϩⲁⲛⲉ
ⲉ..ⲧⲉⲣⲱⲩ ϫⲉ ⲉⲛⲩⲉ .. ⲓⲁ ⲡⲙⲉⲛⲉⲛⲩⲣⲓ.ⲟⲩ ⲉϣⲱⲡⲓ ϯ
ⲧⲁ.ⲓ ⲉϣⲱⲡⲉ ⲙⲉⲛ ⲡⲁⲛⲉⲧ ⲕⲛⲁⲧⲛⲁϥ̄ ⲛⲁⲛⲉⲏⲧ ϫⲉ ⲡⲉⲱϣ ⲉⲣ

→]ⲱϣⲓ ⲉⲡⲉⲕⲟⲩϫⲁⲓ ⲱ̣

2. 'The *oikonomos* (or *hegoumenos*?) of the estate'?

3. Restore **ⲧⲉⲕⲙⲏⲧ[ⲥⲟⲛ?**

Number 7 is a long letter written to a monastic congregation, inquiring about fish and irrigation-works. It closes with a wish expressed in the name of 'the God of the holy Apa Apollo': hence the recipients may have been one of the Apa Apollo monasteries of Middle Egypt, possibly either Bawit or Aphrodito (or Bala'izah?).[3]

inv. 7 18 × 34.5 cm

† ⳁ ⲛ̄ϣⲟⲣⲡ̄ ⲙⲉⲛ̄ ϩⲱϥ ⲛⲓⲙ ⲧⲓ ϣⲓⲛⲉ ⲁⲩⲱ ⲧⲓⲁⲥⲡⲁⲍⲉ
ⲛ̄ⲡⲉϩⲗⲟϭ ⲛ̄ⲧⲉⲧⲛⲉⲙ̄ⲛ̄ⲧⲥⲟⲛ ⲉⲧⲧⲁⲓⲏⲟⲩ ϫⲓ̈ⲛ ⲉⲡⲛⲟⲉ
ϣⲁϩⲣⲁⲓ ⲉⲡⲕⲟⲩⲓ̈ ⲁⲩⲱ ⲙⲁⲕⲁⲣⲉ ϣⲓ̈ⲛⲉ ⲛⲉ̣ⲧ̣ⲛ̣ ⲉⲓⲉ[
ⲛⲉⲛⲣⲱⲙⲉ ⲧⲏⲣⲟⲩ ⲁⲩⲱ ⲛⲉⲧⲛⲣⲱⲙⲉ ⲧⲏⲣⲟⲩ
ⲉⲣⲱⲧⲛ̄ [Broken by fold-line]
ⲉⲧⲛⲉⲥϩⲁⲓ̈ ⲛⲁⲓ̈ ⲉⲧⲃⲉ .ⲁⲁⲧ .... ⲁⲩⲱ
ⲛⲡⲉⲛϣⲟⲩⲟ ⲡⲧⲉⲃⲧ ϩⲛⲛⲉⲣⲛⲛⲱⲛⲉ ⲁⲓ̈[ ]ⲉⲓ
ⲧⲟⲛⲟⲩ ⲉⲧⲃⲉ ⲉⲫⲱϥ ⲛⲉⲙⲟⲟⲩ ⲛ̄ⲧⲁϥⲥⲱⲧⲉ
ⲁⲃϫⲟⲟϥ ⲡϥⲁⲅⲁⲑⲟⲥ ⲙ̄ⲙⲟⲟⲩ ⲛ̄ⲧⲣⲟⲙⲡⲉ
ⲣ̄ⲙ̄ ⲁⲛⲁ̣ ⲟⲩⲱⲃϣ ⲛ̄ⲏ ⲁⲩⲱ ⲧⲓⲡⲓⲥⲧⲉⲩⲉ ⲉⲡⲛⲟⲩⲧⲉ
ϫⲉ ⲉⲧⲛⲉϣⲙ̈ⲧⲓ ⲡϩⲏⲣ ϩⲟⲗⲱⲥ ⲙⲫⲉ ⲡⲛⲟⲩⲧⲉ
ⲛⲟⲩϫ ⲡⲉⲛϩⲓ̈ⲥⲉ ⲉⲃⲟⲗ ⲁⲩⲱ ϣⲁⲡⲟⲟⲩ
ⲧⲃ..ⲉ ⲛ̄ϩⲟⲗⲱⲥ ⲟⲩⲉⲛ̄ϣϭⲟⲙ ⲉⲡⲛⲟⲩⲧⲉ
ⲛⲉⲧⲟⲩⲁⲁⲃ ⲛ̄ⲧⲉⲓⲙⲁⲉⲓⲛ ⲁⲛⲟⲩ.ⲉ.ⲉⲣⲟϥ
ϣⲟⲙⲧⲉ ..ⲧⲛ ⲟⲛ̄ ⲁⲩⲱ ⲉⲓⲥ ϩⲏⲏⲧⲉ ⲧⲉⲧⲛ
.... ⲡⲙⲁ ⲉϣⲱⲡⲉ ϣⲁⲣ........
ⲁⲩⲱ .... ⲑⲛⲛ.ⲉ ⲉⲡⲉⲛⲟⲩⲛⲟⲉ ⲙ̄ⲙⲟⲟⲩ
ⲉⲓⲉ ⲟⲩⲱϩ ⲉⲣⲟⲟⲩ ⲉϣⲱⲡⲉ ϣⲁϥⲥⲱⲕ ⲉⲃⲟⲗ
ⲁⲩⲱ ⲗⲁⲁ̣ⲩ ⲛ̄ⲧⲉⲃⲧ ⲉϣⲁⲧⲛⲉ ϭⲟⲡϥ̄ ⲡⲙⲁⲉ ϣⲁⲧⲛ

[3] J. Gascou, *Documents grecs relatifs au monastère d'Abba Apollôs de Titkôis*, «Anagennesis» I 2 (1981), pp. 219-230 See MacCoull, "The Apa Apollos monastery of Pharoou (Aphrodito) and its papyrus archive," forthcoming in *Le Muséon*.

ϥⲛⲉ ⲛ̄ⲧⲓ ⲉⲃⲟⲗ ⲧⲓ ⲉⲃⲟⲗ ⲧⲉⲧⲛⲉⲥⲛⲟⲩⲁⲓ̈ ⲧⲁⲣⲉ
ⲁⲣⲓⲥ ⲕⲁⲧⲁ ⲡⲛⲟⲩⲧⲉ ⲉⲡⲓ ⲧⲉⲧⲛⲉⲥⲟⲟⲩⲛ ⲉⲡⲛⲟⲉ
ⲉ̣ⲡ̣ⲓ̣ⲙⲁ ⲡⲛⲟⲩⲧⲉ ᴹ ⲫⲁⲅⲓⲟⲥ ⲁⲡⲁ ⲁⲡⲟⲗⲗⲱ ⲉⲃⲉⲣⲟ-
ⲉⲓⲥ ⲉⲣⲱⲧⲛ ⲙⲛ̄ⲛⲉⲥⲛⲏⲟⲩ ⲧⲏⲣⲟⲩ ⲉⲧⲛⲉⲙⲉ ⲧⲱ-
ⲛⲉ ⲉⲛ̄ⲧⲏⲩⲧⲛ̄ ϩⲛ̄ⲧⲓⲣⲏⲛⲏ ⲉⲣⲉⲡⲉⲧⲛϩⲏⲧ ⲁⲩⲱ ⲛ̄ⲧⲉⲧⲛⲉ
ⲉⲓ ϩⲱⲱⲧ̄ ⲧⲏⲩⲧⲛ̄ ⲛ̄ⲧⲉⲧⲛ̄ⲉϣⲛ ⲡⲱⲛⲉⲃ ⲙⲟⲧⲛ̄ ⳨
⳨ⲟⲩϫⲁⲓ̈ ϩⲙ̄ⲡϫⲟⲉⲓⲥ⳨

Before all (else) I greet and salute the sweetness of your honoured brotherhood (pl.), from great to small, and Makare greets you ... all our men and all your men ... to write to me about ... the fish ... greatly about the work of the water ... the year ... and I trust in God ... that God will cast out our trouble ... the sign ... and behold ... a great water being there, if it should flow forth and no fish be caught ... take care that ... The God of the holy Apa Apollo watch over you and all the brothers truly (and) greatly for you in peace, so that you take it to heart and come to me and change (?) Farewell in the Lord.

Also found were thirteen small fragments glued to pieces of cardboard; they appear to include letters (mentioning the common personal names Makare, Victor, Jacob), an account, and a list of names. None is complete enough for determination of either provenance or date.

Finally, an envelope was found to contain dozens of tiny fragments, some resembling inscribed cornflakes, of what appears to be a Subakhmimic text of the Psalms. These fragments await the labours of some patient Coptic Biblical specialist who will work on the jigsaw puzzle of assembling coherent pieces of text and determine the nature of the language and textual tradition. Volunteers would be welcome.

XVII

PATRONAGE AND THE SOCIAL ORDER IN COPTIC EGYPT

Recent research in late antique papyrology over the last fifteen years has pointed the way towards new definitions and a new understanding of *patrocinium* and the adscript colonate as these phenomena actually operated within Egyptian society(1). We now view the adscripticiate as a fiscal-administrative definition, not as a social class. And we now have a clearer concept of how domainial institutions worked during the period of their heyday(2), if not necessarily of their origins. The transformation of the society of Coptic- and Greek-speaking Egypt into a society marked by the institutions of patronage seems to have taken place largely in the fifth century(3), along with the rise of documentary and literary writing in Coptic, the growing recognition of customary law(4), and the entering of Christian ecclesiastical institutions into the fabric of the body politic(5). With the

* I should like to thank Nancy Ševčenko, Jane Baun, Lee Perkins, Patrick Jacobson, and, as always, looking forward to a new life, Mirrit Boutros Ghali (Cant. 2:10).

(1) See especially the work of J.-M. Carrié, most recently his paper *Figures du «colonat» dans les papyrus d'Egypte: lexique, contextes*, «*XVII Congr. int. papirol.*», Naples 1984, III, 939-948, and the literature there cited, in particular the work of J.G. Keenan. The preliminary study of G. Diosdi, «JJP», 14 (1962), 57-72 is unfortunately distorted by Marxist theory.

(2) J. Gascou, *Les grands domaines, la cité et l'Etat en Egypte byzantine*, «Trav. et mém»., 9 (1985), 1-90.

(3) Cf. R.S. Bagnall-K.A. Worp, *Papyrus documentation in Egypt from Constantine to Justinian*, «*Miscellanea Papyrologica*», Florence 1980, 13-23.

(4) See G. Geraci, «Corsi Ravenna», 23 (1976), 227-256 (esp. 243 ff.) and 24 (1977), 197-222 (esp. 203 ff.). On the role of local customs in Coptic law see my article *Coptic Law* to appear in the «*Coptic Encyclopaedia*».

(5) Still thought-provoking are R. Rémondon, *L'Eglise dans la société égyptienne à*

widening of the conception of the juristic person in the legal thought of late antiquity[(6)], we see such Christian institutions (and their individual representatives) standing in patronage relations on both sides of the equation, and in various areas of life. In the enriched environment that was late antique Egypt, the nexus of personal obligations so characteristic of Mediterranean life and the empirical ways in which the profession of Christianity affected these relations became increasingly congruent. In this paper I should like to touch upon three ways in which we can discern patronage at work in the social life of Coptic Egypt: heritable lease or emphyteusis[(7)]; the private monastery or church, under the προστασία or φροντίς of a founding family; and the semantic shift in the meaning of **ⲁⲣⲭⲱⲛ** as it comes to be used as a Coptic loanword, from 'Byzantine magistrate' to '*dhimmi* grandee'.

First a remark on the nature of our sources. Few Coptic documentary papyri date from before the Arab conquest of Egypt in A.D. 641/2; and it is not always safe to reason backwards from the praxis of a communitarian society under alien rule to the praxis of the pre-conquest 'classical age'. Most work on patronage in Byzantine Egypt has been done on the basis of the Greek documents; it is the Coptic evidence I would like to integrate into the picture. However, thanks to the survival of such material as the Vatican and other Coptic papyri from sixth-century Aphrodito[(8)] and some seventh-century Coptic papyri from the Hermopolite, we can at least begin to assess the workings of some institutions that played an influential part in the lives of Coptic-speakers in the bilingual town and rural life of Egypt.

Jean Gascou has recently pointed out[(9)] the variety of vocabulary in Coptic emphyteusis documents that covers the underlying unity of facts: the *pakton* or *phoros* paid (the verb is *syntelei*) by an emphyteutic lessee actually is tantamount to his tax liability, and was regarded globally by the state as really just another form of public revenue, another way to make sure that the tax of that particular category of assessment got paid. Now of course the two major facts about emphyteusis or heritable lease are, first, that it is nearly always extended by an ecclesiastical institution, a church or a monastery; and, second, that *per se* it contains the possibility of improving the property

l'époque byzantine, «Chron. d'Eg.», 47 (1972), 254-277, and his *Les contradictions de la société égyptienne à l'époque byzantine*, «JJP», 18 (1974), 17-32.

(6) See the fundamental study of A. Steinwenter, «Z. Sav. Kanon.», 19 (1930), 1-50.

(7) Gascou (above n. 2), pp. 14-15, cf. 7-10; A. Steinwenter, *Das Recht der koptischen Urkunden*, Munich 1955, 38-39.

(8) See L.S.B. MacCoull, «Chron. d'Eg.», 56 (1981), 185-193.

(9) Above n. 7.

being leased. This latter, combined with the heritability factor, would help a trend to grow whereby ecclesiastical institutions and their representatives would come to be the landlords most beneficent to the Egyptian tenant farmer. Monasteries and churches, thanks to the inalienability of their property, could behave as land entrepreneurs as well as did individuals: witness the Antaeopolite church in P. Michael. 41, in the reign of Justinian, or the Antinoite monastery of Apa Jeremias, in CPR IV, 146 and P. Cair. Masp. II, 67151. It would be interesting if we could analyse more closely the social origins of the clerical lessors and their lay — or clerical — lessees. Unfortunately the prosopography of CPR IV, 128, 146-151, 153, Ryl. 174-176, and BM 1013-1015, 1056, and 1061 does not allow us secure identification of individuals known from other papyri, Greek or Coptic. One lessee is a vinedresser; two are ⲥⲁϩ (scribes); two are deacons, two are priests. The institution of emphyteusis seems to have flourished in the seventh century and continued doing so in the eighth, in the Hermopolite and Antaeopolite.

An interesting Coptic document involving emphyteusis and patronage is BKU III, 400, of uncertain provenance and date (Pachons 6, indiction 7). A certain Psha is asking the priest Apa Phoebammon son of Apa Isaac to look after his, Psha's, family for the period of a year: Psha's wife, son, and sister who is in debt for the ⲫⲟⲣⲟⲥ of her emphyteutic lease. Psha asks Apa Phoebammon to make sure that his sister is not found in default on her payment during her brother's absence. (The reason for the absence is unstated in the document; the editor thinks it might be a prison sentence, but this seems far-fetched). In this document we see an ordinary Copt entrusting his basic financial affairs to a respected cleric. It is clear that the element of trust in representatives of the ecclesiastical body went far towards the strengthening of emphyteusis patronage in the fabric of Egyptian village life.

Ecclesiastical bodies themselves could be under the *patrocinium* of the Coptic *dynatoi*, the landowners who founded their *Eigenklöster* and *Eigenkirchen* on their own properties, sometimes served in them and/or appointed their dependents to do so, and administered their *temporalia* as caretakers (themselves being of either clerical or lay status). A small window into the workings of the Coptic 'proprietary monastery' is afforded by what remains of the papyri of the monastery of Apa Apollos of the Holy Christ-Bearing Apostles of Pharoou at Aphrodito[(10)]. P. Cairo inv. S.R. 3733.19 is a

(10) See L.S.B. MacCoull, «*Acts of the II Intl. Congress of Coptic Studies*», Rome 1985, 159-166; and Eadem, *Missing pieces of the Dioscorus archive*, «*Eleventh BSC Abstracts*»,

letter in which the lawyer-poet Dioscorus describes how his late father Apollos, the founder, had entrusted the curatorship (φροντίζειν) of the monastery (into which he had retired) to his son, and reproaches the *dikaion* of the monastery for procrastination, mismanagement of the property, and lack of reverence. 'Godly thrift' (κατὰ θεὸν εὐτέλεια) is needed to keep the monastery's affairs in good order. From the fragments of the Coptic correspondence of the house we can see how Dioscorus himself took a warm personal interest in the members of the monastic community. P. Cairo inv. S.R. 3733.5, 15, and 20 are his greetings to monks and their families (compare 3733.4, 8, 10, 13, 14, 16, 17). Apparently the Apa Apollos monastery also leased out land (ⲫⲟⲣⲟⲥ is mentioned in the Brugsch/Jkow papyrus of which a photograph survives in the Crum archives in the Griffith Institute, Oxford), represented by its superior in the 550s, Apa Phoebammon. It registered its tenant farmers by *diagraphe*, and paid the land-tax (*demosion*), as we see from another letter of which a copy exists in the Griffith Institute, addressed jointly to the same superior and Dioscorus the curator. Even when Dioscorus was working as a notary on the ducal staff in Antinoe in the 560s, he continued to supervise the monastery's affairs from a distance, as *prostates* (a technical term, as in P. Cairo inv. S.R. 3733.8), making sure that the pagarchs did not attempt extortion (ⲇⲓⲁⲥⲧⲣⲉⲫⲉ) by collecting taxes outside of their competence. All in all, the institution of the proprietary monastery seems, in the classical period, to have functioned benevolently.

And yet, can we see, with hindsight, the seeds of that subjection of the Coptic church, through its temporal institutions, to the financial control of the rich that was to prove so disastrous in the succeeding thirteen centuries[11], a subjection which devalued learning and helped to make the church essentially a department of the Arab/Moslem state[12], acculturated to the ways of the rulers and subservient to maintaing the social position of the Coptic minority *dynatoi*? A clue to this process of change in the nature of patronage can be seen in the semantic shift undergone by the word ⲁⲣⲭⲱⲛ in Coptic between the fifth and the ninth centuries.

In early documents (e.g. Ryl. 272, 273, 310) ⲁⲣⲭⲱⲛ as a Coptic

Toronto 1985, 30 and *More missing pieces of the Dioscorus archive*, (to appear in «Chron. d'Eg.»). The deliberate disappearance of most of the sixth-century Coptic material from Aphrodito is to be deplored. More texts are being made available with the help of computer-enhancement technology (work in progress).

(11) R. Rémondon discerned this already in the last years of his life (above n. 5).

(12) See M. Martin, *Une lecture de l'Histoire des Patriarches d'Alexandrie*, «Proch. Or. Chr.», 35 (1985), 15-36.

loanword means simply a magistrate, a civil servant empowered by the Byzantine government bureaucracy to have authority usually in financial matters, e.g. in cases of default on debts or taxes. He could be an ecclesiastic (as in Ryl. 310) or a layman (though Neilammon of Ryl. 272 cannot be further identified from Greek papyri).

The choice of this loanword is rather a literary one, owed to the Coptic educated and scribal classes' being taught the classical curriculum of Greek literature and history. The Greek word ἄρχων had been used in documentary papyri ever since Ptolemaic times (Preisigke's lemma s.v. in 'Abschnitt 8' is instructive), but seemingly always with a consciously classical ring to it, as when in the third century those of Antinoe refer to themselves as '*archontes* and the *boule* of the famous city of the Antinoites, the New Hellenes'(13). Still in the sixth and seventh centuries, Coptic 'archons' are magistrates who collect fines (CO 43, 295), arbitrate in disputes (CO 189), and protect travellers (Ep. 624.4). But, by a logical semantic progression, ⲁⲣⲭⲱⲛ comes also to mean 'magnate', e.g. in Ep. 162.7 where the writer complains that he is reduced to the impoverished state of a low-class minor monk because the 'archons' stole his inheritance and the whole nest egg he had invested in a ship. (The writer of ST 198 asks the recipient 'not to betray us to the archon': is this an official or a member of the *prostates* class?) A significant text is CO 282. The writer, a bishop, complains that if an archon had written to his correspondent telling him to do something, the correspondent would have obeyed: but no respect is shown to God, 'the God of all', who is above archons.

After the Arab conquest, ⲁⲣⲭⲱⲛ can still occasionally mean 'government official' (who could still be a Christian), as in Bal. 186, one who was sometimes at the same time an ecclesiastic (cf. Bal. 191.7, BM 651). But in the communitarian life of Copts in the Islamic period, when the fiscal designation of 'adscript' or 'client' had given way to the very un-Roman concepts of 'protected person' under 'personal status law', ⲁⲣⲭⲱⲛ in Coptic usage becomes an honorific address of respect for Coptic magnates, sometimes indeed at the same time office-holders, who had maintained and even aggrandized their position by ingratiation with the Moslem rulership (as in ST 170.6, Push. 17.4, BM 1136 and 1140). The notion of 'person in civil authority' attached to the word persisted, as can be seen from the more than forty occurences of ⲁⲣⲭⲱⲛ/ⲁⲣⲭⲟⲛⲧⲓⲕⲟⲛ in the Jeme papyri of the eighth century (including BM 384, VC 8, and CPR IV, 26 and 27 as well as in KRU). These Christian officials, so well placed to do favours to both their

(13) P. Strassb. Gr. 1168, A.D. 258, ed. Wilcken, «Archiv», 4 (1908), 115-122.

co-ethnics and their political rulers, are becoming self-consciously a class of their own: BM 1118, from mediaeval Ashmunein (Hermopolis), where Coptic culture long flourished, is addressed 'To my son the archon, from the archon his father'. The culmination of this process can be seen in the colophon to BM 489, a tetraevangelion written at the White Monastery in A.D. 1112, where one of the donors is described as 'the pious, truly honoured brother, the honourable archon and vizier, Son of Joseph (=Ibn Yusuf)'. Such an official, who donated a deluxe manuscript to the library of Shenoute's monastery, stood at the apex of Coptic patronage in its post-conquest form.

In this brief survey of a few of the ways in which patronage can be seen to have been at work in Coptic society, we have seen how the terminology of patronage situations is understandable only in the context of its own time. In particular, Coptic religious institutions, in their capacities as fiscal entities and as juristic persons, participated in patronage relations in both directions, vis-à-vis both their cultivators and their administrators. *Patrocinium* in one or another of its forms seems to have been a deeply ingrained part of the operation of Coptic society from late Roman times down, indeed, to our own day (reading between the lines of the contemporary 'personal status law'). It is in these patterns that a Coptic *dynatos* or adscript thought when drawing up a contract or arbitrating the complicated counterclaims of a lawsuit. In Coptic Egypt the decorative encomiastic poetry was written, and the opulent architectural sculpture, tapestry, and wall-painting created, to ornament the structure of patronage. Being seen to stand in a patronage relation remained at the heart of Coptic self-identification, perception of the world, and sense of dignity.

XVIII

For Mirrit:

ⲡⲁⲙⲉⲣⲓⲧ ⲉϥϣⲟⲟⲡ ⲛⲁⲓ

THE APHRODITO MURDER MYSTERY

P. Mich. XIII 660–661 (ed. P. J. Sijpesteijn, Zutphen 1977) contain parts of the record of proceedings of a sensational sixth-century trial, involving bribery and possibly the sale of honors, violent murder by hired killers, accusation and attempted whitewashing of local magnates, religious controversy, and the all-important village finances as they affected the Byzantine military presence in the Thebaid. It is also the last recorded law case of Flavius Apollos,[1] former *protocometes*, monk and father of the poet Dioscorus (so identifying the "Fl. ... Apollos ex civ(itate) Afrod(ites)" of 661.11). Since Apollos died in the year A.D. 546/7, we may identify the two dates in the documents, Mesore of the end of the seventh indiction (660.9–10) and Phaophi 8 of the previous sixth indiction (660.15–16), as respectively August of A.D. 544 and 5.X.542.[2] Although already a monk, Apollos testified for the prosecution against a powerful man called Sarapammon, not failing to bring up for tactical reasons the most important event of his, Apollos', own life, a trip to the imperial court at Constantinople.

These papyrus texts, though fragmentary (661 is missing much of its left-hand side, which makes the continuity difficult to follow), deserve further attention. Besides the inherent interest of who was behind the murder mystery, they reveal the complex tensions in the structure of Byzantine Egyptian village life.

The personalities of the people in the case come vividly alive as their manner of speaking is taken down in the texts. First we have one of the accused, Flavius Menas the soldier (*miles*),[3] who is busily denying receiving any money (apparently bribe money); instead he outlines a strange vicious circle of payments (for "laundering" the money, one would infer): Sarapammon has given money to the *boethos*, who has given it to "his" (αὐτοῦ) *meizoteros*, who has in turn paid it back to Sarapammon (660.1–3). Next, Sarapammon, μεγαλοπρεπέστατος and ἐνδοξότατος (and

[1] For his career see J. G. Keenan, *Aurelius Apollos and the Aphrodite village élite*, XVII Congr. intl. papirol. III, Naples, 1984, pp. 957–963. Sijpesteijn's statement (p. 27) that no one in these texts can be identified is incorrect.

[2] The gap in time may actually be closer (which would make more sense), as Bagnall and Worp have called attention to the anomalous wording (*Chronological Systems of Byzantine Egypt*, Zutphen, 1978, p. 62 n. 65). On *epinemesis*, used in Maria's testimony, see CSBE, p. 5 n. 21. The years involved ought to be 542 and 543.

[3] For soldiers as Flavii see J. G. Keenan, ZPE 11 (1973), pp. 61–63.

inlustris),[4] is called on to make a statement. What was this mysterious money for? Sarapammon's reply is bluff and colorful. "I found out," he says, "that some Aphroditans φρατριάζουσι" (660.4) and wished to make the village ... (?), so that they might again φόνοις παρακολουθήσωσ[ιν, and therefore those who had made the φρατρία had required (ἀπητήθησαν) a pound of gold (= 72 solidi) εἰς ἀρχοντικόν." (660.5) This unusual phraseology should be looked at closely.

Sijpesteijn (p. 35) translates: "I did discover that some persons from the village of Aphrodite had made a conspiracy and wanted to make the village desolate(?) so that they again could attend minutely to murders and for that reason the conspirators have been asked for one pound of gold for the government." He interprets this money payment as being a kind of *wergeld*, a fine for murder (p. 29). I think a different interpretation of several points is necessary. First of all, φρατριάζειν and φρατρία are very unusual words in the sixth century (for that matter they are hapaxes in the papyri). Where this noun and verb are used in late antiquity is in Canon 18 of the Council of Chalcedon (Schwartz, ACO II.1, Berlin, 1933, p. 357, ll. 25–29). This canon decrees the punishment of loss of their religious status for clerics or monks who make a συνωμοσία (*coniuratio*) or φρατρία, or concoct trumped-up fakeries, fabricated charges (κατασκευὰς τυρεύοντες), against bishops or their fellow clerics, especially if they do this in a church. The (fifth-century) cultural context of the provision is not hard to discern.[5] What was at stake was the outcome of the empire-wide attempt, to be renewed under Justinian, to ensure that monasteries operated obediently under the jurisdiction of their local bishops. An obvious tactic in opposing an uncongenial ordinary or diocesan would be to discredit him in order to put up a friendly candidate who would let one's own religious foundation alone. Clearly by the 540s in Egypt, when, after the death there in 538 of Severus of Antioch, local Monophysite opposition to serving under Chalcedonian hierarchs was growing to the stage of giving birth to a separate, parallel clergy structure,[6] this type of situation was at boiling point. Might we take it that the illustrious Sarapammon was a well-read Chalcedonian magnate who had detected a Monophysite plan? What sort of plan? Look at the rest of the sentence.

Next: the fragmentary word at the beginning of 660.5 is transcribed by the

[4] No one named Sarapammon is listed in V. Girgis, *Prosopografia e Aphroditopolis*, Berlin, 1938. A Sarapammon is the father of Julius in P. Cair. Masp. III 67353^r (Coptic, from over twenty years later): see L. S. B. MacCoull, BSAC 25 (1983), p. 92.

[5] See L. Ueding, *Die Kanones von Chalkedon in ihrer Bedeutung für Mönchtum und Klerus*, in Grillmeier/Bacht, *Das Konzil von Chalkedon* II, Würzburg, 1953, pp. 569–676, esp. here 611–612.

[6] Cf. D. Bundy, *Muséon* 91 (1978), pp. 45–86; J. Maspero, *Histoire des patriarches d'Alexandrie*, Paris, 1923, pp. 182–190. Jacob Baradaeus, ordained by 542/3, was to travel through Egypt first in the mid-540 s, revitalising twelve sees in the Thebaid alone: while Theodosius, Monophysite Patriarch of Alexandria, languished in Constantinopole from 536 till his death there in 566. Theodora, Aphrodito's patroness, was alive till 548; Jacob's second journey was to be in 577.

editor as [...]ημοιρη, construed as agreeing with τὴν κώμην. I should prefer to restore [πλ]ημοίρη⟨ν⟩ "the Nile flood", a Copticised spelling of πλήμ(μ)υραν. (The word is used by Dioscorus of Aphrodito in his petition P. Cair. Masp. I 67002 II 21.) Translation: "... (and) wished to celebrate (or: to bring about) the Nile flood as far as the village is concerned." Additional papyrological sources are helpful here. It is clear from the cultural context of SPP XV 250ab,[7] a Monophysite "farced" Trishagion with prayers to the abbot St. Shenoute, that the Monophysites successfully appropriated the rites of the annual Nile flood from the Chalcedonians. This was the strongest move they could make to ensure popular support, and it worked: the holy men who could be seen to be bringing about optimal flood levels and the consequent good harvests would stand unshakably high in the hearts of Egypt's farmers.

Next comes the phrase (πάλιν) φόνοις παρακολουθήσωσιν. Although murder is to figure prominently in this case, φόνος can be figurative, connoting "pollution" or "ruin", as well as denoting actual physical killing; while παρακολουθέω is found in the sense of "following, being consequential upon" as well as of "paying attention". "Pollution" is a favorite label to apply to the opposite religious party, and in the days of full-blown anti-Monophysite and anti-Chalcedonian polemics is so used. Translate here "so that they might again be disciples of defilement", i.e. Monophysitism. Here the verb form from ἀπαιτέω is middle, "required for themselves" or "collected".

Further, in fact ἀρχοντικόν can have a technical meaning here, namely "rank" or "order of nobility" (as it does in later Greek), denoting in sixth-century Aphrodito the κόμιτες, συντελεσταί, κτήτορες: the landowning and titled *possessores*. Here the prepositional phrase without an article can mean something like "in keeping with what was required for belonging to the order of nobility".[8] The whole of Sarapammon's testimony in 660.4–5 can be translated as follows: "I learnt that certain people from the village of Aphrodito had formed a 'brotherhood' and wanted to put on the rites of the Nile flood with respect to the village, thus once again following (the party of) defilement, and to this end those who had formed the 'brotherhood' had gotten together a pound of gold in keeping with noble rank." We are dealing with anti-Chalcedonian *dynatoi* taking into their own hands ritual matters of life--and-death importance for the whole community.

[7] See D. Bonneau, *La crue du Nil*, Paris, 1964, pp. 435–437. Bonneau's translation and interpretation can be corrected at many points: no one has noticed the nature of this text as being a Trishagion "farced" with the Monophysite addition "Who was crucified for us", besides being in troparion form with an indicated refrain. See now L.S.B. MacCoull, *SPP XV, 250 ab, a Monophysite Trishagion for the Nile Flood*, JTS 40 (1989), pp. 129–135. P. Lit. Lond. 239 is less openly Monophysite; P. Turner 10 (6th c., from Antinoe) is difficult to pin down doctrinally.

[8] Cf. J. G. Keenan on a possible property or wealth requirement, "Aurelius Apollos", (above n. 1), p. 960 with n. 11.

The life and death are literal, and not only in terms of the harvest: two people have been murdered, one a priest; and the harvest itself is viewed in the context of the συνωνή (661.19), the state-arranged buying-up of grain for maintenance of the Byzantine military garrison (cf. P. Freer 3 for Aphrodito), whose presence was coming to be equated with the forcible imposition of Chalcedonianism. Menas the soldier's denial of involvement in the murders is classic: "I didn't do it, and anyway I was somewhere else at the time, and anyway he died of natural causes, and anyway I don't know anything about it." (660.7–8). The two accusers in the murders then testify: the brother of the victim Victor the priest (a non-Chalcedonian sympathizing priest?), beaten to death by Menas; and Maria, the wife of the victim Heraclius, killed with weapons (ξίφεσι) by *kephalaiotai* (heads of village guilds) suborned by Menas and Sarapammon. (Sijpesteijn does not notice the Biblical turn of phrase used by Maria in her pathetic story, in 660.18: "and I do not know where they have laid them (her husband's bones)", an echo of John 20:2b, ... καὶ οὐκ οἴδαμεν ποῦ ἔθηκαν αὐτόν.) In these first-person tales of violence do we see the actual working of the violent conduct of Chalcedonians towards non-Chalcedonians so dear to the historiography of Monophysite writers? (It has always been hard to find documentary evidence of the much-touted persecutions in the papyri.) This, however, remains speculation.

The testimony of murder and "dirty money" continues in P. Mich. XIII 661. Someone, apparently Sarapammon, declares that Heraclius was killed by popular will as being a συκοφαντῶν (661.7), an informer or slanderer. This notion, this term, will reappear in the petitions written by Apollos' son Dioscorus in the mid-560s, for example in P. Cair. Masp. I 67003.23, where a certain Ezekiel the barber is attacked for having tried to seize land that had been donated to Apollos' monastery of Pharoou; and in P. Cair. Masp. I 67097ᵛ D 39, the *apokeryxis* draft, in which the disinherited daughter is labelled as a συκοφαντρία. In P. Cair. Masp. I 67089ʳ B 3, praise of a duke (probably a fragment of a petition), ὁ συκοφάντης is the enemy of the Thebaid's peace and order, along with those who use weapons (σιδηρῷ) against their ὁμόφυλοι. This is exactly what we have seen happening in the 540s, according to the Michigan texts. *Sykophantes* served as another handy label for your enemy. Now charges of "misrepresenting reality", being a *sykophantes* in that sense, could be levelled against adherents of the opposing religious party as well as against pagans (e.g. by Athanasius: see Lampe, s.v.). Is Sarapammon saying that the world is well rid of Heraclius and his like because they are Monophysites, people who might stand in the way of the all-important process of getting the taxes to Constantinople?

Accusations go in both directions: someone, presumed to be Sarapammon again, alleged to have paid money also to one Letoios (called σοφώτατος, presumably a lawyer), admits that the latter thought him, the speaker, to have perpetrated something παράλογον (661.10). Hence Letoios apparently had to be kept quiet with money. Then we hear from οἱ παρόντες, which must mean "the parties present", not, as with Sijpesteijn, "the *adsessores*". Apollos speaks up, together with a colleague of his, Flavius Psoios (from Hermopolis?), now saying that the sum that has changed hands (or at least been demanded) is as high as four pounds of gold. Though parts of his statement are missing (we never find out, for example, who is the Theodore various people are *excusantes*), he does mention the possibility of going to Constantinople to approach the emperor (661.13): something he had himself recently done, in 541. Would confronting Justinian with a case of local religious violence have influenced policy at the top? Apollos' appearance in this text is tantalisingly brief. We must remember that he was already a monk of his own monastic house. He too would have its interests at heart, to defend it against *sykophantai* of whatever kind.

Before the papyrus breaks off we encounter the συνωνή or *coemptio* of grain on behalf of the state, in a context still of the mysterious money payments. The context is too fragmentary here to determine the exact relationship. Introducing the matter is the party Colluthus (661.18), presumably the Flavius Colluthus of line 13. One would like to propose an identification with the Colluthus son of Christopher who is known from P. Vatic. Copti Doresse 1 and 5 (of A.D. 535/6 and a little later);[9] cf. also P. Mich. XIII 666.3. In this whole imbroglio of bribery and violent death, always in the background is preoccupation with the public revenue, here as it supports the very Byzantine soldiers like Menas the κακοσιώμενος who are involved in the violence.

The text as it stands ends abruptly; there is no exciting revelation of "who did it". Yet we are clearly left with the impression that Sarapammon and Menas have incriminated themselves by their own testimony. The rough, direct narratives of Victor's brother and of Maria, spoken out in open court, tell their own story, as do the tellingly worded disclaimers of the powerful. A clearer understanding of the meanings of words and terms in these proceedings of the Aphrodito murder mystery can reveal aspects of how people in village and administrative life actually behaved to one another during the turbulent years in Byzantine Egyptian history when the confessional lines were being drawn that were to determine for centuries to come the character and the fortunes of Coptic society.

[9] See L. Papini, BSAC 25 (1983), pp, 83–89, and L. S. B. MacCoull, ibid., pp. 91–94. Full publication of the Vatican Aphrodito Coptic papyri is eagerly awaited.

XIX

The Paschal Letter of Alexander II, Patriarch of Alexandria: A Greek Defense of Coptic Theology under Arab Rule

For Professor Ria Stavrides

Berlin papyrus 10677 is the palaeographers' delight. The opulent, hypnotically regular hand in which it is written has become the type example of Alexandrian majuscule[1] "de type copte."[2] It is discussed in every standard handbook of Greek palaeography.[3] And yet the content of this more than five-meter-long document has not been analyzed by historians of the Egyptian Church and of the late antique Mediterranean since its publication in 1910.[4]

This imposing, physically impressive document can be precisely dated to one of three possible years in the first quarter of the eighth century. The terminus post quem is given by the partially preserved outer column, bearing a bilingual Greek/Arabic protocol that gives the formula

> ἐν ὀνόματι τ[ο]ῦ Θ(εο)ῦ [τοῦ ἐλεημόνος]
> καὶ φιλανθρ[ώπου],
> [*bᶜismil*]*lāh ar-ra*[*ḥmān ar-raḥīm*],
> οὐκ ἔ[στι]ν θ(εὸ)ς εἰ μὴ [ὁ θεὸς μόνος],
> Μααμετ ἀπόστ[ολος θ(εο)ῦ],
> [*lā illaha illa Allāh waḥi*]*dun, Muḥammad* [*rasūl Allāh*].[5]

This feature does not appear in the chancery practice of Arab-ruled Egypt, in the designation of official manufacture of the writing material, until it was introduced by the caliph Mo'awiya in the 670s and mandated by the caliph ᶜAbd al-Malik in A.D. 698.[6] Then, thanks to the preservation of the final columns (of a total of eleven) that were innermost when the roll was rolled up, we have the date of Easter being announced: 16 April. Easter Sunday fell on this day in A.D. 713, 719, and 724, before the elimination of bilingual protocols and their replacement by completely Arabic ones in Egyptian chancery documents in A.D. 733.[7] Thus the papyrus can be dated to the first month and a half (the Lenten fast is to begin in February) of either 713, 719, or 724. Ordinarily 724, a leap year, would seem to be ruled out by the correspondence of Mecheir 26, the date given for beginning the eight weeks' fast, with 20 February (to be 21 in a leap year).[8] This, however, is not necessarily the case;[9] a leap year did not have to add an extra day to the

[1] As in G. Cavallo, "Grammata Alexandrina," *JÖB* 24 (1975), 23–54; cf. S. Bernardinello, "Cronologia della maiuscola greca di tipo alessandrino," *Scriptorium* 32 (1978), 251–55.

[2] J. Irigoin, "L'onciale grecque de type copte," *JÖB* 8 (1959), 29–51.

[3] From V. Gardthausen, *Griechische Paläographie*, II (Leipzig, 1913), 250, cf. 104, to, most recently, G. Cavallo and H. Maehler, *Greek Bookhands of the Early Byzantine Period, A.D. 300–800* (London, 1987), 114. See also W. Schubart, *Papyri Graecae Berolinenses* (Bonn, 1911), no. 50; and R. Seider, *Paläographie der griechischen Papyri*, II (Stuttgart, 1970), no. 66 (pp. 168–69 with pl. 36).

[4] The *editio princeps* is by C. Schmidt and W. Schubart, *Berliner Klassikertexte*, VI (Berlin, 1910), no. 5, pp. 55–109 with pls. 1–2 (hereafter SS). The papyrus was bought in Akhmim in 1905; it had been found in the place of the letter's destination, the White Monastery of Shenoute at Sohag, across the Nile from Akhmim, the literary contents of whose library are scattered among many collections in the West. P. Batiffol in *Bulletin d'ancienne littérature et archéologie chrétienne* 1 (1911), 221–23, contented himself with remarking that the text, which he in part summarizes, amounts to "monophysisme Sévérien" (p. 223). Cf. J. van Haelst, *Catalogue des papyrus littéraires juifs et chrétiens* (Paris, 1976), no. 621 (p. 221).

[5] SS, pp. 61.

[6] Cavallo and Maehler, *Bookhands*, p. 114 (no. 52a); cf. SS p. 93.

[7] SS, p. 94.

[8] Bernardinello "Cronologia," 253, repeated by Cavallo and Maehler, *Bookhands*, ibid.; cf. the table in R. S. Bagnall and K. A. Worp, *The Chronological Systems of Byzantine Egypt* (Zutphen, 1978), 98. The other correspondences are the beginning of Holy Week (i.e., Monday of Holy Week) as Pharmouthi 15 = 10 April, and Holy Saturday as Pharmouthi 20 = 15 April. I am grateful to Roger Bagnall and Klaas Worp for discussing points of the chronology.

[9] S. Bernardinello, "Nuove prospettive sulla cronologia del Pap.Grenf. II 112," *Scriptorium* 34 (1980), 239–40. The point is that the scribe could have made, and I think here did make, a mistake, by omitting an alpha.

days before Julian 29 February. Thus 724 remains a possibility. No indiction number survives; the years in question were an 11th, a 2nd, and a 7th indiction respectively. But internal evidence can help in narrowing down the date, as will be seen.

The non-Chalcedonian Coptic patriarch of Alexandria during those years was Alexander II (reigned 705–730). His patriarchate coincided with momentous events in the age of transition from a Byzantine-Coptic to an Islamic-dominated society in Egypt. Alexander II is the subject of an extensive biography in the Arabic-language compilation *History of the Patriarchs of Alexandria,*[10] formerly attributed to Severus of Ashmunein (fl. A.D. 955–987).[11] Even in the later form in which we have it, this Life, originally doubtless written in Coptic but transmitted in Arabic translation,[12] intersects at several points of interest with the material that comes from the patriarch's own hand as contained in his paschal letter.

After the protocol, fragments of the address have also been preserved; legible in both Coptic-style uncials and the tall, impressive Greek chancery lettering is the name Γενναθίῳ, "To Gennadius" (spelled with the fricative to be expected in eighth-century pronunciation). His title, visible in the line of uncials, appears as ⲡⲣⲱ̅ͭ, restored by Schmidt and Schubart as πρωτοπρεσβύτερος (–τέρῳ), but surely more correctly understood as προεστώς,[13] monastic superior, the correct form of address for the head of Shenoute's monastery.[14] We thus know that the holder of this important monastic office in the Egyptian church in the early eighth century bore the Byzantine name of Gennadius. This is a worthwhile addition to the list of known superiors of the "Deir al-Abyad" in late antiquity and the Middle Ages.[15] Since the abbot Gennadius was the addressee of the patriarch's paschal letter, he must have functioned as the disseminator of important ecclesiastical information, such as the date of Easter, for Upper Egypt.

The paschal letter is written in Greek prose of the high style, with long compound-complex sentences, many dependent clauses constructed with

[10] Ed. B. Evetts, PO 5 (Paris, 1947), 48–83 (hereafter Evetts). Also necessary for the *sira* (Life) of Alexander are the editions of the earlier part of the *History of the Patriarchs* by C. F. Seybold: the "vulgate" text in the CSCO (Beirut-Paris-Leipzig, 1904–10), and the earlier recension from the Hamburg ms. of A.D. 1266 (Hamburg, 1912).

[11] The recent pathbreaking research of D. W. Johnson of Catholic University (Johnson, "Further Remarks on the Arabic History of the Patriarchs of Alexandria," *OC* 61 [1977], 103–16) and J. den Heijer of the Netherlands Institute in Cairo and the University of Leiden has shown that Severus had in fact little to do with the compilation that has come down under his name. See J. den Heijer, "Sawīrus Ibn al-Muqaffaʿ, Mawhūb Ibn Manṣūr Ibn Mufarriǧ et la genèse de l'"Histoire des Patriarches d'Alexandrie'," *BO* 41 (1984), 336–47; idem, "L'"Histoire des Patriarches d'Alexandrie': Recension primitive et vulgate," *BSAC* 27 (1985), 1–29; idem, "Mawhūb ibn Manṣūr ibn Mufarriǧ et l'Histoire des Patriarches d'Alexandrie: Notes sur une étude en cours," in OCA 226 (Rome, 1986), 143–57. For social and political background to the *HP,* see M. Martin, "Une lecture de l'Histoire des Patriarches d'Alexandrie," *POC* 35 (1985), 15–36.

[12] The earlier (pre-9th-century) biographies in this collection have not been subjected to as much critical analysis as have later lives. This much seems reasonably clear. The lives of the patriarchs prior to Shenoute II (d. A.D. 1044) were redated in their Arabic versions by Mawhub ibn Mansur beginning in 1088. In a note, Mawhub stated that the biography of Alexander II had been found at the monastery of St. Theodore at al-Manhā at Iblāǧ (Johnson, "Further Remarks," 106–7). Mawhub's collaborator, Michael of Damanhur, is credited with having translated the Coptic material found into Arabic; this is consistent with what we know of the decay of knowledge of the Coptic language by the 11th century and the rise of a consequent era of translation. The findspot may very well be locatable. "Al-Manhā" is the region of the Oxyrhynchite mouth of the Bahr Yusuf, the "Joseph Canal," in Middle Egypt (Yaqut, *Mujma' al-Buldān,* ed. F. Wüstenfeld, IV [Leipzig, 1869], 672). St. Theodore the Stratelates was supposed to have been martyred in the Oxyrhynchite (E. O. Winstedt, *Coptic Texts on St. Theodore the General* [Oxford, 1910], 34, 102), and was a popular saint in that area; his feast was observed in the calendar of Oxyrhynchus of A.D. 535/6: *P. Oxy.* XI 1357.63 or 65 (see note ad loc. p. 42). A church of St. Theodore is attested in the Oxyrhynchite in the early 7th century in *P.Princ.* II 87 (A.D. 612). The bishopric of Oxyrhynchus (Pemje, Baḥnasa) was still flourishing and overseeing monastic activity (in this area so famed for monasticism since the 5th century) in the 10th and 11th centuries; see S. Timm, *Das christlich-koptische Ägypten in arabischer Zeit,* I (Wiesbaden, 1984), 284–90, cf. 300 note 49. In the "al-Manhā" area there exists today a Coptic Orthodox church of St. Theodore, reported to be built on the site of still-visible ancient monastic ruins; Timm, *Ägypten,* II (Wiesbaden, 1984), 715; cf. S. Timm, *Christliche Stätten in Ägypten* (Wiesbaden, 1979), 57. This may well be where the Coptic life of Alexander was written. The Arabic place name "Iblāǧ" is doubtless a corruption of an earlier Greek *epoikion* name, although P. Pruneti, *Centri abitati dell'Ossirinchite* (Florence, 1981) does not appear to provide any leads. (I am grateful to Prof. William H. Willis of Duke University for help on this point.) The life of Alexander was apparently the work of two earlier writers: "George the deacon," syncellus of Patriarch Simon I, who worked during the reign of Anastasius (713–715), and his continuator "John the deacon" (fl. between 744 and 767); Johnson, "Further Remarks," 113.

[13] For προεστώς addressed to the superior of Shenoute's monastery, cf. *P.Cair.Masp.* III 67312.64–65, 96 (A.D. 567). Interchange of ⲟ/ⲱ is common and natural for Coptic speakers and in the Greek of Egypt. See F. Gignac, *Grammar of the Greek Papyri of the Roman and Byzantine Periods,* I (Milan, 1976), 275–77.

[14] Also visible before the name "Gennadius" in the line of larger script are what appear to be the letters ⲏ ⲏ ⲡ with a vertical hasta to the left. SS speculated that they came from the titulature of the sender. The double eta suggests a Coptic word, not a Greek; it could be part of ⲉⲧⲧⲁⲓⲏⲏⲩ, "honored," a title applied to the recipient (the pi is not certain), although that word is more usually found in the postpositive position. As the first eta is not certain, it is possible that the word was ⲁⲣ]ⲭ̣ⲏ-ⲅ̣[ⲱ: ἀρχηγός could also be an abbot's title.

[15] See R.-G. Coquin in *BIFAO* 72 (1972) 169–78.

participles and genitives absolute, and intelligently deployed technical theological vocabulary. Clearly this patriarch deserved the reputation in his biography of being "known for wisdom and learning . . . learned in the Scriptures from his youth" (Evetts, p. 49).[16] As might be expected, Patriarch Alexander makes his timely paschal letter into a mini-sermon, as is nearly always the case in this genre. The scriptural texts from which his homiliary exposition springs are very carefully chosen. In keeping with the practice of earlier Egyptian patriarchs in their paschal letters, the texts chosen answer to needs and events of the times, as will be seen from the remarks on individual points below.

The first thing to consider is the complete text of the letter. In the present translation, which follows the Schmidt/Schubart Greek text (see above, note 4), dots indicate where damage to the papyrus has caused loss of text.[17] A typical formulary opening has been supplied as a restoration.

(Alexander, by the grace of God *papa* of the predication of St. Mark, to Gennadius, *proestos* of the venerable house of Shenoute the archimandrite and prophet.
Before the discourse I greet you and I salute the footstool of the feet of your beloved, Christ-loving fatherhood.)

(Christ of our faith, Easter of the calendar is) the cornerstone. . . . for it would seem as wrong to neglect the feast of all Christendom as to neglect virtue itself. For this is truly the feast of Christ: to purify the soul and to go up on high and to expect grace from heaven.

The occasion: announcing the date of Easter
See then, that now has come the salvific time of announcing: the time has arrived for signaling with a silver trumpet the pure and clear Word, and for me to name for you the coming day of the feast, so we may delight in the promises of faith, not by just hope or love by itself, but rather by both hope and love together, exalted in hope and practiced in love. And so . . . I am again impelled to begin and am led to proclaim the good news among them, and I summon the divine and intelligible light of knowledge to be given me from above by the Father of lights for my comprehension, illuminating my understanding and fitting my stammering tongue to speak clearly. For every ray of the Gospel is divine and utterly clear and unquenchable: for as we study . . . since God has honored our human race also with reason, (so we) conduct ourselves. Everyone who receives this announcement . . . of good news . . .

Preaching of the apostles
. . . and writings from the Scriptures . . . those who were called out of the whole world taught things that were despised by the high-up, yet wondrous to men themselves, things such that they caused the listeners to marvel and be carried away. So great, too, was the power of their words, by the grace of Him who supplied them, to the listeners, that Greek philosophers and rhetors and those (skilled) in the subtly wrought wisdom of this world were not in any way strong enough to overturn their advantage. So those who seemed to be wise were condemned, and shown up as fools by the simple, who flocked to the preaching from out of the whole world.

And who enacted that these things should be wrought intelligently, yet miraculously, if not He according to His will that loves humankind, my Lord and God, Jesus, who is the eternal Light, more than brilliant, intelligible, substantial, enlightening hearts and illuminating perceptions and flashing upon the understanding, in whom we live and move and have our being? He, then, surpasses every word; all wisdom is from Him and exists in Him eternally, as the Scripture says, and, since through it He operates all things in a manner

[16] He came from the old monastery of the Ennaton, outside Alexandria, which one would have expected to continue as a center of learning even more than sixty years after the Arab conquest. The Ennaton (see Timm, *Ägypten*, II, 833–53, s.v. "Dēr az-Zaggāg") remained throughout late antiquity a staunch stronghold of Monophysite loyalty and observance, although Justinian tried to persuade the monks to turn Chalcedonian (see ibid., 837 and the evidence cited there; cf. PG 86, cols. 1103–46). On the other hand, the other great Alexandrian house, the Metanoia (cf. *P.Fouad* 86–89), was taken over by the Chalcedonians; see R. Rémondon, "Le monastère alexandrin de la Métanoia était-il bénéficiaire du fisc ou à son service?," *Studi Volterra* 5 (Milan, 1971), 769–81, and now J. E. Goehring, *Chalcedonian Power Politics and the Demise of Pachomian Monasticism* (Claremont, Calif., 1989), 17–20. Could Alexander's reference to "the instructive memoranda we have recently given out, especially as regards the thunder of . . . the Theologian" mean that he had written a commentary on John? The phrase διδασκαλικαὶ ὑπομνήσεις could indicate a teaching commentary. None, however, has been preserved in any language under Alexander's name.

[17] The editors' indications of biblical quotations and allusions, and of patristic quotations, in SS are taken as given and will not be specifically discussed here. For comparanda on Paschal letters, see J. Quasten, *Patrology*, III (Westminster, Md., 1960), 52; M. F. A. Brok in *VChr* 5 (1951), 101–10; and on this text *DACL* 3 (1937), 1430–33.

befitting God, He has demonstrated that the poor of this world and those who work with their hands are cleansed of every fleshly grossness, and illuminated in their minds, while to the eyes of flesh here below they are deemed worthy . . . (only of being looked down upon).

. . . We shall demonstrate this to the faithful from the Scriptures. For Jesus, Lord and God, performed healings by deed and word and will, as has already been proven, but He never allowed Himself to work miracles by means of His own shadow. But the shadows of the disciples glorified by Him breathed healing upon the sick, as was accomplished by Peter; and (we find that) touching linen cloths and aprons to (an apostle's) face gave back health to the bystanders, as was allowed to happen in Paul's case. Is it not the utmost to be outstripped by such a gift of miracle? He who surpasses the whole intelligible and perceptible creation was willingly outdone by His disciples and ceded the first prize to them, and was not ashamed to be second to them in wonder-working. And since those chosen by them were deemed worthy of very great and exalted mysteries, and have become like cultivators of salvation in the world for every generation, with good, sweet harvests, we have made an approach to them in the instructive memoranda we have recently given out, especially as regards the thunder of the one among them who enjoys the title of "Theologian." And so, as far as possible, we shall ascend to the heights of his thought, as we have been led to it with awe and miraculously.

Texts: Is God visible or invisible? (John 1:14 and 1:18)

What a marvelous thing he experienced, the one who rested on the Lord's breast and was loved by his Master more than the other disciples. He left us this sole legacy, to understand what divine things he taught. He said: "And the Word was God, and the Word was made flesh and dwelt among us, and we beheld His glory, the glory of the Only-Begotten of the Father, full of grace and truth." And then again after that he prepares us to be greatly astonished and, setting a riddle, brings as it were the opposite formulation to perplex our mind, introducing "No one has seen God at any time." And we counter by asking: What are you saying, Theologian, disciple whom God inspired? You sow seeds of divine vision in the world, and yet on the contrary you immediately introduce God's invisibility? Was not the glory of God the Word, as of the Only-Begotten, seen by the faithful, and, as you have borne witness, did He not allow Himself to be touched by our hands? How then can you preach rather that "God has not been seen by anyone at any time"? Who was it who, even before the advent of the Word in the flesh, appeared in many forms to the patriarchs and prophets? Who spoke to Moses from the bush? Or who was it that Isaiah saw above the Seraphim, Ezekiel above the Cherubim, and Daniel carrying a spear above the river of fire? What did your fellow disciple and evangelist Matthew mean to teach when he said, "Blessed are the pure in heart, for they shall see God," if no one has ever seen Him? But you, most studious, are the Evangelist of Thunder, and you cry out like thunder. Let Paul convince you, who cries out with me "Whom no man has seen nor can see."

Christ is God made visible

Well, then, we know clearly that it is shown by the holy Scriptures that the Divine is completely invisible by its own definition, insofar as it exists by nature in the one, holy, and august Trinity. Therefore even Christ's disciples reasonably used the impossible mode of (speaking of) this ineffable and incomprehensible nature in proclaiming it invisible; but straightway they introduced the awesome and exalted mystery of One of the same Trinity which took place for our sake by (divine) dispensation (οἰκονομία) out of love for humankind: and they brought this good news everywhere, that seeing God was quite true, and they made it plain that God's rule is more exact for all, according to the Saviour's saying to Philip, which did not lie, when He spoke to him prescriptively before His Passion, saying, "Have I been so long with you, and you have not known me, Philip? He who has seen me has seen the Father"; and His calling Thomas when he did not believe in the Resurrection and encouraging him to touch His hands and His side, so that he, awestruck, exclaimed "My Lord and my God." And so we, guided in our minds by divine grace and by the apostles whom God chose, are rich enough ever to declare the most important teachings, namely, that God, insofar as He exists by nature and in truth, enables no creature to be fully satisfied and see Him completely. For how could even the Seraphim bear up under the most terrifying (vision)? They cover their faces, that cannot bear the irresistibility of the divine brilliance. It is fearsome, not . . . , but it cannot be seen by any created nature: yet it manifests itself to those who are purified at heart, not as it is, but such as the beholders have capacity to see. And so in one way (God) spoke to Moses, and in another way was seen by Isaiah, and in yet others by Ezekiel and Daniel, not having Himself become different (God forbid!)—for "in Him there is no change or shadow of turning"—but joining Himself to the conditions of the beholders. So even God the Father thought it right to have known by certain people what the term for and the matter of His divinity are, and in the Law and the prophets He revealed Himself through visions and symbols (αἰνίγματα). And He even by the same means pointed to His Only-Begotten Son and the Holy Spirit, but not openly, since human nature was not capable of (receiving) the plain revelation of the one being and divinity of the all-holy Trinity. God the Word, eternally existing in the bosom of the Father, and in these last days having become flesh, as the Gospel says, and dwelt among us, accepted that His glory, as of the Only-Begotten of the Father, should be seen even by human beings, and He gave us grace and truth, showing Himself equal to the Father by His God-befitting actions, and implanting in human minds divine knowledge of the invisible nature; and immediately He granted to everyone to believe "in one God, the Father Almighty," and in Himself, "one Lord Jesus Christ," and in the Holy Spirit, the three being one God, not differentiated by natures (φύσεσι) or beings (essences) (οὐσίαις) (wherefore it would be impious to confess three gods), but rather by substances (hypostases, ὑποστάσεσι) or persons (προσώποις) united into one being, one divinity, one glory, one kingship.

Christological definition

For after His glorious Resurrection He said to the disciples, "Go forth and teach all nations, baptizing them in the name of the Father and of the Son and of the Holy Spirit." He did not teach them to understand (that there was) thereby an addition to the Trinity by means of the Incarnation (ἐνανθρώπησις): rather He was divinely showing that He Himself was one Son and Lord after taking on, from us and for our sake, ensouled flesh, which was itself already truly divinized for the dwelling of the Word in it; even if what is unconfused (τὸ ἀσύγχυτον) is ineffably saved in Him for our sake, it is this that is the differentiation of things that are inseparably hypostatically united, namely, the divinity and the humanity. And in every respect it is constituted as not subject to either numbering or division.

Heretical Christologies

So they would be self-condemned who claim that He existed in two natures after the ineffable union. For this accrues a fourth number to the holy Trinity, and debases the value of the salvific Passion which He willingly accepted for our sake, and alienates God the Incarnate Word Himself from His voluntary and sinless sufferings, juxtaposing disparate things in the flesh alone and in a mere human being.

Others, of the other godless party, lying under the same condemnation and having the equivalent error though it is put in different words, dare to say that as a result of the same union the Lord's body was impassible, and in every way incorruptible: and by this (mere) appearance and illusion (φαντασία) they make a monstrous story (τερατολογοῦντες) the awesome mystery of our salvation. Who of the pious then would not be pained hearing the most discordant opinion of both sides? Who would not introduce (the idea that) this is harmful to the soul's well-being to those who receive it uncritically? But we, to demonstrate the disease in their theology, will make use of the sayings of the Fathers, producing evidence from them in each case of what combats against those (others) and shoots them down and shows that they are weaker, and equips us, the single-hearted, better for uprightness, and ever keeps us stronger on its side.

Patristic proofs

So let the chosen and most brilliant father among the first of holy men come out front now, Felix, who was most holy bishop of the holy church of the Romans, and tell us what he wrote in his letter to Maximus, the most holy bishop who thought the same as he, who was styled (bishop) of the renowned city of Alexandria, and to his clergy, with content as follows: "Concerning the Incarnation of the Word, and our faith: We believe in our Lord Jesus Christ, born of the Virgin Mary, that He is God's eternal Son and Word, and not a man assumed by God so as to be different from Him. For the Son of God did not put on a human being so as to be different from him, but rather, being God, He was perfect, and at the same time was incarnate a perfect man from the Virgin, being God *qua* unchangeable Mind and heavenly Word (for He is God's Word and Wisdom, and thus uncreated and divine); the same became man having joined Himself to human flesh from Mary. We believe in Christ Jesus, confessing Him to be God in

His divine nature, not by participation (μετοχῇ) in divinity: for He is the one who is divinely participated in (μετεχόμενος), having infused the Holy Spirit into the disciples; He himself suffering in His own flesh for our salvation and saving those who believe in Him from their sins." And a little further on: "The Lord born of Mary is one, from Whom comes everything, as Paul says, and He is the Word of God, by Whom everything is, as John says."

And we anathematize those who say that the divinity is passible, and those who say that the crucified Christ was just a man and not God in His entire person (ὑποστάσει, *substantiā*). But we believe that He is the true God, on the one hand suffering in the flesh, while on the other hand remaining without suffering in spirit, He Himself being Son of God and Son of Man in one person (μονοπροσώπως): for He is Only-Begotten *qua* Son of God, in Whom even we who believe are saved.

And Julius, the holy chief shepherd of the same apostolic see, in the same vein of thought gave nearly the equivalent to all in a letter written by him to Prosdocius, saying: "The Son of God is proclaimed, for the perfecting of the faith, as both incarnate of the Virgin Mary and having dwelt among men, not as having operated in a human being (for this is in accordance with the prophets and apostles), (but) perfect God in the flesh and perfect man in the spirit. There are not two sons, one truly-begotten God putting on a human being, the other a mortal man put on by God, but one: Only-Begotten in heaven, Only-Begotten on earth, God in His divine nature, man in His fleshly form (μορφώσει); according to His likeness saving the world through the partaking (μετάλημψις) of His own Spirit, who is given by infusion (lit. insufflation): being God in human frame (σχῆμα), the King of heaven and earth and the netherworld, glorified by all as the one and sole Lord into the glory of God our Father. But if someone says that Jesus Mary's son is a man put on in addition (here from προσλαμβάνω, not simply ἀναλαμβάνω) by God, and unites two persons, let him know that he is a stranger to the true hope. For God the Word, through Whom everything came into being, is the same Jesus Himself, through Whom all things exist, as John and Paul taught, not saying that the Word put on Jesus born of Mary, but that He came into the world, having come into being out of a woman."

Such, then, are the refutations of those who venerate two natures in the one Christ, two natures which not at all correctly introduce two persons (πρόσωπα) for Him. They shy away from naming these persons explicitly, to the point where they are made fun of by everyone; but out of trickery and foolishness they are deceived into positing them, through their assertion (in addition to their other unfortunate expressions) of two natural properties (φυσικὰς ἰδιότητας), thence thinking—those poor people!—that their hidden absurdity will escape the notice of those who understand divine teaching. For who would not clearly understand that "natural property" is substance (ὑπόστασις), that is, person (πρόσωπον)? Come now.

And concerning the Docetists who make the true mystery of Christ a phantom (ἴνδαλμα), we shall again demonstrate from the Fathers' words that what they shamelessly say is impious and foreign to the truth, namely, that the Lord's body became impassible and immortal as a result of the union itself. For the most wise, apostolic hierarch, Dionysius the Areopagite, who was the first to ascend the episcopal throne of Athens, says as follows in the Theological Instructions of the most holy Hierotheos: "Since He came from there out of love for humankind and in accordance with His nature, and truly came to exist, and was called a super-divine man (ἀνὴρ ὑπέρθεος)—may what is beyond understanding and speech be praised by us—and even if in these conditions He remains high exalted and superessential, not only does He share with us without change and without confusion (here ἀναλλοιώτως and ἀσυγχύτως), not having suffered in regard to His surpassing fullness from the ineffable emptying (κένωσις), but, the newest thing of all, He remains highly exalted amidst what is natural to us, and amidst being He is above being, having from us everything that is ours, even more than we."

And Athanasius the Great, who before us in apostolic fashion illuminated this very see, said, in his catechetical discourse about the bodily appearance of our Lord Jesus Christ, as follows: "What did the Lord have to do about this, or what end should there have been for the body, once the Word had come upon it? He could not *not* die, being mortal and offered to death on behalf of all, for which reason even the Saviour prepared it for Himself; nor could He remain dead, because He Himself was the temple of life. And so He died as a mortal, and returned to life through the life in Himself; and His deeds are the sign by which the resurrection is known." And the same praiseworthy father, again, in the third discourse of his book *On the Trinity* against the most impious Arians, relates these things: "Bodily things could not happen in a bodiless being, unless He took a corruptible and mortal body (for holy Mary, from whom the body was, was mortal). Therefore it is necessary that these things also, which are properties of the flesh, be attributed to the One Who suffered and cried and toiled, since He came into existence together with the body."

And Cyril, the accurate teacher of principles, in the first book of his *Thesaurus* says thus in a simile (παραπλησίως): "For since He took a corruptible and mortal body that was also subject to sufferings of this kind, it is necessary to say that He, after (taking) flesh, made His own its sufferings as well, even while it itself bore them while He Himself remained the same. For thus we say that He was crucified and died with the flesh suffering this, not by a property (ἰδίᾳ) of the Word by itself."

Exhortation

Well, then, these few brilliant proofs from the holy Fathers advise us to draw a straight line, treasuring up for another opportunity most of the things that they have studied for piety's sake. But you, lovers of the flawless faith, foster brothers and sisters (σύντροφοι) of the best way of life (πολιτεία), holy offshoots of the Church, be zealous as long as you live to preserve it unadulterated, keeping your mind alert and your intelligence awake, not to fall into the thorns of those who sow them from time to time, and to turn back their poisonous arrows: but intelligently to understand how they hold in contempt the upright teachings of the worthy Fathers which proclaim that Christ is one, and which direct (us) to confess His one incarnate nature and one person and one divine-human operation (θεανδρικὴ ἐνέργεια) and one will (θέλησις); and also (to understand) how the apostolic traditions are despised, those which implant salvation from above for the whole human race, and do not teach us to make mention of "natural properties" (φυσικῶν ἰδιοτήτων) in the one Christ, an invention of newfangled people who conduct themselves in an unholy fashion in the churches, crafty wordsmiths, not theologians (τεχνολογούντων οὐ θεολογούντων). The blessed Paul wrote about them, too, in his first epistle to Timothy, asserting as follows: "If someone teaches differently, and does not come near to the healthful words of our Lord Jesus Christ and teaching in keeping with piety, he is deluded, not understanding, but making himself ill over questions and verbal fighting, from which come envy, strife, evil speaking, suspicions, and a bad waste of time on the part of those who have ruined their minds and been robbed of the truth, who think that making money is piety." And, in a word, the wisdom of the world has done very well to reject the boast of the mystery of Christ, and it treats as of no effect His death, which through His Cross has become lifegiving for us, thinking not to value it as something divine but rather to despise it. I think that the prophetically uttered saying has justly overtaken those who are sick in this way: "Woe to those who are wise in their own eyes, and understanding in their own regard." They are not so beloved by us! But with all free speech and everywhere may those good and pure teachings of the theologian Fathers be spoken, teachings which overthrow the phalanx of the evil-named heretics, I mean the Chalcedonian perversion and the Manichaean insanity of the Docetists, and which edify the holy churches with healthful instruction, according to which the Son and Word of God, being one both before and after the (taking of) flesh, is together confessed and together worshiped as equal and consubstantial with the Father, and the Holy Spirit is numbered with them and adored with them.

And we are bound together with them all (the Fathers) also in the practice of the other virtues, so we may piously reap the fruits of its reward in due time. We shall imitate those who received the five and the two talents: let us take good care of the two, so as also to put our trust in the five: let us manage the five well, so as to be found worthy of still more. We shall abstain from drink, we shall do good works, we shall give thanks to God: for it is the acceptable time, the day for every good work leading to salvation. By good works we shall attract God's mercy, now most of all beseeching Him and making propitiation before His face: (for) since we see that the whole world is beset with misfortunes one on top of another and is running the risk of coming to the end-time which will destroy all things, on account of our many sins up to now, though we are in distress night and day, after singing let us cry to Him: "Lord, let your mercies speedily prevent us, for we have indeed become destitute: help us, O God our Saviour." And equally may He be patient in bearing with our fallings away (παραπτώμασιν), and turn His mercies toward us, and gentle the hearts of those who oppress us (καταδυναστευόντων), and abate the disturbing storms that lower over us, and break in pieces our sufferings at the hands of the mob. And we earnestly entreat Him to give the bond of love and peace to the Church. He himself asks nothing from us, for we have nothing of our own: what He has given, that He seeks. Let us not appear as people who default on a debt to God: we have received a little or a surplus, so let us do that work, not burying the (talent) given but scattering it broadcast to the poor, which is sowing seed in the stomachs of the poor ("He spent abundantly," says the Scripture; "he gave to the poor: his righteousness endures for ever").

The date of Easter

Let us sanctify our own bodies with fasts, calming them with sleeping on the ground, and mortify the flesh with other customary chastisements, and not be altogether enslaved to pleasures of beastly type. And thus cleansing our souls by continence and making them in advance stronger than our emotional appetites, let us fast a pure fast before the Lord, so as to lead a tranquil and quiet life. So let us begin the holy forty days' period of fasting, which is of eight weeks, from the 26th of the Egyptian month of Mecheir, according to the Romans ten days before the Kalends of March, which is February 20; and begin the week of the salvific Pascha from the 15th of the Egyptian month of Pharmouthi, according to the Romans four days before the Ides of April, which is April 10; stopping the holy fast on the late evening of Saturday the 20th of the same Egyptian month of Pharmouthi, according to the Romans seventeen days before the Kalends of May, which is April 15. And let us keep the feast on the holy Sunday at dawn, the 21st of the same Egyptian month of Pharmouthi, according to the Romans sixteen days before the Kalends of May, which is April 16: connecting those (weeks) with the seven weeks of the holy Pentecost, in which, keeping spiritual (all-night) festival (πανηγυρίζοντες) and mystically perfecting our holy performances of sacred rites with unceasing psalms and hymns and odes, we will sing thanks for all to our great God, the Benefactor of our souls, Christ, our Savior and the King of the universe, having fasted the best fast before Him and being found worthy of His love of humankind through His life-giving death and blessed resurrection and glorious ascension into heaven. To Him is due glory, honor, and power, with His undefiled Father and the holy, life-giving and consubstantial Spirit, now and forever and unto the ages of ages, Amen. ☧

"Greet one another with a holy kiss." ☧

☧ I pray that your Christ-loving self, blessed with good spiritual children, may fare well in the Lord. ☧

Alexander II was consecrated to the Coptic patriarchate of Alexandria on 30 Pharmouthi, Diocletian year 420 = 25 April 705.[18] He came to the patriarchate in the wake of a wave of persecution of the Christians initiated by al-Asbagh, son of the governor ʿAbd al-Aziz ibn Marwan (himself son of an earlier caliph), who had died in unusual circumstances the previous week, on Easter Sunday, 19 April. Al-Asbagh was reputed to have pursued the policy of investigating Christian sources and texts[19] for possible insults to Islam, and exacting extortionate taxes, including the first poll tax (*jizya*) on monks, as retribution. On Holy Saturday 705, the story is related by Alexander's biographer, al-Asbagh spat on an icon of the Virgin and Child at a Coptic monastery, with the words "Who is Christ that you should worship him as God?" and was struck dead the next day.[20] The atmosphere at the beginning of Alexander's reign was already tense, and it was to flare up into open conflict on

[18] Evetts, p. 50.

[19] Of interest is his having read to him "the Gospel (*injīl*) in Arabic" and the "books of alchemy (*alkimia*)" (Evetts, p. 51), as well as the *arṭastikāt*, translated by Evetts as "the Festal Epistles." Since we are dealing here with a Festal Epistle by Alexander, this might be of importance, since those of his predecessor Simon I (A.D. 689–701) might already have been under scrutiny by the Moslem regime. This, however, is a mistranslation. The word *arṭastikāt* is obviously a garbled version of some Greek ecclesiastical technical term. It is written differently in nearly every ms.: *arṭastkāt* (emended by Seybold to *anṭaksāt*) in the Hamburg ms. (old recension) of A.D. 1266; *arṭaksāt* in Paris ms. 301/02 ("vulgate" recension, Seybold's CSCO text [Beirut-Paris-Leipzig, 1910], p. 143); *arṭasikā* in Paris ms. 4773; *arṭalsān* (!) in British Museum MS. Or. 1477. Clearly the copyists are getting further and further away from a form they no longer understand. The original must be from the Greek τάξις, and mean "liturgical books." The scribe meant to render *al-ṭaksiyyāt*, "Ordines." It makes sense that what was under scrutiny was the Christian Gospel and liturgy. (I thank Prof. Irfan Shahîd for investigating this point with me.) See also G. Graf, *Verzeichnis arabischer kirchlicher Termini*, 2nd ed. (Louvain, 1954), 74. Metathesis, such as here of *s/k*, is common on Arabic loanwords from Greek. Graf's lemma (*Verzeichnis*, p. 6) of *ārṭstīkā* = (ἐπιστολὴ) ἑορταστική, "Festal Letter," might seem to justify Evetts' translation, seeing that indeed the content of such documents would have been of interest to the regime. This, however, seems more forced than the reading and interpretation "liturgical books." The long *ī* never appears in any of the Arabic versions of the word.

[20] Evetts, pp. 52–54, noticed by A. A. Vasiliev, "The Iconoclastic Edict of the Caliph Yazid II, A.D. 721," *DOP* 9–10 (1956), 23–47. We shall return to this important historical evidence below.

many subsequent occasions. It is the troubled situation in his own times, in which a Moslem governor could express open contempt for the doctrines (which undermined the theoretical foundations of the Moslem state) of the incarnation and divinity of Christ that were proclaimed in Christian images, that prompts Alexander to select the scriptural passages he does as points of departure for his discourse.

Alexander takes as the text of his sermon the apparent conundrum, "Is John the Evangelist contradicting himself?" Specifically, he is addressing the problem of the visibility of God, through the juxtaposition of the texts "we beheld his glory" (John 1:14) and "No man has seen God at any time" (John 1:18). Not only, he affirms, is God visible to us in the fullness of time in the incarnate Lord Jesus, God the Son, but even under the old dispensation the First Person of the Trinity, God the Father, made himself visible to people in Old Testament times, tempering himself to the capacity of the beholders. The Gospel writer, granted by his Lord the gift of convincing eloquence that turns the wisdom of this world upside down, does not contradict himself. God was not only visible under types and visions to the patriarchs and prophets, he was fully visible to ordinary people of the Greco-Roman world in the person of Jesus of Nazareth. The apostles saw the second Person of the Trinity, and were taught by him about the other two; there is no doubt that God, fully the fullness of God, is visible in Jesus Christ.

Why does this early eighth-century patriarch select the problem of the visibility of God? Clearly because he is responding to Moslem attacks on the Christian veneration of depictions of that visible God.[21] The Moslem position, that the utterly transcendent, un-hypostasized god of monarchical monotheism was invisible and undepictable and hence that Christian images were rank idols, was certainly making itself outspokenly felt within the caliphate in the first quarter of the eighth century. In the Life of Alexander in the *History of the Patriarchs,* al-Asbagh's act of contempt for the public display of Christian doctrine and practice was not an isolated occurrence. Beginning in A.D. 709, the richly decorated churches of the Coptic community were stripped of their altar vessels of precious metal,[22] their marble revetments,[23] and their carved woodwork;[24] finally in 721 came the edict of Caliph Yazid II that crosses and images were to be everywhere destroyed.[25] It seems plain that Alexander is telling his flock, who are disturbed by the despoliation of their churches and troubled by accusations that they are wrong to think God could be seen or pictured, to hold fast to what they have always known to be right. The true God did really become incarnate, visible, and saving. To date this paschal letter to A.D. 724, in the wake of the caliph's edict that sought to eradicate the public display of visual forms proclaiming convictions antithetic to those of Islam, would make sense in the context of the times.

In order for this visible, depictable, fully divine Christ to be understood as fully incarnate and thus fully salvific, his incarnation must be understood aright. As the leader of the non-Chalcedonian Christendom of Egypt, Alexander must once again define Christ's person and nature. He singles out Chalcedonian Dyophysitism and Aphthartodocetism as the two extremes of error between which the understanding must steer a correct course. We learn from the Life of Alexander that people of both these positions had been causing trouble during his patriarchate. In the Delta cities and in monasteries of the Wadi Natrun itself, numerous Gaianites (Aphthartodocetists) were active, and the Life relates that Alexander reconciled them to his obedience.[26] It also tells the story of an Alexandrian deacon ("Onopes," clearly a nickname) who, during the reign of al-Walid (705–715), tried to bribe the Moslem governor to get himself made Chalcedonian patriarch. This action provoked a popular uprising, and the repentant Chalcedonian fled to Alexander and was received into his communion.[27] Thus both heresies condemned in the paschal letter were matters of timely concern.[28]

Alexander defines Christ not only by specifying error but by himself spelling out the right position and underpinning his discourse with lengthy quotations from the Fathers. In his own exposition of

[21] See S. H. Griffith, "Theodore Abū Qurrah's Arabic Tract on the Christian Practice of Venerating Images," *JAOS* 105 (1985), 53–73; I. Dick, *Théodore Abuqurra: Traité du culte des icônes* (= Patrimoine arabe chrétien 10; Junyeh 1986). An edition by S. H. Griffith is to appear in the CSCO.

[22] Evetts, pp. 61–62.

[23] Ibid., p. 67.

[24] Ibid., p. 69.

[25] Ibid., pp. 72–73.

[26] Ibid., p. 63.

[27] Ibid., pp. 66–67.

[28] Also troublesome were people referred to as "some who do not believe in the faith of the Coptic Christians, and yet will not pray with the Muslims" (ibid., p. 62). These were probably Chalcedonians; it is highly unlikely that they were leftover pagans.

Egyptian Monophysite Christology, the eighth-century patriarch stands in a long line of tradition. Many of his expressions have earlier parallels in the sixth-century Coptic synodical letter of Damian I, patriarch of Alexandria A.D. 577–607.[29] The scriptural ἐν τοῖς κόλποις ὢν ἀεὶ τοῦ πατρός (SS, p. 72) is, in Damian's refutation of all heresies

ⲟⲩⲇⲉ ⲙ̄ⲡ̄ϥ̄ⲗⲟ ⲙ̄ⲙⲁⲩ ϩⲛ̄ⲕⲟⲩⲟⲩⲛ̄ϥ̄ ⲙ̄ⲡⲉϥⲉⲓⲱⲧ,

"nor did he depart from the bosom of his Father."[30] Alexander's doxological "one *ousia,* one *theotes,* one *doxa,* one *basileia*" (SS, p. 72) and "one incarnate *physis* [Cyril's formula], one *hypostasis,* one *theandrike energeia,* one *thelesis*" (SS, p. 82) are prefigured by Damian:[31]

> ⲟⲩⲫⲩⲥⲓⲥ ⲛ̄ⲟⲩⲱⲧⲧⲉ· ⲁⲩⲱ ⲟⲩⲁⲣⲭⲏ [ⲛ̄ⲟⲩⲱⲧ] ⲧⲉ· [ⲁⲩⲱ ⲟⲩⲙ̄ⲛ̄]ⲧ̄ⲉⲣⲟ ⲛ̄ⲟⲩⲱⲧⲧⲉ· ⲁⲩⲱ ⲟⲩⲉⲟⲟⲩ ⲛ̄ⲟⲩⲱⲧⲡⲉ· ⲁⲩⲱ ⲟⲩⲇⲩⲛⲁⲙⲓⲥ ⲛ̄ⲟⲩⲱⲧⲧⲉ· ⲁⲩⲱ ⲟⲩⲉⲛⲉⲣⲅⲉⲓⲁ ⲛ̄ⲟⲩⲱⲧⲧⲉ· ⲁⲩⲱ ⲟⲩⲁⲙⲁϩⲧⲉ ⲛ̄ⲟⲩⲱⲧⲡⲉ· ⲁⲩⲱ ⲟⲩⲟⲩⲱϣ ⲛ̄ⲟⲩⲱⲧⲡⲉ· ⲁⲩⲱ ⲟⲩⲥⲟⲟⲩⲛ ⲛ̄ⲟⲩⲱⲧⲡⲉ· ... ⲟⲩⲫⲩⲥⲓⲥ ⲛ̄ⲟⲩⲱⲧ ⲙ̄ⲡⲛⲟⲩⲧⲉ ⲡⲗⲟⲅⲟⲥ ⲉⲁϥϫⲓ ⲥⲁⲣ̄ⲝ̄:
>
> (it is) a single nature, a single rule, a single kingdom, a single glory, a single power, a single operation, a single dominion, a single will, a single knowledge . . . one nature of God the Word incarnate [lit. 'that took flesh'].

Damian too condemned the Docetists, ⲉⲧⲧⲁⲩⲟ ⲛ̄ⲟⲩϩⲣ̄ⲃ̄ ⲙ̄ⲙⲁⲧⲉ, "who preach a mere phantom," "like Marcion, Valentinus, Mani, Eutyches":[32] just so does Alexander condemn "the Manichaean *phrenoblabeia* of the Docetists" (SS, p. 83), who by *phantasia* distort salvation into grotesquerie. Although Alexander does not explicitly name or quote his predecessor Damian, in distinction from those Fathers whom he does quote by name ("Pope Felix," "Pope Julius," "Dionysius the Areopagite," Athanasius, Cyril), his exposition clearly stands in the same line of descent. This is all traditional theological language, but in both Coptic- and Greek-speaking Christian Egypt it goes back a long way.

Both Alexander and Damian also deal carefully, if in passing, with the theology of another great Monophysite of the sixth century, John Philoponus. Alexander alludes to the late sixth-century Tritheist controversy in which Philoponus had been involved by warning his flock against differentiating the Persons of the Trinity *ousiais,* by essences/beings (SS, p. 72). The Godhead both of the Trinity and of Christ is so constituted as not to be subject to a numbering operation (SS, p. 73), that is, what we would call a one-to-one mapping of the integers onto it. Closer to the time of the actual controversy, Damian had condemned Philoponus by name ⲓ̈ⲱϩⲁⲛⲛⲏⲥ ⲡⲉⲅⲣⲁⲙⲙⲁⲧⲓⲕⲟⲥ and his ϩⲁϩ ⲛ̄ⲟⲩⲥⲓⲁ, "many beings"), calling him "this blasphemer" (ⲡⲉⲓ̈ⲣⲉ[ϥϫ]ⲓ ⲟⲩⲁ).[33] "Numbering" is not an unfair description of Philoponus' reasoning in the *Arbiter* and *On the Whole and Its Parts.*[34] Unfortunately, it was to lead to his condemnation for what was interpreted as a proto-nominalist positing of three *ousiai* in the Trinity,[35] a fact which gave Moslem controversialists no little *Schadenfreude.*[36] It was important for Alexander in the eighth century to sidestep, if not openly confront, the Moslem imputation of *širk,* "associationism" or "polytheism," to Christians.

In the outright defense of Coptic orthodox Christology, as well as Trinitarian thought, an allied aspect of this concept also comes into play in Alexander's paschal letter. The eighth-century patriarch enumerates the mistakes of the Dyophysites, especially their dividing Christ and making the Trinity into a Quaternity. Their worst error is the positing of two "natural properties," φυσικαὶ ἰδιότητες, belonging to the two natures of Christ supposed to have persisted after the union. This of course refers to the formulation σῳζομένης τῆς ἰδιότητος ἑκατέρας φύσεως, *salva proprietate utri-*

[29] The letter is preserved in Coptic, from a wall inscription, in W. E. Crum and H. E. Winlock, *The Monastery of Epiphanius,* II (New York, 1926), 148–52 (text), 332–37 (trans.) (hereafter *Epiphanius*). A different version in Syriac is transmitted by Michael the Syrian, *Chronique,* ed. J.-B. Chabot, II (Paris, 1901), 325–34 (trans.), 358–64 (text). On Damian and his epoch, see C. D. G. Müller, "Damian, Papst und Patriarch von Alexandrien," *OC* 70 (1986), 118–42.

[30] *Epiphanius,* 150.54.

[31] Ibid., 149.28–30; 150.64–65. The latter passage repeats "and one *hypostasis* and one *prosopon* and one *energeia.*"

[32] Ibid., 151.102–3.

[33] Ibid., 149.19–20; 151.132.

[34] See H. Chadwick. "Philoponus the Christian Theologian," in R. Sorabji, ed., *Philoponus* (Ithaca, 1987), 50, cf. 53. Fragments of these two works, preserved in Syriac (ed. A. Šanda, *Opuscula monophysitica Ioannis Philoponi* [Beirut, 1930], nos. I and IV), are quoted in Greek by John Damascene (PG 94, cols. 744–54); see B. Kotter, ed., *Die Schriften des Johannes von Damaskos,* IV (Berlin, 1982) 50–55. Quotations are also preserved in the Chalcedonian florilegium *Doctrina patrum de incarnatione verbi,* ed. F. Diekamp (Münster, 1907, repr. Münster, 1981), 272–83.

[35] See R. Y. Ebied, A. van Roey, and L. R. Wickham, *Peter of Callinicum: Anti-Tritheist Dossier* (Louvain, 1981).

[36] See M. Steinschneider, "Johannes Philoponus bei den Arabern," *MASP,* ser. 7, 13.4 (1869), 152–76, cf. 220–24, 250–52; A. Abel, "La légende de Jean Philopon chez les Arabes," in *Acta Orientalia Belgica* (Brussels, 1966 [article written 1941]), 251–80.

usque naturae, of the Definition of Chalcedon.[37] The Dyophysites fly in the face of Cyrillian clarity, going from bad to worse: since in Cyril's thought φύσις and ὑπόστασις can become interchangeable, to assert "properties that belong to natures"[38] is the beginning of a slippery slope that leads to two hypostases, two Christs. *Absit.* Here is where Alexander reveals the Coptic layer underneath his Greek. Ἰδιότης is calqued in Coptic by the qualitative of the verb ⲱⲡ, ⲏⲡ, "to count, number, ascribe to": the *property* that belongs to or is ascribed to something (e.g., a nature) is arrived at by a process of numbering.[39] And one cannot perform this operation upon God (παντὸς δὲ ἀριθμοῦ . . . ἔξω καθεστηκότα [sc. θεότης]: SS, p. 73). To Alexander, "natural properties" are just one more absurdity perpetrated by the *technologountes*—the *mutakallimun.*

It is interesting to see this writer, in the first quarter of the eighth century, using and emphasizing the terms μία θεανδρικὴ ἐνέργεια and μία θέλησις (SS, p. 82) in his exposition of Christology. This study is not the place for a detailed history of the various controversies involving these terms which had so disturbed the course of seventh-century Christendom.[40] Suffice it to say that, in using these concepts, Alexander stands in the tradition of a long line of Monophysite discourse that goes right back to Severus of Antioch[41] and indeed to Cyril. Using the supposed near-apostolic authority of (ps.-) Dionysius the Areopagite,[42] Syriac and Egyptian Christological thinkers had grasped the notion of a "single operation" and a "single will" further to express the fundamental insight that it is through the unity of Christ the God-Man that we are saved.[43] As the operational level of Christ's reality represents his essential reality,[44] so one saving operation of God Incarnate represents the fact that it is really God who truly saves. This prevents, as Alexander says, alienating (ἀλλοτριοῦν) God from his own sufferings and debasing their value (παραχαράττειν) (SS, p. 73). Under the pressure of Moslem argument, Alexander feels it necessary to insist in time-honored and patristic terms on the Christian proclamation that we are saved by a God who became actually and effectually human, not a distant spirit who acts on people through prophetic messages and fate. As Alexander would not have been affected by the events of the Monoenergetist controversy, by imperial pronouncements or decisions at Constantinople after 641,[45] he is simply continuing in his own tradition.[46] He most likely obtained his patristic citations, authentic or not,[47] from a Monophysite florilegium in either Greek or Coptic of a type

[37] Quoted from J. Alberigo et al., *Conciliorum oecumenicorum decreta,* 3rd ed. (Bologna, 1973), 86. Christ is to be understood (γνωριζόμενος) *in* two natures, qualified by the famous four adverbs. Of these four, Alexander concentrates on ἀσυγχύτως (his τὸ ἀσύγχυτον) and ἀτρέπτως, in Coptic Damian's ⲛ̄ⲁⲧⲡⲱϣⲛⲉ ⲛ̄ⲁⲧⲧⲱϩ (*Epiphanius,* 150.57, cf. 149.12; SS p. 73, cf. 79–80). Cf. L. S. B. MacCoull, "A Trinitarian Formula in Dioscorus of Aphrodito," *BSAC* 24 (1982), 103–10.

[38] The phrase φυσικαὶ ἰδιότητες is indeed used from the Chalcedonian point of view by Sophronius of Jerusalem (PG 87, col. 3168A) and Theodore of Raithou (PG 91, col. 1497D), as well as by the Lateran Synod of A.D. 649 (ed. R. Riedinger, *ACO,* ser. 2.1 [Berlin, 1984], p. 374). For the non-Chalcedonian usage and understanding cf. J. Lebon, *Le monophysisme sévérien* (Louvain, 1909), 487–88. Compare Alexander's use of πάντα θεοπρεπῶς ἐνεργῶν (SS, p. 66) and θεοπρεπῶν ἔργων (SS, p. 72) for his expression of what appertains to the divine nature.

[39] Compare G. Zoega, *Catalogus codicum copticorum manu scriptorum* (Rome, 1810, repr. Hildesheim, 1973), no. 163 (p. 272), a fragment of the acts of the council of Ephesus, where ⲉⲧⲏⲡ ⲉⲧⲥⲁⲣⲝ "ascribed to/reckoned the property of the flesh" translates *proprietas*/ἰδιότης (of the flesh).

[40] See H.-G. Beck, *Kirche und theologische Literatur im byzantinischen Reich,* 2nd ed. (Munich, 1977), 430–47, and F. Winkelmann, "Die Quellen des monenergetisch-monotheletischen Streites," *Klio* 69 (1987), 515–59.

[41] Hence perhaps Batiffol's quickly applied label of "monophysisme Sévérien" (above, note 4). The phrase is of course that of the title of Lebon's classic monograph (above, note 38).

[42] As in PG 3, col. 1072C. Severus asserted, in a Greek text, that the ancient fathers themselves had proclaimed one energy and one will (Mansi, X, 1117).

[43] In R. Chesnut's words, ". . . the unity in Christ is of greater significance than the duality." By far the clearest exposition of the position being discussed is the section on Severus of Antioch in her masterly work *Three Monophysite Christologies* (Oxford, 1976), esp. pp. 29–34 on "operation" and 20–29 on "will" (the quotation at the beginning of this note is from p. 35). The terminology is quite clear as it is deployed in three different language families, Indo-European (Greek), Semitic (Syriac), and Hamitic (Coptic). Ἐνέργεια is calqued in Syriac by a feminine abstract noun from the root *ʿbd,* "to do, to make"; likewise in Coptic, it comes out as ϭⲓⲛⲣ̄ ϩⲱⲃ, literally "the business of doing work" (when the Greek loanword is not simply borrowed).

[44] See Chesnut's brilliant treatment of the "iconic relationship" between the two levels in Christ: *Christologies,* pp. 34–36. Any introduction of a notional duality into Emmanuel the Saviour, Severus maintains, runs the risk of negating the reality of salvation. Cf. Lebon, *Monophysisme,* 458–66. It is this concept of iconic relationship that makes the Western concern with *communicatio idiomatum* largely irrelevant in Eastern thought.

[45] Neither the *Ekthesis* of Heraclius (638) nor the *Typos* of Constans II (648) would have deterred an Egyptian from proclaiming his own point of view. Nor, a fortiori, would the efforts at union of the Chalcedonian patriarch Cyrus of Alexandria in the 630s have affected the tradition within which Alexander was writing.

[46] As pointed out above, Damian in the 6th century wrote of "one operation and one will" (*Epiphanius,* 148.30).

[47] Neither the letter attributed to Pope Felix nor that ascribed to Pope Julius is authentic, but both were cited by Cyril of Al-

of which we have no preserved example.[48] His acquisition of the pseudo-Dionysian phrase θεανδρικὴ ἐνέργεια would have come via the same sort of transmission.

Both the θεανδρικὴ ἐνέργεια problem and the letter of ps.-Pope Felix are mentioned by another predecessor of Alexander's in the see of Alexandria, in a fragmentary paschal letter in Greek attributed to the Coptic patriarch Benjamin I (626–665), preserved in a recently published Cologne papyrus.[49] Benjamin, eyewitness to the Arab conquest,[50] wrote theological works in both Coptic and Greek; to his Greek epistle may also be compared his (probably originally Coptic) paschal letter of A.D. 642, preserved in Ethiopic transmission.[51] Column I, D line 8 of the Cologne text preserves only part of the word θεαν]δρικήν[(sc. ἐνέργειαν). A little more remains of the next section, in which Benjamin defends adherents of the one-nature Christology against the charge leveled by the dyophysites that they are Theopaschites,[52] by citing Pope Felix's anathema of "those who say that the divinity is passible and mortal, and who say that the crucified Christ is (only) a man" (also cited by Alexander, below). From what remains of it, it appears that the main import of Benjamin's paschal letter of 663 was eucharistic, as the rest of the text describes the proper state of mind and soul for receiving communion. Yet even from these brief mentions it can be seen that the same problems were being dealt with by Coptic patriarchs, whether they had been functioning under Moslem rule only a few years or nearly a century.

One further point relevant to the circumstances of Patriarch Alexander's own time is of interest in his citation from the letter attributed to Pope Felix. "We anathematize," says the text, "those who say that the crucified Christ was a (mere) man" (SS, p. 76). In the first quarter of the eighth century, Moslem controversialists were asserting precisely that. Alexander introduces his quotation from Felix, in a letter supposed to have been addressed to one of his own predecessors in the see of Alexandria, just after his condemnation of the Docetic views of the "Impassibilists." Obviously no one in the third-century world of Pope Felix I was thinking in such developed and sophisticated Christological terms as appear in the text cited. But in the eighth-century world of John Damascene, the problem was neither Docetism nor Theopaschism: it was Islam. It was a topos in Christian-Moslem controversy to show that Islam was a kind of Docetic heresy. The type passage is John Damascene's *Liber de haeresibus* 100.23 (ed. Kotter, IV, p. 61).[53] The Moslems claimed[54] that the Crucifixion was a piece of stage-managed trickery (κρατήσαντες [sc. the Jews] ἐσταύρωσαν τὴν σκιὰν αὐτοῦ [sc. Christ]), involving a mere human being (δοῦλον τοῦ θεοῦ). Whatever the actual genesis of the pseudo-Felix text may have been (perhaps in an anti-Nestorian context), Alexander had a good reason to reply to the Moslems in the same argument by which he refutes the Docetists of his time.

Moving toward the close of his paschal letter, Patriarch Alexander alludes to the sufferings of Egypt's Christians in his own time at the hands of their tyrannical (καταδυναστευόντων) Moslem overlords, sufferings so great that he interprets them apocalyptically, as signs of the approaching end of the world. The cosmos, he says, is afflicted

---

exandria and often used by later Monophysite writers (see SS, notes on pp. 75, 77). It is interesting that, in introducing the citation from the letter supposed to be by Pope Julius, Alexander applies the epithet "apostolic see" to Rome (SS, p. 77).

[48] An Arabic florilegium of this type, expressly said to be translated from the Coptic, containing the letters attributed to Felix and Julius, is preserved in cod. Vat. arab. 101; see A. Mai, *Scriptorum veterum nova collectio*, IV (Rome, 1831), 207–10, and J. S. Assemani, *Bibliotheca Orientalis*, II (Rome, 1721),133–40. See also G. Graf, "Unechte Zeugnisse römischer Päpste für den Monophysitismus im arabischen 'Bekenntnis der Väter'," *RQ* 36 (1928), 197–233.

[49] C. Römer in *P. Köln* V (Cologne, 1985), 215 (pp. 77–106, 322–26). Since Easter is designated as falling on 2 April, the letter is to be dated to A.D. 663, just over twenty years after the Arab conquest.

[50] See C. D. G. Müller, "Benjamin I., 38. Patriarch von Alexandrien," *Muséon* 69 (1956), 313–40.

[51] C. D. G. Müller in AbhHeid (1968), 301–51, with the literature cited by Römer (above, note 49), pp. 84–85 with note 26.

[52] Referring of course to the Monophysite addition to the Trishagion "who was crucified for us." Compare the Chalcedonian argument in Anastasius of Sinai, *Hodegos*, ed. Uthemann, p. 102, that the use of non-Greek languages causes their speakers to fall into the error of Theopaschism. Benjamin also cites the pseudo-Felix in his Ethiopic letter of 642 (Müller [note 51], 326f).

[53] See above, note 34. Scholarly opinion defends the authenticity of this passage; John Damascene must have had firsthand experience of Islam (Kotter, p. 7 with the literature cited in his note 13). Cf. T. F. X. Noble, "John Damascene and the History of the Iconoclastic Controversy," *Religion, Culture, and Society in the Early Middle Ages: Studies in Honor of Richard E. Sullivan* (Kalamazoo, Mich., 1987), 95–116. Compare also the anti-Moslem speech in the Life of the 9th-century Sicilian saint Elias the Younger, accusing Islam of being a tissue of heresies: καὶ τὰ πάθη φαντασίᾳ καὶ οὐκ ἀληθείᾳ τοῦτον [sc. Χριστὸν] ὑποστῆναι φάσκοντες, τὰ Βασιλείδους φρονεῖτε; G. Rossi Taibbi, *Vita di sant'Elia il Giovane* (Palermo, 1962), 34–5, 146–47. This is Basileides' "laughing savior" who substituted Simon of Cyrene for himself on the cross.

[54] Qur'an, Suras 2 and 4.

with one calamity (συμφορά) after another (SS, p. 84). From Alexander's Life in the *History of the Patriarchs* we may gather what some of these calamities may have been.

In May 705 Alexander had himself been held to ransom by the Moslem governor, ʿAbdallah b. ʿAbd al-Malik, against the payment of three thousand dinars by the Christian community. Giving his parole, Alexander was permitted to travel through the Delta cities soliciting the money.[55] Further extortions were perpetrated by the governor Kurrah b. Sharik (709–714), well known from the many papyrus documents from his financial archive.[56] Kurrah once more held Alexander for ransom, occasioning another begging trip, this time to Upper Egypt in quest of another three thousand dinars.[57] A further disaster followed in 715: plague and famine.[58] In 718 came violence, the branding of monks, and the despoliation of church revetments mentioned above,[59] followed by the enforcement of a policy of requiring *sigillia* or travel passes to identify Christian taxpayers by their *idiai* or places of origin.[60] After the accession of the caliph Hisham in 724, a respite may have been granted by the more lenient policies of the governor ʿUbaid Allah,[61] but Alexander was not yet aware of it. After all, he remembered the doubling of the poll tax (*jizya*)[62] and its imposition for the first time on monks at about the time of his own consecration to the patriarchate.[63] When he quotes the Bible in this section of his letter, he quotes a verse of Psalm 78 (79), the context of which reads: "O God, the heathen are come into thine inheritance: thy holy temple have they defiled . . . We are become a reproach unto our neighbours, a scorn and derision to them that are round about us . . . Pour out thy wrath upon the heathen that have not known thee . . . Wherefore should the heathen say, Where is their God? Let him be known among the heathen in our sight . . ." (Ps. 78:1, 4, 6, 10). In 725/6, about a year and a half after the date suggested for this paschal letter, the desperate Copts revolted.[64] It was not the first time, and was not to be the last.

Patriarch Alexander was conscious of himself as the successor of illustrious men on the throne of Alexandria. He explicitly refers to Athanasius the Great as his predecessor ἀποστολικῶς[65] "upon this very see" (SS, p. 80). When he closes his paschal letter with the scriptural quotation "Greet one another with a holy kiss" (Rom. 16:16a; 2 Cor. 13:12; SS, p. 87), he must have been aware that this very quotation was Athanasius' favorite ending for his paschal letters.[66] Alexander, who also had suffered for the sake of his flock, is consciously following in the footsteps of Athanasius, the originator of the custom of the yearly paschal letter to all of Egypt.

The paschal letter of Patriarch Alexander II stands as an impressive testimony to the knowl-

[55] Evetts, pp. 55–56.

[56] Ibid., pp. 56–64. On the Kurrah archive see H. Cadell, "Nouveaux fragments de la correspondance de Kurrah ben Sharik," *Recherches de papyrologie* 4 (1967), 107–60; Y. Ragib in *JNES* 40 (1981), 173–87.

[57] Evetts, pp. 58–59.

[58] Ibid., p 67: date given as Diocletian year 431, a 13th indiction.

[59] Ibid., pp 68–69.

[60] Ibid., pp. 69–70. Papyrus documentation of such *sigillia* is well known: e.g., *P. Lond.* IV 1540, 1633, 1419.1328 ff. The Coptic petition CLT 3 records the request of 8th-century monks for such a travel permit. The Life of Alexander relates the sad story of a young man whose *sigillion* was eaten by a crocodile; Evetts, p. 70.

[61] Evetts, pp. 74–75. See N. Abbott, "A New Papyrus and a Review of the Administration of ʿUbaid Allāh b. al-Ḥabḥāb," in G. Makdisi, ed., *Arabic and Islamic Studies in Honor of H. A. R. Gibb* (Cambridge, 1965), 21–35.

[62] In addition to the standard research on the Islamic poll tax (D. C. Dennett, *Conversion and the Poll Tax in Early Islam* [Cambridge, 1950, repr. New York, 1973] is the classic work), its roots might be sought in more than one late Roman source in addition to the *laographia* of Roman Egypt. The root *j-z-y* means "compensation"; the tax was conceived of, not only as a headcount of the non-Moslem population (in 8th-century Greek papyri "poll tax" is rendered ἀνδρισμός), but also as a kind of compensation to the state for its "protection" of the *dhimmis*. The state has in essence suffered an injury to its body politic by having non-Moslems within it. For different conceptions of "compensation" in the Hellenistic law reflected in papyri, see R. Taubenschlag, *The Law of Greco-Roman Egypt in the Light of the Papyri*, 2d ed. (Warsaw, 1955), 426, cf. 277. A "protected person" paying this tax is a dependent of the state as a whole, as a *mawlaʿ* (client) is the dependent of a patron; cf. P. Crone, *Roman, Provincial and Islamic Law* (Cambridge, 1987), 35–42, 77–88. The poll tax is not a wergeld, the equivalent of the "protected person's" buying his life from the state.

[63] Evetts, p. 51.

[64] Cf. L. S. B. MacCoull, "Sinai Icon B. 49: Egypt and Iconoclasm," *16. Internationaler Byzantinistenkongress,* II.2 (Vienna, 1982), 407–14.

[65] Alexander consciously views patriarchs as the successors of the apostles, as seen in his graceful introductory passage (SS, pp. 67–68), where he praises Christ's humility in taking the second place to his own apostles in wonder-working, and describes the vocation of the apostles' successors as that of being φυτουργοὶ σωτηρίας for each succeeding generation. He may also have been aware of the new weight being placed upon the Arabic translation of "apostle," *rasūl,* in the context of Moslem polemic. Compare the protocol.

[66] For the Coptic, see L. Th. Lefort, *S. Athanase: Lettres festales et pastorales en copte,* CSCO 150–51 (Louvain, 1955), vol. 150, pp. 22, 44, 67.

edge, intelligibility, and vitality of Greek in Egypt nearly three generations after the Arab conquest. The history of the death of Greek in Egypt has not yet been written. It can and should be traced through documents: administrative documents such as bilingual papyri; literary documents such as the el-Moallaqa inscription,[67] the letter of Benjamin in *P. Köln* V 215, and the present letter; and liturgical documents such as hymns and saints' lives.[68] Greek did not vanish from the administrative and cultural life of Egypt the moment that the edict banning its use in the government chancery in 715 was promulgated. A complete list of all extant Greek/Arabic bilingual documents does not yet exist, though efforts have been made.[69] The major bilingual administrative documents need to be studied in depth: for example, the great trilingual (Arabic/Greek/Coptic) *homologia* of *APEL* III 167, and bilingual tax lists such as *PERF* 595 and 609, all dating to the first half of the eighth century. Purely Greek documentary papyri are attested until the 780s. Egypt very gradually de-Hellenized at different rates in different areas of cultural life. Hymns in very poorly construed Greek continued to be written by Copts up through the ninth century;[70] Greek antiphons, versicles and responses, and even troparia,[71] continue fossilized in the Coptic Orthodox liturgy until the present day. By now it is clear that there was no ironclad equation between Greek-using = Chalcedonian and Coptic-using = Monophysite. Greek is thought to have lived on in the society of the nome towns, now become provincial capitals under the Arab-controlled administration.[72] Our Berlin papyrus can take its place in this chain of evidence, as part of the story of the *Nachleben* of Greek in Egypt from 642 to 1956.

The paschal letter of Alexander is of importance for two reasons. First, it is an elaborate exposition of Egyptian Monophysite theology that is written, not in one of what are ordinarily labeled as the usual culture-carrying languages of the Monophysite churches (Syriac, Armenian, Coptic, Ethiopic), but in Greek. Second, it is a defense of the principle of icon veneration that is written, not, like the other principal iconodule texts, by a Chalcedonian (such as John Damascene in Greek or Theodore Abu Qurrah in Arabic), but by a non-Chalcedonian, the head of a Monophysite community. After eighty years, it deserves to be known in its historical context, for its content as well as for its appearance.[73]

[67] See L. S. B. MacCoull, "Redating the Inscription of el-Moallaqa," *ZPE* 64 (1986), 230–35.

[68] The famous B.M. ms. add. 37534, the Miracles of Sts. Cosmas and Damian from the monastery of St. Mercurius at Edfu, dated to the 11th century, may not have been produced in Egypt; its hand resembles those known from Palestine. I am grateful to Mr. Thomas Pattie of the British Library for the chance to inspect this ms. Similarly, the famous Vat. gr. 2200 of the *Doctrina Patrum* is apparently Hagiopolite, not, as had been thought by E. A. Lowe (*Scriptorium* 19 [1965], 15), Egyptian; L. Perria in *RSBN* 20–21 (1983–84), 25–68.

[69] See K. A. Worp in *Aegyptus* 65 (1985), 107–15, in summary recapitulating earlier literature.

[70] The many extant examples deserve to be collected and studied: e.g., P. Berol. 11763; *PSI* IX 1096; P.Vindob.Gr. 42377 (cf. MacCoull in *ZPE* 69 [1987], 291–92); Ryl 25–28, 35–37, 39, 53, and *P.Ryl.* III 466.

[71] I. Borsai in *Studia Musicologica Academiae Scientiarum Hungaricae* 14 (1972), 329–54; O. Burmester in *OCP* 2 (1936), 363–94.

[72] R. S. Bagnall in *Journal of Roman Archaeology* 1 (1988), 200–201.

[73] For help on various points I should like to thank Roger Bagnall, Monica Blanchard, Berenice Cavarra, Sidney Griffith, Ofer Livne, Irfan Shahîd, Lucas Siorvanes, Klaas Worp, and the anonymous reader for *DOP;* and, as always, Mirrit Boutros Ghali (Cant. 5:16; Isa. 19:2).

Papyri are cited according to J. F. Oates et al., *Checklist of Editions of Greek Papyri and Ostraca*³ (Atlanta, 1985), and A. A. Schiller, "A Checklist of Coptic Documents and Letters," *BASP* 13 (1976), 99–123.

Addendum: On the *History of the Patriarchs*, see now J. den Heijer, *Mawhūb ibn Manṣūr ibn Mufarriǧ et l'historiographie copte-arabe: Etude sur la composition de l'Histoire des Patriarches d'Alexandrie*, CSCO Subsidia 83, Louvain, 1989. On the life of Alexander at al-Manhā (above, note 12), cf. ibid., p. 98, with note 51, p. 122.

XX

Notes on the social structure of late antique Aphrodito

We know more about the city of Aphrodito (it called itself a *civitas*, *P.Mich*. XIII 661.11) than about any other site in Roman/Byzantine Egypt, with the possible exceptions of Oxyrhynchus and Hermopolis. Certainly we know more about Aphrodito in the Late Antique period, including the first hundred years of Umayyad rule, than about any other Egyptian settlement (except Apollonopolis Ano in the post-conquest decades). Material is abundant, and continuity is on the whole easy to perceive. This knowledge is based on the chance finds of papyri made early in this century; the site of Kom Ishqaw has never been scientifically explored by excavation (a first survey is hoped for). Yet up to the present few questions have been asked about the specific nature of social and economic life in this city (except for taxation matters), and little has been formulated describing the activities which sustained the community and the social links which made it up. (At least to-day no one would write an article entitled 'The Byzantine servile state in Egypt'[1] so perhaps we are more able to ask questions of this kind of the material we have. One hopes to do for the analysis of Aphrodito something of what Professor Le Roy Ladurie has done for Romans.)

In magisterial fashion E. Patlagean[2] has given us a picture of the various occupations practised in a typical Late Antique society of Asia Minor. Regrettably, her book does not include Egypt within its scope: but it provides a set of models from which to work. In the following tables I summarize, following a classification similar to that of Patlagean, the categories of occupation, service, and rank found in the Aphrodito papyri of the sixth to eighth centuries[3], giving a figure for the number of persons known by name to be found in each occupation.

An asterisk indicates that the occupation or rank concerned is found only in the eighth century, after the conquest. A double figure (e.g. 23+27) indicates a figure for the sixth century followed by a figure for the eighth century.

THE 'UPPER CLASS' (landowning aristocracy, *possessores*, 'propriétaires')

κόμες/-ης 7	μειζότερος 2	πατρίκιος 8
κτήτωρ 33	μείζων 15	συντελεστής 11

66

SERVICES:

PRIVATE SERVICES

ἀρχισταβλίτης 1*	λογογράφος 8*
βουκελλάριος 1	λογόφορος 1
γραμματεύς/γραμματικός 4	φορολόγος 1
διδάσκαλος 2	νομικός 11+4
ἐκβιβαστής 16	νοτάριος 4+15
ἐντολικάριος 1	συμβολαιογράφος 7
ἰατρός/ἀρχιατρός 14+4	σχολαστικός 7
ἱπποκόμος 3	ταβελλίων 10
καλλιγράφος 1	τροφός 1
κουρεύς 2	ὑπογραφεύς 4
	φροντιστής 1

PUBLIC SERVICES, NON-GOVERNMENTAL

βαλανεύς 1	πυργοφύλαξ 3
γραμματηφόρος 7	ῥιπάριος 5
θυρουρός/φρουρός 4	ῥωγευτής 1
νεκροτάφος 1	ταφρωρύχος 1
ποταμίτης 1	φύλαξ 9

CHURCH SERVICES

ἀναγνωστής 6	παραμονάριος 1
διάκονος 18+6	πρεσβύτερος 79+83
ἐπίσκοπος 1	στυλίτης 1
μοναχός/μονάζων 31 m., 2 f.	ὑποδιάκονος 2
οἰκονόμος 2	ψαλμῳδός/ψάλτης 1+1

THE CIVIL SERVICE[4]

ἀπαιτητής 5	κριτής 1
βερεδάριος 34*	λογευτής 1
βοηθός 15	μαγίστηρ 2
δεσποινικός 1	πολιτευόμενος 10[5]
δικασπόλος 1	πρυτανεύς 1
διοικητής 7	ῥεφερενδάριος 1
εἰρηνάρχης 1	σιτομέτρης 4
ἔκδικος 4	σύνδικος 4
ἐμβολάτωρ 1	τίρων 1
ἐμβολάρχης 3*	τοποτηρητής 4
ζυγοστάτης 2+4	υποδεκτης 10+5
κελλάριος 3*	χρυσυποδέκτης 1+4
κῆρυξ 2+2	ὑπουργός 26*
	χαρτουλάριος 12

THE MILITARY, AND MILITARY OFFICIALS

ἀκτουάριος 2
ἀπλικιτάριος 1
ἀποπραιπόσιτος 3
ἀρχίφρουρος 1
βικάριος 5
δομεστικός 3
εἰρηνικός 2
ἐξκέπτωρ 1
ἐξπελλευτής 3
ἐπιμελητής 1
καγκελλάριος 1
καστρησιανός 2
κελλάριος 3
κηνσίτωρ 4
κομμενταρήσιος 7
κομμωνίτωρ 1
μαγιστριανός 3
νουμεράριος 3
ὀπτίω(ν) 2
ὀφ(φ)ικιάλιος 2
ὀρδινάριος 1
παλατῖνος 1
πραιπόσιτος 1
πράκτωρ 4
πριμικέριος 2
προρουράτωρ 4
σιγγουλάριος 18
σκρινιάριος 3
σπαθάριος 1
στατιωνάριος 1
στρατίαρχος 5
στρατιώτης/στρατηλάτης 23+27
στρατιωτικός 6
σύμμαχος 12*
ταβουλάριος 1
τακτόμισθος 1
ταξιώτης 2
τεταγμένος κ. Ἀφρ. 1
τοξοδαλμάτης 1
τρακτευτής 4
τριβοῦνος 1
φαρανίτης 4

FOOD:

GATHERING

ἀγρευτής 1
κύρτος 1

SALE OF FOOD

ἁλοπώλης 1*
ἀρτοπράτης 1
κυμινοπώλης 4
λαχανοπώλης 1
ὀρβιοπώλης 9+2
φοινικοπώλης 1
χεδριοφόρος (?) 1

SALE OF STAPLE COMMODITIES:

ἐλαιοπώλης 2
οἰνοδεσπότης 1
οἰνοπράτης 6

SALE OF FOODSTUFFS BY MAKERS:

ζυτουργός 1
καθαρουργός 16+2
μάγειρος 9
χοιρομάγειρος 3
μυλωνάρχης/-ος 4

TEXTILES

γέρδιος 5*
λινοϋφος 5+2

CLOTHING

βαφεύς 2+7
γναφεύς 8+5
καυνακοποιός/-π`.κος 2

ῥάπτης 4+4
σκυτεύς 3+4

CRAFTS

ἀργυροποιός 1*
ἀσπιδοποιός 3*
ἐργαστηριακός 1
ἐργάτης 56*
κεραμεύς/κεραμοπλαστής 3
σελλοποιός 4*
σιβένινος 19*
σιδηρεύς 8*

σιδηροχαλκεύς 5
συντεχνίτης 2*
τεχνίτης 1+29
τυλάριος 2
χαλινάριος 4*
χαλκεύς 11
χειρότεχνος 3
χρυσοχόος 13

BUSINESS

ἐξωπυλίτης 1*
ναύκληρος 1
πιστικός 25*

πραγματευτής 18
τραπεζίτης 1*
χρυσώνης 2

BUILDING TRADES

γλύπτης 1*/γλυφευτής 2
λατόμος 1
μηχανάριος 1
μυλοκόπος 2
οἰκοδόμος 6+5
πισσουργός 1

πλινθευτής 1
πλινθοποιός 1
τέκτων 11+7
τροχοβόλος 1
ὑδραγωγός 1

RIVER TRADES

καλαφάτης 21*
κυβερνήτης 3
ναυπηγός 3*
ναύτης 1+54

πακτωνοποιός 7
πακτωνοπράτης 3*
πολυκωπικός/-ίτης 7

BASIC PRODUCTION**

αἰγοβόσκος 1
μηλονόμος 1
ἀμπελουργός 2
ἀρωτρητής 1
γεωργός 71
ἐλαιοκόμος 2
ἐλαιουργός 6+6
καμηλίτης 9+3

μελισσουργός 7
ὀνηλάτης 2
ποιμήν 37
ποιμὴν καὶ ἀγροφύλαξ 19+2
πρίστης 12*
πωμαρίτης 1
ταυρηλάτης 2

** This does not include, of course, all the persons listed (e.g. in a tax register like *P.Flor.* III 297), giving no occupation, whom one assumes to be γεωργοί. This does not alter the picture given by the final table.

Grosso modo this gives the following rough breakdown:

landowning class	76	5 %
services, excluding church	156	10.6%
church	239	16 %
civil service	172	11.6%
military	174	11.8%
food: production and sale	250	17 %
textile and leather	51	3 %
crafts	165	11.2%
business	48	3 %
building trades	41	2.8%
river trades	99	6.7%

Patterns of occupation

More study has been devoted to the activities of trades on the great estates of Late Antique Egypt[6] than has been done on a place-by-place basis. A few observations can be made about specific occupations and the role they played in the life of the community of Aphrodito.

A pattern similar to that in the very different agricultural conditions of Syria[7] seems to have obtained in Egypt, at least in our area: jobs connected with the olive-oil industry tended to run in families (whether legally obliged to do so or not is unclear). In sixth-century Aphrodito we find the families of Victor and of Hermauos and Elisabeth engaged in this trade. Victor, ἐλαιουργός in *P.Flor.* III 297.134, is the father of Mousaios and Psaios, ἐλαιοκόμοι in *P.Flor.* III 297.421 and 297.130 respectively. Elisabeth the ἐλαιοπώλισσα (see Youtie/Hagedorn in *ZPE* 7 [1971] 30; cf. *BL* VI 26) of *P.Cair.Masp.* III 67287 IV 23 and her husband Hermauos of *P.Flor.* III 285.6, ἐλαιουργός, are the parents of the ἐλαιουργοί Aur. Kyriakos and Matthaios, of *P.Flor.* III 285.6 (A.D. 552) and *P.Vatic.Aphrod.* 6.3 respectively. A three-generation family of oil-workers is found in the eighth century, all ἐλαιουργοί: the elder Pnei (*P.Lond.* IV 1420.134 [A.D. 706] and 1552.2) and his son Leontios (*P.Lond.* IV 1420.142) are followed by Leontios's son Pnei (*P.Lond.* IV 1562.4), according to the most common naming-pattern found in Egyptian society. An ἐλαιουργεῖον was located on Isis Street in Aphrodito in the mid-sixth century (*P.Flor.* III 285.11): perhaps the dwellings of these workers were located near it, as in Syria (cf. Tchalenko *Villages* I.409-410).

For the textile industry, in the sixth century we find three generations of dyers in the persons of Poulos or Paulos son of Horus (*P.Cair.Masp.* III 67288 II 14) and his son Mousaios son of Paulos (*P.Cair.Masp.* II 67134 v 1). In the eighth century, Philotheus, βαφεύς in *P.Lond.* IV 1459.20, is followed by his two sons Paulos and -ol (*P.Lond.* IV 1454.8 and 1558.9 respectively). Dyeing was in traditional Egyptian opinion a disagreeable profession; perhaps this quality of undesirability contributed to confining the craft within families.

In small retail trade, Martes son of Mousaios in the sixth century (*P. Cair.Masp.* II 67146.2), κυμινοπώλης, and his wife Thekla are the parents of Aur. Mousaios, again named for his grandfather (*P.Cair.Masp.* III 67328 IV 30 and VII 4, 24, A.D. 521), also a κυμινοπώλης. This pattern in small business is far from unexpected in a village society.

About the church, a sizeable piece of the city, and its personnel it is unfortunately difficult to say anything concrete. I can discern no patterns in which priests tend to be related to other priests and/or to clerics in minor orders or monks. The names borne by these people for the most part are so common as to rule out identification. In the present stage of research it is also too early to make observations about the origins and social status of clerics in late antique Aphrodito[8]. (Or, indeed, about possible relationship between social status and Chalcedonianism or non-Chalcedonianism. There appear to be no hard and fast boundaries.) Victor son of Besarion[9] was a bilingual aristocrat, a member of the first family of Aphrodito, first cousin to the lawyer and poet Dioscorus; other priests were illiterate, though a cleric can appear as ὑπογραφεύς for an illiterate non-cleric.

An occupation that is not found at Aphrodito is anything to do with the making and, indeed, the distribution of papyrus. A local factory could have existed[10], and the characteristic physical appearance of most especially sixth-century papyri from Aphrodito argues local manufacture (the locality may of course have been located not within the city itself). But evidence is lacking.

Monastic establishments in the Aphrodito area (see below) must also have had their characteristic occupations. The same trades appear in the Pachomian writings[11]: tailor, smith, carpenter, dyer, tanner, cobbler, gardener, copyist, camel-driver, weaver, palm leaf mat maker. A monastery too was a village, or a city.

Nothing is said in the documents about the free/unfree status of people in these small trades and occupations. Nothing exists in Late Antique Egypt remotely like a document of *commendatio*[12]. The notion of **ϭⲁⲩⲱⲛ** as a status category in Coptic law still needs explication[13]. Between the structure of texation at Aphrodito and the network of clientage and dependence, connections still remain to be drawn.

Patterns of landholding

From the Freer papyri especially, we can obtain a good picture of how great and small monasteries owned land in many farmsteads *(topoi)* and received rents in money and in kind. The Aphrodito area was dotted with as many as 66 monastic establishments[14], not to mention the six at Antinoe[15]. A survey of monastic landholding at Aphrodito may complement the work already done on the economic activities of churches[16].

The well-known monastery of Apa Sourous[17] owned land in twenty *topoi*, as follows:

Topos	*P.Freer*
Abakit	1.7.29
Abaktou	2.2.24
Atretos	1.3.32
...esh	2.2.31
Ide...	1.5.10
Isakiou	1.3.27-28
Karour	1.5.11
Khinanemph	2.1.31
...oriou	1.7.19
...ostrakinou	1.7.20
Pareitos	2.1.27
Phanaom	1.7.18
Pheneos	1.7.16, cf. 14
Poimenos	2.2.26, 27
Psebetos	1.3.31
Psin	1.7.1
Psintase	2.1.24, 2.2.1
Romanos	2.2.17
.sir.os	1.5.9
Tilampon	1.6.10

Holdings of land are attested for other Aphrodito monasteries as well:

Apa Zenobios

Topos	*P.Freer*
Kalau	2.1.23
Parab/ Leonidon	2.2.6-7
Pherko	2.2.19-20
Pilemonos	2.1.21
Promauotos	2.1.33
Syladokon	2.1.7-8
tou Anachoretou	2.1.3-4

This monastery also rents an unnamed holding to a doctor, *P.Freer* 1.6.27.

Monastery of Sminos

Alapame	2.2.3
Makariou Harpokra	2.2.3
Psoiou Paniskou	2.2.5

Monastery of Porbeos

Psauman	2.3.1

An institution often noticed in Late Antique Egypt is the growth and function of the church as a landholder. The prosperity of the monasteries of the Aphrodito region can be discerned from the extent of these holdings as recorded in the documents. The rents from holdings of the monastery of Apa Sourous alone come to more than 137 art. grain (some amounts are lost), besides oil and wine.

Continuity and change

There is little evidence across the hundred years of transition to the Arab period. Dated papyri are as follows:

582/602	*P.Michail.* 55
585	*P.Cair.Masp.* I 67111
after 585?	*P.Cair.Masp.* III 67325 (1 leaf)
585/600	*P.Mich.* XIII 664
589 (date uncertain)	*SB* VI 9144
598	*P.Vatic.Aphrod.* 1
613-641	*P.Mich.* XIII 665
685/705	*P.Lond.* IV 1447
699/705	*P.Lond.* IV 1412[18]

There is no real evidence to tell us how Aphrodito weathered the wrenching storm of the Arab conquest[19]. We may assume that personal freedom of movement still was within the grasp of the ordinary inhabitant of the Upper Egyptian nomes (cf. *P.Bu.*). This period saw changes in occupation at the village and city level: as has been seen from the first set of tables, certain occupations cease after the sixth/seventh centuries, while others are found only in the eighth.

The following occupations and titles are attested at Aphrodito only after the conquest:

ἁλοπώλης	ναυπηγός
ἀργυροποιός	πακτωνοπράτης
ἀρχισταβλίτης	πιστικός
ἀσπιδοποιός	πρίστης
βερεδάριος	σελλοποιός
γέρδιος	σιβένινος
γλύπτης	σιδηρεύς
ἐμβολάρχης	σύμμαχος
ἐξωπυλίτης	συντεχνίτης
ἐργάτης	τραπεζίτης
καλαφάτης	ὑπουργός
κελλάριος	χαλινάριος
λογογράφος	ψάλτης

The Latinate Justinianic bureaucracy has withered away. But the new *veredarii*, with their Latin title, are all Arabs (see *P.Lond.* IV, Index of Persons, and Bell, *P.Lond.* IV pp. xxiv-xxv), couriers of the *cursus publicus* which was to be put firmly in the hands of the conquerors. Twenty such couriers are attested for Aphrodito. The κελλάριοι and the σελλοποιοί are Arabs: perhaps looking after the occupying troops. In the eighth century the new, Arabic-derived title ἀμαλίτης/-ται appears, apparently also for government carriers or porters. In *P.Lond.* IV 1447.140, 190 (A.D. 685-705) we meet the first Ἀραβικος νοτάριος attached to the governor's staff, at Aphrodito[20]; while the notaries for Greek and Coptic and the physician are Christians (cf. *P.Lond.* IV 1375.6-7, A.D. 711: ... και τῶν συνόντων ἡμῖν ὑπουργῶν Ἀράβων τε και Χριστιανῶν και διαφορῶν προσώπων ...). Of the παλλικάρια (attendants) of the governor (cf. Bell, *P.Lond.* IV p. 360), two are Arabs, one presumably a Copt, called Sisinnios (*P.Lond.* IV 1447.13).

In the post-conquest period at Aphrodito we of course meet the μαυλεύς, *mawla*, the client of a member of the new governing class[21]. A person with this designation always bears an Arabic name (22 are attested in the Greek and Coptic papyri) and usually represents himself or herself as being attached to the *symboulos* (governor). Much more work is needed to elucidate the fate of the old

Graeco-Coptic upper class, the skilled class, as its patterns of occupation and office-holding changed, and as its members entered upon new status categories while trying to make a successor form of the Late Antique patron-client relationship work for them. (For example, Coptic accountants were to be indispensable to the caliphate.)

What remains to be done is a survey of monastic landholding in the Aphrodito area in the period after A.D. 642. The great house of Apa Sourous, north of Aphrodito (cf. *P.Cair.Masp.* I 67087.6), is attested often in the tax codex of *post* A.D. 716, *P.Lond.* IV 1419, under the designation '*ousia* of Apa Sourous'. Holdings in the *topos* of Phanaom (Phanaϩom) reappear, attested as follows, with assessments:

Topos name	*P.Lond.* IV 1419 line	Amount
Phanaom	1143	1 nom. 8¼ ker.
Phanaom kai Keratas	1149	1 nom. 8¼ ker.
" " "	1152	3 nom. 19¼ ker.

Other eighth-century *topoi* attested for this monastery are: Baphe, Kertout, Paniske(i), Piene, Pine (*sic*), Plan, Pnam, Teiae, and Teneete Patei, total assessment (amounts preserved) coming to almost 13 solidi (12 nom. 22 1/12 ker.). The monastery of Apa Sourous may also be the place of origin of P.Yale inv. 1804, a 32-leaf monastic account-book apparently shortly post-conquest in date.

Other survivals are the monasteries of Psempnouthios (*P.Freer* 2.1.10; *P. Lond.* IV 1419.363, 1002; in the sixth century it is listed for a rent of 6 art. grain plus 3/4 art. reeds; in the eighth, it is taxed at 15 art. grain and the large money sum of 35 nom. 13½ ker.), Taroou or Tarouth (*P.Freer* 1.2. 27, 30, 32, 33 and *P.Lond.* IV 1419.639, 1144, 1150, 1153; sixth-century figure 29 art. grain; eighth century, for the *topoi* Neon Ktema and Son of Collu-thus/Piah Kollouthou, 4 nom. 7 ker.), and Pharoou, apparently administered by the family of Dioscorus in the sixth century (*P.Michail.* 40.9; *P.Cair.Masp.* II 67176 recto + P.Alex.inv. 689; *P.Cair.Masp.* III 67353 recto: the last three are in Coptic).

If we can take the unusual name Psimanobet as a clue (cf. Maspero/Drioton, *Baouit* [Cairo 1932] Inscr. 128, ⲯⲓⲙⲁⲛⲱⲃⲉⲧ ⲡⲣⲙⲭⲏⲕⲟⲟⲩ; cf. the spelling Ψιμπανοβετ in *P.Cair.Masp.* II 67150.2, 7 and the commentary on *P.Freer* 1.7.4-5; the spelling Ψιβανοβετ occurs in the eighth century), the family of Dioscorus the poet continued into the reign of Heraclius (Maria, wife of Jacob, and Enoch are children of one Psimanobet in *P.Mich.* XIII 665). It can be discerned to have survived in the Arab period as well: in *P.Lond.* IV 1419.527, 539, 550, 906 the total assessment for one Psimanobet comes to 20 art. grain plus 15 nom. 15¼ ker. Between A.D. 641 and 716 evidence is lacking[22].

When a complete guide to the Aphrodito archives is made (the currently projected one will be limited to the sixth/seventh century material), it will of course include a prosopography of who was who, with attestations and dates. With such a tool to aid research, it will become easier for the present-day scholar to map out the nexus of existence that encompassed the inhabitants of Aphrodito. It is hoped that the realities of what it was like to be human in this Late Antique city will be more clearly seen and felt by those who take the trouble to examine the documents[23].

NOTES

1. H.I. Bell in *JEA* 4 (1917) 86-106. I should like to note here that Professor James Keenan and I came to our reading of Le Roy Ladurie quite independently!

2. *Pauvreté économique et pauvreté sociale à Byzance, IVe-VIIe siècle* (Paris/ The Hague 1977) 159-163.

3. The principal sources are: *P.Cair.Masp.; P.Flor.* III; *P.Lond.* IV and V; *P. Mich.* XIII; *P.Michail.; P.Ross.-Georg.* IV; *P.Vatic.Aphrod.;* and *P.Freer,* the papyri originally in L.S.B. MacCoull, *Greek and Coptic papyri in the Freer Gallery of Art* (Diss. Catholic University 1973) (to be republished by Jean Gascou and MacCoull in *Travaux et mémoires* [Paris]). This list is not complete: there are many Aphrodito papyri in other, minor collections (see J. G. Keenan in this number of *BSAC*, p.). J. Gascou has now (June 1983) compiled a complete listing of all Byzantine Greek papyri from Aphrodito, alphabetical by collection. For a few brief notes on Aphrodito, see Jones *LRE* II.847-848; Braunert, *Binnenwanderung,* 327-328.

4. On this and the following section see the thought-provoking remarks of T.F. Carney, *Bureaucracy in traditional society: Romano-Byzantine bureaucracies viewed from within* (Lawrence, Kansas, 1971) I.78-83, II.47-76, 117ff., 176 ff. (I owe this reference to the kindness of Professor E.A. Judge of Macquarie University.)

5. See now H. Geremek, 'Les πολιτευόμενοι égyptiens sont-ils identique aux βουλευταί?,' *Anagennesis* 1 (1981) 231-247.

6. E.R. Hardy, *The large estates of Byzantine Egypt* (New York 1931) 122-132; see now J. Gascou, *Les grands domaines, la cité et l'Etat en Egypte byzantine (5e, 6e et 7e s.)* (Paris, to appear) [Now published, Travaux et Memoires 9 (1985) 1-90.]
7. G. Tchalenko, *Villages antiques de la Syrie du nord* (Beirut 1953-1958) I.372-373, 407-410.

8. What needs tp be done is a work along the lines of R.W. Mathison, *The ecclesiastical aristocracy of fifth-century Gaul: a regional analysis of family structure* (Diss. Wisconsin 1979).

9. Cf. L.S.B. MacCoull, 'Documentary texts from Aphrodito in the Coptic Museum *SOCC* 16 (1981) 205-206. (These texts should be ascribed to the second find at Aphrodito, that of 1905.)

10. Cf. N. Lewis, *Papyrus in classical antiquity*^{2} (Oxford 1974) 116-117.

11. L.Th. Lefort, ed., *Oeuvres de S. Pachôme et de ses disciples (CSCO* 159-160, Scr.Copt. 23-24) (Louvain 1956).

12. M. Bloch, *Feudal society* (Chicago 1968) 262; cf. J.G. Keenan, 'On village and polis in Byzantine Egypt,' *Proc. XVI Intl.Congr.Papyrol.* (Chico 1981) 479-485. Highly unsatisfactory is B. Bachrach, 'Was there feudalism in Byzantine Egypt?,' *JARCE* 6 (1967) 163-166.

13. Cf. A. Steinwenter, *Das Recht der koptischen Urkunden* (Munich 1955) 16-17.

14. P. Barison, 'Ricerche sui monasteri dell'Egitto bizantino ed arabo secondo i documenti dei papiri greci,' *Aegyptus* 18 (1938) 95-122 for Aphrodito; A. Calderini, *Dizionario dei nomi geografici e topografici dell'Egitto greco-romano* I.2 (Madrid 1966) 325-335 for Aphrodito. These two works urgently need both to be updated and to be supplemented by Coptic evidence.

15. P. Barison 1938 (previous note) 86-90 for Antinoë.

16. E. Wipszycka, *Les ressources et les activités économiques des églises en Egypte du IVe au VIIIe siècle (Pap.Brux.* 10) (Brussels 1972).

17. *P.Mich.* XIII 667 and the references cited by Sijpesteijn p. 89.

18. Cf. R.S. Bagnall/K.A. Worp, *The chronological systems of Byzantine Egypt* (Zutphen 1978) 127-128 and the addenda et corrigenda.

19. Cf. W.H.C. Frend, *The rise of the Monophysite movement* (Cambridge 1979) 358.

20. *P.Lond.* IV preface p. xli n.

21. See P. Crone, *Slaves on horses* (Cambridge 1980) 49ff. and n. 349; one looks forward to the appearance of her work on late Roman and Arab clientage. [See now P. Crone, *Roman, Provincial and Islamic Law* (Cambridge 1987)]

22. A street in sixth-century Aphrodito was named 'the street of the house of the old man Psimanobet, the ancestor' (i.e. Dioscorus's great-grandfather): *P.Lond.* V 1691.5-6, cf. Calderini *Dizionario* I.2.323-324.

23. I should like to thank Klaas Worp, James Keenan, and Robert Markus; and the libraries of the German Institute and the Franciscan Centre, Cairo.

XXI

ADDITIONS TO THE PROSOPOGRAPHY OF APHRODITO FROM THE COPTIC DOCUMENTS

For eighty years historians have been well informed about the life and institutions of Aphrodito (Coptic Jkow, modern Kom Ishgaw), a community that flourished between the fifth and the eighth centuries, thanks to major finds of papyri between 1901 and 1905. These papyri were, as one would expect the records of a bilingual society to be, written in both Greek and Coptic. But unfortunately, nearly all the Aphrodito documents published, with the exception of some eighth-century tax records and the like, have been the Greek ones only. The Coptic remain unknown. Indeed, in describing the *Nachlass* of Lefebvre's finds that came to the Egyptian Museum in 1905, the preface to *P.Cair.Masp.* III (1916) states that the late Jean Maspero left behind him from the Lefebvre material 'some boxes ... containing *only* Coptic papyri.' [Emphasis added.] These boxes have not yet been found. The Museum *Journal d'entree* shows that no numbers were ever assigned to them; the *Registre provisoire* entry corresponds to no known place; and efforts to search the storage areas have been obstructed by the administration. But from unread material and from some items that fortunately found their way safely abroad we can glimpse at least a few more transactions conducted by the inhabitants of sixth-century Aphrodito, this time in Coptic.

The first group consists of *P.Cair.Masp.* II 67176^{r}, a *parachoresis* or cession of land in Dioscorus's hand, joined with its lower half P.Alex. inv.689; and *P.Cair.Masp.* III 67353^{r}, an arbitration (*mesiteia*), not in Dioscorus's hand but paralleling *P.Lond.* V 1709, an arbitration that deals with different people. The second group are Coptic papyri in the Vatican Library, presented in 1961 by Jean Doresse after they had disappeared in the process of transfer to the Coptic Museum and been sold on the antiquities market. They are known under the siglum *P.Vaticani Copti Doresse*.

First, the family and transactions of Mesiane. *P.Cair.Masp.* II 67176/ Alex.inv. 689 and *P.Cair.Masp.* III 67353 are both concerned with legal actions involving Anoup son of Apollo and Julius son of Sarapammon, and their mother (ⲧⲉⲩⲙⲁⲁⲩ) Mesiane. This last is an unusual name, recorded only once, in ST 264.7, a letter about *misthosis* mentioning an Apa Sarapion. No place or date are given by Crum for the ST text, but a deacon Sarapion is mentioned in *P.Cair.Masp*. III 67288 IV 34, where he pays 3 solidi (no date given). Hence the ST document may possibly be also from Aphrodito. An Abba Anoup, perhaps the same man after having entered the monastic life (a passage treated in these documents), figures in *P.Cair.Masp*. III 67342. Julius is harder to place: the only Sarapammon known at Aphrodito was the man who was involved in a murder case in *P.Mich*. XIII 660 and 661 (of A.D. 543/4?)[1]. Representing the monastery's side in the transactions of this group is one Apa Papnoute: he appears thirteen times. Hitherto no ecclesiastic by this name has been known at Aphrodito.

P.Cair.Masp. III 67353^{r} is, as has been said, an arbitration: it begins with the exact same phrase as *P.Lond*. V 1709: ⲕⲁⲧⲁ ⲙⲉⲥⲓⲧⲉⲓⲁⲥ ⲧⲣⲟⲡⲟⲛ ⲁⲓⲥⲱⲧⲙ ⲉⲑⲩⲡⲟⲑⲉⲥⲓⲥ ⲛ̄..., *viz*. 'I have heard the depositions of the following witnesses:' and continues with their names: 'Paulos son of X., Theophilos, priest and monk, Chrestes son of Paham, and Leontios son of Apollo.' None of these four can be identified with anyone previously known at Aphrodito. Without a patronymic Paul cannot be further identified with the bearers of this name in Girgis's *Prosopografia* (a work which badly needs to be replaced) and *P.Vatic.Aphrod*.; perhaps we should also think of the Paul who is the bridegroom of Patricia in Poem 24 Heitsch of Dioscorus of Aphrodito[2]. Theophilos and Chrestes remain unidentified. A soldier named Leontios and a *singularius* of the same name both appear in *P.Cair.Masp*. III 67287 (no date), paying 2½ and 3 keratia respectively, but the identifications cannot be made. We should note that *P.Cair.Masp*. III 67353^{r} mentions a fifteenth indiction (A.D. 566), and the dating clause at the bottom of P.Alex.inv. 689 has been read by Professor K.A. Worp as yielding a date of 28.x.569. These two documents would thus span a time period of four consecutive years, A.D. 566-569. The arbitration hearing preceded the cession of land before Anoup and Julius became monks.

Second, the family and transactions of Tsyra. One Tsyra daughter of Sabine is a principal figure in *P.Vatic.Copti Doresse* 1, along with her late husband Christophoros son of Pesynthios (?) and their son David. A

Tsyra is mentioned in *P.Vatic.Aphrod.* 4.29, but there seems to have been some confusion in transcription involved: the Tsyra mentioned by a witness as being 'the aforementioned' may not be the same as, hence an error for, the Tirenat mentioned in 4.15; probably not, as Tirenat's patronymic is Phoibammon. The Greek document is quite fragmentary at its beginning, and all we can say is that perhaps the same person was mentioned in passing in the Greek, which is a sale of a house. The rest of the family members do not seem to be identifiable. Could the Colluthus son of Christopher mentioned in line 26 be the Aur. Kollouthos/Christophoros, a *syntelestes*, who figures in *P.Mich.* XIII 666.3? The witnesses to this document are Victor son of the late Phoibammon (also a witness to *P.Vatic.Copti Doresse* 5.45), Theodosios son of the late X., Victor Apater the priest, and John the *hegoumenos*. The notary is called George. Now we know of a Victor/Phoibammon who was priest of the holy catholic church of Apa Mousaios at Aphrodito in *P.Mich.* XIII 667.41-42; he is known from *P.Michael.* 40 (A.D. 540) and *P.Lond.* V 1661 (A.D. 553). Unfortunately the person here is not titled priest.

The next two do not suffer identification. For John the *hegoumenos*, all we can say is that an Apa John appears in *P.Cair.Masp.* III 67325 IIv 11 (A.D. 585), and two deacons called John in *P.Vatic.Aphrod.* The name is too common to permit going further. Also, although George is a common name, no notary called George signs a document previously known from Aphrodito.

A Colluthus is also mentioned in *P.Vatic.Copti Doresse* 5.2-3. He occurs twice together with the name apparently of his brother, Mark: Colluthus and Mark. It is interesting to observe that the names of a Colluthus and a Mark are joined in tandem in two poems of Dioscorus of Aphrodito, 17 Heitsch and 13 Heitsch; the former is addressed explicitly to Count Colluthus, the pagarch, son of Apa Dios, 'together with Mark, the judge', while the latter is also to Colluthus 'and Mark, the judge' (*dikaspolos*). The name Mark alone occurs in *P.Vatic.Copti Doresse* 5.9, and 'my late husband Mark' in 5.32-33. (A Mark signs in 5.50, but this is not the same person.) Even if this Mark were the pagarch treated in Dioscorus's encomia, he cannot be identified with the two bearers of this name in Girgis or the one in *P.Vatic.Aphrod.* Now it seems that the spouse of this Mark in *P.Vatic.Copti Doresse* 5 is Taham daughter of Promauo, of 5.42. A Taam is known from Syene (*P.Lond.* V 1723.15, A.D. 577), but not from Aphrodito.

Other names that occur in this collection of papyri are no more unusual than Jacob, John, Constantine, George: too common to admit of identification. There remains an Isakios, interesting in that that is the name of the bridegroom addressed in Dioscorus's epithalamium 23 Heitsch, called 'of a famous father' and 'strong of spirit'. Could this be the same as the Aurelius Isakios son of John who appears as a *ktetor* in A.D. 548 in *P.Cair.Masp*. III 67283 II 25? Probably not, as the epithalamium, probably from the 560s, would have belonged to an earlier stage of the person's career.

These two groups of Coptic documents alone, hitherto not integrated into the Aphrodito archive, yield a total of 27 names of persons (not counting patronymics), of whom perhaps eight have at least a possibility of identification. But most of these people are new to us. The projected 'Guide to the Aphrodito Archives' being planned by Professor Klaas Worp and his colleagues will, of course, be planned to include a complete and up-to-date prosopography of all residents at Aphrodito at various periods, with their attestations. I hope the information in this paper and in the other studies of Aphrodito Coptic material now being conducted will underline the importance of incorporating all of the available Coptic evidence into our knowledge of this important ancient city.

XXII

SINAI ICON B. 49: EGYPT AND ICONOCLASM

With one plate

Everyone dealing professionally with Late Antiquity, in whatever area, will sooner or later have to come up against the phenomenon of Iconoclasm. We have recently been reminded[1] that it is the cult of the saints even more than Christology that lay at the basis of iconoduly as a part of the fabric of human life (Peter Brown's epoch-making article on the holy man in JRS 1971 has itself generated in ten years what Brown himself has termed '... a respectable academic light industry'[2]). In the realm of pure art-history the experts remind us that icons were still being produced (and iconophile literature composed) under the caliphate, while the 'home provinces' were riven by controversy[3]. This paper will attempt to place Sinai icon B.49 of S. Mercurius within the historical context of eighth-century Umayyad Egypt, using both documentary[4] and literary[5] Coptic sources.

Only in 1956 did Vasiliev begin to ask the question of what was happening in those provinces lost to the Arabs[6]: and so far as Egypt was concerned what he principally did was to extract stories of persecution and revenge from Severus of Ashmunein's History of the Patriarchs (of which more has been published since, in an edition which we hope will be improved by the finding and incorporation of many more MSS. (the work of J. den Heijer, University of Leiden)). In the subsequent 25 years a great deal more Coptic evidence has become available, especially from the Pierpont Morgan MSS., and it is to this that we must turn later in this paper.

First, to clear up the matter of the inscription on Sinai icon B.49: ⲟ ⲁⲅⲏⲟⲥ ⲙⲣⲕⲩⲣⲏⲟⲥ. Weitzmann misinterpreted the inscription as owing its lack of an epsilon to acquaintance with Arabic (The Icons, p. 79). In fact the inscription is in Sahidic Coptic, in which language the merging of ⲉ with the 'murmur-vowel' or sh^{e}wa is perfectly easily indicated by omission in the spelling[7], with or without a visible supralinear stroke. (The vertical lettering precludes such a stroke here.) B.49 is one of the few icons Weitzmann will agree to attribute to a Coptic hand. Even without stylistic analysis, the simple fact just indicated would tell us that the work is Coptic.

B.49 would also appear to be the earliest known equestrian representation of S. Mercurius[8]. I suggest that Mercurius, the slayer of Julian the Apostate, became regarded in post-conquest popular piety as the defender of the increasingly anxious Christian inhabitants (so Meinardus in SOCC 15 (1972/3) 115: I agree). 'Mercurius' as a baptismal name in Egypt becomes popular only in the post-conquest period, as we see from the papyri[9].

Let us now ask the question of the <u>Sitz im Leben</u>, the use, of this particular work of art in the Egypt of the eighth century, the world we know from the account-books of <u>P.Lond.</u>IV. In the hagiographical sources we have many anecdotes relating how people felt about icons and what part they played in their lives. Orlandi has shown that most of the 'cycles' that may have come down to us in 9th-10th century MSS. were in fact composed, with great care as works of literary art and didactic purpose, in the seventh (spanning the trauma of the conquest) and eighth centuries, and reflect the historical realities of that time[10]. While the stories purport to be set in a sort of 'Early-Christian' (Constantinian/Theodosian) world, they display innumerable (and charming) retrojections of later historical conditions and the practices of a later age: To begin with the material associated with S. Mercurius himself[11]:

> 'And he (sc. Constantine) wrote it in every place that they should build ⲙⲁⲣⲧⲩⲣⲓⲟⲛ in the name of the holy ones in every ⲭⲱⲣⲁ and every ⲉⲡⲁⲣⲭⲓⲁ , and that they inscribe (ⲥϩⲁⲓ) the icons of the holy ones on ⲥⲧⲩⲗⲗⲏ and put them in their ⲁⲩⲗⲏ (pl.) and their bedrooms and their ⲉⲣⲅⲁⲥⲧⲏⲣⲓⲟⲛ for a ⲃⲟⲏⲑⲓⲁ for those in them, and they should pray to them (ⲙⲛ ⲛⲉⲧⲛⲁϣⲗⲏⲗ ⲛϩⲏⲧⲟⲩ). ... And so (ⲗⲟⲓⲡⲟⲛ) they depicted (ⲍⲟⲅⲣⲁⲫⲉⲓ) the image (ⲗⲟⲓⲙⲏ[ⲛ]) of S. Mercurius in many places in the city of Rome as a protector (ⲱⲥ ⲡⲣⲟⲥⲧⲁⲧⲏⲥ ⲛⲁⲩ).'(<u>Miracula</u> §13)

> 'After this the man called a wise ⲧⲉⲭⲛⲓⲧⲏⲥ and gave him ten pounds of choice gold and precious stones of great value to make (ⲥⲙⲓⲛⲉ) the ⲗⲟⲓⲙⲏⲛ of S. Mercurius with his ⲕⲟⲛⲧⲁⲣⲓⲟⲛ in his right hand. He caused it to be set (ⲧⲟϭⲥ) with diamond stones and caused to be made (ⲥⲙⲓⲛⲉ) also his likeness (ϩⲓⲕⲟⲛ) with gold and chrysolith stones ... And when he had made the ϩⲓⲕⲱⲛ he brought it to the church ... and put it in front of the ϩⲓⲉⲣⲁⲧⲓⲟⲛ (<u>Miracula</u> §39).

> (For making a new coffin for the body of Mercurius) '...And the head of the coffin (ⲙⲁ ⲛⲉⲛⲕⲟⲧⲕ), he fixed inside it (ⲁϥϣⲱϥⲧ ⲉϩⲟⲩⲛ ⲉⲣⲟⲥ) some images (ⲛϩⲉⲛϩⲓⲕⲱⲛ) with green stones the colour of leek, with three crosses of gold, with three ⲥⲫⲣⲁⲅⲓⲥ of silver.' (<u>Miracula</u> §45)

(Note the various Coptic words for 'icon' or 'image'[12].) This certainly sounds like the world of the late sixth/early seventh century[13] (cf. Orlandi's introduction p. 10: ' ... piuttosto la situazione dell' Egitto al tempo in cui fu redatto il testo primitivo.').

Another window on this world can be opened by examining the story of the widow Euphemia, a 'sub-plot' to the encomium on the Archangel Michael attributed to Eustathius of Thrace[14]. Euphemia says to her dying husband:

> (§23) 'I wish you to order a ⲍⲱⲅⲣⲁⲫⲟⲥ to ⲍⲱⲅⲣⲁⲫⲉⲓ me the ⲗⲓⲙⲏⲛ of the holy Archangel Michael, on a piece of wood: I shall put it in my bedroom, the place where I sleep, and you will give (or 'entrust') me to it (ⲛⲅⲧⲁⲁⲧ ⲉⲧⲟⲟⲧϥ) for safekeeping (ϩⲱⲥ ⲡⲁⲣⲁⲑⲩⲕⲏ), so that when you die it will watch over (ⲣⲟⲉⲓⲥ) me, and it will (2 fut.) save me from the ⲉⲡⲓⲃⲟⲩⲗⲏ of the Unjust One, that is the devil, and from every human temptation (ⲡⲉⲣⲏⲁ).' So (§25) ' ... a ⲍⲱⲅⲣⲁⲫⲟⲥ came and he instructed him to ⲍⲱⲅⲣⲁⲫⲉⲓ the image of the Archangel Michael on a tablet (ⲡⲟϭⲉ), and they gilded it with choice gold and precious stones whose value was great. ... And she rejoiced over it like one who has found great riches.'

And in the husband's death scene:

> (§27) '... He took her hand, he put it upon the hand of the holy Archangel Michael whose image was depicted (ⲍ.); he cried out saying: O Archangel Michael, ... behold, I give you Euphemia my wife now as a ⲡⲁⲣⲁⲑⲩⲕⲏ, so that you will watch over her ...' (§28) '... After these things she took the piece (f.) of wood with the ⲗⲓⲙⲏⲛ of the Archangel Michael inscribed (ⲥⲏϩ) on it, she put it (f.) in her bedroom where she slept; she continued offering it (f.) costly perfumes, with a lamp (ⲫⲁⲛⲟⲥ) before *him* (ⲙⲡⲉϥⲙⲧⲟ, m.) at all times, and she used to ⲡⲣⲟⲥⲕⲩⲛⲉⲓ before *him* (ⲛⲁϥ, m.) three times a day asking him to help her.'

Apparently the most loving possible gesture was to entrust the person you loved to the safekeeping of an icon.[15]

What reached Mount Sinai sometime in the iconoclast eighth century was not a gilded and jewelled *objet de grand luxe*, a Late Antique Fabergé, but a simple painted panel. There is some factual basis for the notions of 'impoverishment' and 'descent in quality' that get attached to later works of the art of the Copts: the conquerors kept themselves to themselves and appropriated the revenues; there was not gold to spare for precious images for those in a state of clientage[16]. Icon B.49 may possibly have been made as a presentation-piece for the fortress-monastery of Sinai. What I wish to emphasize is that this image was created by a human being whose society was in deep trouble, heavily threatened[17]. Far from being able to be distracted by notions of the 'uncircumscribability' of divine power, *baraka*, the eighth-century Christian Egyptian needed to open as many windows as possible upon the unseen, to have a very thin 'permeable membrane' through which divine grace could pass, to hold on tight to his or her 'invisible friends'. This mounted saint (with stirrups, note) with arrestingly concentric face, hair, nimbus, with accompaniments of fantastic foliage and animal, with his angel ally and his enemy (a disguise for the caliph?) under his feet, was depicted as a prayer for help in the midst of a society whose holy tradition was being placed under heavy stress — heavier, perhaps, than elsewhere. Syriac, e.g., survived as a spoken language; Coptic did not, and we still do not understand why. Here in the language of visual art is an indication of what life was like where people could not afford to argue about matters of the human soul's life and death.

Sinai icon B. 49: St. Mercurius

NOTES

*I should like to thank Archimandrite Dionysios on Sinai for greatly facilitating my studies; and, as always, Mirrit Boutros Ghali (Canticles 8:7).

1. N. Gendle, 'The role of the Byzantine saint in the development of the icon cult,' in S. Hackel, ed., *The Byzantine saint* (=*SSTS* 5) (London 1981) 181-186. Cf. *idem*, review of Ch. von Schönborn, *L'icône du Christ* (Fribourg 1976), *ECR* 10 (1978) 164: '... a concrete indication of the historical, political and social context of icon theory ...'

2. P.R.L. Brown, '*Mohammed and Charlemagne* by Henri Pirenne,' *Daedalus* 103.1 (Winter 1974) 25.

3. K. Weitzmann, *The monastery of Saint Catherine at Mount Sinai: The icons*, I: 6th-10th c. (Princeton 1976) 5, cf. 7.

4. Oaths on icons turn up already in sixth-century papyri: e.g. *P.Lond.* V.1674.73 (by Dioscorus of Aphrodito, *ca.* A.D. 570; on the verso is his Greek-Coptic glossary), ἔμπροσθεν τῶν ἁγίων ; cf. *P.Varsov.* 29, ἐπὶ ἱερά , interpreted as referring to images. Oaths by the saints (e.g. John, Ep 162; Phoebammon, ST 111) in Coptic documents imply the presence of an icon. See E. Seidl, *Der Eid im römisch-ägyptischen Provinzialrecht* II (=*MB* 24) (Munich 1935) 145 ff.

5. Essentially what I want to do here is in a small way what Sebastian Brock (who deliberately, of course given the nature of his study, left Coptic out of his field of reference) has done for Syriac in 'Iconoclasm and the Monophysites,' in A.A.M. Bryer/J. Herrin, edd., *Iconoclasm* (Birmingham 1977) 53-57. We badly need a corrective to the too-often-repeated old view of the 'Monophysite' distaste for pictures, e.g. R.J.H. Jenkins, *Byzantium: the imperial centuries* (London 1966) 81: '... the monophysites could never accept the making of images. ... they were also strongly opposed to Mariolatry...' (Late Antique people were *not* Low Church Anglicans.) *Contra*, S. Gero, 'Cyril of Alexandria, image worship, and the *vita* of Rabban Hormizd,' *OrChr* 62 (1978) 97 (with n. 109): 'The Coptic Church in the medieval era was decidedly iconophile...' (When is "medieval", though?) The old view unfortunately still appears in many standard textbooks, e.g. M. Cramer, *Koptische Buchmalerei* (Recklinghausen 1964) 93-94 (counterweighted at least by Kl. Wessel, *Koptische Kunst* (Recklinghausen 1963) 165, cf. 192).

6. A.A. Vasiliev, 'The iconoclastic edict of the Caliph Yazid II, A.D. 721,' *DOP* 9/10 (1956) 23-47.

7. For the phonology: F.T. Gignac, *A grammar of the Greek papyri of the Roman and Byzantine periods*, I: *phonology* (Milan 1976) p. 238 for ⲁⲅⲏⲟⲥ/ⲁⲅⲓⲟⲥ ; 237-239 for ⲓ > ⲏ ; on the basis of natural Coptic inter-

ference in the Greek of Egypt.

8. Cf. O. Meinardus, 'The equestrian deliverer in Eastern iconography,' OrChr 57 (1973) 142-155, and idem,'St. Mercurius - Abu's-Saifain: a study of cult and art,' SOCC 15 (1972/3) 107-119, pls. 18-23. Ninth- to eleventh-century representations are known: cf. J. Leroy, Les mss. coptes et coptes-arabes illustrés (Paris 1974) 184 ff. (pl. 105.1, caption reversed) and 188 ff. (pl. 106.1, wrong caption).

9. S.v. in F. Preisigke, Namenbuch (Heidelberg 1922, repr. Amsterdam 1967) and D. Foraboschi, Onomasticon alterum papyrologicum (Milan 1971) (for the Christian saint, that is, not the pagan god). We are handicapped by the lack of a Coptic Namenbuch (two are in progress), but see e.g. the indices of personal names in Crum/Steindorff KRU (eighth-century documents from Jême/Thebes) and Crum BM and Ryl (both pre- and post-conquest material). It does not seem possible to discern a regional preference for this name. It appears once in the Arsinoite (in a restoration), in J.M. Diethart, Prosopographia Arsinoitica I: S. VI-VIII (Vienna 1980) no. 3474 (with n. 448); 3 times at Aphrodito (P.Lond.IV); once at Apollonos Ano. At the present day there are thirty-two Coptic Orthodox churches in Egypt of the dedication of S. Mercurius (of which 5 are in Cairo, 2 in Alexandria, the rest scattered): S. Timm, Christliche Stätten in Ägypten (=Beih.z.TAVO B.36) (Wiesbaden 1979) 160. This makes Mercurius the fourth most popular saint in Egypt (after S. George, the Virgin, and S. Michael), and greatly outdistancing his other equestrian colleague S. Theodore Stratelates (tied with S. Mark at 19 each).

10. E.g. most recently in his paper 'Un testo copto sull'invasione araba dell'Egitto' at the II International Congress of Coptic Studies, Rome, 25 September 1980; and in 'The future of studies in Coptic biblical and ecclesiastical literature,' in R.McL. Wilson, ed., The future of Coptic studies (=CS 1) (Leiden 1978) 143-163, esp. 156, and 159: '... how the Coptic mind responded to the problems that existed during the eighth and ninth centuries.'

11. T. Orlandi/S. di G. Camaioni, Passione e miracoli di S. Mercurio (Milan 1976): review article by G. Godron, 'A propos d'un récent ouvrage concernant Saint Mercure,' IFAO Livre du centenaire (Cairo 1980) 213-223.

12. See G. Godron's forthcoming article on the etymology of Coptic λιμην, to appear in BSAC 25.

13. Cf. Averil Cameron, 'The artistic patronage of Justin II,' Byzantion 50 (1980) 62-84, esp. 83 on icons. See my forthcoming article on the panegyric by Dioscorus of Aphrodito on the icon of Justin II.

14. In T. Orlandi et al., *Quattro omelie copte* (Milan 1977).

15. The icon subsequently does all the appropriate things: confuting the devil, flying, exuding branches of olives (to eat which heals the sick) etc. For another flying Coptic icon cf. T. Orlandi, 'Un encomio copto di Raffaele arcangelo ("Relatio Theophili"),' *RSO* 47 (1972) 211-233.(dated to the 7th-8th centuries, p. 213). Miracles of healing by Coptic icons have been collected in the dissertation on healing in Coptic hagiography by Mme. G. Godron.

16. P. Crone, *Slaves on horses: the evolution of the Islamic polity* (Cambridge 1980) 55, cf. 29. Cf. M. el-Abbadi, 'The revenues of Egypt at the conquest,' paper at the XVI International Congress of Papyrology, New York 1980.

17. I.M. Lapidus, 'The conversion of Egypt to Islam,' *Israel OrStud* 2 (1972) 248-262 uses antiquated methodology and out-of-date narrative sources: no papyri at all. What is needed is an effort, for Umayyad Egypt, along the lines of R.W. Bulliet's *Conversion to Islam in the medieval period* (Cambridge (Mass.) / London 1979): perhaps beginning with an analysis of the names and lineages in the indices of *P.Lond.*IV, *P.Apoll.Anô*, the volumes of Grohmann, and the rest of the Kurrah ibn Sharik material. At any rate, what did happen in the eighth century before the rulers turned their backs on the Mediterranean? Coptic revolts: in A.D. 725/6, 739, 748/9-750/1 (Lapidus p. 256).More broke out in 752/3, 762/3, and 773, and the last was not until 832 (p. 257).

ADDENDUM

This is far from the last word, of course, on the Coptic connection on Sinai, and/or the light that artistic production within Egypt may throw on the period of Byzantine Iconoclasm. (I believe numerous art historians may be willing to consider an Egyptian origin for many of the eighth-century Sinai icons.) In the bindings of at least four of the Arabic codices in the Sinai library have been discovered stuffings, or stiffenings, in the manner of the Nag Hammadi binding cartonnage, made with Coptic, Greek, and Arabic documentary papyri and parchments. In a letter of June 1980 Professor A.S. Atiya of Utah confirmed to me that he had mounted at least one set of these binding materials under glass, but on my last trip to Sinai the mounts could not be located. (The MSS are: Ar. 131, Gospel lectionary ca. 13th c., with Arabic and Greek papyri; Ar. 161, Catholic Epistles and Acts, 12th c., with Arabic; Ar. 175, lections from the Catholic Epistles and Acts, A.D. 1225, with Coptic; and Ar. 190, Horologion, ca. 13th c., with Greek and Coptic. There may be more.) When these documents have been located and read, we will have more concrete facts about the making of, and what went into, the cultural life on Mount Sinai in a world polarised between Byzantine Iconoclasm on the one hand, and the growing Islamisation of Egypt and Syria/Palestine on the other. I hope the finding of such facts will be of use to cultural historians interested in placing these objects within their social context.

XXIII

The Coptic Cambyses Narrative Reconsidered

APART FROM A FEW individual encounters with particular philological problems,[1] no serious attempt at reevaluation of the text known as the 'Coptic Cambyses romance' ('narrative' would be a preferable term) has been made in more than thirty years.[2] Research in late antique social history has made scholars more aware of the communal, and especially historiographical, ambiguities of the non-Chalcedonian Eastern Mediterranean in what are viewed as the troubled years of Justinian's successors. Attention has recently been drawn to the divided Heraclian world as it faced the Islamic threat;[3] and, by implication, to special qualities in the literatures (and *Fachliteratur*) composed either for the Heraclian court or in the awareness of the imperial struggles. It is worth while to look at *BKU* I 31 in this context.

The transmission of an *unicum* in a MS. without known provenance must, without further evidence, remain dark. But a few notes on points already noticed by earlier scholars may help us to see our way better to new conclusions.

First of all, be it agreed that Cambyses' problematic nickname ⲥⲁⲛⲟⲩⲑ, "'cowardly', in our language," is of Syriac origin (Jansen 33): this will provide an important lead toward placing the story and its probable redactor.[4] A Semitic background is also invoked for the use of ⲉⲓⲣⲏⲛⲏ in the opening formula of (quoted) letters.[5] In point of

[1] *E.g.* W. Vycichl, "Was bedeutet 'Sanuth' im koptischen Kambyses-Roman? Ein weiteres Beispiel des *nomen agentis* qattāl im Koptischen," *Aegyptus* 36 (1956) 25–27.

[2] H. LUDIN JANSEN, *The Coptic Story of Cambyses' Invasion of Egypt: A Critical Analysis* (*AvhOslo* 1950.2), remains the standard, and about the only, work (cited hereafter by author's name alone).

[3] H. A. Drake, "A Coptic Version of the Discovery of the Holy Sepulchre," *GRBS* 20 (1979) 381–92, esp. 389–90, and in T. Orlandi, B. A. Pearson, H. A. Drake, *Eudoxia and the Holy Sepulchre: A Constantinian Legend in Coptic* (*Testi e Doc. Stud. Antich.* 67 [Milan 1980]) 162–66, 173–77.

[4] Not cited by Jansen is J. Schwartz, "Les conquérants perses et la littérature égyptienne," *BIFAO* 48 (1949) 65–80, esp. 75–78.

[5] Since the work of L. Dinneen, *Titles of Address in Christian Greek Epistolography to 527 A.D.* (Washington 1929), we have the excellent studies of H. Zilliacus, *Unter-*

fact, a look at Coptic documents of both pre- and post-conquest date will provide a picture of how frequently, and where, such usage is found alongside the more usual ϯϣⲓⲛⲉ, ϯⲁⲥⲡⲁⲍⲉ-plus-epithets formulae.[6] Apart from biblical quotations, 'peace' is found just as often at the close of a letter as in the greeting (*KOW* 300.21; *VC* 114.16, 22; 116.11). Crum noticed in 1939 (*VC* 100.1) that as a greeting it is found more often in texts (*e.g.* *BM* 546.1, 606.1, 1128.4, 1164.1, all greetings) from Ashmunein and the Fayum (this latter is borne out by Krall in *MPER* V 25, 35), not from the Thebaid. (Kahle attributed the instances in *Bal.* 256.5, 262.1 to Muslim writers!) Dating in these documents is often not explicit; but we cannot infer a post-conquest date just from the 'neutral' opening ⲉⲛ ⲟⲛⲟⲙⲁⲧⲓ ⲧⲟⲩ ⲑⲉⲟⲩ.

To reflect on Egyptian-Syrian contact in the period after the setting up of a separate, parallel non-Chalcedonian clerical structure[7] is to be led to the Syrian presence most visibly embodied in the later period in the Monastery of the Syrians, still extant today in the Wadi Natrun, and its relations with its country of origin and the outside world. What is now 'Deir-es-Suriani' originated as the doublet or 'Theotokos' monastery of St Bishoi's in the Gaianite controversies of the sixth century, and was restored in Benjamin I's patriarchate after *ca* 620.[8] There were monks in Scetis with Syriac educations in the troubled first half of the seventh century: troubled above all by a Persian invasion. Hence the Syriac nickname of Cambyses, and the preoccupation with 'Persian invaders'.

In such a late antique context we may perhaps explain the hitherto puzzling occurrence in the Cambyses narrative of the name ⲅⲁⲗⲗⲓⲕⲟⲥ (ⲛⲉⲣⲣⲱⲟⲩ ⲛⲅⲁⲗⲗⲓⲕⲟⲥ, "the kings of the Gauls," 6.15). Byz-

---

suchungen zu den abstrakten Anredeformen und Höflichkeitstiteln im Griechischen (Helsinki 1949), and "Zum Stil und Wortschatz der byzantinischen Urkunden und Briefen," in *Akten VIII. Int. Kongr. Papyrologie* (Vienna 1956) 157–65. From the New Testament point of view see J. L. White, *The Form and Function of the Body of the Greek Letter*² (Missoula 1972) and *The Form and Structure of the Official Petition* (Missoula 1972), with C. H. Kim, *The Form and Structure of the Familiar Greek Letter of Recommendation* (Missoula 1972).

[6] Still awaited is A. Biedenkopf-Zaehner, *Der koptische Brief* (to appear). Note that not every writer whose style, especially in a letter, contains biblical echoes is Semitic by background. [Now published in *Untersuchungen zum Koptischen Briefformular* (Würzburg 1983).]

[7] W. H. C. Frend, *The Rise of the Monophysite Movement* (Cambridge 1979) 274–76, 283–95; D. D. Bundy, "Jacob Baradaeus," *Muséon* 91 (1978) 45–86. P. Gray, *The Defense of Chalcedon in the East* (Leiden 1979), unfortunately stops at A.D. 553.

[8] H. G. Evelyn White, *The Monasteries of the Wadi 'n-Natrun* II (New York 1932) 316–18, 319–21. It is well to remember that the famous patriarch Damian (A.D. 578–607), in whose patriarchate so much Coptic literature was produced, was a Syrian by extraction.

antine relations with the Merovingians in the late sixth and early seventh centuries had been warmly complex since Justin II's truce with Sigibert of Austrasia (A.D. 571–3: see Dölger, *Regesten* I no. 24). Such a man as the poet Venantius Fortunatus moved easily about between both worlds. 'The kings of the Gauls' (*not* the 'Galatians' of Asia Minor, as Jansen 16) were hardly unknown figures to an Egyptian public, and most especially so since Heraclius' treaty with Dagobert in about 630 (Dölger, *Regesten* I no. 202).[9]

I would accordingly suggest an alternative set of hypotheses to explain the why and wherefore of this still-puzzling text. (By now it must be clear that the notion that the tale and/or its redactor cannot be Christian must be set aside.)[10] The redactor, I propose, was a Syrian monastic settler in Scetis during the patriarchate of Benjamin I, working in about the decade 630–640. Out of reminiscences of Herodotus (in very old school curricula), 'popular epic', and the Bible, and out of very real memories of the trauma of the Persian occupation of 617–627,[11] he stitched together a tale of warning for the Monophysite population, casting the character of 'Cambyses' as the villain to represent the real present threat, the Caliph 'Umar (died A.D. 634). (Syria fell to the Arabs in 637;[12] night was about to fall, albeit slowly, over what was left of late antique Egyptian polite culture.) No more frightening figure could be used than that of the traditional wicked Nebuchadnezzar/Cambyses fused with the all-too-recent apparition of Khosro II Aparvez.[13] The fable was a call to

[9] *Cf.* H. St L. B. Moss, *The Birth of the Middle Ages* (Oxford 1935) 198; J. Richards, *Consul of God: The Life and Times of Gregory the Great* (London 1980) 212–16; *Chron. Fredegar* 4.62–65 (*MGH SS.Rer.Merov.* II 151–53).

[10] Jansen 49 and 56 assigns the work to a second-century B.C. Jewish author. I believe the points raised in the present article will help to demonstrate the unlikeliness of this thesis.

[11] *Cf.* E. K. Chrysos, "The Date of Papyrus *SB* 4483 and the Persian Occupation of Egypt," *Dodona* 4 (1975) 343–48. It is a matter of great regret that there is no text volume to accompany the plates in J. de Menasce, *Ostraca and Papyri* (*CInscrIran* III.4–5 [London 1957]). On the whole question of invocations and their absence or presence under different regimes, see now R. S. Bagnall and K. A. Worp, "Christian Invocations in the Papyri," *Cd'E* 56 (1981) 112–33.

[12] M. A. Shaban, *Islamic History I (600–750)* (Cambridge 1977) 31; *cf.* P. Crone and M. Cook, *Hagarism* (Cambridge 1977) 88–91, with a highly controversial stress on 'ethnicity'.

[13] We know a good deal about relations between Egypt and other regions occupied by the Sassanian invaders, specifically John the Almoner's poor-relief for Palestine, as witnessed by the so-called ϵΤΜΟΥΛΟΝ ostraca: K. Galling, "Datum und Sinn der graeco-koptischen Mühlenostraka im Lichte neuer Belege aus Jerusalem," *ZDPV* 82 (1966) 46–56 and 239; *cf.* Frend (*supra* n.7) 339–40; and, earlier, G. R. Monks, "The Church of Alexandria and the City's Economic Life in the Sixth Century," *Speculum* 28 (1953) 353.

Egyptians, and in its wide appeal could have been heard even by Chalcedonians as well as their non-Chalcedonian countrymen.[14]

There is no 'Matter of Egypt'. Yet out of the epic material of the Bible and the classical curriculum of the schools, the unknown author of the Cambyses narrative constructed a cry of warning in the face of an unprecedented kind of invasion. But perhaps not quite unprecedented: the historical Cambyses had both invaded Egypt and cut it off from contact with Greek culture until the coming of Alexander. This writer of the Heraclian age was well aware that a second such break would be deadly. "Constantinople . . . and Alexandria spoke the same religious language . . . their chroniclers continued to live in a Byzantine world, as though . . . the Arab conquest was an interlude.[15] . . . key Christological terms . . . existed only in Greek."[16] Without the fruitful atmosphere of debate, the eloquence of the schools that was the very fabric of the late antique mind, the excellence in word that mapped out an excellence of spirit, survival alone awaited the later copyist and readers of the tale of Cambyses and 'the brave Egyptians' (8.23).[17]

[14] *Cf.* Drake (*supra* n.3) 391–92. For a much-needed corrective to earlier views of 'collaborationist Copts', see now J. Moorhead, "The Monophysite Response to the Arab Invasions," *Byzantion* 51 (1981) 579–91.

[15] Compare the oath-formula "by the health (ⲟⲩϫⲁⲓ) of our rulers" (ⲛⲉⲛϫⲟⲉⲓⲥ/ⲧⲉⲝⲟⲩⲥⲓⲁ/ⲛ̄ⲉⲣⲣⲱⲟⲩ [who rule over us] ⲕⲁⲧⲁ ⲕⲁⲓⲣⲟⲥ, "for the time being": E. Seidl, *Der Eid im römisch-ägyptischen Provinzialrecht* II (*MünchBeitr* 24 [1935]) 141–43.

[16] Frend (*supra* n.7) 357–58.

[17] I should like to thank the libraries of the German and French Archaeological Institutes at Cairo for help in preparing this paper; and, as always, Mirrit Boutros Ghali (*cf.* Haydn, *The Creation*, no. 24).

XXIV

EGYPTIAN ELEMENTS IN THE CHRISTUS PATIENS

The Euripidean cento which has come to have attached to it the short title Χριστὸς Πάσχων or *Christus Patiens*[1] has been variously dated and attributed since the early Renaissance[2]. Turn-of-the-century orthodox textual criticism, largely oriented toward using this text as a tool for Euripidies studies, has tended to ascribe the work to a twelfth-century Byzantine author[3]. The editor of the recent *Sources Chrétiennes* edition has revived scholarly debate by reaffirming support for the traditional attribution to Gregory Nazianzen[4]; while recent literary-critical study of the work has not entirely rejected this opinion[5]. In this paper I should like to examine the text of the *CP*, and in particular the 1100 lines out of 2600 that were not taken from Euripides but originally composed by the centonist, with a view to discovering further clues that may provide evidence for dating and localising the work.

A brief summary of the content of the *CP* will be in order. It falls into three principal sections or 'acts': the Passion, Entombment, and Resurrection of Christ, corresponding to the three days of the Paschal triduum. While the figure of the Virgin Mary functions in the foreground as protagonist[6], nearly all the biblical personages known to take part in the Gospel passion narratives are given a voice[7], in the manner of a Bach passion. A chorus (possibly more than one) plays its antique role, both commenting on the events and engaging in dialogue with the principal figures. The Virgin is informed by a messenger of the betrayal and condemnation of her Son, and brought to Calvary, where Christ entrusts John to her care. (The centonist does not attempt to render all of the 'seven last words'.) John, Joseph of Arimathea, and Nicodemus come to take Christ's body for burial, while the Virgin laments. After keeping vigil, she is joined by the Magdalen, and both proceed to the tomb where they find, first the angel, and then the risen Christ[8]. A messenger relates the supernatural events of the night and, in direct discourse, we hear the reactions of the soldiers, the chief priests, and Pilate. Finally, Christ appears to the holy women, proclaiming in his risen body his real presence and his gift of the Holy Spirit as a commission to the world. The work ends with a twofold prayer by the poet, first to Christ to redeem him from his sins, and then to the Virgin to protect him from evil and be his advocate before the judgement of her Son. The closing phrases of the piece are a salutation or *chairetismos* to Mary.

The thirty-line prologue to the drama especially repays close consideration. The author announces his intention to tell the Passion story κατ' Εὐριπίδην (1.3), in view of the hearer's veneration for the models of (classical) literature (ἀκούσας εὐσεβῶς ποιημάτων, 1. 1: there follows a semantic shift on εὐσεβῆ in 1.2; the writer loves plays on words). Now Homeric centos were common in Late Antiquity[9]: Euripidean were not. In view of the popularity of Euripides in Egypt as evidenced by the abundant papyri[10], and the range of plays drawn upon by the centonist (cf. Tuilier 1969:19-20), one begins to think of Egypt as a likely place of composition for the work[11]. Christ is styled ζωοποιός (1.21) and ζωοποιήσαντα (1.23), a characteristically Egyptian epithet for the persons of the Trinity[12]. The use of ἔνδικος (1.18) to describe divine judgement foreshadows the frequent use throughout the poem of terms characteristic of the 'legalese' of fifth- and sixth-century documentary papyri. And the language, as well as the doctrinal implications, of lines 24-25 is important: 'If the Logos had remained ἀκένωτος, she (Mary) would not have been the mother of the Δεσπότης.' (Almost a foreshadowing of 'Adam lay ybounden'.) 'Ακένωτος, a rare word, is used in the (pseudo-Apollinarian) *Metaphrasis Psalmorum,* 74:9, which has been demonstrated to be the work of a late fifth-century Chalcedonian Egyptian poet[13]. This is to be the first of many telling points of correspondence.

The epithet πάναγνος (1.29), used of the Virgin, is one of very many παν-compounds used throughout the work (in the original sections): e.g. πανδερκέστατον (1.1412), cf. Nonnus *Paraphr.Joh.* 12.165; παγκόσμιον (1.2111); πανόλβιον (1.2440), a favourite adjective of Dioscorus of Aphrodito (e.g. Heitsch XLII 12.1); πανένδικος (1.2543). The use of παν-compounds is a characteristic stylistic trick of Nonnus, his later follower Dioscorus of Aphrodito, and other 'wandering poets' of the Egyptian school of the fifth and sixth centuries[14]. Also similar to Dioscorus' practice of fancy compound formation is the *hapax* λαμπροπυρσόμορφος (l.2055): compare *P.Cair.Masp.* I 67097 F 17-26, e.g. 20 πρασινοπάντιμε λαμπρόβιε and the other compounds in the passage[15]. This sort of poetic language does not fit well in the fourth century[16]; it is known from fifth- and sixth-century Byzantine Egypt.

In line 187 the messenger styles Saint John Ἐπιστήθιος, the one who leaned on Jesus' breast. This is a very rare word: it occurs (in this meaning) first, it seems, in one of the homilies of that shadowy figure 'Eusebius of Alexandria' (*PG* 64.47A), a name attached to a collection of possibly fifth-century (or early sixth-century) Egyptian Greek sermons by the secretary John who collected them[17]. Little as we know of the exact historical milieu of the 'Eusebius' parallel, the occurrence is tantalising.

In line 1420 one encounters the odd phrase τὸ πρόσωπον τοῦ λόγου in the meaning of 'the point of what is being said'. This is a usage known from sixth-century documentary papyri: e.g. *P.Cair.Masp.* I 67057 II 29, from Aphrodito. Also characteristic of papyri of the period is the use of Latinisms drawn from the administrative 'officialese', and such words turn up in the *CP* as well: e.g. for κουστωδίας in line 2383 compare *P.Oxy.* II 294.20; *P.Ryl.* II 189.2; *BGU* II 341.3; *P.Aberdeen* 78.4 (these usages are, however, somewhat earlier)[18]. Likewise one finds ταχύδρομος (l.1952) (frequent in the *Dionysiaka),* which also evolves into an administrative title (e.g. *P.Oxy.* XXXI 2561.20). The impression gained is one of a writer familiar with usages that are at home in the world of the documentary papyri.

It seems clear that the epithet διφυής (in l.1795, μήτηρ τοῦ διφυοῦς) points to a Chalcedonian position on the part of the author. The term itself, being Cyrillian (Lampe *s.v.*), of course antedates the hardening of specific doctrinal positions and the setting up of separate parallel clergy structures. But it has roots in the Egyptian (and Jacobite) liturgical usage (*PG* 36.700, cf. 94.1473C), and is found in both the *Apophthegmata* and in documentary papyri (e.g. *P.Warren* 10.16). (Compare also the sense of *Metaphrasis Psalmorum,* προθεωρία 86, on the Incarnation.) We seem to be once again at home in late fifth-century Egypt[19].

A striking line which has attracted the attention of commentators is 2164: κακοῦ γὰρ ὑπόστασις οὐκ ἔνεστί τις. The line is really a trimeter condensation of a formulation long current in Athenian and Alexandrian Neoplatonic thought, especially rooted in Proclus' treatise *De malorum subsistentia* (ed. D. Isaac, Paris 1982): τὸ κακόν is a παρυπόστασις, not something that exists in and of itself. Just this sort of commonplace of the schools would come readily to the pen of a *doctus poeta* with an Alexandrian educational background (as in the case of Dioscorus of Aphrodito and his probable teacher John Philoponus). Ἐνειμί in this type of sense is also found in the Job commentary of the Alexandrian deacon Olympiodorus, who wrote *ca*. A.D. 500. Perhaps this fact furnishes another scrap of background.

The closing prayer to the Virgin (11.2572-2602), in its thirty lines balancing the thirty lines of the prologue[20], reaffirms the central importance in the *CP* of a developed Mariology[21]. (The Virgin herself proclaims her perpetual virginity [e.g. 11.67-68] and her painless childbirth [e.g. 11. 429, 987], concepts evolved in the early sixth-century Egyptian tradition[22].) Mary's assumption into heaven[23] is described metaphorically: ἀφθαρσίας...ἐστολισμένη (1.2575)[24]. Elements in this hymnlike prayer recall the empress Sophia's prayer to the Virgin in Corippus[25]; and are especially reminiscent of motives and invocations in the Coptic *Theotokias*[26], particularly those referring to the incarnation of the Word. The prayer ends with a supplication to the Virgin as advocate (πρέσβιν εὐπρόσδεκτον, cf. *P.Oxy*. VIII 1151) at the Last Judgement and protector from evils and torments: cf. *P.Ryl*. III 470 and the Der Bala-'izah liturgical papyrus. (The poet is almost prefiguring the ending of the *Stabat Mater*.[27])

From such evidence as the foregoing I believe it is possible to put forward the suggestion that the *Christus Patiens* was composed in Egypt in the late fifth or early sixth century, by a probably Chalcedonian author. Relationships with Nonnus (especially the *Paraphrase of the Gospel of John)* and the hexameter *Psalter Paraphrase* are easy to discern. Noticeable features of the vocabulary are shared with documentary papyrus usage. In late antique Egypt the infrastructure of classical literary and rhetorical education was certainly there: and why should the Monophysites have all the good tunes?[28]

NOTES

1. Variously in the MS tradition: τὸ σωτήριον πάθος or τὸ ... κοσμοσωτήριον πάθος of Jesus Christ.

2. A. Tuilier, 'La datation et l'attribution du Χριστὸς Πάσχων et l'art du centon,' *Actes VI*[e] *Congr.int. études byz.* I (Paris 1950) 403-409; F. Trisoglio, 'Il Christus patiens. Rassegna delle attribuzioni,' *RSC* 22 (1974) 351-423.

3. So Brambs' Teubner edition of 1885 and his Munich thesis (publ. Eichstatt 1883). This judgement was enshrined in Krumbacher.

4. A. Tuilier, *Grégoire de Nazianze, La passion du Christ* (=*SC* 149; Paris 1969). Reviewers, e.g. J. Grosdidier de Matons in *Trav. et Mém.* 5 (1973) 363-372, were not in agreement.

5. F. Trisoglio, *La passione di Cristo* (Rome 1979).

6. F. Trisoglio, 'La Vergine Maria come protagonista del Christus patiens,' *Marianum* 41 (1979) 199-266; *idem*, 'La Vergine ed il coro nel Christus patiens,' *RSC* 27 (1979) 338-373.

7. F. Trisoglio, 'I deuteragonisti del Christus patiens,' *Dioniso* 49 (1978) 11-187.

8. Cf. P. Bellet, 'Testimonios coptos de la aparición de Cristo resucitado a la Virgen,' *Estudios bíblicos* 13 (1954) 199-205.

9. Crusius in *PW* 3 (1899) 1929-1932; E.A. Clark, *The golden bough, the oaken cross* (Chico 1981) 5-6, 8=9, 102-105.

10. See especially B.E. Donovan, *Euripides papyri* (=*ASP* 5; New Haven/ Toronto 1969). More papyri have come to light since Donovan's study was written. On the use and re-use of Euripides in Egypt see C.H. Roberts in *Mus.Helv.* 10 (1953) 270.

11. For points of comparison in style cf. also the works discussed by Alan Cameron, 'Pap.Ant. III.115 and the iambic prologue in late Greek poetry,' *CQ* n.s. 20 (1970) 119-129.

12. E.g. in invocations: R.S. Bagnall/K.A. Worp, 'Christian invocations in the papyri,' *Cd'E* 56 (1981) 112-133, 362-365.

13. J. Golega, *Der homerische Psalter* (Ettal 1960). The term appears also in Isidore of Pelusium (and, later, in Sophronius). Tuilier's translation and note miss the point (as they do in many places).

14. Other Nonnianisms: γηθόσυνος (1.958), μυστήπολος (1.2171), αὐτόριζον (1.2397; parallels in *Paraphr.Joh.*)

15. See L.S.B. MacCoull, 'The imperial *chairetismos* of Dioscorus of Aphrodito,' *JARCE* 18 (1981, appeared 1984) 43-46.

16. Already in 1934 Albert Vogt, in a review of V. Cottas' *L'influence du drame 'Christos Paschon' sur l'art chrétien d'Orient* (Paris 1931), in *RQH* 1934.505-508, hypothesised an origin for the *CP* in early seventh-century Palestine, possibly the monastery of S. Saba. He thought the work might have been composed as an anti-monothelete tract. This is at least on the right sort of track.

17. D.J. Sheerin in *VigChr* 30 (1976) 16-17 with n.80; cf. J. Leroy in *Sacris Erudiri* 19 (1969-70) 46-47. M. Gronewald in *ZPE* 34 (1979) 22-25 has shown that *P.Lond.Lit.* 245 (provenance unknown) is to be identified as a piece of this corpus, and that the text was in a state of confusion already in the later sixth century. A possible set of *termini post* and *ante quem* could be provided by this papyrus. Cf. ἐπιστήθιος in the hymn reproduced in Pitra *Analecta sacra* 1.506 (dated by Maas fifth-sixth century).

18. S. Daris, *Il lessico latino del greco d'Egitto* (Barcelona 1971). Cf. κούστωρ in *P.Erlangen* 110.5.

19. The doctrinal point has been raised of the non-occurrence of the term θεοτόκος, and explanation given for metrical reasons: cf. A. Saija, 'La metrica di Dioscoro di Afroditopoli,' *Studi A. Ardizzone* 2 (Messina/Rome 1978) esp. 840-845 on trimeters. This is a dangerous argument from silence: a text as late as the eighth-century inscribed lintel of el-Moallaqa (see MacCoull, art. to appear in *ZPE*) has been dated to the period of Athanasius partly on the basis of the non-appearance of θεοτόκος. The concept is paraphrased in other words in the *CP* (e.g. 1.928). However, the question of metre in the *CP* is an important one. I think that on the basis of evidence like that collected in F.T. Gignac, *Grammar of the Greek papyri of the Roman and Byzantine periods* I-II (Milan 1976--), nearly all the phonological and other peculiarities noticed by critics (e.g. values of vowels, use of ἐν) can be accounted for in a way consonant with my Egyptian hypothesis. The language and metre are surely not Prodromic.[Now published in *ZPE* 64 (1986) 230-235. In this volume study XIV.]

20. The closing speech of the risen Christ (11.2504-2531) is also just under thirty lines (nearly all original: the two borrowed lines are from the *Bacchae*, an arresting transfiguration).

21. The incompatibility of the *CP* with a fourth-century milieu was noticed by J. de Aldama, 'La tragedia "Christus patiens" y la doctrina mariana en la Capadocia del siglo IV,' *Mélanges Danielou* (Paris 1972) 417-423, also on the basis of the highly developed Mariology.

22. G. Giamberardini, *Il culto mariano in Egitto* 1 (Jerusalem 1975) 236 (*P.Ryl.* III 467), 175-178. Cf. Ep 600.12-19. The use in the *CP* of the *Protevangelium of James* (11.563f., 1530) has been noticed (Tuilier 1969:67 with n. 3 - 68 with n.1). This is a work that originated in Coptic and was transmitted in that language.

23. Cf. A. Campagnano, *Omelie copte ... sulla Vergine* (Milan 1980) 151-195. Also noteworthy is the epithet in l.2576, ἀγήρως. For the feast in the sixth century cf. *P.Oxy*. XI 1357.45, the calendar of Oxyrhynchus. On the characteristic Egyptian identification of the Virgin Mary with 'the other Mary' at the tomb (Mt 28:1), as here in the *CP* (l.1989), cf. Campagnano's text, pp. 58-59.

24. Cf. S.P. Brock, 'Clothing metaphors as a means of theological expression in Syriac tradition,' in M. Schmidt et al., edd., *Typus, Symbol, Allegorie bei den östl. Vätern* (Regensburg 1982) 11-38. Also, Dioscorus of Aphrodito in *P.Cair.Masp*. I 67024 v 11: see L.S.B. MacCoull, 'The isopsephistic poem on S. Senas by Dioscorus of Aphrodito,' to appear in *ZPE*. The scriptural echo is 1 Cor 15:53, δεῖ γὰρ τὸ φθαρτὸν τοῦτο ἐνδύσασθαι ἀφθαρσίαν. [Now published in *ZPE* 62 (1986) 51-53.]

25. Averil Cameron, *Fl. Cresconius Corippus: In laudem Iustini Augusti minoris* (London 1976) II.52-69, esp. 52-60. Note 55-56: *credula verbum / concipiens*.

26. DeL. O'Leary, *The Coptic Theotokia* (London 1923) 1a (incarnation of Logos), 12a (incarnation of Mediator), 21b ('one nature of God the Word incarnate'!). It is astonishing to run across the famous lines from the *Hippolytus*, πλεκτὸν στέφανον ἐξ ἀκηράτου / λειμῶνος, 're-woven' as an offering to the Virgin Mary (cf. Tuilier 1969:48-49). George of Pisidia writes in the *Expeditio Persica* III 379-380: σοὶ τόνδε πλεκτὸν στέφανον ἐξ ἀκηράτου / λειμῶνος ἄρτι τῆς ἀληθείας φέρω (I owe this last reference to Dr David Frendo).

27. I have not specifically treated the debate as to which came first, the *CP* or Romanos (cf. Tuilier 1969:39-47). See the excellent literary treatment of the Romanos poem by E.C. Topping, '"Mary at the Cross": St. Romanos' kontakion for Holy Friday,' *BS/EB* 4 (1977) 18-37. It may be observed that the Virgin's lament language, so much noticed by critics, has much in common with Coptic laments: see M. Cramer, *Die Totenklage bei den Kopten* (Vienna/Leipzig 1941).

28. A first version of this paper was given at the Byzantine Studies Conference, Cincinnati, November 1984. I should like to thank Kent Rigsby, Kenneth Snipes, Alan Cameron, David Frendo, and Stephen Morse for their help.

XXV

THREE CULTURES UNDER ARAB RULE: THE FATE OF COPTIC*

'... aucune voix ne s'est encore élevée pour dénoncer le "genocide culturel", l'"évacuation du champ historique" de la nation copte.'
J.-P. Péroncel-Hugoz, *Le radeau de Mahomet* (Paris 1983) 125

From none other of the Byzantine provinces that were to pass under Arab domination do we have such abundant documentation as has come from Egypt. Studies on Egypt in the period of transition from Byzantine to Arab government have brought out aspects of what happened to the existing administration of the province and of the steps taken by the new rulers to deal with their subjects. In this paper I shall attempt to deal with the phenomenon of the three *cultures* -- cultures carried by languages, that is, the Greek-speaking, Coptic-speaking, and Arabic-speaking spheres of thought and action -- being politically governed by an element just arrived in its new-found strength in the old Mediterranean world.

Several pieces of the puzzle became displaced and rearranged after A.D. 642. The moving of the capital, the administrative seat and centre, from Alexandria to the newly-created camp town of Fustat was done surely more for strategic and tactical reasons than out of any feeling of anti-Alexandrian reaction. For a very small invading army to achieve effectual control over an inhabited land-corridor stretching all the way to Aswan, it needed more than just a toehold on the sea. A point at the head of the Delta, that meeting-place of Upper and Lower Egypt, made geopolitical sense. And it made manpower sense as well as psychological sense to co-opt local talent: there is very little, if any, hard evidence in the papyri for any wholesale flight of the 'Byzantine' (=Chalcedonian) Greek-speaking, office-holding upper classes. We must not make retrojective inferences from late narrative sources. We must rather exploit the abundantly factual papyri (and other MSS.) to ascertain the facts of cultural change.

First to consider is the staffing of the local administration.

Everyone since Bell and Becker[1] has been agreed that it remained in Christian hands. Even if the well-known Flavius Atias ('Atiya), active from the 690s well into the early eighth century, was at the top of the hierarchy, he was not necessarily evidence that 'the islamicisation of the higher officialdom had begun earlier than had previously been thought'[2]. Atias might well have been a Christian Arab, brought from Mesopotamian (non-Chalcedonian) circles especially to deal with the Coptic population. However, even if Atias were a Muslim, the Coptic- and Greek-speaking lower administrators continued to put into practice their characteristically shrewd survival move: it does not matter who visibly bears the chief title as long as the actual work is done by members of one's own group. (No Egyptian government before or since could survive without Coptic financial expertise.[3])

It is a very good point, one I have raised before now, to look for onomastic evidence[4] for conversion to Islam of members of this professional bureaucratic class. (There seems to be very little.) It is also a good point to call attention to documents such as Grohmann's great trilingual, *APEL* III 167. This document leads directly to the heart of the matter of 'three cultures', specifically to the phenomena of bilingualism/trilingualism in various social registers and of the language shift, matters to which I shall return at some length. For the moment let us look carefully at the text of *APEL* III 167 with an eye to determining the historical occasion that gave rise to this document. It will be seen to make a telling point about the policy of rulers toward ruled.

APEL III 167, which opens with a Christian invocation, is a ϩⲟⲙⲟⲗⲟⲅⲓⲁ between villagers and a representative of the governor; the indiction number is unfortunately not preserved. The operative verb in lines 10-11 is ϫⲓ ⲛ̄ϭⲟⲛⲥ, 'use violence' (in the technical legal sense of βία), which Grohmann translated as 'oppressed'. Most of the negative forms are in restorations, e.g. in lines 9-10 and 10-11. The point is that this *homologia*, signed by some sixty witnesses, was elicited by a classic device of control: requiring those controlled[5] to swear (line 12; note that the verbs ⲱⲣⲕ or ⲁⲛⲁϣ are not used) that nothing wrong has happened[6]. Further analysis of the prosopography might make up for the loss of the indiction-number in line 1 and of the governor's name in lines 4-5: to date this document would give us another landmark in Umayyad administration.

A trilingual document such as *APEL* III 167 leads immediately to the whole question of language use in various departments of the chancery, in different regions, at different times, in varying social and administrative contexts. Perpetually seized upon by historians are the edict of the prefect 'Abdallah b. 'Abd-al-Malek in A.D. 698, imposing the use of Arabic in the official chancery, and the caliph Walid I's prohibition of the use of Greek in A.D. 715[7]. Praxis, of course, was not totally obedient to edicts enacted in the capitals. A complete list of Coptic/Arabic bilingual documentary papyri has yet to be compiled (though the present writer has begun assembling one): still, consideration of materials for such a list will show that within the 'three cultures' monolingualism was far from being the only state of affairs, and that Coptic/Arabic bilingual documents (as opposed to liturgical codices, which operate in their own world and respond to another set of needs) occur at quite late dates. *PERF* 577, perhaps of 20.v.674, is a bilingual *sigillion* of Rashid b. Khaled[8]; *PERF* 609 of A.D. 751/2, just after the transition to Abbasid rule, is a trilingual Coptic/Greek/Arabic tax list, as is *PERF* 595; while *PERF* 628 is a bilingual Coptic/Arabic list of taxpayers. (As the language shift begins to occur in the ninth and tenth centuries we find writing exercises, syllabaries, abecedaria and wordlists, such as *PERF* 185, 199, 202 and 204. I shall return to this subject below.[9])

I began with the incomparable fullness of the Egyptian documentation[10]. It is especially full on two matters of central importance to the realm of 'three cultures': first, conscript service (and resistance to it); and second, once again, the language shift. I shall now consider each of these in turn.

The eighth-century papyri tell us about the inner workings of the *cursus*, the annual Arab naval expedition against Byzantine forces (particularly Constantinople), in which the ships were built by Coptic shipwrights[11] and crewed by Coptic rowers, all of whom were forcibly and systematically conscripted from up and down the length of the Nile Valley[12] and sent to serve under Arab military commanders. How did this arrangement work out? At the battle of Phoenix off Alexandria in A.D. 654/5, the Coptic sailors did not fight[13]; while in Maslama's sea attack on Constantinople in September 717, they deserted to the Byzantines[14]. Clearly anti-Chalcedonian feeling was not a deciding factor in the conscripts' behavior. If the Arab commanders had counted on their non-Chalcedonian subjects' supposed dominating hatred of Chalcedonians, or expected their support for new masters against former enemies, they were handed a surprise. They could not assume that to conscript the bodies of Copts was also to obtain their allegiance. There were holes in the system[15].

No one has yet been able to account for the fact of the death of the Coptic language. It died at different times in different contexts; but what Persians, Greeks, and Romans (not to mention Ottomans) could not do[16], the Arabic language, openly and in itself the carrier of an alien faith, did: Coptic died. The stages of its death remain to be charted[17], and cogent reasons for its death[18] have yet to be brought forward. There are many historical situations in which one language is used in the job market and another in the home. A few theories to account for the death of Coptic (alone of all the languages of the Christian East) have been advanced, but none satisfies. One is that the multiplicity of Coptic dialects led to such an unmanageable situation of mutual unintelligibility that Arabic replaced the clash of dialects out of sheer convenience[19]. Another is that Coptic was used in a purely pragmatic register for monastic services and hence naturally atrophied as an *Umgangssprache*[20]. Still another, perhaps a variant of the preceding, is that the fundamental and pervasive anti-intellectual stance of the Coptic mentality[21] engendered a cultural laziness (there is some truth in this) that ensured the victory of the language brought and used by the wielders of political control. I have as yet evolved no adequate explanation. (There is much anthropological literature on the phenomenon of language death, but it does not seem to illuminate the problem of Coptic.) But some stages in the fate of this autochthonous strand among the 'three cultures' can be followed.

Everyone is aware of the assertion in one of the prefaces attributed to Severus of Ashmunein[22] that Coptic was ceasing to be understood by the ninth to tenth century. By the tenth century we have some, though sparse, evidence for the phenomena of (as it were) 'Karshuni', or Arabic texts transcribed in Coptic script[23], which would of course have come first in time, and then 'reverse Karshuni', or Coptic texts rendered in Arabic script[24] (a phenomenon seen in churches at the present day). Sinai cod.ar. 116, written by a (presumably Chalcedonian) monk from Damietta in A.D. 995/6, is a Greek/Arabic gospel lectionary whose Greek hand shows Coptic affinities and whose Greek phonology betrays Bohairic Coptic influence[25].

Nomenclature has already been pointed out as a matter of importance, of labelling, within the 'three cultures'. Alongside the persistence of Graeco-Coptic given names, there appeared, at an as yet undated stage, the phenomenon of Arabic 'renderings' of such names (e.g. Bishai for Evangelos)[26]. In the Berlin Arabic MS. or.oct. 194 fols. 49v-50v there are lists of masculine and feminine names in which, e.g., Makarios is rendered as Sa'id, **ⲕⲓⲣⲓⲕⲟⲥ** (understood as being from **ⲕⲏⲣⲩϫ**) = Bishara, Johanna becomes Sitt al-Fadl, **ⲁⲅⲁⲑⲟⲥ** Abu-'l-Kheir, Theophanos = Abu-'l-Farag, and the 'Nico-' in Nicodemus produces Manṣur[27]. The only further step in camouflage would be the adoption of deliberately ambiguous Arabophone descriptive names like 'Samir' or 'Habib'. The pseudepigraphic *Apocalypse of Samuel of Kalamun*[28], a text to which I shall return, laments '... they give the names of them ['those of the *hijra*'] to their children, leaving aside the names of the angels, the prophets, and apostles and the martyrs.' (Unfortunately this text has never yet been securely dated. One looks forward to the results of the research of Fr Javier Martinez.)

By the time of the thirteenth- and fourteenth-century compilers of *scalae* and 'introductions' (grammatical sketches based on Bible and liturgy)[29], after centuries of what Graf called 'die schriftlose Zeit', Coptic was of course a totally dead language. I need not summarise here recent scholarship on the subject of these encyclopaedists[30]. Suffice it to say that these writers sought 'the usefulness of the upright Coptic people/folk' (*awlād al-sha'b al-qibtī al-mustaqīm)* (Mallon 1907:221/229: Abu Ishaq b. al-Assal) and decried the fact that 'for the people of this our time in this our land, *bilad al-qibtiyya wa-al-diyar al miṣriyya,* their language has become forgotten and it is very hard for them to learn it ... and that others have not abandoned their language as we have ours' (Athanasius of Qus, ed. Bauer, pp. 245/305)[31]. Formulations like those, albeit late[32], surely speak against any hypothetical 'cultural affinity' between conquerors and conquered[33]: Athanasius goes on to lament in biblical language how the Copt who would learn Coptic 'does not understand what he is saying ... and, as the apostle says, has become a foreigner in his essence' (*ibid.*) because of the 'lordship of the *umma al-'Arab*'. Language was the carrier of each of the three cultures.[34]

I conclude with additional passages from the *Apocalypse of Samuel of Kalamun*, a text whose postulated Coptic original, date[35], and cultural milieu of origin remain undetermined. (Martinez opts for the eighth century.) It is a passionate outcry against the swamping of one language, seen as the carrier of the patristic heritage, by another, regarded as the carrier specifically and in its essence of non-Christian forms of thought and feeling. Previously there had not been an open link between language and religion in the culture of Egypt. (We are before the controversy on the pre-existence of the Quran, itself a response to Christian ways of thought.) This is an extraordinary text any way you look at it. If the original had been in Coptic, would it have reached its audience with intelligibility? It is, on the other hand, a deep irony that it should be preserved only in Arabic.

> They have abandoned the beautiful Coptic language in which the Holy Spirit spoke through the mouths of our fathers; they teach their children from infancy to speak Arabic and glory in it. Even priests and monks dare to speak Arabic, and be proud of it, right inside the *heikal* (sanctuary). ... Woe to every Christian who teaches his son from childhood the language of the *hijra*, making him forget the language of his ancestors. ... All at this time are abandoning this (Coptic) language to speak Arabic and glory in it, up to the point where one would not even know them for Christians any more, but would take them for barbarians. And those of al-Sa'id who still know and speak Coptic are looked down upon and harmed by their brother Christians, who speak Arabic. ... Whoever shall dare to speak the language of the *hijra* inside a church shall be cut off from the laws of the holy fathers. ... When Christians shall dare to speak the language of the *hijra* right at the altar, they are blaspheming against the Holy Spirit and the Trinity: seven times woe to them! ... Whoever remains aloof from the actions of the *hijra* and does not resemble them shall save his soul.[36]
>
> (*ROC* 20 [1915-17] 379-380, 382-383)

Perhaps if this advice had been followed before it was too late, there might have been even more than three cultures under Arab rule.

NOTES

* This paper was originally presented at the Colloquium on Papyrology (FIEC), Dublin, in August 1984, as the response to a paper by Professor M. el-Abbadi of the University of Alexandria. I should like to thank Andrew Cappel of Yale University, Sidney Griffith and Monica Blanchard of Catholic University, and Stephen Morse of The Rockefeller University for their help.

1. H.I. Bell, preface to *P.Lond.* IV (1910) xvii-xli; idem, 'The administration of Egypt under the 'Umayyad Khalifs,' *BZ* 28 (1928) 278-286; C.H. Becker, 'Grundlinien der wirtschaftlichen Entwicklung Ägyptens,' *Klio* 9 (1909) 206-219. For a critique of K. Morimoto, *The financial administration of Egypt in the early Islamic period* (Kyoto 1981), see now J. Gascou, 'De Byzance à l'Islam: les impôts en Egypte après la conquête arabe,' *JESHO* 26 (1983) 97-109, esp. on this point, 101-102.

2. K.A. Worp in *CPR* VIII (Vienna 1983) 196-197 with p. 197 n. 1. On Arabs in Egypt from Ptolemaic to early Byzantine times see I. Shahid, *Rome and the Arabs* (Washington 1984) 5, 7, 57-59 with notes, 174.

3. Cf. Y. Artin, 'Signes employés dans la comptabilité copte ...,' *Bull.Inst. d'Egypte* ser. 2,10 (1889) 285-298; S.Y. Labib, *Handelsgeschichte Ägyptens* ... (Leiden 1965) 217, citing b. al-Ḥağğ.

4. Along the lines of R. Bulliet, *Conversion to Islam in the medieval period* (Cambridge 1979), but using evidence from the papyri, as here in *APEL* II 117-118.1-2. Cf. L.S.B. MacCoull in *Akten d. XVI.Intl.Byzantinistenkongress* II.5 (Vienna 1982) 413 (note 17); R.S. Bagnall in *BASP* 19 (1982) 105-124 on the earlier process of Christianisation of the society. Is *PERF* 1181 of 8.vii.1036 evidence for a conversion?

5. Here, subject to tax: Grohmann's interpretation of ⲠⲈⲚⲆⲒⲔⲀⲒⲞⲚ in line 7 as 'our dues' (in tax assessment) might, however, be questioned: not 'dues' exactly but more like 'rights'. Grohmann cites as parallels *P.Lond.* IV 1349.20 and 1380.11. Those passages run: (i) [Kurrah to Basil] 'We have not ordered you to be lazy and eat, but rather we have ordered you to fear God, to guard your faith, and to look after the *dikaion* of the *amir al-mu'minin*'; (ii) '... without neglect to see to the *dikaion* of the *amir al-mu'minin* with skilled management (κυβέρνησις) and good will (καλοθέλεια)'. At least in this context the word does not refer to a 'juristic person'.

6. On the often-treated subject of freedom of movement see Schiller's comments on P.Bu in *JARCE* 7 (1968) 113-118.

* 7. Greek continued, of course, to be used. For a Greek inscription in the highest of style datable to Pachon 12, indiction 3, year of Diocletian 451 = 7.v.735 see L.S.B. MacCoull, 'Redating the inscription of el-Moallaqa,' to appear in *ZPE*. It would be illuminating exactly to pinpoint the first time the era of Diocletian is called the era of the Martyrs, which latter seems not to have been used in documents (the earliest use in a colophon appears to be A.D. 861/2): this question is the subject of a forthcoming article by K.A. Worp and the present writer. Greek was used for Easter festal letters by eighth-century Coptic patriarchs (e.g. P.Berol. 10677, in *BKT* VI). It may well have lived on in the society of the nome towns, as Roger Bagnall has suggested.

8. See K.A. Worp in *BSAC* 26 (1984) 100-101. British Library MS. Or. 6201 (A) 2 mentions Rashid as well (14th indiction, ?=732/3); it is from the Hermopolite.

9. Cf. also *PERF* 79, 82, 83, 91, 628, 629. There is an unpublished Coptic/Arabic bilingual document in the Theresianum Academy at Vienna (so Wessely in *SPP* I.1). A corpus of these documents would be a real contribution to social history. Cf. also below, note 20. On the interpenetration of terminology see A. Grohmann, 'Griechische und lateinische Verwaltungstermini im arabischen Aegypten,' *Cd'E* 7 (1932) 275-284.

10. Cf. J. Gascou in *JESHO* 26 (1983) 105-106.

11. *P.Lond.* IV 1410; B.M. Kreutz, 'Ships, shipping, and the implications of change in the early medieval Mediterranean,' *Viator* 7 (1976) 79-109 esp. 94, citing A.M. Fahmy, *Muslim naval organisation in the Mediterranean* (London 1960) 106-107.

12. *P.Lond.* IV passim (e.g. 1393), and, besides *P.Apoll.*, the Coptic portion of the Papas archive from Edfu (being published by MacCoull) and an additional Greek Edfu document in Cairo being published by Gascou. Cf. Bell in *JEA* 12 (1926) 265-281. [Now published in Acts XVIII *Congr. Papyrol.* 2 (Athens 1988) 141-160. In this volume study XI.]

13. A.M. Fahmy, *Muslim sea-power in the eastern Mediterranean* (London 1966) p. 87 with n. 7, citing Tabari (ed. de Goeje) I 2870.

14. E. Eickhoff, *Seekrieg und Seepolitik zwischen Islam und Abendland* (Berlin 1966) 34, citing Theophanes (ed. de Boor) 396-399.

15. On Coptic revolts in the Umayyad period cf. MacCoull in *Akten d.XVI. Intl. Byzantinistenkongress* (above note 4) 413. The years A.D. 829-830 saw the revolt of the Bashmurites (Severus of Ashmunein, *History of the Patriarchs* [ed. Evetts, *PO* 10 (1915)] I.20 = pp. 487-496.) Cf. N. Abbott, 'A new papyrus and a review of the administration of 'Ubaid Allah b. al-Habhab,' *Studies ... H.A.R. Gibb* (Cambridge 1965) 21-35.

16. A. Mallon in *Mél.Univ.St.Joseph* 1 (1906) 109.

* ['Redating the inscription of el-Moallaga', now publised in *ZPE* 64 (1986) 230-235. In this volume study XIV. K.A. Worp, "The Era of the Martyrs", in R. Pintaudi, ed., *Miscellanea Papyrologica* (Florence 1990) 375-408; see also MacCoull in *DOP* 44 (1990) 27-4. In this volume study XIX.]

17. Amateur work like W. Bishai, 'The transition from Coptic to Arabic,' *Muslim World* 53 (1963) 145-150 needs to be replaced. Also on the persistence of Coptic, we must realise that the often-repeated travellers' tales of villages in Upper Egypt where Coptic was still spoken in the eighteenth to nineteenth centuries are mostly wishful thinking: these Anglican and other clerics were relating what their co-religionists back home wanted to hear.

18. Unsatisfactory is G.C. Anawati, 'Factors and effects of Arabization and Islamization in medieval Egypt and Syria,' *Levi della Vida Conference 4: Islam and cultural change in the Middle Ages* (Wiesbaden 1975) 37-39. J. den Heijer (Leiden) and S. Rubenson (Lund) are working on this problem.

19. W. Macomber, paper at ARCE, spring 1982.

20. T. Orlandi, 'Coptic literature,' to appear in *The roots of Egyptian Christianity* (Philadelphia 1986); cf. his comments in R.McL. Wilson, ed., *The future of Coptic studies* (Leiden 1978) 159. But (in an earlier period) compare the trilingual conversation-manual (P.Berol. 10582) republished by J. Kramer in *PTA* 30 (Bonn 1983) 97-108: the situation covered is the quite practical one of travelling. [See now T. Orlandi, "Coptic Literature", in J. Goehring, B. Pearson, eds., *The Roots of Egyptian Christianity* (Philadelphia 1986) 51-81.]

21. J. Timbie, *Dualism and the concept of orthodoxy in the thought of the monks of Upper Egypt* (diss. Pennsylvania 1979) esp. 229-233; cf. 216-224, 227-228.

22. *History of the Patriarchs* (ed. Evetts, *PO* 1 [1907]) pref. III (p. 115). It has now been proven that this passage was not written by Severus: J. den Heijer, 'Sawīrus ibn al-Muqaffa', Mawhūb Ibn Manṣūr Ibn Mufarriǧ et la genèse de l'"Histoire des Patriarches d'Alexandrie",' *BiblOr* 41 (1984) 336-347.

23. P. Casanova, 'Un texte arabe transcrit en caractères coptes,' *BIFAO* 1 (1901) 1-20; for the hand cf. M. Cramer, *Koptische Paläographie* (Wiesbaden 1964) nos. 26 and 27 (but in the present case the MS. itself could possibly be a little later than the work it embodies). -- It is astonishing to encounter, in this apophthegmatic text, what must have been an original Coptic **π2λλο** rendered by **ϭϣ-ϣειϸ**, a word with utterly different resonances. -- Compare *PERF* 603 and 174.

24. G. Galtier, 'Coptica-arabica: un manuscrit copte en caractères arabes,' *BIFAO* 5 (1906) 91-111. In the Coptic medical papyrus published by Chassinat (Cairo 1921) several Arabic names of ingredients are written in Arabic letters within the Coptic text: cf. L.S.B. MacCoull, 'A checklist of Coptic medical papyri,' (to appear) dating it to the early eighth century.

25. Colophon in D. Harlfinger et al., *Specimina Sinaitica* (Berlin 1983) Tafel 22; cf. G. Garitte, 'Un évangéliaire grec-arabe du Xe siècle (cod.Sin.ar.116),' in K. Treu, ed., *Studia Codicologica (=TuU 124)* (Berlin 1977) 207-225; Garitte does not perceive the part-Coptic milieu.

26. Note the names in *PERF* 819-822, poll-tax receipts of A.D. 878-9.

27. I am grateful to Professor H.-M. Schenke and Dr Chr. Elsas for photographs of the MS., and to Andrew Cappel for help with the Arabic. The same phenomenon is also found in British Library MS. Or. 1325 fol. 261a: I thank Dr E. Silver for permission to work with this MS.

28. Ed./tr. J. Ziadeh in *ROC* 20 (1915-17) 374-404, with remarks by F. Nau, 405-407. The principal MS. (there are five) is Paris arab. 150.20r-31r (copied in A.D. 1606!), bought in Cairo by Vansleb. The present quotation is from p. 394 (tr.). Cf. also p. 396: '... those who abandon the names of the saints to give alien names to their children shall be excluded from the benediction of the saints.'

29. A. Mallon in *Mel.Univ.St.Joseph* 1 (1906) 109-131, 2 (1907) 213-264 was the first to outline the field and identify some of its principal figures.

30. G. Bauer, *Athanasius von Qus: Qiladat at-tahrir fi 'ilm at-tafsir* (Freiburg 1972); A. Sidarus, *Ibn ar-Rahibs Leben und Werk* (Freiburg 1975); idem, 'La philologie copte-arabe au moyen age,' in *8e Congrès des arabisants et islamisants* (Aix-en-Provence 1976) 267-281; idem, 'Coptic lexicography in the Middle Ages: the Coptic-Arabic *scalae*,' in Wilson, ed., *The future of Coptic studies* (above note 20) 125-142.

31. We know Athanasius' dates now: he signed a document found at Qasr Ibrim (dated 20 Mecheir A.D. 1372): J.M. Plumley, *The scrolls of Bishop Timotheos* (London 1975) 21, 23-25, 36; and cf. J.-C. Garcin, *Qus* (Cairo 1974) 251 with n. 3.

32. Most MSS. of the grammatical works (above note 30) are eighteenth- and nineteenth-century, which says something about the dark years of Coptic cultural history.

33. With respect to Syria, one might possibly make a case (as has been done): Syriac is after all a Semitic language. Coptic is not (*pace* Vycichl et al.).

34. The monuments of the twilight are sad. The fourteenth-century *Triadon* (new ed. P. Nagel, Halle 1983) is in part a plea for the revival of a language long dead; the Life of John of Phanijoit, who recanted his apostasy in the late twelfth century, is a translation from the Arabic.

35. Nau in *ROC* 20 (1915-17) 406 hypothesized an eighth-century Coptic original, on what basis he did not state. Fr Martinez opts for the first half of the eighth century, based on parallels with the Ps.-Macarius.

36. Once again I should like to thank Andrew Cappel of Yale University for help with the Arabic text.

XXVI

*THE STRANGE DEATH OF COPTIC CULTURE**

To the June 1981 neomartyrs of Cairo

It is still possible to be born in Mardin or Mosul (or in Detroit) and speak Syriac as your mother tongue. It is just possible, or was until twelve years ago, to be born in Abyssinia and have some sort of meaningful relationship with Ge'ez. It is of course quite possible to be born in Thessalonica or Erevan, or Boston, Paris, Fresno, California, or Queens, New York, and speak Armenian or Greek. It is not possible to be born in Egypt and understand a single word of Coptic; it has not been possible for eight hundred years. Why is this the case?

The Coptic culture of Christian Egypt, which had flourished in high originality and creativity in the sixth and early seventh centuries, was more thoroughly submerged than was any other of the high cultures of the Christian Orient by the effects of the Arab/Islamic conquest. A particularly troubling and unexplained feature of this cultural extinction is the death of the Coptic language, a degree of death not undergone by any of the other indigenous languages of Oriens Christianus. With frightening rapidity Coptic culture lost touch with a past about which it had long been ambivalent. This ambivalence had much to do with the pervasive anti-intellectual stance of the Coptic ethos, a disposition the roots and causes of which have never been made plain. The consequences of the Coptic devaluation of learning were to be tragic even up to the present day. Coptic culture in effect self-destructed.

It should be plain that I am investigating the phenomenon of cultural death through that of language death, as language, especially in a world that passed from province to *ahl al-dhimmi* to *millet*, has been *par excellence* the carrier of culture and of identity. The cognitive style of the Coptic mind, its ways of classifying and conceptualising, are embedded in the Coptic language. The death of that language is the loss of a whole way of being human; the story of its death needs to be told. As a documentary papyrologist, I am investigating the materials for that story through collecting and tracing the historical context of Coptic/Arabic bilingual documentary papyri. (The subtitle of this paper might be 'From the documentary papyrologist's point of view'.) The persistence of Coptic as a viable and practical *Umgangssprache* can be followed through tax receipts, marriage contracts, requisitions, orders for payment, cadasters, sales, loans, leases, writing exercises, wordlists, and of course private letters. Such linguistic continuity, and the access it provided to the life of past times even after it had become plain that the Arab domination was there to stay, for a while permitted what Robert Browning has called '...continuity of values and ideals and terms of reference.'[1] When the continuity was broken, it was broken irreparably and for all time. When around 1800 the bishop of Abutig, just south of Assiut, tried to write a letter in Bohairic, he had used an Arabic scala in manuscript and was making obvious direct calques from Arabic in his head.[2] When around 1900 a railway official in Luxor tried to write a letter in Bohairic to impress a French inspector, he had to use Labib's folk dictionary, with extremely comic results.[3]

The question of the death of Coptic is not exactly the same as the question of the Arabicisation of Egypt or of the imposition and then domination of the Arabic language, although the matters are of course interrelated. In more than one historical situation it has been the case that the language of the political conquerors is used in public life and for upward social mobility, while the language of the conquered is spoken within families and written in private letters. 'Abd-al-Malik decreed by edict the imposition of Arabic by the end of the seventh century; the real shift seems to have occurred in the late eleventh to early twelfth, if not before. Nothing happened overnight. And in studying bilingualism in Copto-Arabic society let me state that, as a documentary papyrologist, I must leave on one side the large and rich sphere of textual bilingualism in Bible and liturgy. That is a whole different field from that of the persistence of Coptic in daily life. We now know that the first translation programme to produce Gospel texts in Arabic was carried out under Melkite auspices in Syria/Palestine in the late eighth to early ninth centuries, both as pastoral purposes to be used in churches in an area where Arabic already dominated, and with a view to carrying religious apologetic into the camp of the conquerors[4]: this is the work of Sidney Griffith of Washington. The question of the first appearance of an Arabic Bible in Egypt, made by and for the use of Non-Chalcedonian Copts in their own regional variety of Arabic and translated from whatever Coptic, Greek, and Hebrew texts may have been at hand, has hardly been investigated at all, let alone provisionally answered.[5] Then bilingual liturgical codices, with varying degrees of bilinguality, were produced in Egypt gradually over time. This is a field in which I claim no competence; but it will yield rich results for some future qualified social historian of medieval Egypt.

To return to the documentary papyri. We come up against the question of 'register.' In what context, for what purpose, dealing with what subject-matter, by whom to whom, did one use which language, Coptic or Arabic? (Or a juxtaposition of both.) The most immediate and most important area of direct contact between conquerors and conquered was, of course, the running of the local financial administration. The genres of document mentioned earlier give an idea of the areas in which Coptic remained a viable medium of useful communication. Coptic/Arabic bilingual tax registers and tax receipts are found throughout the eighth century and into the early ninth (e.g. *PERF* 609, 595, 628, 690, 686, 707, 709, 633 in the Vienna collection; Ryl 236, 237, 259, 401, and 116 from the Hermopolite; BM 1050 from the Hermopolite and 565 and 685 from the Fayum). Some exist dated as late as A.D. 942 (CPR IV 13) and 1006/7 (Ryl 464). The two areas of the Fayum and the Hermopolite nome (the area of Ashmunein) appear to have been Coptic language strongholds until quite late, although this impression is partly dependent on the nature of our sources, the two great papyrus finds of the late 1880s having come from just those two areas. (Minya remained a town of Coptic merchants until forty years ago.)

To what extent did the conquerors learn the language of the conquered? Again we have evidence from those two regions of Coptic linguistic strength, the Hermopolite and the Fayum. From the latter come BM 580 and 584, letters dated by the editor (Crum) to the ninth to tenth century. The confessional identities of writers and recipients are unmistakable from their names: Ali, Ahmed, Mohammed ibn Abdullah, Abd el-Jabbar. These letters are written *in Coptic* by Moslems to Moslems. Along with the Coptic language, the writers have acquired at least some of the forms of epistolary *politesse* that come with it, conveniently including the (possibly) ambivalent opening formula 'In the name of God first'[6]. Formulas of 'greeting all the brothers' and 'may God forgive me', quite at home already in Christian Coptic, could of course be filled in by Moslem readers with their own content. In BM 580, Ali for one has not learnt Coptic very well: he has mastered the formula 'I greet you with my whole soul', ϩⲛ̄ⲧⲁⲯⲩⲭⲏ ⲧⲏⲣⲥ̄, but he keeps making the noun *psyche* and its modifier masculine. This document thus seems likely to be actually from the hand of the Moslem writer/sender, rather than to have been dictated to a Coptophone village scribe, at least one who knew his job. Also cases of apparent Coptic language learning by Arabs are the numerous examples of letters written in Coptic by Moslem officials to their Christian subjects. From the Hermopolite in the later eighth century (ca. A.D. 764-770) we have the archive of Severus son of Bane and his brother Papostolos, from the village of Bousiris: Ryl 117, 214, 346, 378, 383, BM 1167, 1168, 1169. Severus receives letters and orders in Coptic from the officials Yezid ibn Abd-ar-Rahman and Hisham ibn Belal; and one of the signers of a document in his archive acknowledging the discharge of a debt is Najjih, the Arabic interpreter (in Coptic transcription ⲧⲏⲣⲕⲟⲩⲙⲁⲛ: Ryl 214, Pachons 10, 3rd indiction = probably A.D. 764). Only from the degree of proficiency of the hands and the linguistic competence can one venture to decide whether these communications were dictated to Coptic chancery employees or were actually penned by the officials themselves.[7] By the eleventh century, as we shall see shortly, the existence of Coptophone local village scribes employed by the Arab chancery can hardly any longer be credited.

In epistolography too we see the other side of this phenomenon of who was learning whose language. One can watch the progressive infiltration of Coptic letter-writing, and documentary composition in general, by Arabised and even Islamised phraseology. From the 'Peace be with you' -- ϯⲣⲏⲛⲏ ⲛⲁⲕ -- of the late seventh century (already in the Apollonos Ano Coptic papyri) to the 'your servant, may God pardon him' of the tenth we see new values and new attitudes at work in the old language (a few examples among the many extant are BM 545 [see Crum's note p. 267a n.1], Ryl 309 [written by Bishai son of Shenoute], 349, 362, 372, 373). In Ryl 376 and 379 (10th c.) the bilingual Christian writers, Severus son of Agene and David son of Abraham (Daoud ibn Ibrahim), of Ashmunein, sign in Arabic; while in ninth-century Edfu Coptic signatories still signed in Coptic when acting as witnesses to Arabic sale contracts executed among Moslems (e.g. *APELI* 56.27-29), as well as calling in Moslems to sign their own contracts.

In one interesting area we can watch the progress of the language shift within inner-Coptic community circles themselves. In the late tenth to early eleventh century there seems to have been an outbreak of chicken-stealing and black magic at Hermopolis, a city referred to by its bishop John as 'the Christ-loving city (ϯⲡⲟⲗⲓⲥ ⲙⲙⲁⲓⲡⲉⲭ(ⲣⲓⲥⲧⲟⲥ)) of Shmoun': P. Berol. 5568.2-3 and Ryl 267. In these two parallel papyrus documents written in good Sahidic, the bishop writes to his flock that cases of chicken theft have come to his attention; and he threatens the thieves in Biblical language with every possible curse out of the Old and New Testaments, while saying that 'the innocent will go free.' In references to 'the good of our souls' and 'our custom' (ⲥⲏⲛⲏⲑⲓⲁ = συνήθεια) we can see the religiously defined community coalescing in self-awareness when it is a question of wrongdoing amongst their own. In a Leipzig paper document also from Hermopolis, this time written in an uncertain Arabic, the bishop, Abraham, threatens with excommunication a priest who has gone so far as to traffick in sorcery (and, it seems, make himself ill in the process).[8] This prelate is clearly unused to writing Arabic, and was perhaps dictating his encyclical to a Christian scribe who was new at the language and translated from Coptic as he went along. And yet, to reach his flock, Arabic was the language this bishop used.[8a]

As late as the late eleventh century we have the persistence of viable documentary Sahidic Coptic in the Hermopolite: the so-called Teshlot papyri preserved at Leiden.[9] These documents are the family archive of the villager Raphael, a man of property and local entrepreneur whose will ensured that there would be at least one more prosperous generation of Christians in his part of the nome. In no. 11 of the archive we have the case of a Christian, Raphael's son Agathon, writing in Coptic to another Christian, their neighbor Sisinnios: Sisinnios then turns the papers over and writes his reply to the letter, with perfect ease, in Arabic. Thus by the 1060s A.D. the Christian community in Egypt is moving with fluency between both languages in the conduct of its daily affairs: but all the other papers of Raphael's archive are in slightly oddly spelt but still good Sahidic. Already in the reign of al-Mustansir the minor country gentry, with brothers and sons in the Church, were doing this and seeing nothing odd in it. The age of the translations had not quite begun[10]; although the feeling that a language is in and of itself the carrier of values and ways of perception had been articulated nearly three hundred years before, as we shall find when we look at the Apocalypse of pseudo-Samuel of Qalamun.

The late Coptic speech of the Hermopolite nome maintained itself nearly as a separate dialect, to which Kasser has given the siglum 'H' for 'Hermopolitan.'[11] The main literary witness of this Ashmunein dialect is one of the hands of the still unpublished Pierpont Morgan Library papyrus codex M636, which on the basis of an Arabic protocol on one of the leaves has the *terminus post quem* of A.D. 849-856. The text, amounting to the commonplace-book of a sermon-writer made up of paraphrases of Biblical passages (some perhaps metrical) and indices to the Psalms, must thus have been composed, most likely in a monastic community, in the late ninth century.[12] It has been suggested by Kasser[13] that this speech was a semi-artifical, 'hothouse-forced' attempt to establish a new 'post-Sahidic' literary medium in the late Abbasid period: but it seems more a question of peculiar orthography.[14] What is necessary to obtain a notion of the kind of Coptic that remained in use in this area until late is to compare the 'H' of the Morgan codex with the language of the Ashmunein documentary papyri so abundant in the Vienna, Rylands, Leiden, and British Library collections. Above all, Coptic communication had to remain intelligible, at least within the Christian community: and the degree of intelligibility can be assessed only by studying the Hermopolite, and the Fayumic, Coptic dossiers as a whole.

The very latest Coptic documents of all are marriage contracts, certainly a matter of importance to the life of the community. They are (perhaps) twelfth to thirteenth century. A paper document from Esna once in the collection of Sir Alan Gardiner[15] was dated by the first editor to Year of the Martyrs 663 = A.D. 946, but the date was corrected six years later[16] to Martyrs 963 = A.D. 1246. The deacon ⲡⲁϣⲁⲉⲓⲣ (?=Abu-'l-Kheir, i.e. Agathon) son of Abu-'l-Farag (Theophanes) is marrying his first cousin, Sitt al Baha; and there are Arab witnesses (ⲙⲛⲧⲣⲉ ⲛⲁⲣⲁⲃⲓⲕⲟⲛ)'from the ⲉⲑⲛⲟⲥ who are set over our land' (11. 22-23) (this is reminiscent of the eighth-century oath clauses wherein people swear 'by the health, *oujai*, of those who happen to rule over us at the moment, *kata kairos*).' In an Ashmunein paper document[17] dated by the editor to Martyrs 925 = A.D. 1209, P.Berol. 11348, we have the marriage contract of Petros son of Pisente (so far so good), who is marrying a girl called Sitt al-Ward ('Rose'), whose father has the name, jarring in this context, of Rashid ibn Abu-'l'Badr. (And yet the man had to have been a Christian.) All the witnesses to this contract are Coptic clerics; and lines 51-52 have the proviso 'Christ being king over us' (ⲉⲣⲉ ⲡⲉⲭ̅ⲥ̅ ⲱ ⲛⲉ[ⲣⲣ]ⲟ ⲉϩⲣⲁ[ï ⲉϫⲱⲛ]) : compare the wistful phrase at the end of the witnesses' signatures in BM 673 of A.D. 987 (Fayum; 11, 10-11): 'May the Lord Jesus Christ be witness for all of us', a phrase which also appears in the Teshlot papyri. (In the Berlin document the two rhos are in a restoration, and I do not yet have a photograph.) The difficulty in dating the Berlin document lies in its giving the name of the reigning patriarch of Alexandria as John, which does not square with A.D. 1209. If the first figure of the three numerals were to be read as a ϕ = 500 (which is quite possible), and the immediately preceding squiggle were to be a symbol for ⲥⲁⲣⲁⲕⲏⲛⲱⲛ or the like,[17a] it would yield a Hijra date of = A.D. 1147, when there was indeed a patriarch John. The problems with both documents remain; but they speak eloquently of the social history of the Copts not far from the time when Francis of Assisi himself sat at Damietta trying to convert the Sultan of Egypt.

Finally, in the 'subliterary' realm, we can trace, on papyrus, parchment, and paper, the gradual encroachment of Arabic upon Coptic even in the schools, and the gradual shift in degrees of language familiarity in different subject areas. There are many extant examples of Coptic/Arabic bilingual writing exercises, from individual letter-forms and syllables to epistolary greetings. Then, first come the transcriptions of Arabic texts into Coptic letters, the writing-system they knew, and then at last the Coptic texts, no longer understood, are transcribed into Arabic script,[18] so they can at least be read aloud. How, after all, is a language transmitted? In the home, especially by women, and in the school. At some point or points over time, one generation stopped passing on to the next what it had once known.

How late did the production of writings in Coptic go on? This is the usual question asked by historians. Scriptoria went on, as we know from the White Monastery in the ninth century and the Wadi Natrun in the eleventh (see now Fr. Ugo Zanetti's catalogue of the St Macarius MSS.); metaphrasis from Sahidic into Bohairic went on; hagiography and homiletic went on, at first originally composed, then copied. Professor Tito Orlandi has recently made a case for the idea that, at least through the ninth century, Coptic literature continued as a kind of 'underground literature', putting in concealed protests against the Islamic government disguised as Scriptural parables or the like.[19] I shall return to this when I touch on Coptic apocalyptic literature. As to who was the last original Coptic author, the extant sources are still far from being completely explored, and the answer probably lies somewhere in Graf's 'schriftlose Zeit' between the letters of Patriarch Mark III in the early ninth century and the first translation projects of the twelfth (e.g. the early canonists). What exercises the cultural historian is the shift in the whole value structure, the ideological framework if you will, that came about in Egypt when it became apparent that the Islamic domination was there to stay. To quote from a Byzantinist, '...values and attitudes which had previously been contextually impossible now come to dominate and to determine the appearance of the culture.'[20] For Greeks under first Roman and then Turkish rule it can be said that '...only when this fact has penetrated' [i.e. that all political hope is gone] '...that the cultural archaizing really gets under way. If the present is unsatisfactory, it is tempting to rummage around in the past to see what you can find to preserve self-respect.'[21] Exactly the opposite happened in the case of Coptic Egypt. As opposed to what happened in other subject communities of the Near East, for whom monasteries and schools functioned to emphasize awareness of their own learned tradition, Coptic monasteries never became centers of resistance, identity, or self-image, and schools were painfully neglected. Only when Gaston Maspero pointed out in the 1890s that they should do so did any latter-day Copts -- who of course did not know Coptic -- try to 'rummage around in their past.'

In what areas, then, did creative production in the Coptic language persist at all? Quite early in Umayyad times, first of all, we encounter Coptic apocalyptic, that (perhaps) descendant of the demotic oracles blended with a dash of Syriac scripturality that has recently been so well studied by Javier Martinez.[22] In the ps.-Athanasius we find the ravages of the Islamic rulers attributed, as in John of Nikiu, to human sinfulness on the part of the Coptic community, especially to lax standards among monks and clergy (from simony to fornication). In the Apocalypse of pseudo-Samuel of Qalamun, dated by Martinez to the first half of the eighth century and preserved by a painfully ironic fate only in Arabic, we have an eloquent outcry against the swamping of the Coptic language by Arabic. As: 'They have abandoned the beautiful Coptic language in which the Holy Spirit spoke through the mouths of our fathers...Woe to every Christian who teaches his son from childhood the language of the *hijra,* making him forget the language of his ancestors...Whoever shall dare to speak the language of the *hijra* inside a church shall be cut off from the laws of the holy fathers.'[23] This appendix, probably written somewhat later than the main text, already eloquently articulates the principle dear to Herder and Romanticism that a people's identity resides in its language.[24]

Writing of a high literary quality in early mediaeval Coptic is to be found in the hymnography and folk poetry, the funerary laments preserved in tombstone inscriptions, and the odd bits of liturgical 'creative writing' found in Coptic prayer-books. The *floruit* of much of surviving Coptic poetry, from scriptural paraphrases and hymns in praise of saints to the Ballad of Archellites, has been placed in the tenth century.[25] The art of the quatrain as it is wrought in Sahidic Coptic is surprisingly affecting in its simplicity, recalling the 'Ambrosian stanza' or Prudentius: an unheard Schubert or Brahms (or Hugo Wolf) setting comes to the ear of the reader of 'A crown of pure gold is on the head of Queen Mary, / A crown of precious stones is on the head of Mary Queen' or 'Four teachers, four wise men are ours: Athanasius and Cyril the Great, Pachomius and Apa Shenoute.' It would be a worthwhile study to investigate the Coptic cultural milieu that gave rise to these *Lieder,* in which we hear the authentic singing voice of a people. The vision of death as an unbridgeable gulf of human separation calls to us from the eighth- and ninth-century grave inscriptions: 'O voyage from which there is no return, O cutting apart for which there is no coming together.'[26] Not the Greek garden of *refrigerium* is in these poetic laments, but a one-way trip to *Amente.* And occasionally in liturgical MSS. one encounters eloquently worded references to the oppressive social situation. In an eleventh-century codex in Prague[27] we find a prayer in Sahidic to be delivered 'from all plots of the evil kings, who have risen up against us...and from the hidden and the open enemy', and intercessions 'for prisoners and captives and those in disgrace (ⲘⲚⲦϬⲖⲒⲰ) and those who detain them in sour bitterness (ⲘⲈⲦϨⲈⲘϪ).[28] Al-Hakim had left scars.

Coptic continued as the vehicle for other kinds of writing as well. The White Monastery scriptorium (being reconstructed by Professor Orlandi), in the ninth century, copied and passed on the Alexander Romance as well as all those sermons. And we have a fair amount in Coptic of what is called 'alchemy'[29] -- actually mostly recipes for making dyes, pigments, and paste stones for ornament, important for the textile industry and the jewellery craft that has always been the province of minorities. Though full of Arabic words for substances, the Coptic alchemical texts pass on great helpings of Coptic *Kulturgut:* 'the master says,' they repeat over and over: 'the teacher (ⲡⲥⲁϩ) says', even 'the master Hermes says.' These texts are deeply rooted in what Helen Waddell called the leaf-mould of antiquity. What does not appear in Coptic, and when it does appear does so only in Arabic, is apologetic, anti-Moslem defences of Christian faith and life. The concept that the Christian faith ought to be spoken for, in expository prose at any rate, in a language that is in and of itself a carrier of that faith, did not come to birth among Non-Chalcedonian Christian Egyptians, except for fragments of the *Questions of Theodore* (ca. A.D. 680-690) and anti-*ethnos* fables in the Coptic *Physiologus.*[29a] There was to be no Coptic Abdisho, no communal regrouping, no Coptophone historiography: nothing.[30]

At the time of the thirteenth-century encyclopaedists and compilers of *scalae* and so-called 'Introductions to Coptic', the language was dead, and the issue was a dead letter. From John of Samanoud on, the *scala* writers were fighting a battle that was already lost.[31] And by the Ottoman period even the bare copying of Coptic script has degenerated in the MSS. into the mere drawing of shapes: the words are not understood. There is much anthropological writing on the phenomenon of language death, but none of the theories I have ever encountered seems to fit what happened to Coptic: dialectal unintelligibility; restriction to a purely practical and rote-memorised monastic sphere of use; simple laziness (to quote Barry Lopez: '...ignorance, poverty of spirit, indolence, and the threat of anonymity and destitution':[32] perhaps that comes closest). What did happen was that, for reasons which remain both unclear and unexplored, learning never became a holy act in Coptic culture. Learning for its own sake never became a thing of positive value. The comparison with Syriac or Armenian is sad. No Roman Vishniac with a camera and a time-machine could ever capture images of rows of Coptic schoolboys swaying back and forth over their texts. The historical roots of this Coptic devaluation of learning are still to be sought: its consequences have been disastrous.

'Language,' it has been said, 'lasts longer than stone or law.'[33] The Coptic language reflects and embodies a millennial and intimate interaction with a particular Mediterranean and Valley landscape, with all that implies about a particular set of perceptions and rhythm of life. And yet: we are for the dark. In Egypt it is an offence punishable by imprisonment to teach, study, or promote the Coptic language in any form, even the debased rote memorisation of the few words of liturgy that remain, garbled into street-Cairene-Arabic pronunciation. Elsewhere in the Near East it has been shown that an ancient, primarily liturgical language can come to new life and operate with success in a modern nation. The example will not be heeded. The techniques of awareness have been thrown away. ⲁⲣⲉⲧⲏ, 'excellence', has never become a Coptic loanword. [34] It is the parable of the talents: what you have been given, you must use. 'So full of sleep are they when they leave the way.'

Notes

* A first version of this paper was delivered at the Colloquium on Late Antiquity and Early Islam, University of London, June 1986.

I am grateful to Professors Averil Cameron and John Matthews for inviting me to participate in the Colloquium. I should also like to thank Sebastian and Helen Brock and Cyril and Marlia Mango, without whose hospitality in Oxford I could not have written this paper; and the Griffith Institute and the Oriental Reading Room of the British Library, whose resources made the research possible. Thanks also to Georgina Robinson, Monica Blanchard, Sidney Griffith, and Stephen Morse for fruitful discussion. And, as always, to Mirrit Boutros Ghali, in the hope that ⲁⲣⲉⲧⲏ will be perceived while there is still time.

1 In *Greece old and new* (New York 1983) p. 111.

2 Ryl 461, a fascinating document.

3 G. Legrain, *Une famille copte de Haute-Egypte* (Brussels 1945) 122-123, with Vergote's comments, 124-126.

4 S.H. Griffith, 'The Gospel in Arabic: an inquiry into its appearance in the first Abbasid century,' *OrChr* 69 (1985) 126-167; and see now, for a slightly earlier colophon, Y. Mimaris, *Catalogue of the new Arabic MSS. of St. Catherine's Monastery, Mount Sinai* (in Modern Greek) (Athens 1985) no. 16, p. 27, photos 19, 20, 21 (A.D. 859).

5 J.F. Rhode, *The Arabic versions of the Pentateuch in the church of Egypt* (St Louis 1921); K. Samir, in *OCA* 218 (1980) 104-105, and *idem*, 'Arabic sources for early Egyptian Christianity,' in B.A. Pearson/J.E. Goehring, edd., *The roots of Egyptian Christianity* (Philadelphia 1986) 86-89. Cf. the work of R.-G. Coquin on the Canons of Hippolytus in Egyptian Arabic, in *PO* 31.2 (Paris 1966) 297-301, cf. 433-437.

6 See L.S.B. MacCoull, 'Coptic documentary papyri as a historical source for Egyptian Christianity,' in Pearson/Goehring, *Roots* (above n. 5) 42-50.

7 Further examples, all from the Fayum, are BM 598, Suleiman to Ali; 634, from Qasim; 638, from Daoud ibn Abd-al-Jabbar; 662, to Abu al-Leith; and 664, to Ayoub ibn Mohammed from Yusuf. Clearly Ryl 324 (8th to 8th c.), in which Mohammed writes in Coptic to Victor appointing him tax-collector to work for the government, was for its part processed through a Coptic chancery scribe. In Arabic cf. the *baqt al-Qibt* attested at Hermopolis in A. Grohmann, 'Ein arabischer Steuerpapyrus...,' *In memoriam Carl Schmidt* (Berlin 1939) 52-53 (=Wien Ar. 330.2). More bilinguals are *BKU* III 403; 436 (A.D. 880); 478, written by one Sa'id to a Christian recipient in Coptic.

8 K. Reinhardt, 'Eine arabisch-koptische Kirchenbann-Urkunde,' *Festschrift G. Ebers* (Leipzig 1897) 89-91. The Coptic document in Berlin is published by G. Steindorff, 'Eine koptische Bannbulle...,' ZÄS 30 (1892) 37-41. Cf. BM 633, from the Fayum.

8a For bilingual magic see Bilabel/Grohmann *Kopt.u.arab. Texte* (Heidelberg 1934) 123 (PSR inv. 500/1): to be dated later than 700.

9 M. Green, 'A private archive of Coptic letters and documents from Teshlot,' *OMRO* 64 (1983) 61-122. I am grateful to Dr. Jürgen Horn of Göttingen for discussing these documents with me at the International Congress of Papyrology at Athens in May 1986. See now L.S.B. MacCoull, 'The Teshlot papyri and the survival of documentary Sahidic in the eleventh century,' forthcoming in *OCP.*

10 We need some sort of quantitative study on the interrelation between language predominance and conversion, especially mass conversion. There is very little evidence for individual converts in the documents between the seventh and the eleventh centuries: probably Abu-Jabbar son of Markos in BM 707; perhaps Qasim son of Abla (Apollos?) in BM 666; probably not Hale son of Pegosh in BM 1036, thought by Crum to be = Ali. Cf. *PERF* 1181 of 8.vii.1036 A.D.

11 R. Kasser in *ZÄS* 92 (1966) 106-115; in *BIFAO* 73 (1973) 85-86; in *Muséon* 93 (1980) 68, cf. 59; in *OLP* 6/7 (1975/76) 285-294.

12 I am grateful to Monica Blanchard of the Institute of Christian Oriental Research, Catholic University, for making available to me the late Fr T.C. Petersen's photostats of Morgan MS. M636, together with his transcriptions and copies of Grohmann's letter with the dating information and of a letter for Sir Herbert Thomson with his opinion of the contents. I have formed the impression that some of the biblical paraphrases are metrical, i.e., are actually hymns. We shall return to Coptic hymnography below.

13 R. Kasser in *ZÄS* 92 (1966) 106-115 (above n. 11).

14 See W. -P. Funk in E.Ch. Welskopf, ed., *Soziale Typenbegriffe im alten Griechenland* 7 (Berlin/DDR 1982) 283-320, esp. 284.

15 H. Thomson, 'A Coptic marriage contract,' *PSBA* 34 (1912) 173-179.

16 See next note.

17 G. Möller, 'Ein koptischer Ehevertrag,' *ZÄS* 55 (1918) 67-74. I failed to take account of the dating problems in my article on the early Morgan marriage contract in *Actes XV*[e] *Congr. intl.papyrol.* 2 (Brussels 1979) 116-123.

17a Not in K.A. Worp, 'Hegira years in Greek, Greek-Coptic and Greek-Arabic papyri,' *Aegyptus* 65 (1985) 107-115. Usually, but not always, a *hijra* date used in a Christian text without the explicit designation 'of the Saracens/Arabs' is flagged by a phrase like *tirompe tai,* 'this year.' Professor Worp's and my joint study, 'The Era of the Martyrs,' will appear in *Miscellanea Papyrologica* (Florence 1989). In gravestones it is found late 8th c.; in colophons 9th c.

18 See L.S.B. MacCoull, 'Three cultures under Arab rule: the fate of Coptic,' *BSAC* 27 (1985) 61-70. For writing exercises cf. e.g. *PERF* 185, 199, 202, 204.

19 T. Orlandi, 'Testo copto sulla dominazione araba in Egitto,' *Acts II Intl. Congr.Copt.Stud.* (Rome 1985) 76-84, and in Pearson/Goehring, *Roots* (above n. 5) 78-81; J. Martinez, *Pseudo-Athanasius* (below, n. 22) II.267-274.

20 J. Haldon, 'Some considerations on Byzantine society and economy in the seventh century,' *ByzForsch* 10 (1985) 76.

21 B.P. Reardon, 'The Second Sophistic,' in W. Treadgold, ed., *Renaissances* before the *Renaissance* (Stanford 1984) 39-40.

22 J. Martinez, *Pseudo-Methodius and Pseudo-Athanasius: Eastern Christian apocalyptic in the early Muslim period.* (2 vols.; Diss. Catholic University 1985). The Coptic text of ps. -Athanasius will appear, with translation and notes, in the *CSCO.*

23 From J. Ziadeh's text and translation in *ROC* 20 (1915-17) 394. By the fourteenth century Athanasius of Qus was to lament, 'For the people of this time in this land, their language has become forgotten...Others have not abandoned their language as we have ours.' -- G. Bauer, ed., *Qiladat at-tahrir fi 'ilm at-tafsir* (Freiburg 1972) 245, 305.

24 I cannot date the first appearance of the popular tradition that, because of the Flight into Egypt, the infant Christ learned to speak Coptic (i.e. Egyptian).

25 H. Junker, *Koptische Poesie des X. Jhdts.* (Berlin 1908-1911); A. Erman, *Bruchstücke d.kopt. Volkslitteratur* (Berlin 1897). We need re-editions with commentaries.

26 M. Cramer, *Die Totenklage bei den Kopten* (Vienna/Leipzig 1941).

27 V. Hazmuková, 'Miscellaneous Coptic prayers,' *ArchOr* 8 (1936) 318-333 and 9 (1937) 107-145. I quote from the text as paragraphed by Hazmuková, 2.16-3.2 and 5.11-13.

28 Compare P. Strassb.Copt. inv. 171, 'May Christ give you the ⲡⲁⲣⲣⲏⲥⲓⲁ to speak out before the archons and the ⲉⲝⲟⲩⲥⲓⲁ and the sultan who has desired to seize our church' (transcription in Crum's Notebook 108 in the Griffith Institute, Oxford).

29 See L. Stern, 'Fragment eines koptischen Traktates über Alchimie,' *ZÄS* 23 (1885) 102-119. The Bodleian papyri MS.Copt. a.2. (P) and a.3. (P) are still unpublished, and I should like to thank the authorities of the Bodleian Library Oriental Reading Room for permission to study and publish them. See now L.S.B. MacCoull, 'Coptic alchemy and craft technology in early Islamic Egypt: the papyrological evidence,' in *The Medieval Mediterranean* (Minneapolis 1988)

29a A. van Lantschoot, ed., *Les "Questions de Théodore"* (Studi e Testi 192; Vatican City 1957); idem, 'A propos du *Physiologus*,' in *Coptic studies in honor of W.E. Crum* (Boston 1950) 339-363, esp. 343-344: 'if they say: "There is no Son of God, God has not taken a wife or begotten a son" ' (obviously the old Moslem argument): the Christian is to counter with the example of the parthenogenetic bee. Also 351-352: the enemies of the Christians are the ⲉⲑⲛⲟⲥ, the wolves.

30 Cf. L.S.B. MacCoull, 'Coptic sources: a problem in the sociology of knowledge,' *BSAC* 26 (1984) 1-7.

31 MacCoull, 'The fate of Coptic' (above n. 18).

32 B. Lopez, *Arctic dreams* (New York 1986) 310.

33 P. Howard, *The state of the language* (New York 1985) 139.

34 M. Drew-Bear, *Le nome Hermopolite* (Missoula 1979) p. 69.

XXVII

Approaches to Coptic Studies

We are all classicists. Everyone reached by these words by virtue of his or her vocation, not duty or accident of baptism but calling, is a classicist of one persuasion or another. As classicists whose particular affinity is with the Late Roman East, we are fortunate to be living in a very exciting time for our special varieties of classical studies. In Peter Brown's words, we are no longer struggling to free ourselves from the weight of the dead hand of post-Renaissance Humanism; and in Marc Bloch's words, we are no longer, or at least less, suffering from a bad case of *folie des origines*, of the compulsive need to pick apart every text or work or art to find what fossils it might contain from some sort of Harnackian sub-Apostolic world. We are more receptive to the achievements of what has recently been termed the 'Age of Spirituality'. It is with this set of attitudes in mind that I should like to examine with you some of the narrow viewpoints from which our field has in the past been regarded, some of the very partial interpretations by which it has been limited or fixed, and to suggest ways in which we can draw more balanced, nuanced, insightful, and, I hope, true maps of where we have been and where we are going.

Let us, like Cosmas Indicopleustes, consider our picture of the world. The high Byzantine church plan, as it developed into a classic articulation of the material and immaterial universe, the participation of the face-to-face Mediterranean world of glory and patronage in the very structure of the courts of heaven, was that with four domes inscribed within the arms of an equilateral Greek cross, with the fifth or great dome overarching all the central space. In the Society for Coptic Archaeology we bring together four traditions: (1) the international school of Late Antique studies that began with Peter Brown's *Augustine of Hippo* and now embraces and inspires scholars on all continents and writing in all major languages -- a French, a German, an Anglo-American tradition -- and from all angles from jurisprudence to art history; (2) the classics of New England, especially papyrology, which latter is my special gift; (3) the Christian tradition from Mabillon to Charles Williams and from John Damascene to John Meyendorff; and (4) what I like to call *genius loci*, i.e., Coptic studies practised in their native place: for it becomes clear that only under the light of these skies can one perceive the world in which the papyri were written, the capitals carved, the tapestries woven, the icons painted, the liturgies composed. We bring together the four activities of love and scholarship and the arts and worship. With this sort of conceptual structure in mind, let us look at the four principal side-spaces that have been most studied in recent years, and then try to look up and see the mosaic of the central dome, its meaning, and the nature of the space it defines.

First, because it is most 'in the news', let me take Nag Hammadi. Professor Robinson never ceases to remind us that, if the '70s were the decade of the Qumran Scrolls, the '80s will be the decade of the Nag Hammadi Codices. These Egyptian Gnostics perhaps burying their books to escape the wrath of the orthodox are presented to us as the Zen dropouts of Late Antiquity, the crazies of the ancient world. Elaine Pagels's *The Gnostic Gospels* is featured in The New York Times, only to have Raymond Brown dash popular hopes of sensational new stories of sex and women's lib. Characters in Lawrence Durrell's *Monsieur* sit about in darkened rooms reading -- the *Pistis Sophia*. Gnosticism is fashionable: and in the minds of many beginning graduate students and much of the so-called 'educated public', whoever they are, the words 'Coptic' and 'Nag Hammadi' are absolutely synonymous. In the academic world the unfortunate upshot of this situation is that people try to teach themselves enough Coptic to read bits of text -- or, worse yet, read long tractates in translation only -- and then write involved and 'relevant' (to what?) expositions of what they take to be the, or a, Gnostic world-view appealing to 'modern alienated man' and based on no hard evidence whatever of what we know about the realities of life in the ancient world. A good way to get a job in the so-called 'History of Religions' field is to go into Nag Hammadi studies. *This does not make you a Coptic scholar*. Now we appreciate and honour the people who have done so much to create a whole new field. With all respect to the tremendous and uniquely important efforts made on behalf of these invaluable documents by our dedicated colleagues all over the world, and bearing in mind the worlds of work still to be done, we must remember that Coptic studies do not begin and end with Nag Hammadi, and that the two are *not* synonymous. The ongoing work of interpreting these texts must be done by scholars not attracted by fashion or utility but steeped in classical thought and its social background.

Second, Bible and specifically New Testament. It is often reiterated, with a touch of sadness, that Coptic is a sort of stepchild of New Testament studies, owing to the fact that students in various seminaries are often obliged to take one or two smattering-courses in languages of the Eastern Empire in order to learn more at first hand about the early versions of the New Testament: how they circulated in the ancient world, and how the surviving versions are used in the never-ending work of textual criticism and exegesis. Again, this is only one side of the story. The exclusively clerical picture of Coptic *Schrifttum* is not a true one, even when it spills over into the areas, just beginning to be investigated for their historical value and for their own sake, of hagiography and homiletic. What we must look for is aspects of what happened to the culture of the ancient world when it became totally interpenetrated with widely varying canonical texts, how the imagery in the midst of which people lived acquired the richness we see in Coptic Textiles or sculpture, in the poetry of Dioscorus of Aphrodito, in the phraseology of legal documents, in the utter naturalness of the formation of the Late Antique Mediterranean *koine*. In the world of the Coptic Bible we are not playing a sterile *Glasperlenspiel* of shifting counters: we are seeing how a whole literature and a whole fabric of daily life could acquire a relationship to the Word of God as totally at ease as that of Dorothy L. Sayers or P.G. Wodehouse.

Our third side-chapel is what I would like to call 'the petering-out of Egyptology'. Again, the academic world is so structured that students of hieroglyphic are required to read a year or so of Coptic in order to understand the reconstruction of what they are doing with Pharaonic and Demotic paradigms and writing-systems. Translation from (and into!) Coptic is encouraged as an activity giving the Egyptologist a greater familiarity with the ways in which the ancient language operated. Coptic itself is not viewed, as of course within these limits it would not need to be, as the language of a whole society, indeed as one of the languages of a multi-lingual social mix. It is laid on the Egyptologist almost as an extra burden of oddities: one is reminded of the (I hope apocryphal) classical master who said 'This term you are to have the privilege of reading the *Oedipus Coloneus*, a veritable treasure-house of grammatical peculiarities'. We can only hope that this picture will be brightened by a greater recognition in the standard curriculum that the world, the Egyptian world, did not end with Alexander (or take a giant leap over to 'Amr or Saladin with nothing in between), any more than the 'classical' world ended with Hadrian or the 'ancient' world with Gregory the Great. And let us remember that the 'patriotically Coptic' overemphasis on the Pharaonic heritage is only the reverse of the situation I have just been describing. (People are still being baptised 'Sesostris' and 'Amenhotep'.) And we might also hope that, given their preoccupations, Egyptologists will not always be too busy to teach Coptic -- *as Coptic*.

This categorising of Coptic as a pure linguistic tool leads us to the fourth domain, one represented nowadays by a growing volume of writings by an increasing number of scholars: the domain of the linguists. These are very, very intelligent people, who have taken up Coptic as a rare example of a well-documented language not of one of the major families but 'its own thing', who tend to talk only to one another in extremely abstruse terminology bristling with newly-invented categories and employing all the latest devices (in every sense) of the social scientists and the cliometricians. They are very concerned to demonstrate that our knowledge of Coptic has heretofore been simplicistic and our 'models' (favourite word'!) inadequate, our analyses based on unquestioned assumptions, our readings superficial, our categories drawn from notions that do not apply. Now by and large all this is a healthy thing. If our classically-educated spectacles are in danger of becoming what Cyril Mango called 'distorting mirrors', let this be pointed out. Most of all, if we cannot read the texts adequately then we have no discipline at all. (As my colleague Roger Bagnall has remarked, 'How many Copticists are there?' and 'How many people know Coptic?' are completely different questions.) The danger in viewing Coptic as a province of linguistics lies in its becoming isolated behind an impenetrable wall of jargon, tricked out in the appurtenances of fashion but forgetting what we have come to call 'the mentality of the documents'. The new grammars and lexica being produced now with so much excitement have their *raison d'etre* in the monuments themselves. We must ask the questions these people are asking, and some derived ones too: what *is* a liturgical language and how does it affect the people whose spiritual life takes place in one? And so on. Let us ask these questions mindful of our responsibility to the entire field.

As a quick flashback, let us take a look at the answers implicit in these approaches to the question so often discussed nowadays of 'what are the uses of history?' (we are all historians too). In its way Nag Hammadi is the legacy of the '60s when everything had to be 'relevant' (again, to what?): the shock-value of the illuminating anachronism is sought for at the expense of comprehension of the texts on their own terms. The New Testament critics and their school give us a totally clerical and hence shrilly confessional picture of Coptic society: *everything* has to be religious, *everything* has to be a Christian symbol. The tiresome, not to say distressing, one-sidedness of this view is self-evident. (I have seen someone confronted with a perfectly straightforward grain receipt say, 'Well, it must be a liturgical text ... or else magical!') The Egyptological or modern-sons-of-the-Pharaohs approach tends to be self-defeating in that without meaning to it does what we try to avoid: it passes over that intervening thousand years in which ancient society really did come into its own, substituting a sort of mental picture of squatters among the ruins. And modern linguists, who deny any sort of historicism while they invoke the shade of de Saussure, need to be reminded of what was going on outside the magic circle of sound-changes. It is a matter for rejoicing that we are no longer the prisoners of the emotionally charged value-judgements of previous generations. (The heirs of Maspero and Bell do not write about '...decadence...*bizarrerie*...morass of absurdity' or even, we hope, *byzantinische Untertänigkeit*.) The responsibility lies with us, to show that our field is not a forgotten backwater or an outlandish religion but a vital branch of the great vine of classics. Coptic history too has both its particularisms, its sets of conceptual structures that need to be understood, and its particularities, its *wie es eigentlich gewesen*. We are to show awareness of both.

Now that we have lit a candle in each of the side-chapels, to try to throw a little light on their structure and decoration, let us stand with Anthemius of Tralles in his Great Church and look upwards to grasp the space of the central dome. What should be our approach to this 'entire field' that appears to include so many sub-specialities, so many partial viewpoints, indeed sometimes so many communication problems? As in all 'area studies', each blind man tends to think that his is the only part of the elephant. If it be endurable to introduce yet another metaphor, let me put into your hands Coptic as a key: the key that for us unlocks the door that swings inward into the world of Late Antiquity. Surely it has become clear from the research of recent years that the language, literature, institutions, and culture of Coptic Egypt are to be approached within the context of Late Antiquity that makes them intelligible. The phonology and morphology of the language, the theological and aesthetic resonances of the texts, must always be kept in perspective in the world of that Coptic-speaking, and indeed multilingual, Egypt that formed a part successively of the Late Roman and Umayyad Empires. Art and liturgy are not just 'particularism' (in the surface sense); theology and preaching are not 'nationalism' (a ghost we can all be thankful that A.H. M. Jones has finally laid). In other words, we must find and keep our balance and sharpen our sensitivity to the whole world of the Mediterranean *koine* (and not believe everything we learned in school and/or everything we read!). Coptic puts into our hands a unique tool, a unique lens for 'seeing the true nature of the transformation of the classical inheritance in the Late Antique world, both in Greek and in the vernacular languages of the Near East (P.R.L. Brown)'. The religious, administrative, visual and textual material with which as professionals we have to deal every day forms a totality of exceptionally privileged richness in our corpus of evidence for what it was like to be human in the years from, say, 300 to 800. It is this historical approach I follow in my own work as a practising papyrologist. As the phrases in a document succeed one another, organically growing to articulate an exact meaning, as through the process of making the words 'happen' on paper I can enter into the mental processes of the scribe who composed the original, I am doing what Wilamowitz did, or Bentley, or what anyone in the ancient world did when he or she read a poem or a will aloud or sued their cousin's brother-in-law. When a scholar analyses homilies, or liturgical structures, or hagiographical storytelling, he or she is doing in a way what Shenoute did in his community: making the word live. And we can hope that when future art historians look at book illumination or sculpture, fresco or wood-carving, they will be indulging in fewer condemnatory preconceived value-judgements and instead *opening their eyes to see* what the Late Antique Egyptian saw at a festival, in church, at home, at his landlord's birthday party or the enthronement of an ecclesiastic.

How people were happy and unhappy, how they saw their world through linguistic structures, forms of thought and art and belief: these are the persistent realities, the themes of iconographical consistency and variation amongst which we move. The point of this *ekphrasis*, of this description of our interior space, has been, I hope, to delineate a vision like that of Braudel's Mediterranean, of that history of Late Antique Egypt that yet remains to be written. To elaborate the metaphor, the sharing of all of our various fields of scholarship is like a liturgical procession through this inner space. As a scribe used a single script to write the three languages of Byzantine Egypt -- Latin, Greek, and Coptic, in one basic hand -- as a chanter blended terms from three languages to create a unified hymnody, let us carry our awareness of the wholeness of this world into all our work. As regards the several ways of constructing *Coptic* lays, *not* every single one of them is right. *Recta sapere et ... semper consolatione gaudere*. We are all classicists.

And, as classicists, let me put it to you that, in Sir Frederick Kenyon's words when they were rediscovering Bacchylides from the papyri almost a hundred years ago, we are living in and living through the days of the Renaissance all over again; with this very important difference: that we do not want to lay, as I said, the dead hand of triumphant Humanism on everything we touch, everything we create. The most basic -- I cannot too strongly emphasise *basic* -- tasks of our field remain to be done. Above all, the provision of usable texts. The *Corpus Scriptorum Christianorum Orientalium* of Louvain/Washington is an admirable beginning: but still just a beginning, and only, like the *Patrologia Orientalis,* for religious literature. We need the fundamental labours of the textual critic -- the Lachmann and Mommsen, the A.E. Housman of the future -- to provide us with our shelf of Teubner and Oxford and Guillaume Bude texts (though perhaps this is temporarily to beg the question of who and what constitutes a classical author). We need a *Checklist II* of documentary material; and people to edit it. When the entire Pierpont Morgan collection is completely published in critical editions we will know more, and not just regard the textual *problemata* as peculiarities of exclusively a translation-literature. And we are only beginning to ask questions about liturgy:in contrast to what has been done for the West and even for Greek and Syriac, we know little about the dates and origins of the various elements of the liturgies, about their role in teaching, about how people prayed in Sahidic and how the Bohairic Mass supplanted it, about what it means to carry on your spiritual life in a liturgical language that you have to *learn* (like learning to compose classical poetry in order to get a good job in the bureaucracy? Surely more). And we need a study comparable to that done so brilliantly for Syriac on the role of tradition as a shaping force in Coptic *Geistesgeschichte*. And at every moment we must assess our discipline's 'intellectual loves' with an eye to the type of person who will be attracted to the field. Credibility above all.

I cannot do better than to leave you with some words of the master of us all, Ulrich von Wilamowitz-Moellendorff. These are excerpts from 'Wilamowitz's Catechism for Classicists' (1914-1930):

> Thou shalt have reverence for tradition.
> Lies cry for refutation.
>
> The linguistic use is decisive.
> The individual is always deviation from the usual.
>
> Be not too grand to work like Mr Dryasdust.
> *Non fumum e fulgore sed e fumo dare lucem.*
>
> It is not enough *quid traditum acceperimus* (Lachmann's *recensio*): one must make certain *quale sit*, which leads to the question, *quomodo traditum sit*.
>
> Even what is absolutely not worth knowing thou shalt not despise, because it may relatively lead to recognition of what is worth knowing. But thou shalt treat rubbish as rubbish.
>
> *Nil in arte parvum.*
> *Minima non curat praetor.*
> *Nec scire fas est omnia.*

XXVIII

Coptic sources:
A problem in the sociology of knowledge

'... und der griechische Geist von der national-koptischen Barbarei noch keineswegs überwuchert ist.'

C. Schmidt/W. Schubart, in *BKT* VI *(Altchristliche Texte)* (Berlin 1910) 109.

'... the poverty of the Coptic vocabulary and the utter lack not only of literary style but of intelligent argument in Coptic writings show that those who used this language had learnt nothing of Greek culture.'

J.G. Milne, *A history of Egypt under Roman rule*³ (London 1924) 255.

'... Copti, utpote ingenio speculativo minus praediti, ...'

M. Jugie, *Theologia dogmatica christianorum orientalium* 5 (Paris 1935) 458.

'*Ubi sunt*' has become, in mediaeval studies, a generic name for the sort of literary work, usually poetic, that rhetorically laments the disappearance of famous entities of the past. In this introductory paper to the Society's fiftieth-birthday number of the *Bulletin* I should like to raise a few *ubi sunt* questions about puzzling gaps in the extant material that goes at present to make up the body of Coptic source texts from which we draw our knowledge of the world of late antique Egypt. In particular, I should like to focus attention on six principal areas: a major patristic author, Cyril of Alexandria; the pseudo-Dionysian corpus; later Greek philosophy; canon law and synodical collections; historiography; and poetry.

The most important thing an Egyptian religious thinker could do was to be seen to be a loyal son of Cyril of Alexandria, the 'great illuminator'[1]. It is astonishing that, apart from a couple of homiletic works[2], the 'Ερωταποκρίσεις preserved in the Cheltenham papyrus codex[3], and the (falsely attributed) commentary on the Apocalypse contained in Pierpont Morgan Library MS. M 591, almost nothing of Cyril, this central and surely bilingual Egyptian church father[4], has been preserved in Coptic. None of his important and large-scale exegetical or expository works has, according to the present state of our MS. knowledge, come down to the present day in the Coptic language. Yet Coptic Cyril texts existed in earlier periods[5]. There are extant witnesses to a transmission that was still alive in comparatively recent centuries: scribal subscriptions to Cod.Vat.arab. 126 (copied in A.D. 1688/9), fol. 238, attest to a long list of Cyril's works in Coptic collated by the scribe from at least four separate codices[6]. What has become of these MSS. since they were seen by a scribe from Assiut in the late seventeenth century? In addition, a great amount of Cyril's theological work is extant in Ethiopic, another major transmission-language of the Monophysite thought-world[7]; not to mention Syriac[8] and Armenian[9]. The lack of a *Cyrillus Copticus* is a serious and distressing gap in Coptic patristic literature.

Since the early sixth century the corpus of Neoplatonic writings fathered in late antiquity on to the figure of Dionysius the Areopagite, Paul's convert of Acts 17:34, had an extraordinary influence owing to its supposed apostolic origin. A great amount of the pseudo-Dionysius exists in Syriac[10], and is being edited and published by G. Wiessner of Göttingen[11]. Of the Latin *Nachleben* after Eriugena there is here no need to speak. What surprises the student of Neoplatonic thought in late antique Egypt[12] is the fact that no pseudo-Dionysian writings have yet turned up transmitted in the Coptic language. Surely with that characteristically Egyptian concern with the orderly structure of things unseen, a Coptic translator of these much-discussed works would not have been far to seek[13]. One can only hope that further manuscript discoveries will fill in this blank area in the map of Mediterranean thought in the Monophysite provinces.

This topic leads us directly to the next consideration, that of the Greek, especially Aristotelian[14], philosophy basic to the school curriculum, both the *Organon* and, in particular, the ubiquitous *Eisagoge* of Porphyry. Again, among the languages of the non-Chalcedonian world it is Syriac that is our principal line of transmission[15]. Nonetheless, the heritage of philosophy underlay learning in Egypt as elsewhere: both Shenoute the monastic rhetorician[16] and Cyril the master dialectician[17] remembered and used their training. Once again, no Coptic version of the *Eisagoge* has yet been found. In the age when Boethius was attempting to give the West the *Organon* and so much more besides, Egyptian thinkers, in particular John Philoponus (surely another bilingual[18]), were perpetuating these intellectual tools in their own milieu[19]. Even if only as students' helps, these materials must have existed in the schools of late antique Egypt. It is the bad luck of our transmission that we cannot yet see the shapes and hear the resonances of the categories of Greek thought as they took shape in the Coptic language-structure.

Between the sub-apostolic materials taken over whole from the Greek[20] and the Arabophone compilations of the thirteenth and fourteenth centuries[21] lies a jungle of silence in the history of Coptic canon law and its sources, a chasm dubbed by Graf 'die schriftlose Zeit'[22]. As evidence for the actual practice of Coptic ecclesiastics in the seventh and eighth centuries, we have, of course, the Coptic legal documents on papyrus[23], a source resolutely ignored by the few canonists who have touched on the field. (The current hope of constructing a *Corpus iuris canonici Copticum* is both unprofessional and ludicrous without this source work.) But from Chalcedon to the late Middle Ages we have in Coptic not a single equivalent to the historically rich mass of synodical compilations in Syriac[24] that yield to the researcher such abundant information on the practical concerns of Christian hierarchs under the Islamic domination. It is to be hoped that lurking somewhere under the general rubrics 'Historica' or 'Canon Law in handlists of Coptic MSS., still in their infancy[25], there may be found *Synodica Coptica* that will make centuries of committee-meetings open to the investigations of historians of what happened after A.D. 642.

Of historiography in Coptic, either sacred or secular, only the smallest fragments are as yet known. The fact that Eusebius single-handedly changed the shape of the writing of history is reflected in the Egyptian milieu by a very few scraps of MS.[26]; while Coptic elements of an indigenous *Historia Ecclesiastica* have now been collected[27] and help to form an idea of the sort of materials that underlay the post-conquest narrative sources. But so far as we know there was no Coptic Agathias, no school of classicising writers who put speeches into the mouths of exemplary figures of the past. The *Paschal Chronicle* is in Greek. There never was a Coptic Bede. Most surprisingly of all, we have no Coptic example of what used to be called the 'monkish chronicle', a year-by-year running compilation detailing how in such a year a comet was seen, the flood and harvest were bad, someone's army marched through, the abbot died, and so on. Communities keep records. Alongside a monastic account-book like the compilation of receipts and documents copied into P.Yale inv. 1804 (from Aphrodito) we might hope to find a papyrus or parchment codex containing at least a summary of local events that affected a monastic settlement. And also on the historiography front, where is the possible Coptic original of John of Nikiu?

There exists no people without a poetry. Of Coptic poetry almost nothing whatever is known. The Manichaean psalms are written in a form of verse[28]; after them we have nothing until Junker's *Koptische Poesie des 10. Jahrhunderts* (Berlin

NOTES

1. For the expression, ⲣⲉϥⲣⲟⲩⲟⲉⲓⲛ, *GospEg* 88.28; cf. P. Bellet in R.McL. Wilson, ed., *Nag Hammadi and Gnosis* (=*NHS* 14) (Leiden 1978) 64-65. On Cyrillianism see P.T.R. Gray, *The defense of Chalcedon in the East* (Leiden 1979) 5-6, 104, 119.

2. Ed. M. Chaîne in *Mél.Beyrouth* 6 (1913) 493-528; E.W. Budge, *Miscellaneous Coptic texts* (London 1915) 139-146, 717-724; H. de Vis, *Homélies coptes* II (Copenhagen 1929) 158-202.

3. W.E. Crum, *Der Papyruscodex saec. VI-VII der Phillippsbibliothek in Cheltenham* (Strassburg 1915) esp. pp. 4-12, 145-154.

4. E.R. Hardy, 'The Patriarch Cyril and the Coptic monks,' in L.S.B. MacCoull, ed., *Coptic studies presented to Mirrit Boutros Ghali* (Cairo 1979) 6-10.

5. E.g. the *Thesaurus de Trinitate:* see N. Charlier, 'Le "Thesaurus de Trinitate" de S. Cyrille d'Alexandrie,' *RHE* 45 (1950) 35; citations of the exegesis at innumerable places in the Bohairic Gospel Catena (ed. P. de Lagarde [Göttingen 1886, repr. Osnabrück 1971]). Cf. J.-M. Labelle, 'Saint Cyrille d'Alexandrie: témoin de la langue et de la pensée philosophiques au Ve siècle,' *RSR* 52 (1978) 155.

6. A. Mai, *Scriptorum veterum nova collectio IV* (Rome 1831) 249-250 lists letters, and excerpts from the dialogues, scripture commentaries, controversial and expository works. Are the attestations in W. Riedel, 'Der Katalog der christlichen Schriften in arabischer Sprache von Abū 'l Barakāt,' *Nachr.Göttingen* phil.-hist. Kl. 5 (1902), esp. foll. 224a, 238b, 239b of MS. D, to works in Coptic? Probably not. At that late date night had fallen over the old polite learning. (And yet the seventeenth-century scribe of Assiut had access to large amounts of Coptic texts.)

7. Continuing editions by B.M. Weischer in the series *Qerellos: "Dass Christus einer ist"* (Bonn 1966 and Wiesbaden 1977); *Der Prosphonetikos "Über den rechten Glauben"* (Hamburg 1973); the Melchizedek homilies (Wiesbaden 1980). *

8. E.g. the letters published by R.Y. Ebeid/L.R. Wickham in *CSCO* 359-360 (Louvain 1975); and the commentary on Luke edited by Chabot, *CSCO* 70 (Louvain 1912) and 140 (Louvain 1953, tr. R.M. Tonneau). Also the *Contra Julianum* ed. E. Nestle (Leipzig 1880); Pusey's text of the *De recta fide* (Oxford 1877); and still more of the exegesis.

9. E.g. F.C. Conybeare's edition of the *Scholia on the Incarnation* (London 1907).

10. The Sinai MS. is numbered 66 in the (useless) catalogue of M. Kamel (Wiesbaden 1970), p. 153.

11. Cf. also J.M. Hornus in *Parole de l'Orient* 1 (1970) 69-93.

12. E.g. the forthcoming study by S. Karren on Damascius' life of Isidore as a witness to Egyptian intellectual life: cf. *Sixth BSC* (Oberlin 1980) 43.

13. Perhaps some transmission took place as early as the fifth century: see H. von Cranenburgh in *Muséon* 76 (1963) on use of ps.-Dionysian material in the *Historia Lausiaca*.

14. As is well known, a bit of Plato turns up in the Nag Hammadi corpus: *Rep.* 588B-589B (Codex VI.5): see J.M. Robinson, ed., *The Nag Hammadi Library* (New York 1977) 290-291.

15. See the Erlangen dissertation of A. Freimann, *Die Isagoge des Porphyrios i.d. syrischen Übersetzung* (1897). The translation is mid-seventh century, by one Athanasius of Balad.

16. Cf. W.C. Till, 'Griechische Philosophen bei den Kopten,' *Mélanges Maspero* 2 (Cairo 1934) 165-175.

17. J.-M. Labelle, 'Saint Cyrille d'Alexandrie...,' (above note 5) *RSR* 52 (1978) 142 (esp. use of Porphyry in the *Contra Julianum*), 145-148; *ibid.* 53 (1979) 25, 28, 34, 38-40.

18. L.S.B. MacCoull, 'John Philoponus and Dioscorus of Aphrodito,' paper at the Ninth International Conference on Patristic Studies, Oxford, September 1983.[Now published in *Studia Patristica* 18 (same as Panegyric 580f). In this volume study IX.]

19. On Philoponus' *Eisagoge* commentary see Gudeman in *RE* 18 (1916) 1772; and Kroll, *ibid.* 1794-5 for the Syriac.

20. W. Riedel/W.E. Crum, *The canons of Athanasius* (London 1904, repr. Amsterdam 1973).

21. For a survey and citation of the published works see O. Meinardus, 'A study on the canon law of the Coptic church,' *BSAC* 16 (1961-2) 231-242. Nothing has been done since.

22. G. Graf, *GCAL* I.557. His melancholy remarks still hold true.

23. The great collection remains W.E. Crum/G. Steindorff, *Koptische Rechtsurkunden des 8. Jhdts. aus Djême (Theben)* (Leipzig 1912). Indispensable are the works of A.A. Schiller, esp. 'Prolegomena to the study of Coptic law,' *Arch. d'Hist. du Droit Orient.* 2 (1938) 341-365; and see the forthcoming article 'Coptic Law' in the *Coptic Encyclopaedia* (by L.S.B. MacCoull).**
[Now published in *The Coptic Encyclopaedia* (New York 1991).]

24. J.B. Chabot, *Synodicon Orientale* (Paris 1902); A. Vööbus, *The Synodicon in the West Syrian tradition, CSCO* 367-8 (Louvain 1975), 375-6 (Louvain 1976); *idem, Syr. Kanonessammlungen* in *CSCO Subs.*, 307 and 317 (Louvain 1970). No work like that of Kaufhold and Selb is yet possible for Coptic; there are no sources. (Only some Arabic attestations were published by Assemani: Graf, *GCAL* I.480-481).

25. See the survey of S. Kent Brown in *ARCE Newsletter* 114 (Spring 1981) 11-17.

26. W.E. Crum, 'Eusebius and Coptic church historians,' *PSBA* 24 (1902) 68-84.

27. D.W. Johnson, *Coptic sources for the History of the Patriarchs of Alexandria* (diss. Catholic University, Washington, 1974); *idem*, 'Further remarks on the Arabic history of the patriarchs of Alexandria,' *OC* 61 (1977) 103-116. Could a fragment like P.Duk.inv. C 58 (to be published by the present writer in *BASP*) be a bit of such a source? [Now published in *BASP* 20 (1983) 137-141.]
28. See T. Säve-Söderbergh, *Studies in the Coptic Manichaean Psalm-book* (Uppsala 1949).
29. Ed. O. von Lemm (St Petersburg 1903). [Now ed./tr. P. Nagel (Halle 1983); Eng. tr by L.S.B. MacCoull forthcoming.]
30. E.g. by DeL. O'Leary in his *Fragmentary Coptic ḥymns* (London 1924), *The Coptic Theotokia* (London 1923), *The Difnar of the Coptic Church* (London 1926). This mine of texts remains unexplored.
31. See L.S.B. MacCoull, 'The Coptic archive of Dioscorus of Aphrodito,' *Cd'E* 56 (1981) 185-193.
32. D.W. Johnson has recently (at the Claremont symposium on 'The Roots of Egyptian Christianity') referred to Coptic writings as 'one of the dullest literatures ever created by man'. Indeed.
33. I should like to thank Robert Markus, who, with his musician's ear, listened.

* And *Homilien und Briefe zum Konzil von Ephesos* (Wiesbaden 1979).

**And, of course, A. Steinwenter, *Das Recht der koptischen Urkunden* (Munich 1955).

XXIX

Towards an Appropriate Context for the Study of Late Antique Egypt

In memory of Michael Kenny

Classicists and papyrologists have derived much benefit from the recent thought-provoking article by Professor Deborah Hobson of York University, 'Towards a Broader Context for the Study of Greco-Roman Egypt.'[1] Urging as it does a greater interdisciplinary collaboration among people who read Greek, i.e. classicists, on the one hand, and social scientists who work with other periods of Egyptian history and with other non-modern, non-industrial societies, on the other, Hobson's paper, with its anthropological awareness, has begun to stimulate further social-science-oriented work that some are already styling 'the New Papyrology.'[2] Whether papyrology, that *Hilfswissenschaft* whose development has kept pace with our century, be new or old, in this paper I should like to suggest some directions toward which Hobson's exhortations might be somewhat redirected, for even greater benefit to those who deal with Greco-Roman culture and its Mediterranean-wide effects. If there truly has been a new papyrology in the last twenty-five years, it has been the coming into its own of the papyrological study of Late Antiquity, roughly the period A.D. 300-650, long scorned by classical philologists.[3] In this recent research we have indeed seen work of a much more interdisciplinary nature, and more linkages with the history of Egypt before Alexander the Great and after the Islamic conquest. It is with this Late Antique period specifically in mind that I should like to examine Hobson's two main arguments, in order to mark out further paths of enquiry and, indeed, to step even further out of the system for a critical perspective on Late Antique historical and papyrological studies.

The first of the two principal arguments in 'Broader Context' asks for a firmer integration of Greco-Roman papyrological studies into the entire

[1] *Echos du Monde Classique/Classical Views* 32 (1988), 353-363; hereafter 'Broader Context.'

[2] James G. Keenan, 'The "New Papyrology" and Ancient Social History,' paper at the American * Philological Association, San Francisco, December 1990, to appear (revised and expanded) in *Ancient History Bulletin*; D. P. Kehoe, 'Comparative Approaches to the Social History of Roman Egypt,' *Bulletin of the American Society of Papyrologists* 26 (1989), 153-156; B. W. Frier, 'A New Papyrology?,' *ibid.*, 217-226. We already have to contend with the 'New Philology' (see *Speculum* 65 [1990]), and 'poststructuralist' classics (see the book of the same name edited by A. Benjamin [London-New York, 1988] and M. Mullett's excellent article, 'Dancing with Deconstructionists in the Gardens of the Muses: New Literary History vs. ?,' *Byzantine and Modern Greek Studies* 14 [1990], 258-275).

[3] Cf. L. S. B. MacCoull, 'Verso una nuova comprensione dell'Egitto copto,' *Studi e Ricerche sull'Oriente Cristiano* 13 (1990), 3-17; also Keenan 1990 (above n.2). For a brilliant characterization of Late Antiquity see M. Roberts, *The Jeweled Style* (Ithaca, 1989).

* Now published in *Ancient History Bulletin* 5 (1991) 159–169.

history of Egypt, from Pharaonic to Islamic and modern. Of course this sounds unexceptionable. There are, however, consequences of this line of thought that the Late Antique scholar is aware cannot be pressed too far. Hobson begins by stating that papyrologists read Greek, i.e., are classically trained, and thus (a) are interested in the matter preserved on papyrus because it is in Greek, and (b) take note only incidentally of the Egyptian aspects of such matter because it is owing to the accident of the climate of Egypt, and nowhere else, that papyri were preserved there (and not in, e.g., Italy or Asia Minor).[4] She then emphasizes the necessity of understanding these papyri as 'documents of the history of Egypt itself',[5] not just as pieces of classical (Greco-Roman) history. The other side, however, of this line of argument is a return to the old-fashioned scholarly attitude that played up the 'uniqueness of Egypt', a viewpoint that permeated earlier papyrology congresses[6] and has more recently been set aside.[7] In our salutary awareness of the local particularity of Egypt we do well to remember that it was Hellenism that gave the local, the particular, the chance to flower and the ability to endure.[8]

Historians of the Mediterranean world from Alexander to the Umayyads are of course trained as classicists because the classical education, with its combination of philology and ancient history, is the only possible doorway into the discipline. This is as it should be. I submit, in a reorientation of this trend of thought, that what Late Antique scholars, indeed papyrologists who specialize in Late Antiquity, become interested in is not a geographical *place* (Egypt) but rather a slice of *time*: the period A.D. 300-650, or 450-750, in the Mediterranean world. Granted that papyri are, owing to climatic accident, found in Egypt[9] and reflect the realities of that place. But they cannot, and Egypt cannot, be understood in geographical isolation.[10] For the Late Antique

[4]'Broader Context,' 353-354.

[5]'Broader Context,' 355.

[6]See the progression from C. Preaux, 'Les Raisons de l'originalité de l'Egypte,' *Museum Helveticum* 10 (1953), 203-221, to N. Lewis, 'The Romanity of Roman Egypt: A Growing Consensus,' *Atti dell'XVII Congresso Internazionale di Papirologia* (Naples, 1984), 1077-1084.

[7]Recent discussions of the historiography are found in the congress volume *Egitto e storia antica dall'ellenismo all'età araba* (Bologna, 1989): G. Geraci, 'L'Egitto romano nella storiografia moderna,' 55-88; A. Giardina, 'Egitto bizantino o tardoantico?,' 89-103; H. Heinen, 'L'Egypte dans l'historiographie moderne du monde hellénistique,' 105-135.

[8]See G. W. Bowersock, *Hellenism in Late Antiquity* (Ann Arbor, 1990), with its useful distinction between Hellenism and Hellenization.

[9]A few in Israel (Nessana, Khirbet Mird, Wadi el-Murabbat) and Syria (Dura-Europus); carbonized papyri have been found in Greece (Derveni) and Italy (Herculaneum).

[10]'It is for linguistic reasons, primarily, that the history of Egypt is compartmentalized,' writes Hobson ('Broader Context,' 354), to urge the usefulness of Ancient Egyptian and Demotic on the one hand (passing over Coptic, so often relegated to departments of religion and Oriental studies) and

period one must learn, besides Coptic, also Syriac, Armenian, Ge'ez, Hebrew, Arabic and sometimes even Persian in order to understand Greco-Roman-Coptic-Byzantine Egyptian society in its total context. For example, law or monasticism or land use in Egypt cannot be understood without reference to those same phenomena in the other provinces of the late Roman Empire.[11] How much the more is this true for matters of intellectual history such as theology and philosophy, or for economic studies which need to compare the data from papyri with those from from epigraphy. For Roman Egypt the comparative method, so well discussed by Frier (1989; above n.2), will do quite well. But for Late Antiquity the comparative method needed is comparison with other areas of Late Antiquity.

Hobson's *mise en scène* was a lecture on an Egyptian antiquity site ('Broader Context,' 353). It is indeed illuminating to look at the lectures and conference programs of benefit to, and attended by, scholars of Late Antique Egypt. In fact they learn comparatively little from the programs of, for example, the American Research Center in Egypt, almost exclusively Pharaonic and Islamic in content. They go tirelessly to congresses of Byzantine studies, patristic studies, Christian archaeology, Coptic studies, Syriac studies, Christian Arabic studies, Armeno-Georgian studies, and even canon law, not to mention the Late Antiquity workshops and seminars at such places as Princeton and London. Even more than being in touch with colleagues who work on, e.g., Demotic/Saite and Arabophone/Abbasid periods of Egyptian history, what Late Antique people demonstrate a need for is contact and interchange with Syriacists, Armenianists, Ethiopicists, historians of the Sasanian empire, philosophers (especially those who deal with the Eastern Christian churches), patristicists and theologians, even Merovingianists, and those Late Antique historians working mostly with Latin and Greek who, in their interdisciplinary and 'new-wave' way, are continually enlarging our knowledge of the late Roman world. These specialists, and their colleagues working on Greece, North Africa, Palestine, Italy, Asia Minor, the Caucasus, in the span of time A.D. 300-750, would give anything to have the kind of documentation with which papyrologists deal:

Arabic on the other. But classicists working in the Late Antique period cannot manage with Greek and Latin alone. The point is temporality, not geography; and temporality in the sense of what languages were being used at a certain period in the late Roman world, not of an isolation of Ancient-Egyptian-Demotic-Coptic-speaking culture from Greek-and-Latin-speaking culture in a single place (Egypt).

[11]Hobson calls attention, in the context of the unity of Egyptian culture, to the illogicality of jurists' terming native Egyptians *peregrini*, 'foreigners' ('Broader Context,' 355; from the Roman law point of view). Attention might be drawn to the extent to which the second-class-citizen Christian Copts of the present day, lineal descendants of the ancient population, are regarded as aliens in contemporary Egypt by the Moslems, themselves descendants of new arrivals from Arabia who intermarried with apostates from Christianity.

the taxation records of a city, the business archives and private letters of an individual. And yet it is in these just mentioned areas of specialty that the most innovative work is being done, and it is from them that 'new' (or old) papyrologists can most profitably draw models for their own research.[12]

The second of the main points of 'Broader Context' is the emphasis on the anthropological paradigm.[13] Granted that this has been all the rage for fifteen years or so. In 1975 classicists and papyrologists, including the present writer, sat in on seminars reading *Saints of the Atlas* and monographs on quantifying holiness in Southeast Asia, works on the rural family, on Cathar heresy and on Vlach transhumance, and derived immense profit from the enlarged horizon gained thereby. This phenomenon seems to be part of the postmodern world, in which it is well seen by many to criticize the dominance of that classical curriculum which until very recently defined the universe of discourse for all educated men and women in the West, and to seek for enlightenment from the formerly undervalued.[14] It is true that the relaxing of the strict boundaries of that classical curriculum (temporally defined) is one of the things that has helped to make Late Antiquity not only a legitimate, but even a 'hot', field. It seems to be a function both of the versions of irony and distance characteristic of postmodernism and of the way Late Antiquity used to be pictured (as 'decadent') in older scholarship that leads our contemporaries to be attracted to that very period, to put emphasis on rhetoric, the roles of women, the use of *spolia* and the like.[15] Yet it is time

[12]Examples would be too numerous to list, but might include such work as analyzing the social origin of clergy and other elites, reading saints' lives and homilies as documents of social change, reattributing long-known narrative historical texts, analyzing the rhetoric of fiscal and legal documents, or trying to identify the audience for various genres of texts both literary and documentary. Papyrologists are now aware of the dangers of letting the accepted methodology determine the questions they ask (cf. Frier, 'New Papyrology?' [above n.2]; Keenan, '"New Papyrology"' [*ibid.*]; cf. A. Megill, *Prophets of Extremity* [Berkeley, 1985], 107). Empirically it likewise becomes clear that, as far as ancient historians are concerned, the whole 'Hellenistic' thousand-year period is best grasped in the slice-of-time fashion, not piecemeal by geographic areas.

[13]'Broader Context,' 358-362.

* [14]A. Grafton's *From Humanism to the Humanities* (Cambridge, 1986) will be found eye-opening with respect to the recent nature and political program of the 'classical humanist' curriculum. A century ago the first use of anthropology by classicists (see below) was part of 'the century-long process, which began at the end of the seventeenth century and gathered force throughout the Enlightenment, to dethrone the cultures of classical antiquity from the privileged position they had enjoyed since the Renaissance' (R. Ackerman, *J. G. Frazer: His Life and Work* [Cambridge, 1987], 63).

[15]Cf. C. Geertz in *The New York Review of Books*, November 18, 1990, 19, on *episteme* vs. *doxa*; A. J. Wharton in *Gesta* 29 (1990), 5: 'With the dislodging of the fact, rhetoric usurps the place of reason as the most powerful means of persuasion. .... The Modernist distance to the objectified past has been superseded by a Postmodernist relation to history which is both nostalgic and unmediated.' Illustrative are A. Megill, D. N. McCloskey, 'The Rhetoric of History,' in *The Rhetoric of the Human Sciences*, ed. J. S. Nelson et al. (Madison, 1987), 221-238; and D. Preziosi, *Rethinking Art History* (New Haven, 1989).

* See now R. Ackerman, *The Myth and Ritual School: J.G. Frazer and the Cambridge Ritualists* (London – New York 1991), and *idem*, in W.M. Calder III, ed., *The Cambridge Ritualists Reconsidered* (Atlanta 1991) 1–19.

to ask what, if anything, the next paradigm will be. After anthropology, what?[16]

It is at this point that a look at the history of the discipline of papyrology, as a part of classics, is useful. While papyri had always turned up as chance finds,[17] roughly a century ago the first directed searches specifically for papyri were undertaken.[18] This purposeful exploration took place just after the first set of attempts by classicists to put anthropology to work for them, in the work of the so-called 'Cambridge Ritualists', and the first impact of early ethnography on classical studies.[19] As recent re-evaluations of those earlier scholars have shown, the present is not the only time when classicists have had to deal with the application of social-science parallels and methods to their own subject matter, and to evaluate the fitness of the tool for the task.[20] At the present moment the fashion is to regard Greco-Roman culture as as 'other' as possible, in reaction to the older view of it as directly generative of our own reality[21] (hence one aspect of the controversial 'rewriting of the canon'). This may well change.

To return to Hobson's first point: a primary reality of the field of papyrology, one just beginning to stretch at the temporal edges, is that its practitioners are classicists, people dedicated to understanding Greco-Roman culture, and how that culture both evolved in its surroundings and affected its surroundings. One of the perennial ailments afflicting classicists is dissatisfaction with the closed universe of their discipline and a renewed search for whatever adjoining field can supply them with a new approach to the West's oldest (since the Alexandrians) subject matter. Classicists seem to feel that what they do and what they stand for is no longer valued by the 'real

[16]The prefaces in A. Cameron, ed., *History as Text* (London, 1989) continually remind the reader of the 'flight from objectivity' (cf. above, n. 15) and of how everything is constructed by means of something else; the 'Postlude', entitled 'What Next with History?,' offers no suggestions.

[17]Cf. R. Pintaudi and M. Gigante in *Miscellanea Papyrologica in occasione del bicentenario dell'edizione della Charta Borgiana*, ed. R. Pintaudi et al. (Florence, 1990), v-viii.

[18]See E. G. Turner in *Excavating in Egypt: The Egypt Exploration Society, 1882-1982*, ed. T. G. H. James (Chicago, 1982), 161-163.

[19]See Ackerman, *J.G. Frazer* (above n. 14), and S. Peacock, *Jane Ellen Harrison: The Mask and the Self* (New Haven, 1988). Worth reading are Ackerman's acute remarks about the incorporation of anthropology into 'the armory of classical studies' (129), together with his hilarious footnote 3 on p. 326.

[20]Even F. R. Leavis, in a different context, had things to say about 'queering one discipline with the habits of another' (quoted from A. Kernan, *The Death of Literature* [New Haven, 1990], 41).

[21]Cf. L. O. Mink's '"apperceptive mass" of familiarity with the *otherness* of a period or culture...', in *After the Reformation*, ed. B.C. Malament (Philadelphia, 1980), 4. For a Late Antique slant on this generative aspect, the current debate, for example, about the disappearance of the author (A. Kernan, *The Death of Literature* [New Haven 1990]) is really just Late Antique Neoplatonism coming back in through the back door (no doubt to the posthumous delight of C. S. Lewis, Tolkien, and other upholders of the 'subcreation' of secondary worlds).

world': so begins a search *for* value, an effort *to be valued*.[22] This dissatisfaction comes from putting the cart before the horse. Before the approaches comes the dedication. Classicists pursue their characteristic activity, research leading to original contributions to knowledge about the ancient world, because of their commitment simultaneously to the subject matter of the classics and to their view of that subject matter as exercising a particular effect on the human beings exposed to it.

Classicists are, deep down, still Platonists, and believe, first, that the achievements of Greco-Roman culture are intrinsically valuable and ennobiing, and second, that since the mind becomes like what it contemplates, the most excellent human activity is seeking to understand that ancient culture and its effects on all other places and times. As classicists study one body of documentation, namely in this case papyri from Egypt, and thus become papyrologists, immersed in the realities disclosed by those papyrus texts, they have the freedom to weigh various approaches, fitting each to its most adaptive end. To be a practicing papyrologist is to question the world in a very immediate way.[23] Papyrologists are not, for example, going to fall into the currently fashionable trap of trying to show that it is all about, and only about, power. The business of making a coherent text keeps them honest.

There were many strands in Late Antique (or Hellenistic) Egyptian society,[24] and the understanding of each benefits from redefining problems, rejuxtaposing pieces of evidence, breaking boundaries. Hence Late Antiquity, with its transvaluation of what 'classics' had been thought to consist of, has become the most pathbreaking area within papyrology.[25] It is important to consider whether, in enlarging our tool-kit, the offered tool of analysis is at all congruent with the job in hand.

The teacher of three generations of North American papyrologists (and of Professor Hobson and the present writer), the late C. Bradford Welles, taught all his students, not that Egypt was one country, but that the Mediterranean

[22]Cf. J. Z. Smith: 'What rules ... is an overwhelming concern for assigning value, rather than intellectual significance...', in *Drudgery Divine* (London, 1990), 46. Likewise A. Bloom: 'The permanent human tendency is to doubt that the theoretical stance is authentic and suspect that it is only a covert attachment to a party,' in *Giants and Dwarfs* (New York, 1990), 17.

[23]See H. C. Youtie, *The Textual Criticism of Documentary Papyri*, 2nd ed. (London, 1074).

[24]As there are in the Egypt of today so revelatory to the social-science-minded: Professor Hobson's amusing impression of classicist papyrologists lost in the Fayum ('Broader Context,' 356) might be balanced by other observations, e.g. that it is the case that certain other papyrologists have never met any *indigènes* who were not Francophone and Jesuit-educated. Pursuing Late Antique papyrology in the field tends to have more to do with *l'aristocratie du Levant* than with Professor Hobson's innocents abroad. Cf. M. Martin, 'Note sur la communauté copte entire 1650 et 1850,' *Annales islamologiques* 18 (1982), 193-215.

[25]Cf. Megill, *Prophets of Extremity* (above n. 12), 113-116, 341-342.

was one world. It is in the Late Antique period that the Greco-Roman classics come into their most vivifying state of being, their perfect moment. Late Antique papyrologists are not so much detained by either the 'Egyptianness' or the 'otherness' of what is in their papyri: they are trying to uncover and recover a vanished sensibility whose echoes still have the power to astonish the reader/beholder and to make us think. The paradigm has long since shifted, and a good thing too. As Peter Brown pointed out at the birth of Late Antique studies in our time, Augustine never tired of making his discourse stick by demanding *Da mihi amantem*: Give me a person who is in love: he or she will understand what I mean.[26]

[26] P. Brown, *Augustine of Hippo* (London, 1967). -- I should like to thank M. Blanchard, J. G. Keenan, D. Krueger, and J. P. Thomas for their helpful discussion; and L. Perkins and the Lauinger Library of Georgetown University for support and facilities.

SCHOLAR'S LYRIC
(On reading the Triadon)

In the West it happened very gently,
from Venus' Eve to early Ambrose,
when the verb-endings sang to one another.

In the East it happened by the very nature
of the languages, Clement, Methodius,
the echoing inflections of parallel thought.

Fortunatus heard it when he saw
the imperial image transfigured in light;
        from Ephrem to Romanos the acclamations

sang each to each like Gabrieli,
picked up between the lines of the papyri,
the Coptic "Book of the Cries in the Night".

When it flowered in the West, the students
of the University of Paris singing,
they rejoiced and called it "the scholars' lyric".

The tongues of court and church, school and courtyard,
of love and wine and the Day Offices,
        flowed together: "O come, Desire of nations".

Surely in the East the same images
of gardens and eagles, grape-clusters and cities,
quickened the eloquent silence of the desert.

Two sources and one hypostatic union
for a language of indomitable pride
        that gloried in the Word's first words in time.

And so when I rise singing from your arms
I am rejoicing in a great tradition:
when Kipling's daffodil is reborn in Coptic
        it is the Greek words that rhyme.

INDEX